Microsoft®

Money 2004

Gina Carrillo

Part 1
Getting Started . . . .

Part 2
Understanding the Basics .

Part 3
Exploring Your Home Page . . . . .Pg. 36

Part 4
Working with Your Accounts . . . . .Pg. 44

Part 5
Managing Your Account Activity . . . . .Pg. 68

Part 6
Managing Your Budget . . . . .Pg. 102

Part 7
Creating a Debt Reduction Plan . . . . .Pg. 120

Part 8
Managing Your Investments . . . . .Pg. 132

Part 9
Analyzing Your Finances .Pg. 148

Part 10
Managing Your Taxes . . . . .Pg. 160

Part 11
Planning for the Future . . . . .Pg. 174

Part 12
Planning for and Managing Major Purchases . . . . . .Pg. 202

Part 13
Money Extras . . . . .Pg. 212

Contents

Introduction xi

1 Getting Started 2

Opening Money 4

Importing Quicken Files 6

Setting Up Your Password 7

Setting Financial-Tracking Information 9

Specifying Financial Priorities and Accounts 10

Entering Account Information 12

Setting Up Accounts Online 15

Entering Your Income Information 16

Selecting the Bills You Pay 18

Entering Living Expenses and Bills 19

2 Understanding the Basics 22

Using and Customizing the Toolbar 24

Using Menus 26

Creating a New File 29

Opening a File 30

Backing Up Your Files 31

Printing 32

Setting Up or Changing Your Password 33

Getting Help 34

Getting the Latest Financial Updates 35

3 Exploring Your Home Page 36

Using Alternative Views 38

Customizing the Task List 39

Modifying the Order of Categories 41

Collapsing or Expanding Categories 42

Changing Your Default Home Page 43

4 Working with Your Accounts 44

Reviewing and Updating Account Information 46
Sorting Accounts 49
Tracking Frequent-Flyer Information 50
Adding a New Account 52
Closing and Reopening Accounts 54
Deleting an Account 55
Adding Spouse/Partner Accounts 56
Viewing and Organizing Account Categories 58
Adding a New Account Category 60
Renaming or Deleting an Account Category 61
Creating Account Classifications 62
Entering Payee Information 63
Adding a New Payee 64
Deleting a Payee 65
Setting Up Accounts Online .66
Getting Online Statements 67

5 Managing Your Account Activity 68

Recording Account Transactions 70
Adding a New Bill 72
Adding a New Deposit or Paycheck 74
Adding a New Transfer 76
Adding a New Investment Purchase 77
Modifying Bill or Deposit Information 78
Deleting Bill or Deposit Information 80
Setting Up Accounts for Electronic Pay 81
Paying Bills or Transferring Funds Online 82
Writing and Printing Checks .83
Reviewing Paid Bills 86
Searching for Account Transactions 87

Setting Up or Changing Bill Reminders 90
Balancing Accounts 91
Reviewing Projected Cash Flow 96
Adding to the Cash Flow 98
Editing the Cash Flow 99
Experimenting with Cash-Flow Scenarios 100

6 Managing Your Budget 102

Creating a New Budget 104
Viewing Budget Reports 110
Adding Withdrawals or Deposits to Your Budget 111
Reallocating Funds 112
Updating Budget Information 114
Viewing Different Budget Periods 117
Setting Up Reminders to Keep You on Budget 118
Revisiting the Cash-Flow Forecast 119

7 Creating a Debt Reduction Plan 120

Specifying Which Accounts to Pay Off 122
Editing Account Information 123
Creating or Deleting an Account 124
Putting More Toward Your Debt 128
Viewing Your Debt Reduction Plan Results 129
Putting Your Debt Reduction Plan Into Action 130

8 Managing Your Investments 132

Reviewing Existing Investments 134
Recording Cash Transactions for Investment Accounts 136
Recording Investment Transactions 140
Adding New Investments 142
Updating Investment Prices 146
Finding Investment and Financial News 147

9 Analyzing Your Finances 148

Viewing Reports 150

Customizing Reports 154

Creating a Favorite Reports List 158

10 Managing Your Taxes 160

Entering Your Tax Information .162

Reviewing Possible Tax Deductions 165

Reviewing or Estimating Capital Gains 168

Reviewing Your Filing Status and Tax Rates 170

Exporting Tax Information 171

11 Planning for the Future 174

Entering Your Family Information 176

Entering Income Information 178

Specifying Taxes and Inflation .181

Entering Savings and Investment Information 182

Reviewing and Changing Savings Contributions 184

Reviewing and Changing Life Insurance Policies 186

Entering Expected Returns on Investments 187

Setting Up Homes and Assets .188

Reviewing and Changing Your Debt Information 190

Reviewing and Changing Expenses 192

Reviewing and Changing Your Plan Results 196

Putting Your Plan into Action .201

12 Planning for and Managing Major Purchases 202

Determining How Much House You Can Afford 204

Taking Inventory 207

Comparing Loans 209

13 Money Extras .212

Exploring Money Services 214

Checking Your Credit 218

Numbers and Symbols 220

Glossary 220

Index 226

Easy Microsoft® Money 2004

International Standard Book Number: 0-7897-3070-7

Library of Congress Catalog Card Number: 029236730703

Printed in the United States of America

First Printing: November 2003

06 05 04 03 4 3 2 1

Trademarks

All terms mentioned in this book that are known to be trademarks or service marks have been appropriately capitalized. Que Publishing cannot attest to the accuracy of this information. Use of a term in this book should not be regarded as affecting the validity of any trademark or service mark.

Warning and Disclaimer

Every effort has been made to make this book as complete and as accurate as possible, but no warranty or fitness is implied. The information provided is on an "as is" basis. The author and the publisher shall have neither liability nor responsibility to any person or entity with respect to any loss or damages arising from the information contained in this book.

Bulk Sales

Que Publishing offers excellent discounts on this book when ordered in quantity for bulk purchases or special sales. For more information, please contact

U.S. Corporate and Government Sales

1-800-382-3419

corpsales@pearsontechgroup.com

For sales outside of the U.S., please contact

International Sales

1-317-428-3341

international@pearsontechgroup.com

Associate Publisher
Greg Wiegand

Acquisitions Editor
Stephanie J. McComb

Development Editor
Nicholas J. Goetz Jr.

Managing Editor
Charlotte Clapp

Project Editor
Tricia Liebig

Copy Editor
Kate Shoup Welsh

Proofreader
Linda Seifert

Technical Editor
Mark Hall

Team Coordinator
Sharry Lee Gregory

Interior Designer
Anne Jones

Cover Designer
Anne Jones

Page Layout
Susan Geiselman

Dedication

To my loving and supportive mother and daughter—thanks for believing in me!

Acknowledgments

I would like to thank first and foremost my mother and daughter, to whom I dedicate this book. Without their constant love, support, and encouragement, I would not be where I am today. Thanks Mom, for providing the foundation on which I've built my career. I am truly grateful for all you do for me. I would also like to acknowledge my tough little daughter. You have been a trooper the past few years with all of the challenges we have faced. Thank you, sweetie. And of course, I can't forget all of my friends that have each helped in so many different ways, especially Michelle and Arnold, Nancy, Linda, Carrie, Maria, Mike and Molli, Madeline, and all my friends in Austin and Florida. Thank you all for being there for me!

I also would like to thank the wonderful folks at Que Publishing for giving me so many great opportunities to write and edit for them. A huge thanks to my acquisitions editor, Stephanie McComb; development editor, Nick Goetz; project editor, Tricia Liebig; copy editor, Kate Welsh; technical editor, Mark Hall; and project coordinator, Sharry Lee Gregory for putting all their time and effort into making me look good. Also, thanks to the indexers, proofreaders, designers, and layout technicians. I truly enjoy working with all of you!

—Gina Carrillo

About the Author

Gina Carrillo has enjoyed 10 years of professional experience as a technical writer, analyst, editor, Web designer/developer, and instructor. She works full-time as a technical writer and application analyst, writing software system manuals, developing online help and company Web sites, and writing technical documentation. Gina has also helped develop a certification program for technical communicators at the University of South Florida, where she is a part-time RoboHelp and Technical Editing instructor. While not working or teaching, Gina also is an author and technical editor for Que Publishing and Sams Publishing. She is the author of *Easy Web Pages, 2nd Edition* and is the technical editor for *Teach Yourself Microsoft FrontPage 2000 in 10 Minutes, Teach Yourself to Create Web Pages in 24 Hours*, and *Easy Microsoft FrontPage 2000*.

Tell Us What You Think

As the reader of this book, *you* are our most important critic and commentator. We value your opinion and want to know what we're doing right, what we could do better, what areas you'd like to see us publish in, and any other words of wisdom you're willing to pass our way.

As an associate publisher for Que Publishing, I welcome your comments. You can email or write me directly to let me know what you did or didn't like about this book—as well as what we can do to make our books better.

Please note that I cannot help you with technical problems related to the topic of this book. We do have a User Services group, however, where I will forward specific technical questions related to the book.

When you write, please be sure to include this book's title and author as well as your name, email address, and phone number. I will carefully review your comments and share them with the author and editors who worked on the book.

Email: `feedback@quepublishing.com`

Mail: Greg Wiegand
Associate Publisher
Que Publishing
800 East 96th Street
Indianapolis, IN 46240 USA

For more information about this book or another Que title, visit our Web site at `www.quepublishing.com`. Type the ISBN (excluding hyphens) or the title of a book in the Search field to find the page you're looking for.

1 Each step is fully illustrated to show you how it looks onscreen.

It's as Easy as 1-2-3

Each part of this book is made up of a series of short, instructional lessons, designed to help you understand basic information that you need to get the most out of your computer hardware and software.

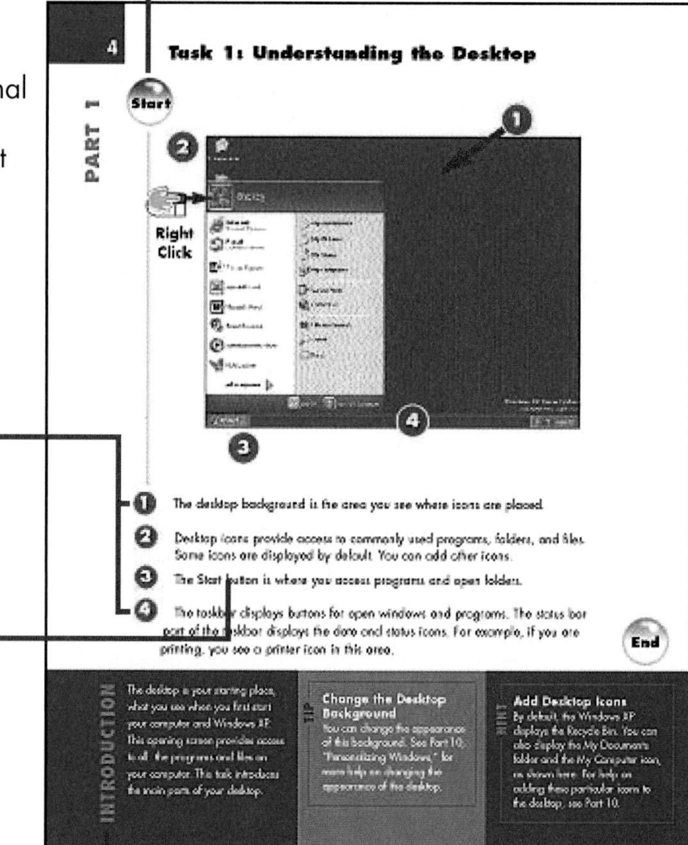

1 The desktop background is the area you see where icons are placed.

2 Desktop icons provide access to commonly used programs, folders, and files. Some icons are displayed by default. You can add other icons.

3 The Start button is where you access programs and open folders.

4 The taskbar displays buttons for open windows and programs. The status bar part of the taskbar displays the date and status icons. For example, if you are printing, you see a printer icon in this area.

INTRODUCTION The desktop is your starting place, what you see when you first start your computer and Windows XP. This opening screen provides access to all the programs and files on your computer. This task introduces the main parts of your desktop.

TIP **Change the Desktop Background** You can change the appearance of this background. See Part 10, "Personalizing Windows," for more help on changing the appearance of the desktop.

HINT **Add Desktop Icons** By default, the Windows XP displays the Recycle Bin. You can also display the My Documents folder and the My Computer icon, as shown here. For help on adding these particular icons to the desktop, see Part 10.

2 Each task includes a series of quick, easy steps designed to guide you through the procedure.

3 Items that you select or click in menus, dialog boxes, tabs, and windows are shown in **bold**.

Introductions explain what you will learn in each task and **Tips and Hints** give you a heads-up for any extra information you may need while working through the tas

drop

How to Drag:
Point to the starting place or object. Hold down the mouse button (right or left per instructions), move the mouse to the new location, then release the button.

See next page:
If you see this symbol, it means the task you're working on continues on the next page.

End Task:
Task is complete.

Selection:
Highlights the area onscreen discussed in the step or task.

Click:
Click the left mouse button once.

Right-click:
Click the right mouse button once.

Click & Type:
Click once where indicated and begin typing to enter your text or data.

Double-click:
Click the left mouse button twice in rapid succession.

Pointer Arrow:
Highlights an item on the screen you need to point to or focus on in the step or task.

Introduction to *Easy Microsoft Money 2004*

Finances are usually not a fun topic to discuss, unless you're Donald Trump. Chances are the reason you bought this book (or are contemplating buying it) is because you need some help managing your finances. Am I psychic? Nope, just an educated guess. I think it's safe to say that with today's economy and the rising costs of living expenses, education, and taxes, we could all use a little help managing our finances.

You're in luck because help is available and right in your hands. *Easy Microsoft Money 2004* can help you learn how to take control of those financial reins using Microsoft Money 2004. You can track your incoming and outgoing funds, analyze your spending habits, track your investments (or learn about investing), create a plan to get out of debt, and save for the future. In some cases, you can also download statements, check your credit, and set up bills to pay online. You no longer have to write yourself notes to remember to pay your bills on time; *Easy Microsoft Money 2004* can teach you how to set up reminders so that you won't forget. As if all this financial control wasn't enough, you can even get a head start on your taxes and have Money determine for which deductions you might be eligible. It's like having a personal accountant right at your fingertips, but much cheaper, of course.

Even if you already have a hold on your finances, you can use Money to keep all your financial information in one central place, and run a report at the click of a button to tell you everything you need to know about your finances, any trouble areas you might run into down the road, and how to plan for that dream vacation or a nice retirement. You will learn how to do all these things and great deal more with this book. *Easy Microsoft Money 2004* walks you through each task at your own pace, and you don't have to worry about any confusing financial double talk. And even if you run across a word you aren't too familiar with, there's a handy glossary at the back of the book to define unfamiliar terms. All this information is offered to you in simple terms with simple, step-by-step procedures that will have you singing the praises of financial control in no time. In other words, you'll learn how to manage your finances, the Easy way. But before you start doing your happy dance, we have some work to do. So let's get started...

PART 1

Getting Started

Before you can start crunching numbers, analyzing your finances, getting out of debt, or planning for that dream home, you must complete a setup process so that Microsoft Money has all the information it needs to work for you.

First, you have to let Money know if there is an existing Money file it can update, a Quicken file to import, or a brand new Money file to create. Then you use the Setup Assistant, which prompts you for all of your personal and financial information. If you don't already have your banking, bills, personal, and paycheck information ready, go get that information now. Also, if you want to include your spouse's or partner's information, get all of his or her information too.

If you had a previous version of Money and have already entered most of your personal and financial information, you won't need all of that information at hand. Money automatically brings in the information from any previous versions of Money. However, if you want to add to what you already have, get that information together now. Be sure you have Microsoft Money 2004 installed and ready to run because this book starts out with the assumption that Money has already been installed. If you haven't installed it yet, do that now and come back when you are finished.

Microsoft Money 2004 Setup Assistant

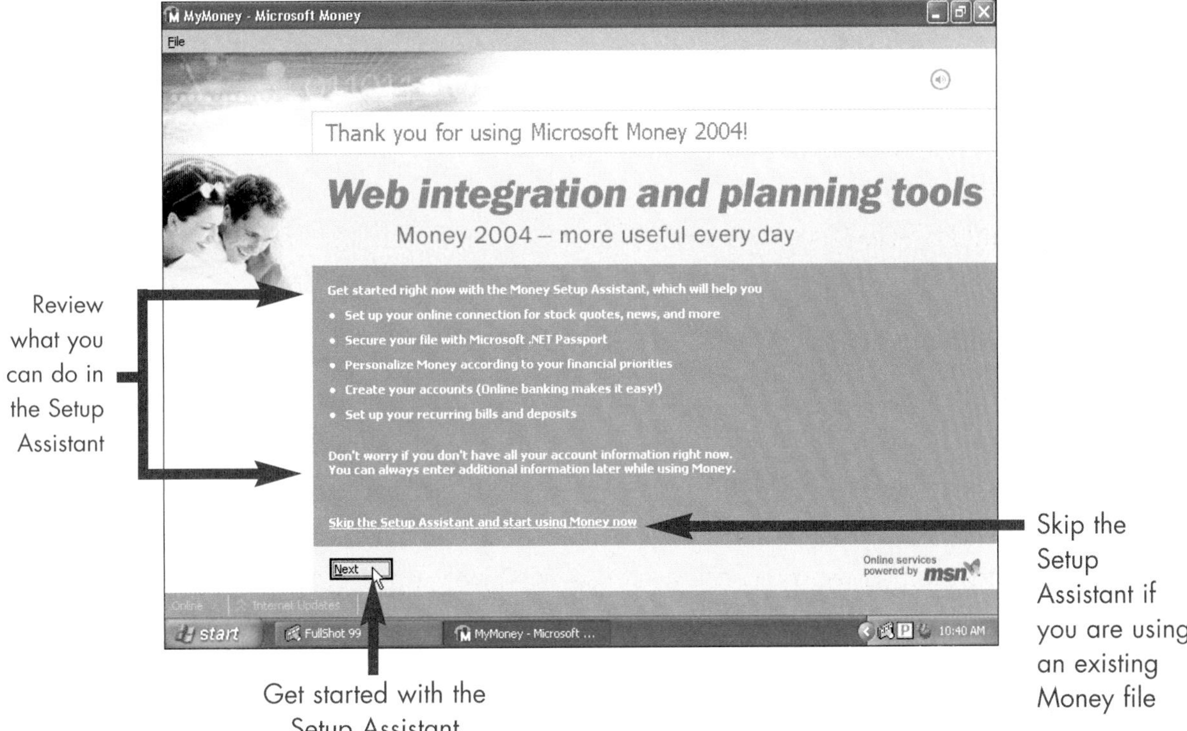

Opening Money

1 Double-Click
2 Click
3 Click
4 Click

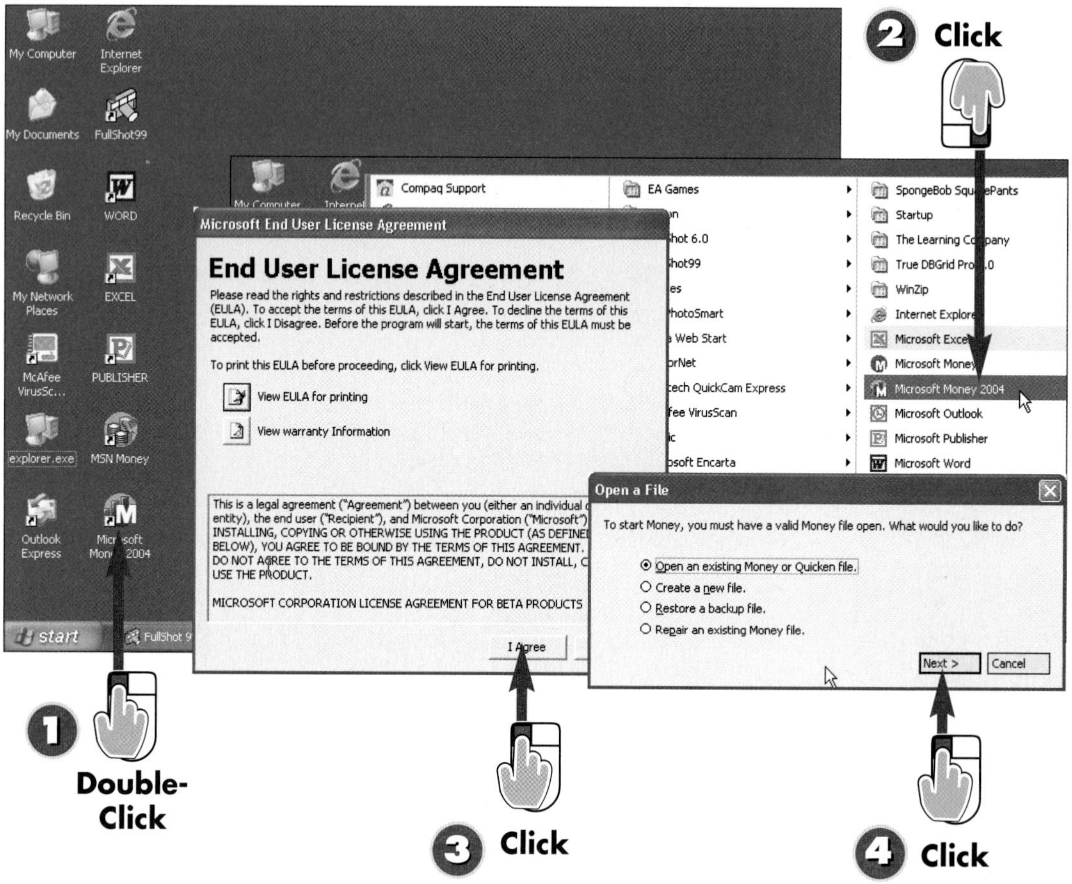

1. From your desktop, double-click the **Microsoft Money 2004** icon.
2. Alternatively, from your Windows taskbar, click **Start**, **All Programs**, and then choose **Microsoft Money 2004**.
3. If an End User Agreement dialog box appears, read the agreement and click **I Agree**.
4. If a Money file is already set up on your computer, choose **Open an existing Money or Quicken file** and click **Next**.

INTRODUCTION

When you installed Money, the installation setup should have placed a Money icon on your desktop. You can open Money by double-clicking this icon or by using your Windows Start menu. After you start Money, you are prompted to either open an existing file or create a new one. If you have a Quicken file you would like to import and use, skip to the next task.

TIP

Seeing the EULA
If this is the first time you've used Money 2004, the End User Agreement (EULA) will appear. If you have used Money 2004 before now, you won't see this agreement again.

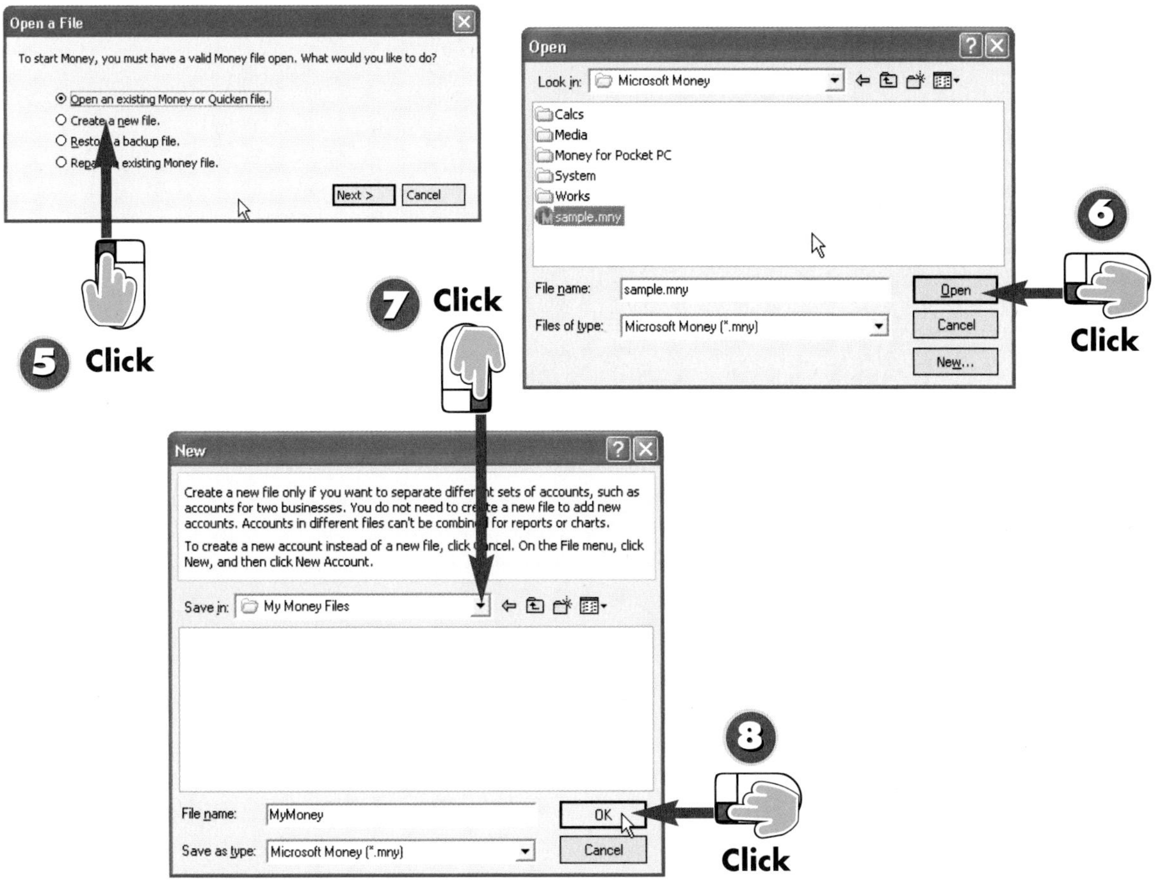

Open a File

To start Money, you must have a valid Money file open. What would you like to do?

- Open an existing Money or Quicken file.
- Create a new file.
- Restore a backup file.
- Repair an existing Money file.

Next > Cancel

5 Click

Open

Look in: Microsoft Money

Calcs
Media
Money for Pocket PC
System
Works
sample.mny

File name: sample.mny
Files of type: Microsoft Money (*.mny)

Open Cancel New...

6 Click

7 Click

New

Create a new file only if you want to separate different sets of accounts, such as accounts for two businesses. You do not need to create a new file to add new accounts. Accounts in different files can't be combined for reports or charts.

To create a new account instead of a new file, click Cancel. On the File menu, click New, and then click New Account.

Save in: My Money Files

File name: MyMoney
Save as type: Microsoft Money (*.mny)

OK Cancel

8 Click

5 If you want to create a brand new Money file, choose **Create a new file** and click **Next**.

6 If you are opening an existing Money file, click the **Look in** down arrow and locate the .mny file you need. Then click **Open**.

7 If you are creating a new Money file, click the **Save in** down arrow and locate the folder in which you would like Money to save your new .mny file.

8 Type a name for the new Money file in the **File name** box. (Be sure to keep the .mny extension.) Then click **OK**.

TIP

What Happens Next?

If you are using an existing Money file, Money displays information telling you that it is copying your previous .mny file and converting it for use with the 2004 version. If you are creating a new Money file, you will see information about Money and its features. Click **Next** to cycle through the windows until Money is finished upgrading your file information or displaying its feature information.

TIP

Already Set Up?

If you have already gone through Money's setup process, you can skip ahead to Part 2.

Importing Quicken Files

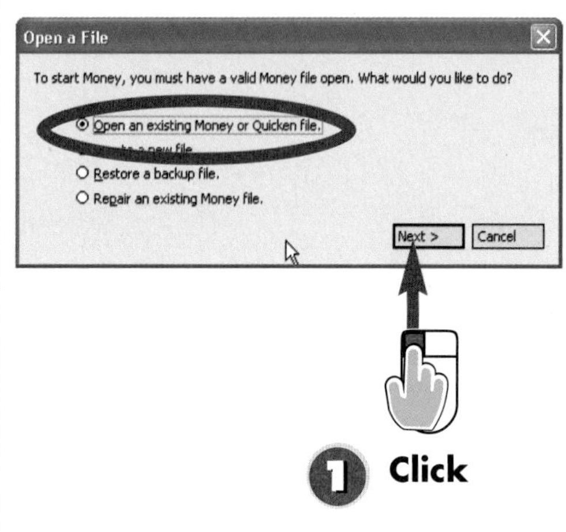

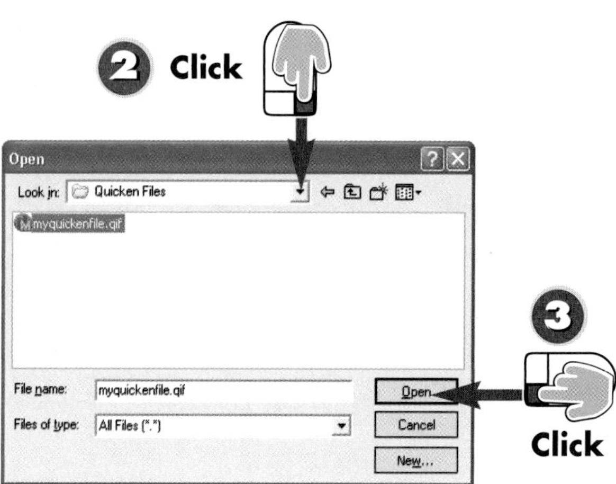

1. After you start Money and agree to the terms in the End User Agreement), choose **Open an existing Money or Quicken file** and click **Next**.
2. Click the **Look in** down arrow and locate the Quicken file you want to import.
3. Click **Open**, and click **Next** in each window that appears until Money finishes converting your file and displaying its feature information.

INTRODUCTION

If you have used Quicken in the past to manage your finances, you can use the information you entered into Quicken by importing the information into Money. Money gives you the option of importing a Quicken file when you start Money for the first time. You can also import Quicken files once you have already gone through the entire setup process. If you already set up a .mny file in the preceding task and don't have a Quicken file, skip to the next task.

TIP

Importing Quicken Files
If you want to import your Quicken file after setup is complete, open Money; then, from the **File** menu, select **Import Quicken file** and follow the prompts. The remainder of the import process is the same as it is in this task.

Setting Up Your Password

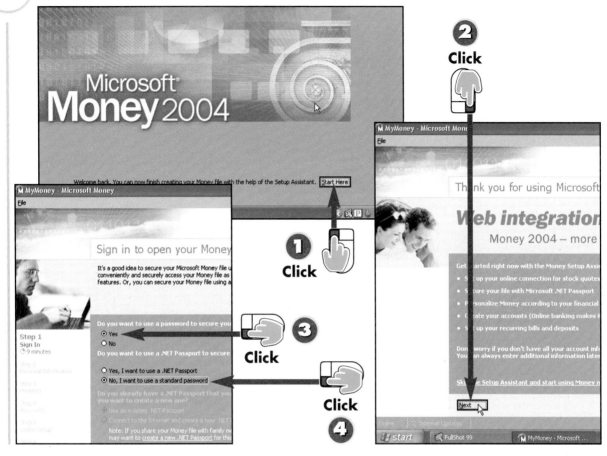

1. Click **Start Here** to start the Setup Assistant.
2. Review the information you will see during the setup process and click **Next** to continue.
3. To set up a standard password, click the **Yes** option button under the first question.
4. To use a .NET password, click the **Yes** option button under the second question. To create and use a standard password, click **No** and skip ahead to step 7.

See next page

INTRODUCTION

After you've opened Money and created or imported a file, Money launches the Setup Assistant, which asks you if you want to secure the financial information on your PC by setting up a password. You can set up a standard password, or if you already have a .NET password, you can use it. You can also set up a new .NET password, but you will need to connect to the Internet to do so. You do not have to set up a password to use Money, though doing so is a good idea; if you decide not to create a password now, rest assured that you can do so later if you change your mind. If you do set up a password, be sure to write it down in a safe place because you are required to enter it each time you enter Money.

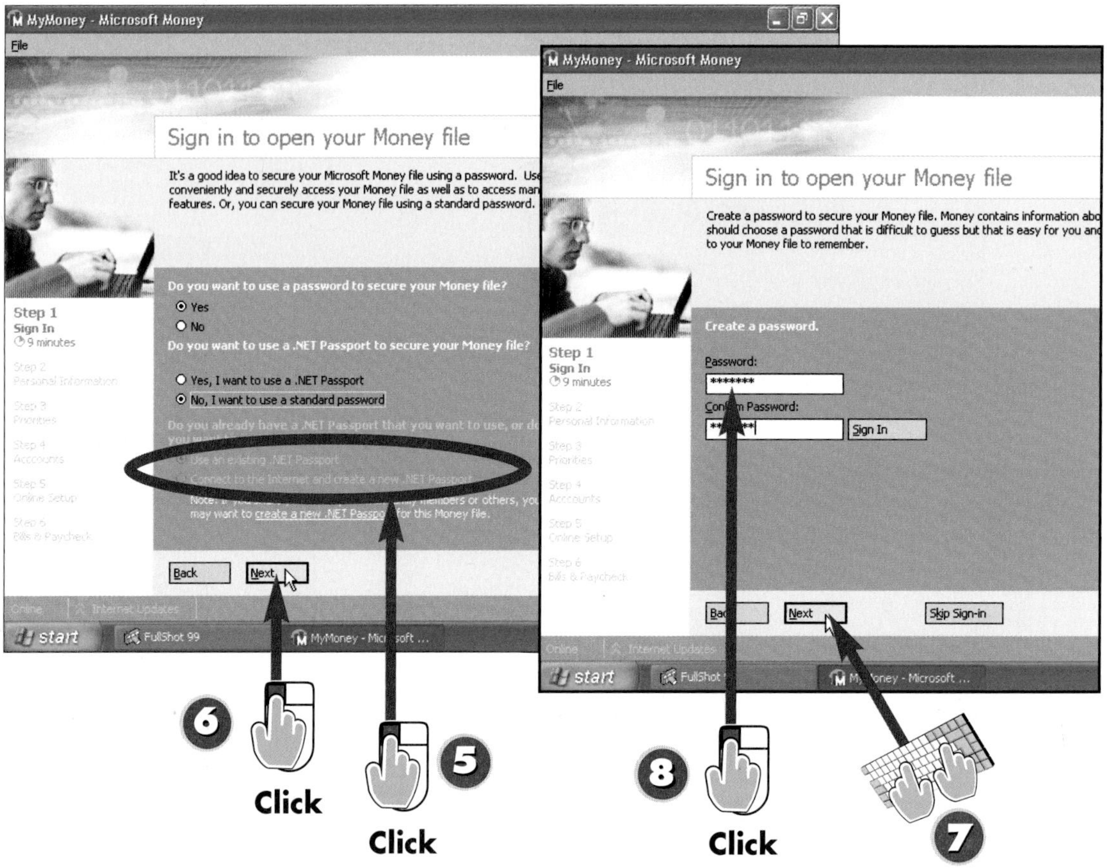

5. If you already have a .NET Passport, click **Use an existing .NET Passport**. To create a new .NET Passport, click **Connect to the Internet and create a new .NET Passport**.
6. Click **Next**.
7. Click in **Password** and type your new password, then click in **Confirm Password** and type it again.
8. Click **Sign In** and then click **Next**.

TIP

Skipping Setup
You can skip the Setup Assistant by clicking **Skip the Setup Assistant and start using Money now** on the screen shown in step 2, but I don't recommend it. Entering all your information now will save you time later.

TIP

Disabling Audio
If your PC has sound, you'll hear information about each window of the Setup Assistant. To turn off these voice commands, click the sound icon in the upper right corner of Money and select **Turn All Audio Help Off**.

TIP

Skipping the Sign-in
If you don't want to bother with signing in at this time, click **Skip Sign-in**.

Setting Financial-Tracking Information

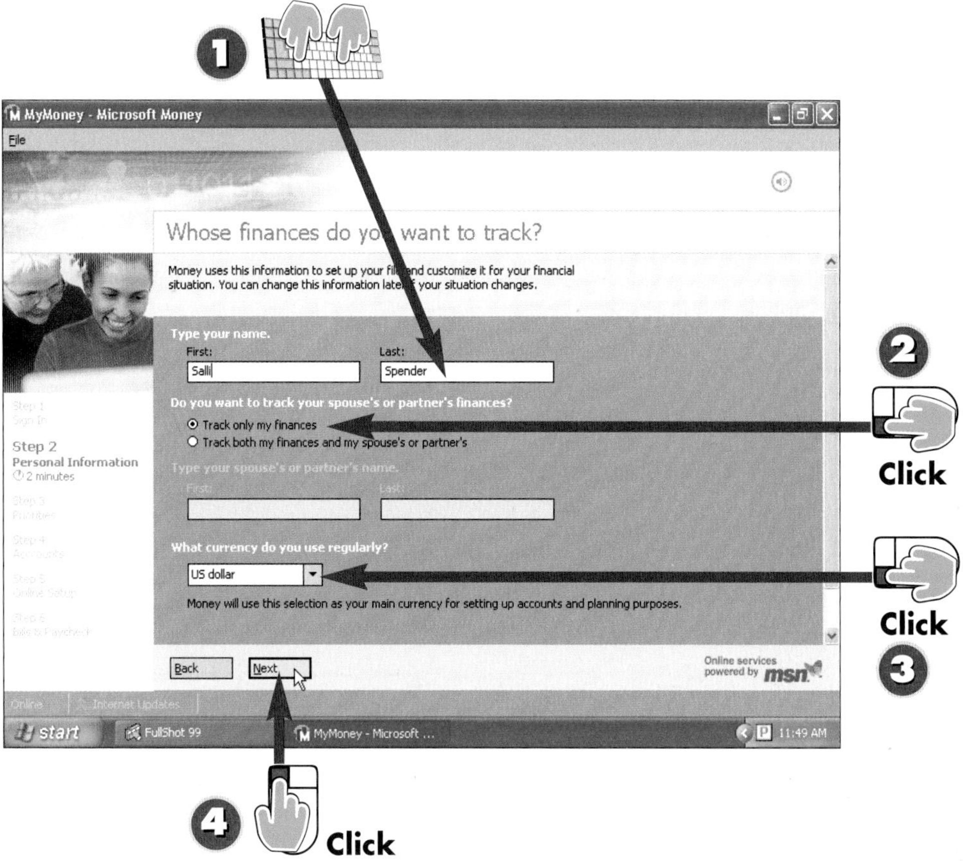

1. If your name does not already appear in the **First** and **Last** text boxes, click in those boxes and type your first and last name.
2. Select **Track only my finances** or select **Track both my finances and my spouse's or partner's** and type his or her name in the **First** and **Last** boxes.
3. Specify what kind of currency you use by selecting it from the **What currency do you use regularly?** drop-down menu.
4. Click **Next**.

INTRODUCTION

After asking you whether you want to set a password, Money's Setup Assistant prompts you to select whether you want to track just your own financial information or to include that of your spouse or partner, if applicable. You can also select the type of currency you want to track.

Start

Specifying Financial Priorities and Accounts

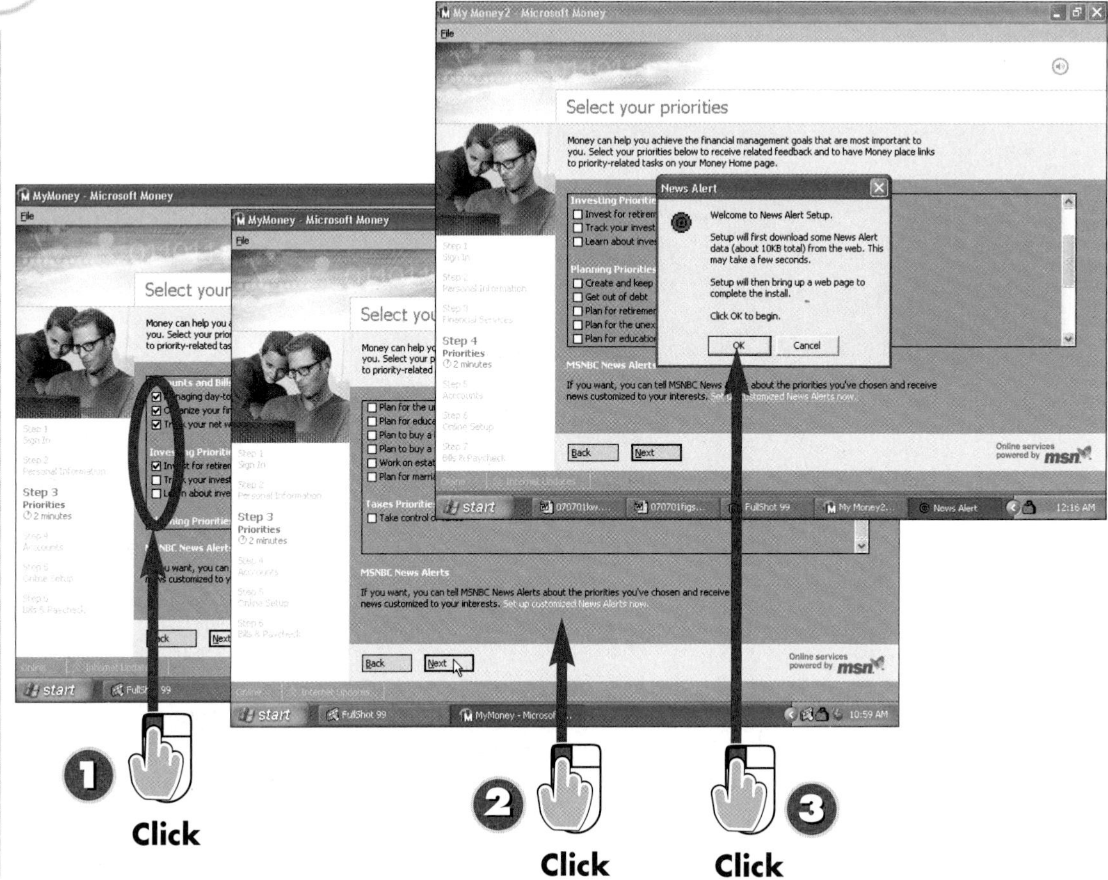

1. Select your goals or financial preferences by clicking in the desired check box(es) under each category. (Use the scrollbar to see all the options.)
2. To receive information via email about select financial interests, click **Set up customized News Alerts now** (be sure you are connected to the Internet).
3. A message appears telling you that Money will download the necessary files; click **OK**, or click **Cancel** to stop the installation.

INTRODUCTION

After you specify whose financial information you want to track, Money asks you to specify your financial priorities. When doing so, think about your financial goals and needs, and select the options that interest you. What you select will determine what information is included on your home page, which is created when you are finished with the Setup Assistant. The more options you select here, the more categories appear on your home page. (You can always change your selections later, as discussed in Part 4, so don't worry about selecting something you're not sure about.)

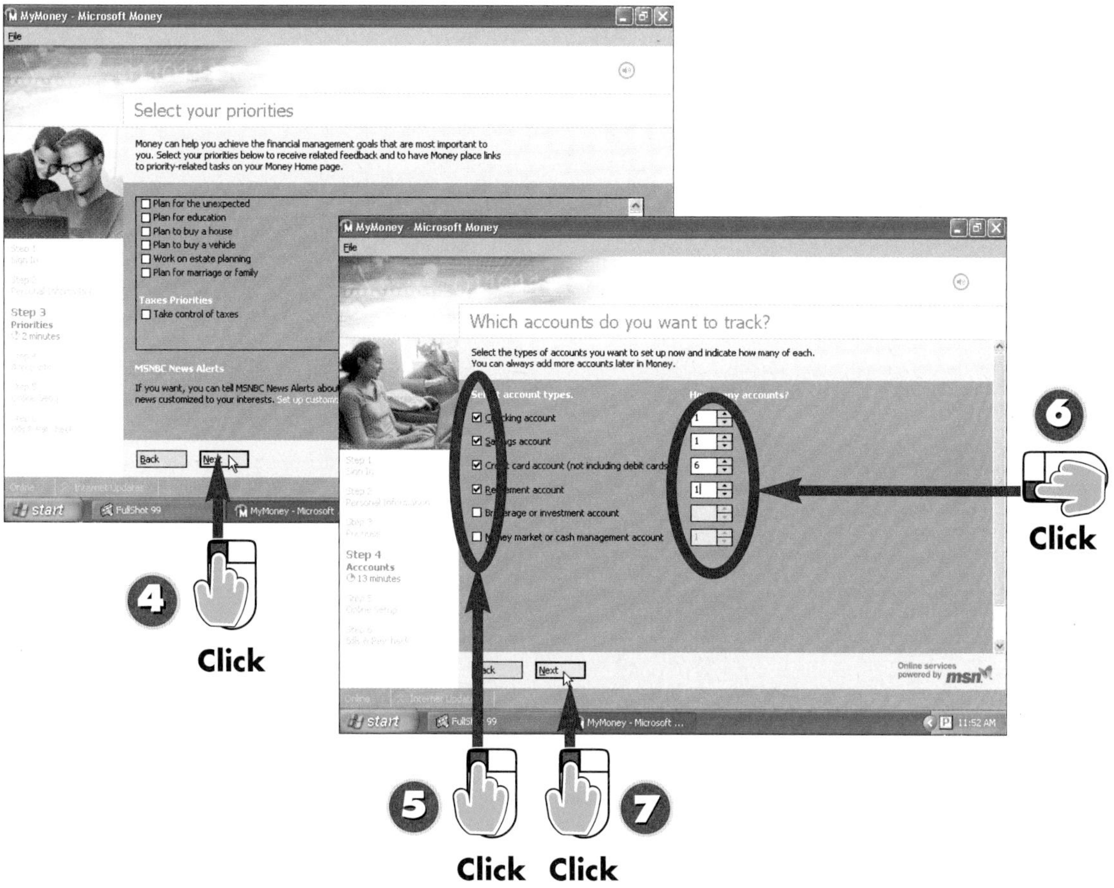

4 When you are finished making your selections, click **Next**.

5 Select the types of accounts you have—checking, savings, and so on—by clicking the appropriate check boxes.

6 Next to each account type, specify the number of accounts you have by typing the number or by clicking the up/down arrow buttons.

7 Click **Next**.

TIP

Understanding Priorities
When you select a check box in the **Priorities** area, Money displays a description of the selected option. If, after reading the description, you are not interested in the option, click the check box again to deselect it.

TIP

Changing Your Settings
Remember, you can always change the options you select at a later time (see Part 4 and beyond) if you change your mind.

TIP

Importing or Upgrading?
If you imported information from Quicken or upgraded a previous version of Money, this may be your last step. If so, click **Finish** on the Congratulations window and skip to Part 2.

Entering Account Information

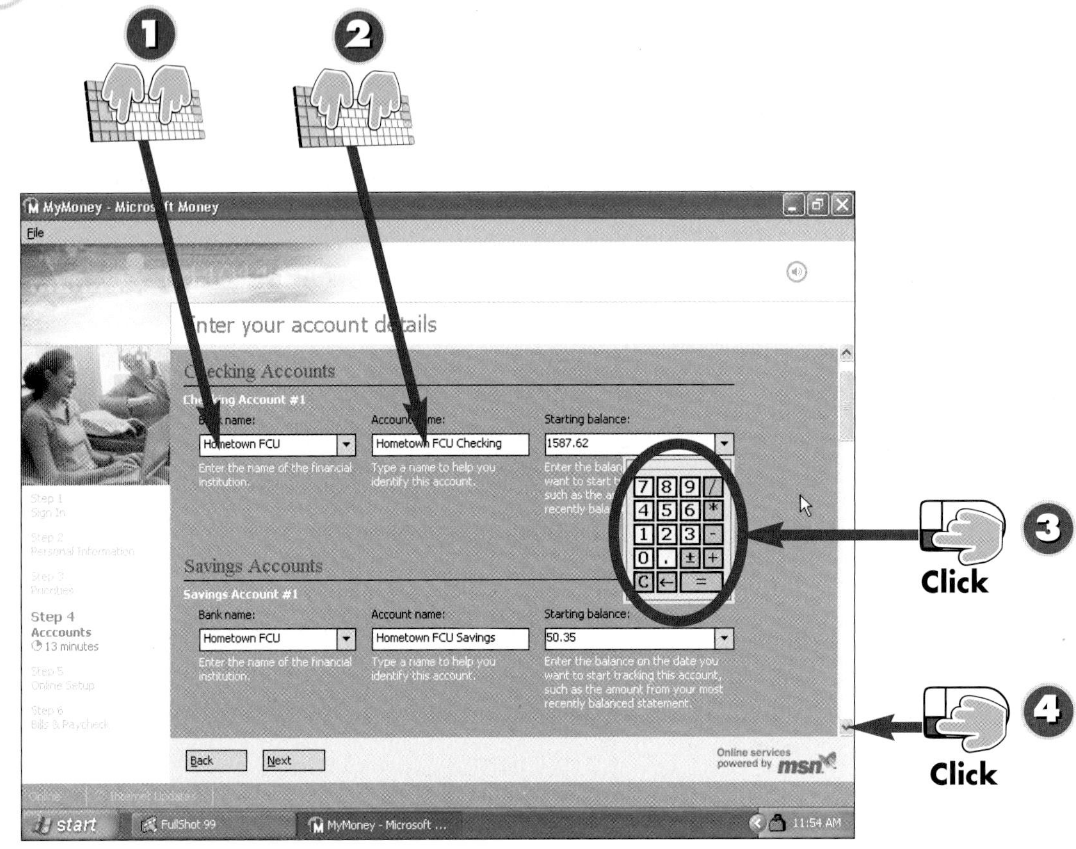

1. For each bank account, type the bank's name in the **Bank name** box. Alternatively, click the down arrow and select the name from the list, if it appears there.
2. Type a name for each bank account in its **Account Name** box. This name is used simply to identify the account within Money.
3. For each bank account, type your current balance or the balance of your last statement in the **Starting balance** box, or click the down arrow to enter the balance.
4. When you finish entering bank-account information, scroll down to the next category.

INTRODUCTION

After you specify your financial priorities, you must enter your accounts information. The types of accounts for which you are asked to enter information appear because of the selections you made in the previous task. So, get out those checking, savings, retirement, credit card, and loan statements, and get ready to plug in some information about each account. (If you don't have information for all of your accounts, you can enter it later; to learn how, see Part 4 and beyond.)

TIP

Entering Balances
To enter account balances, you can either type the dollar amount in the **Starting balance** box or click the down arrow next to it and click the numbers on the key pad (don't forget the decimal).

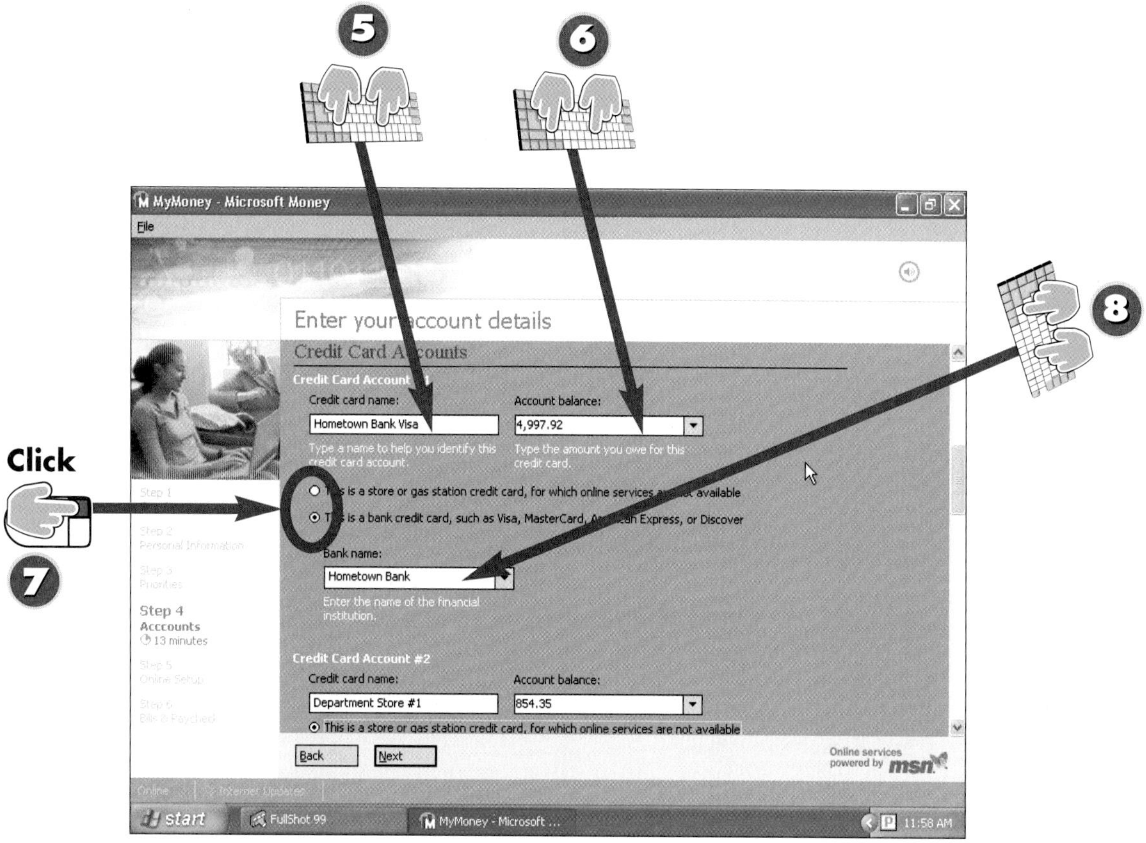

5 For each credit-card account, click in the **Credit card name** box and type the credit card's name.

6 For each credit-card account, click in the **Account balance** box and type the current balance or the balance of your last statement.

7 For each credit-card account, select whether the card is a store card or a bank card.

8 If the credit card is a bank card, click in the **Bank name** box and type the name of the bank.

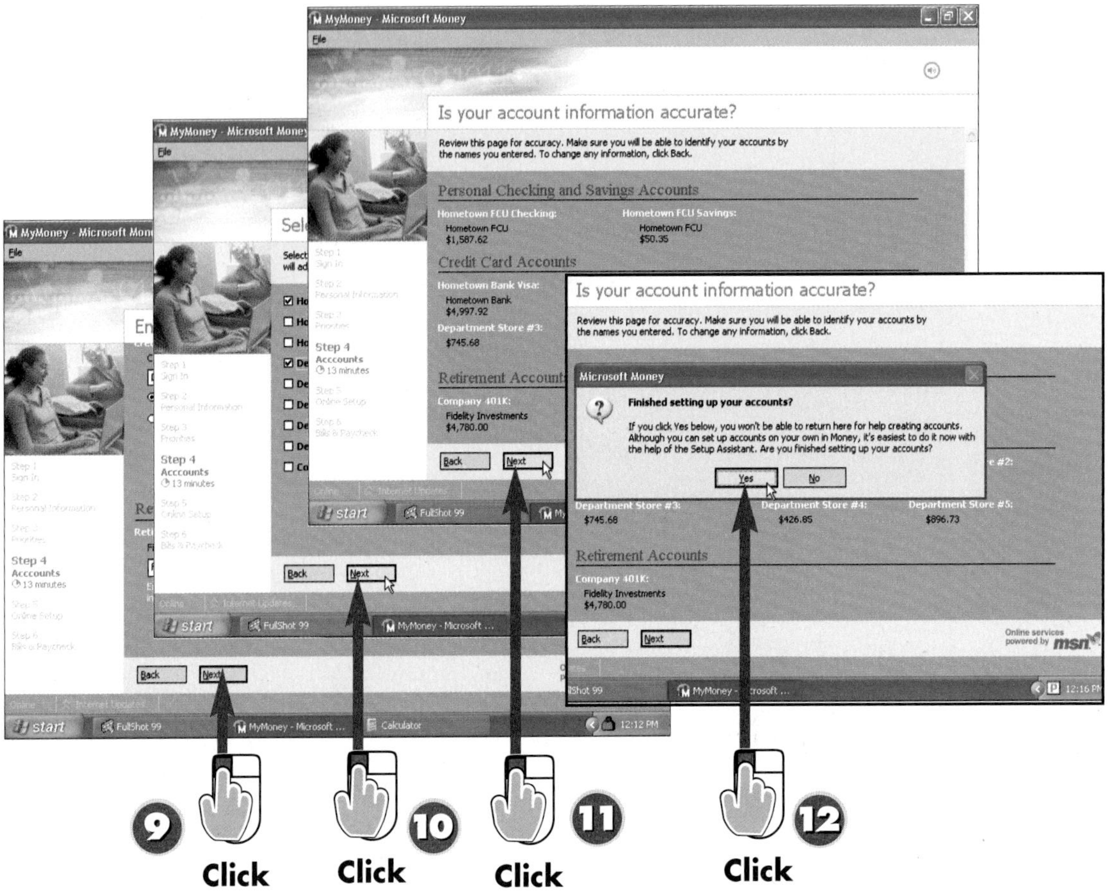

9. If you have retirement accounts, enter the information for those accounts just as you did for your other accounts; click **Next** when you are finished.

10. Click the check box next to the accounts you access most often and click **Next**. The accounts you select will be used to create a Favorites list.

11. Review all your account information, scrolling down if necessary, and click **Next**.

12. If you are finished setting up your account information, click **Yes**, and then click **Next**. If you still have changes to make, click **No**.

TIP

Changing Your Information

To make changes or add more accounts, click **Back** until you reach the window you need, make the desired changes, and click **Next** until you return to the summary window.

HINT

Updating Accounts Later

If you later find that you want to change account information or add a new account, you'll have many chances to do so after you are finished with the Setup Assistant (see Part 4 and beyond).

Setting Up Accounts Online

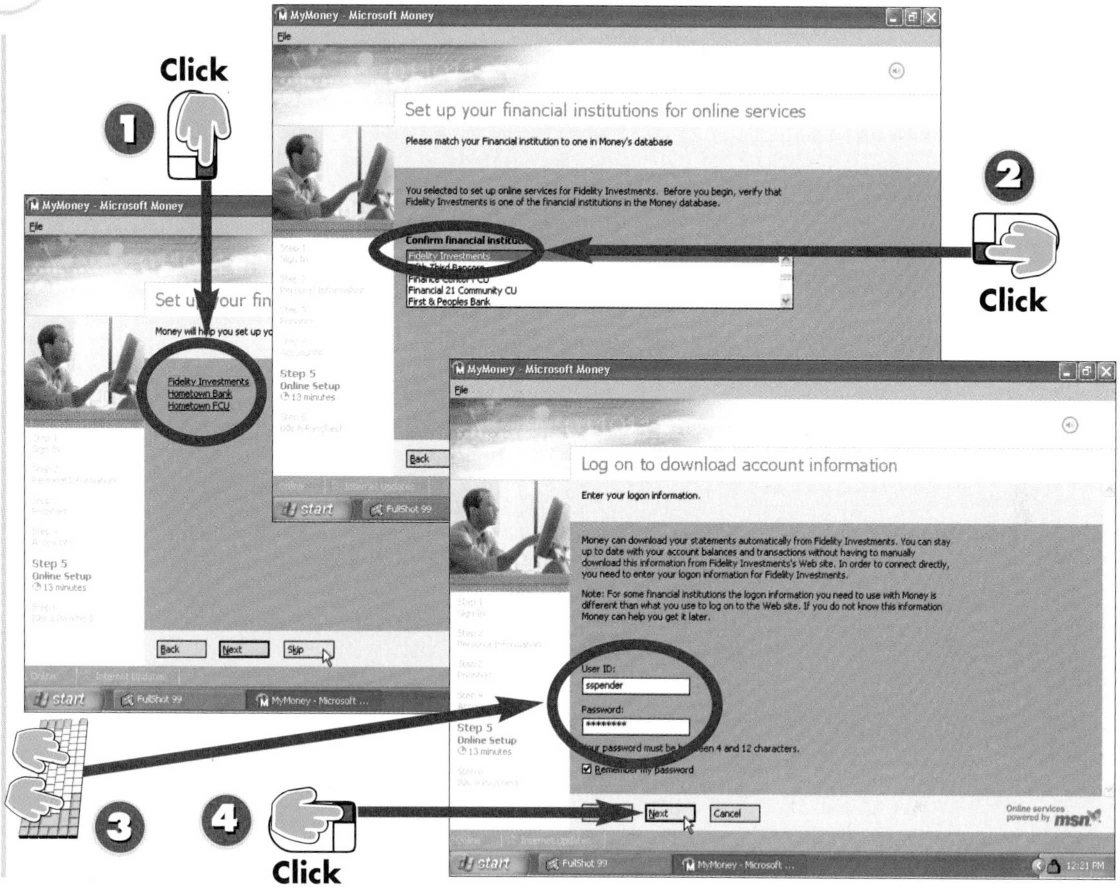

1. Click an account for which you would like online services set up. If you do not want to set up online services, click **Skip**.
2. Confirm the name of the account you want by selecting it from the list. A message appears telling you that Money is downloading information about your account.
3. In the **User ID** and **Password** boxes, type your information. (If you don't have this information, click **Back** and skip the online services setup for now.)
4. Click **Next**. A progress message tells you Money is updating account information and finalizing the online setup.

INTRODUCTION

After you enter your account information, Money determines whether any of your accounts are eligible for online services, compiles a list of eligible accounts, and enables you to select which accounts you would like to set up online. That way, you can download statements and account information, so that your financial information is kept up-to-date. If you don't want to set up accounts online, you can skip this portion of the setup process. Be sure your PC is connected to the Internet before you begin this task.

TIP

Setting Up Other Accounts

If you have other accounts that are eligible to be set up online, and you want to set them up now, repeat this task for each account.

Entering Your Income Information

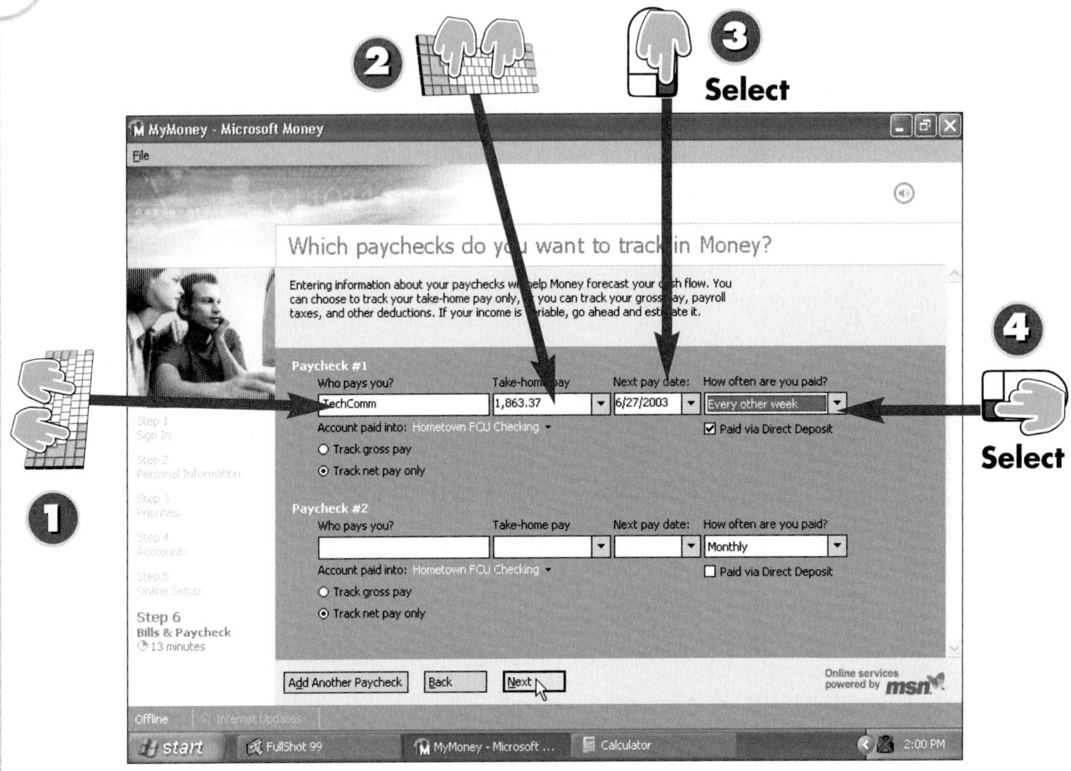

1. Click in the **Who pays you?** box and type the name of your employer or source of income.
2. Click in the **Take-home pay** box and type your net or gross pay.
3. Click in the **Next pay date** box and enter the date on which you will next be paid.
4. Click the **How often are you paid?** down arrow and select the frequency with which you are paid.

INTRODUCTION

After you finish setting up online services, Money's Setup Assistant asks you to enter information about your income. So, pull out any income information you want to include: paychecks, 1099s, child support, social security, and so on. Include any regular income you can count on and that you use to pay your bills and living expenses.

TIP

Tracking Net Pay
Tracking your net pay instead of your gross pay enables Money to better estimate your cash flow.

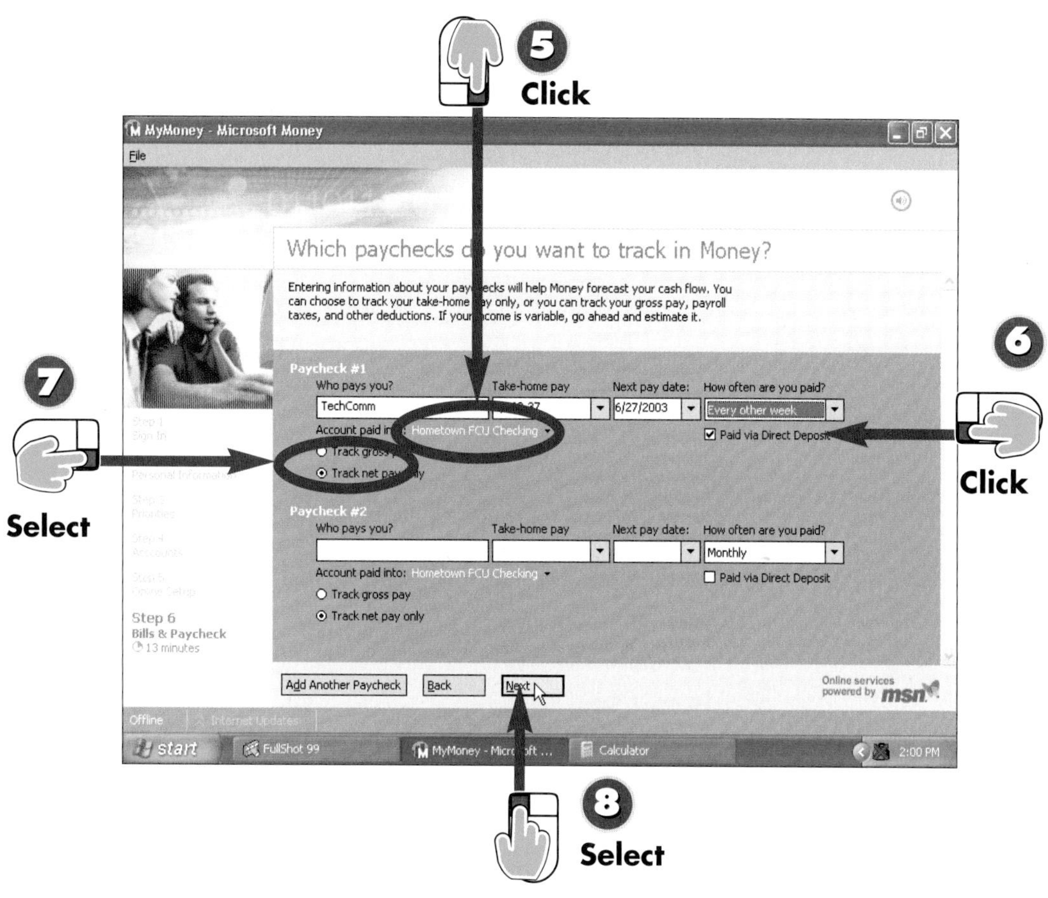

5 Click the **Account paid into** down arrow and select the bank account into which your paycheck is deposited.

6 If your paycheck is automatically deposited into your account by your employer, mark the **Paid via Direct Deposit** check box.

7 Select either **Track gross pay** or **Track net pay only**.

8 If you have another paycheck or source of income, enter that information in the **Paycheck #2** area by following steps 1–7. When you are finished, click **Next**.

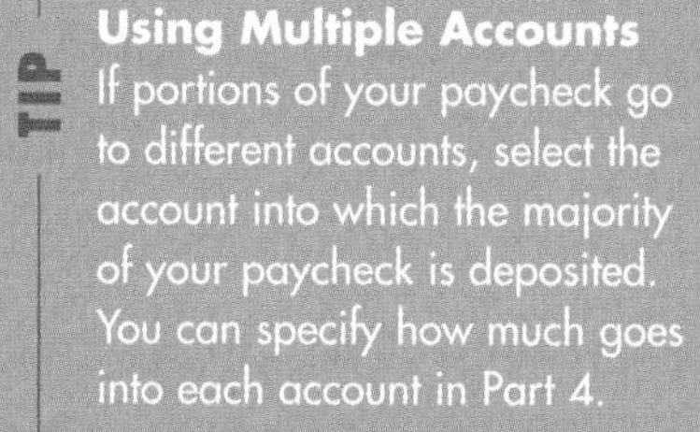

TIP

Using Multiple Accounts
If portions of your paycheck go to different accounts, select the account into which the majority of your paycheck is deposited. You can specify how much goes into each account in Part 4.

HINT

Adding More Paychecks
If you need to add even more paychecks, click **Add Another Paycheck** and enter the required information by following steps 1–7.

Selecting the Bills You Pay

Start

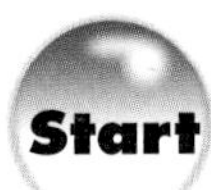

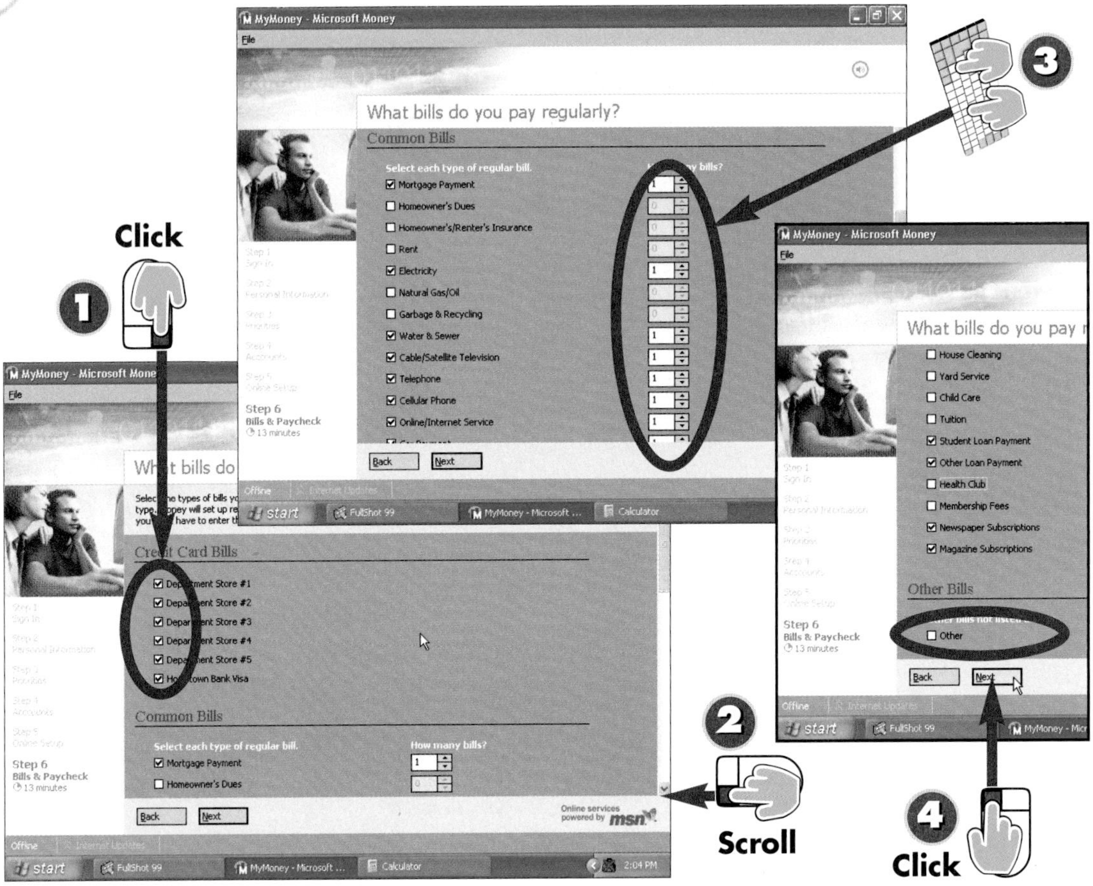

1. If applicable, select the credit-card bills you pay by clicking in the check box next to each credit card name.

2. Scroll down and click the check boxes next to all the other bills you have.

3. In the **How many bills?** column, type the number of bills you have for each bill type.

4. If you don't see a bill type for a bill you want to add, click the **Other** box. When you are finished, click **Next**.

End

INTRODUCTION

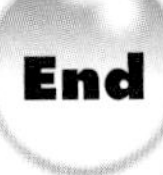

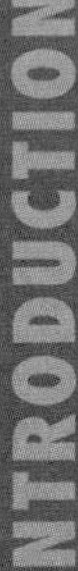

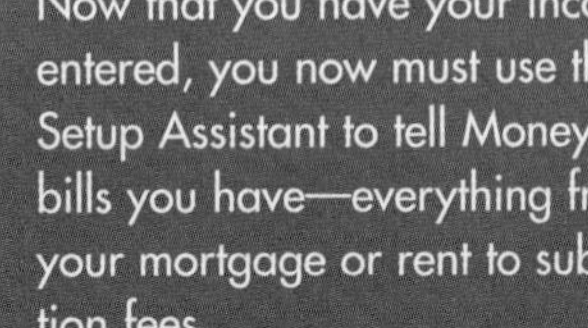

Now that you have your income entered, you now must use the Setup Assistant to tell Money what bills you have—everything from your mortgage or rent to subscription fees.

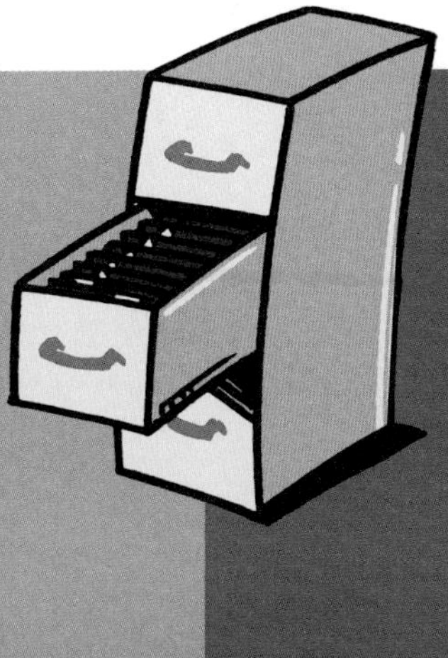

Entering Living Expenses and Bills

1. In the **Payee** box, type the name of the creditor or person/place you pay.
2. In the **Estimated amount** box, type the amount you pay.
3. In the **Next due date** box, type the date on which you will next pay the bill.

INTRODUCTION

The last thing the Setup Assistant prompts you to do is to enter the details about all of those bills and living expenses you selected in the preceding task. You'll need to know the names of the creditors or payees, approximately how much you pay them, the frequency with which you pay them, and the due dates for each bill and/or expense.

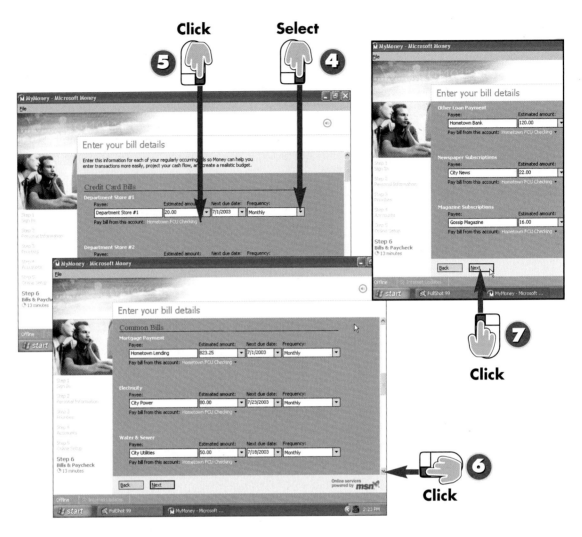

4. Click the **Frequency** down arrow and select how often you pay the bill.

5. Click the **Pay from this account** down arrow and select the bank account from which the bill is paid.

6. Scroll down and enter information about each bill/expense just as you did in steps 1–5.

7. When you finish adding bill information, click **Next**.

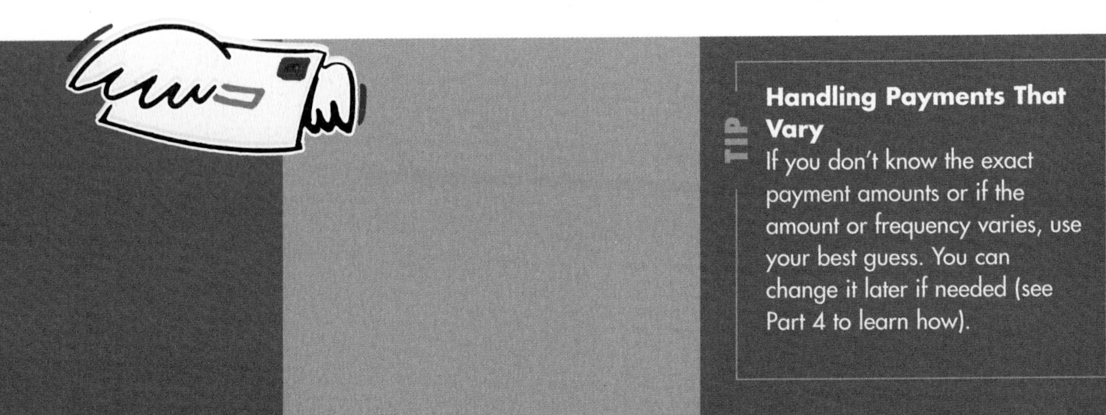

TIP

Handling Payments That Vary

If you don't know the exact payment amounts or if the amount or frequency varies, use your best guess. You can change it later if needed (see Part 4 to learn how).

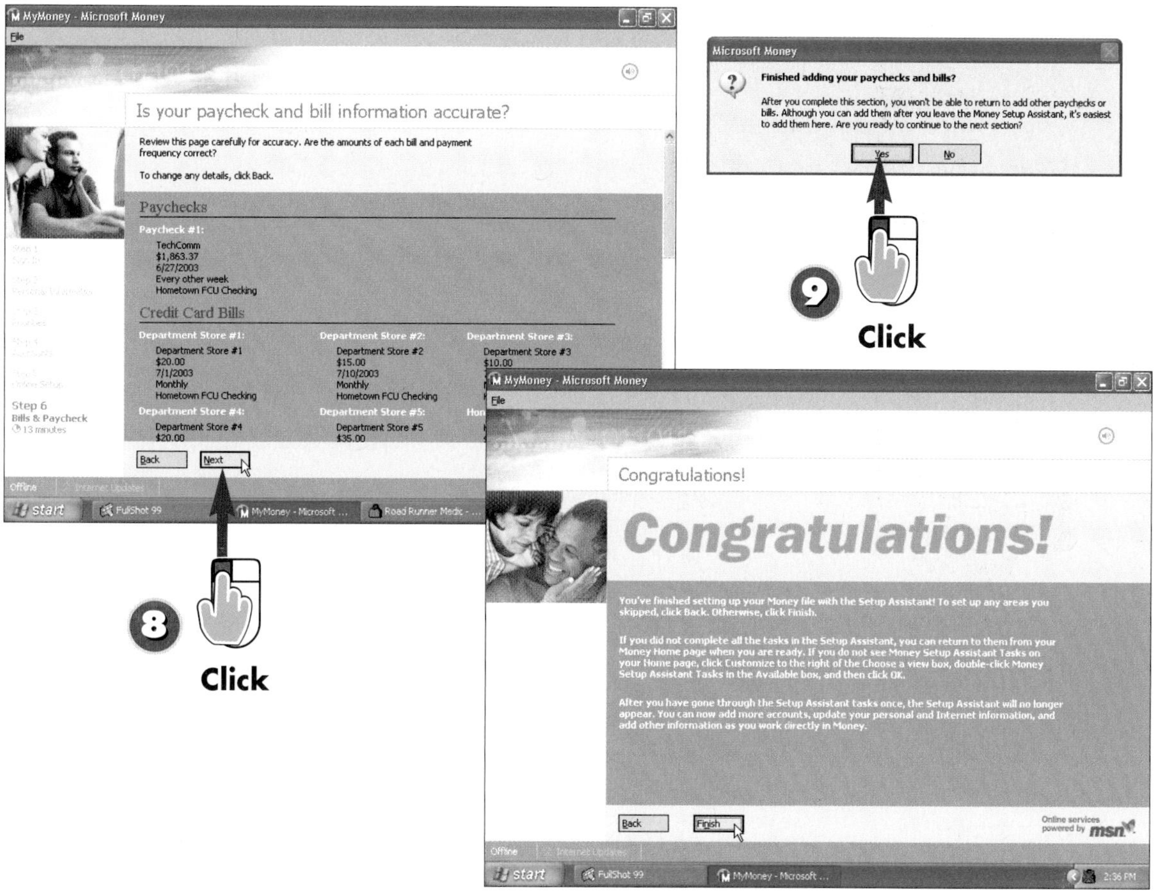

9 Click

8 Click

8 Review all your bills and expenses and click **Next** when you are finished.

9 A message appears asking if you are finished. Click **Yes**.

10 Click **Finish** to complete the setup process and close the Setup Assistant.

HINT

Changing Your Information

If you need to add, remove, or change bill/expense information, click **Back** until you reach the window where you can make the desired adjustments. Then click **Next** to return to the bills detail or bills summary window.

PART 2

Understanding the Basics

You made it through the setup process; now it's time to learn some basic Microsoft Money functionality. After you go through the Setup Assistant and each time you enter Money from then on, the first window you see is your home page. From your home page you access all of Money's features. In this part, you'll learn how to use the toolbar and menus that appear at the top of the home page to get around in Money. You'll also learn how to open and create new Money files—for example, to use for different businesses or for managing finances for properties. Lastly, you will learn about backing up your files, printing information, setting up or changing your password, getting help, and getting the latest Money and quote updates.

The Microsoft Money Home Page

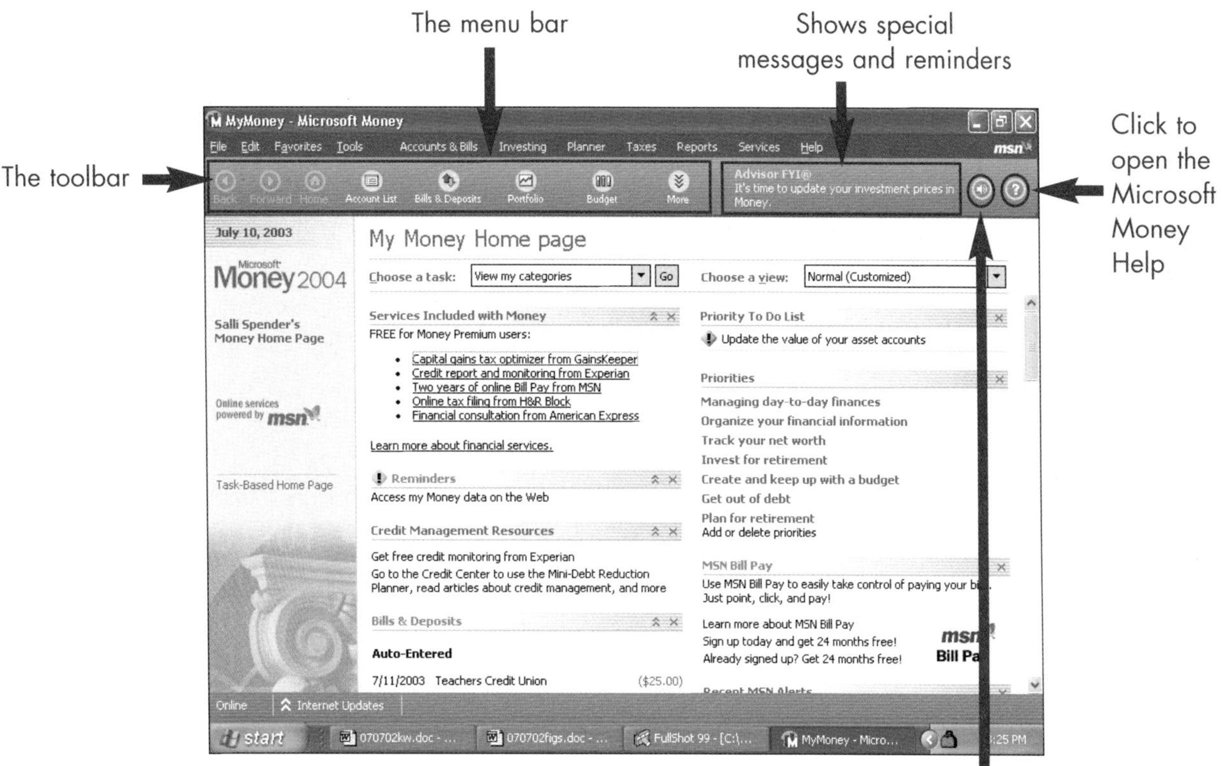

Using and Customizing the Toolbar

Start

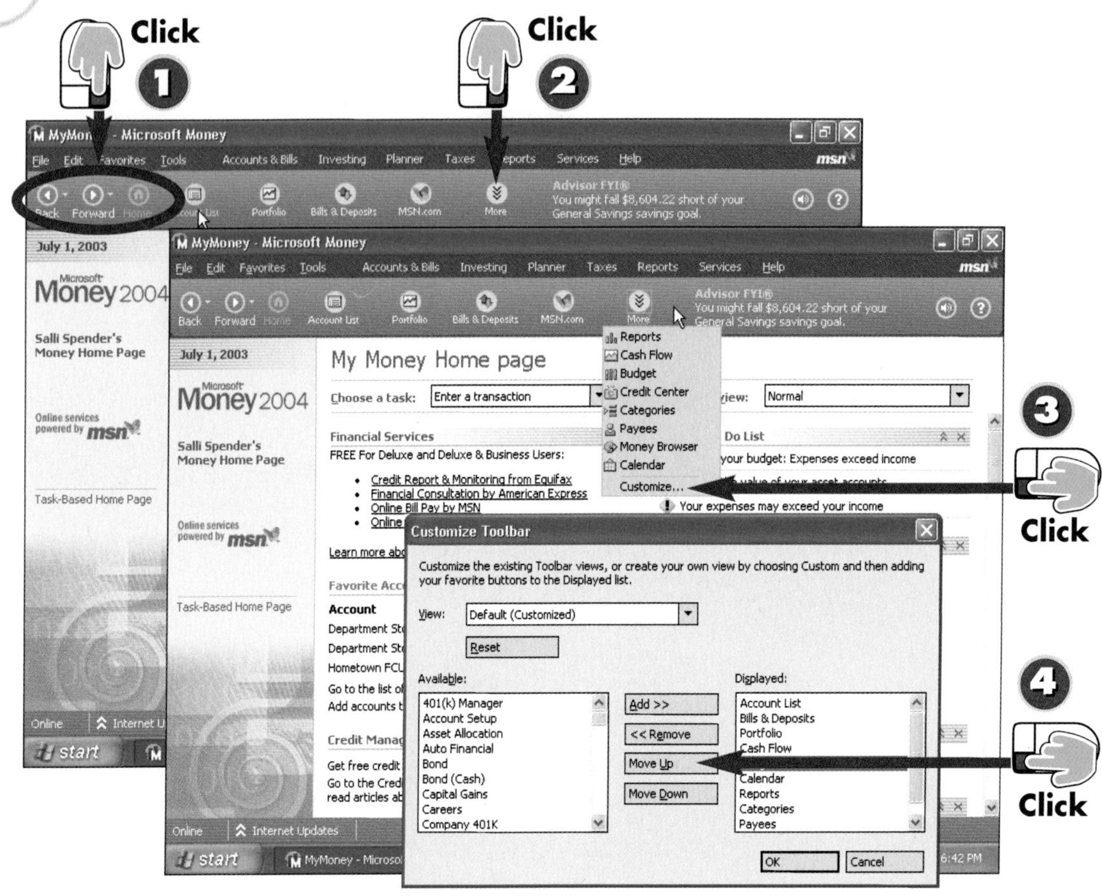

1. Use the first three buttons on your toolbar to move forward and backward or to get return to your home page.

2. Hover your mouse over the buttons on your toolbar to see a brief description of each one. To see all the displayed buttons, click the **More** button.

3. To customize your toolbar, click the **More** button and choose **Customize**.

4. To move a button from the More list to the main toolbar, click the button under **Displayed**. Cick **Move Up** repeatedly until the button is where you want it.

INTRODUCTION

Money's toolbar enables you to access all kinds of information at the touch of a button, and accessing your information can be even easier if you customize what buttons appear on the toolbar. If you're not already there, open your Money file so that you are looking at your home page.

TIP

The Customize Toolbar Dialog Box

Buttons already on your toolbar or in the More list appear in the **Displayed** list in the order they appear onscreen. For example, if Account List is the first name in the list, then the Account List button will be the first button on the toolbar. Buttons not on your toolbar or in the More list appear under **Available**. Only four buttons (give or take) are visible on the toolbar; to see the rest, you must click the **More** button.

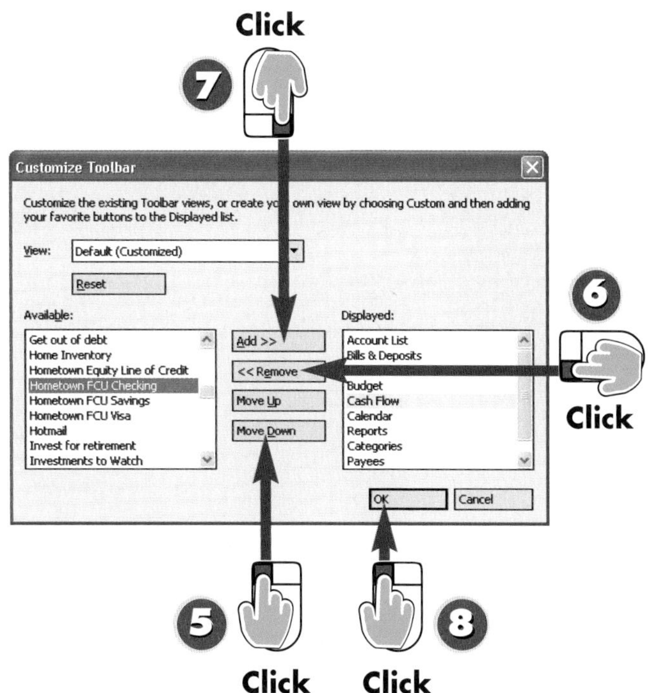

5 To move a button from the main toolbar to the More list, click the button under **Displayed**. Click **Move Down** repeatedly until the button is where you want it.

6 To remove a button from the toolbar and the More list, click the button's name under **Displayed** and then click **Remove**.

7 To add a button that is currently not displayed on the toolbar or in the More list, click the button's name under **Available** and then click **Add**.

8 When you are finished arranging, adding, and removing toolbar buttons, click **OK**.

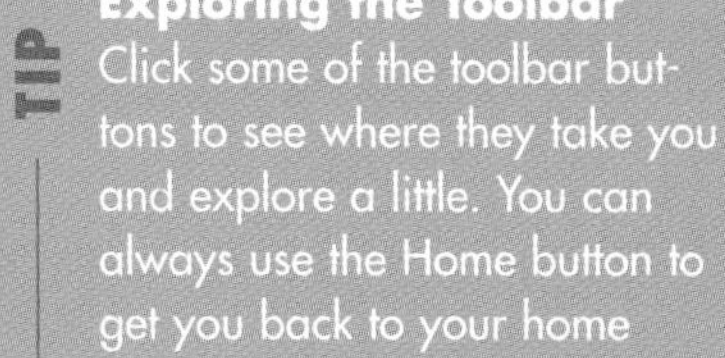

TIP

Exploring the Toolbar

Click some of the toolbar buttons to see where they take you and explore a little. You can always use the Home button to get you back to your home page.

HINT

Adding Buttons for Accounts

Notice that you can add to your toolbar buttons for the accounts you entered during setup. By adding buttons to the toolbar for your accounts, you can quickly access the accounts you use a lot.

Using Menus

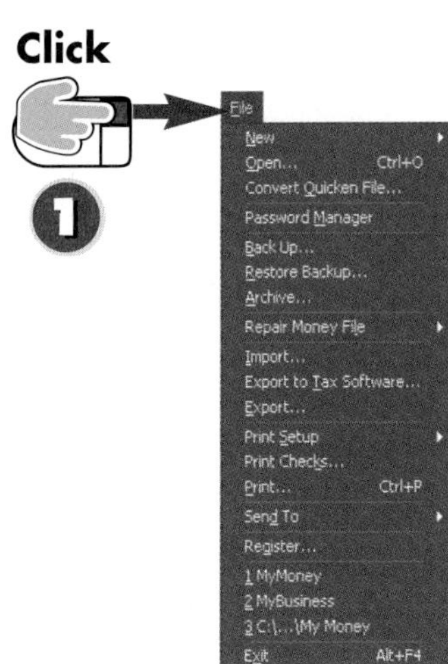

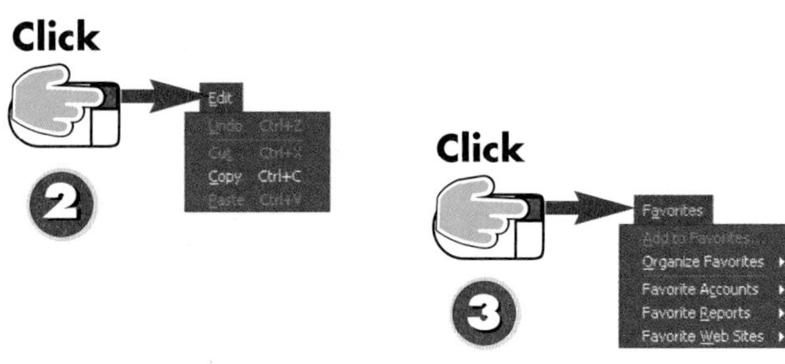

1. Use the **File** menu to open and create new files and accounts, convert Quicken files, manage passwords, and more.

2. Use the **Edit** menu to reverse an action, and to cut, copy, or paste text.

3. Use the **Favorites** menu to change to, view, and organize your favorite accounts, reports, and Web sites.

INTRODUCTION

Now that you're familiar with the toolbar, you're ready to explore the menus. Everything you accessed from the toolbar can be accessed from the menus, and much more.

HINT

Keyboard Shortcuts

Some functions have shortcut commands that you can use instead of using menus. If a function has a shortcut, it appears next to the menu command used to launch the function. For example, to undo an action, you can either open the **Edit** menu and choose **Undo** or press **Ctrl+Z**.

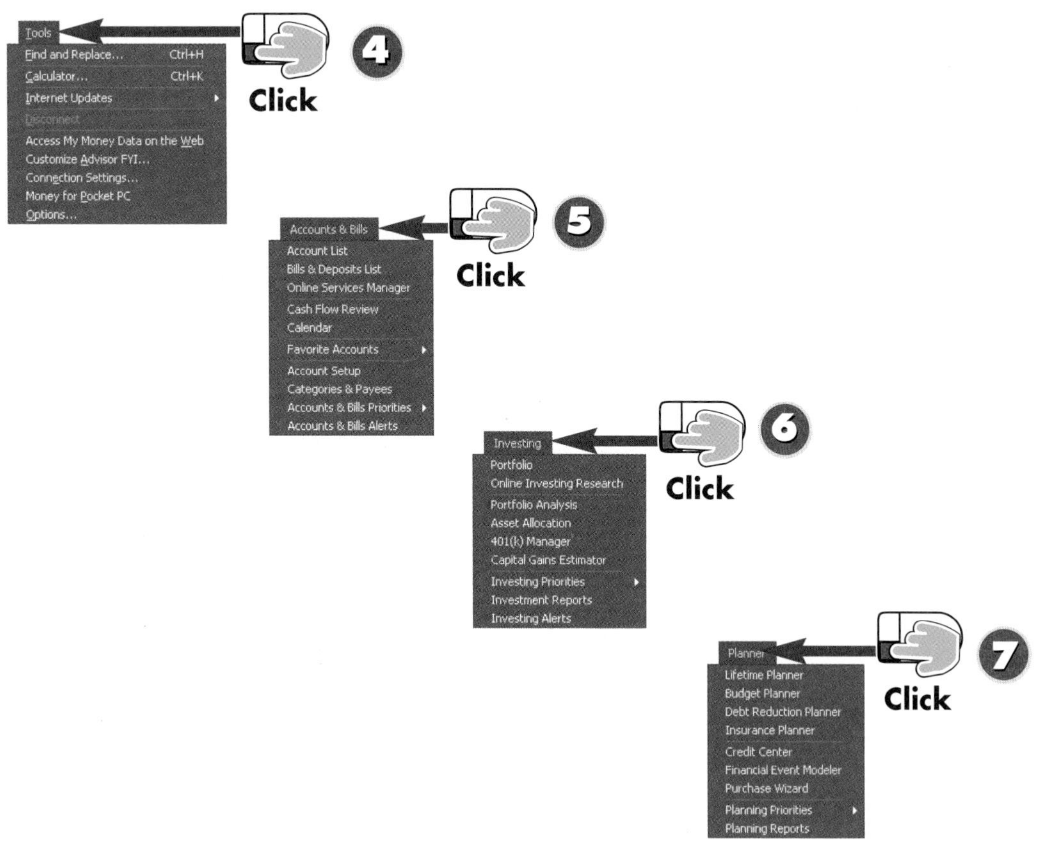

4 Use the **Tools** menu to access utilities such as Find and Replace and Calculator, as well as to update files and customize Money settings.

5 Use the **Accounts & Bills** menu to access, change, and manage all your accounts and bills information.

6 Use the **Investing** menu to access all information related to your own investments, as well as to investments in general.

7 Use the **Planner** menu to access all planners (for example, for creating budgets and debt reduction plans).

See next page

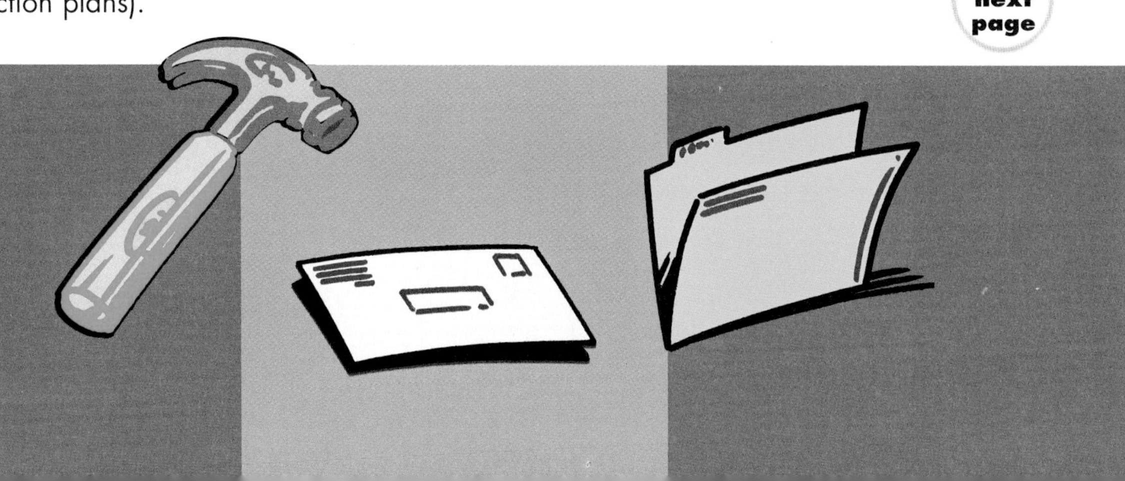

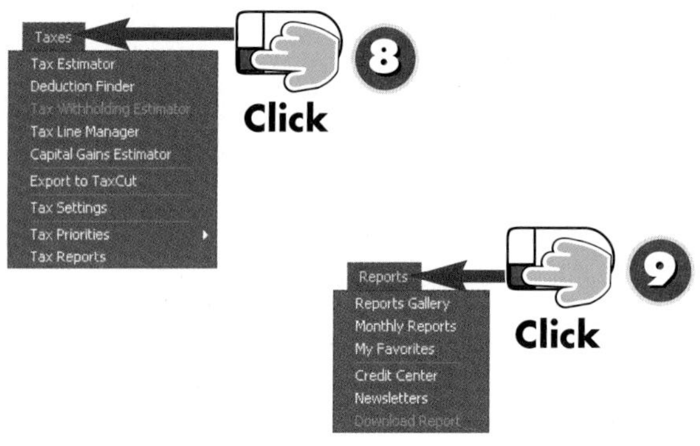

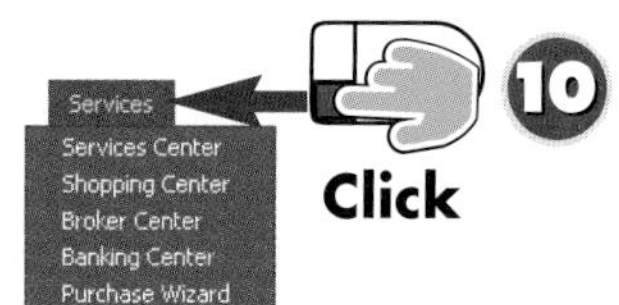

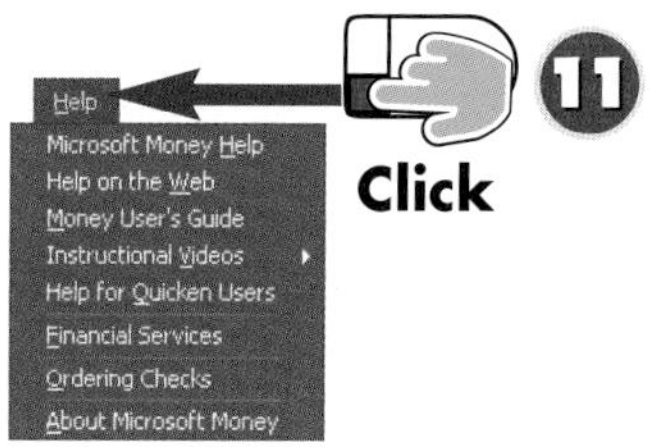

Help
Microsoft Money Help
Help on the Web
Money User's Guide
Instructional Videos
Help for Quicken Users
Financial Services
Ordering Checks
About Microsoft Money
Click
11

8 Use the **Taxes** menu to access all information related to your taxes, exporting tax information, and tax advice in general.

9 Use the **Reports** menu to access all kinds of reports, such as pie charts that outline your income and expenses.

10 Use the **Services** menu to access information about services Money provides, financial-management information, shopping links, and banking sites.

11 Use the **Help** menu to access the online help, the user manual, mini-videos to see how functions work, and other useful information about using Money and its services.

TIP

Finding Out More

For more detailed information about Money's various menus, review the Microsoft Money Help or, better yet, go exploring on your own.

Creating a New File

1. To create a new file, open the **File** menu, choose **New**, and select **New Account**.

2. Click the **Save in** down arrow and select the folder in which you want Money to save your new file.

3. Type a name for the new file in the **File name** box. Then click **OK**.

4. Using the Setup Assistant, set up your new file just as you did your original file in Part 1.

INTRODUCTION

If you want to create a new Money file—for example, to manage separate income and expenses or if you have a business that you want to keep separate from your personal finances—you can easily do so. Money allows you to create as many Money files as needed.

TIP

Skipping the Setup Assistant
When you create a new file, you are prompted to use the Setup Assistant. If you do not want to use this tool, click **Skip the Setup Assistant and start using Money now**.

Opening a File

Start

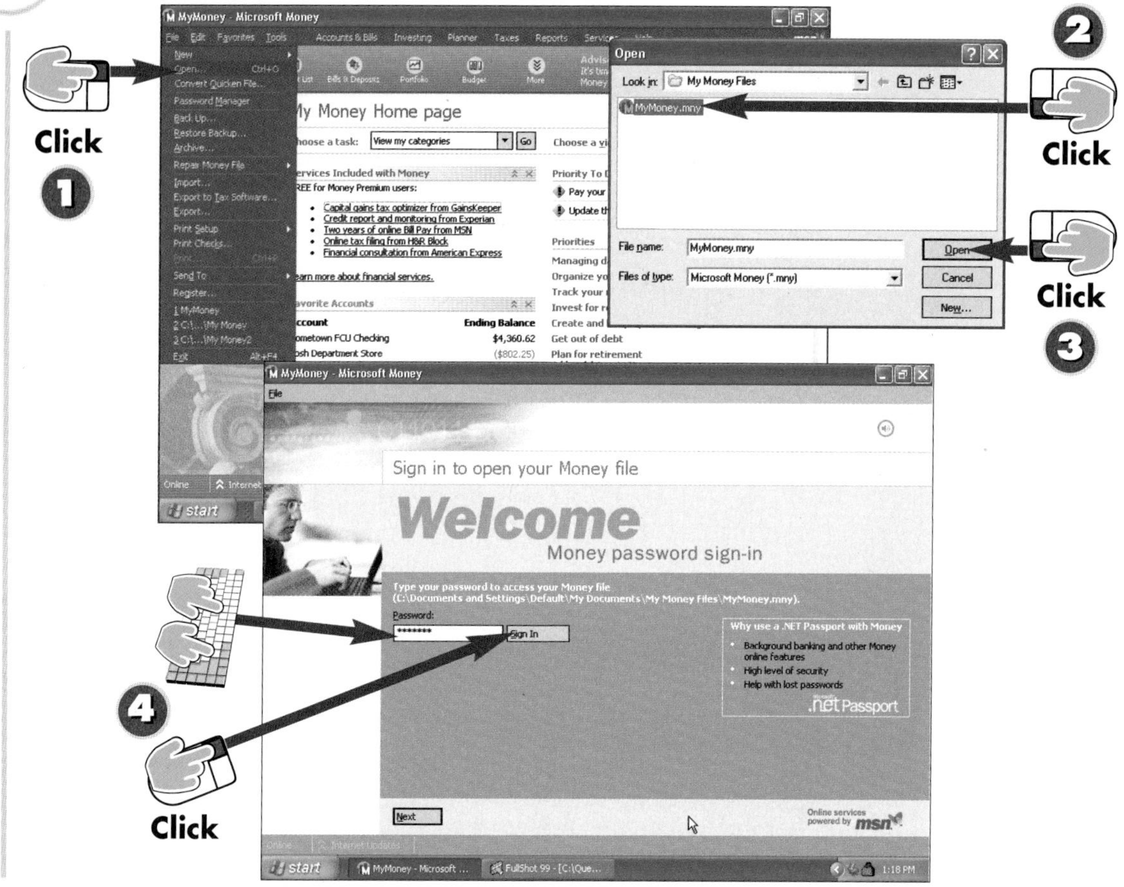

1. To open an existing Money file, open the **File** menu and click **Open**.
2. Click the **Look in** down arrow, locate the folder in which your Money file resides, and then select the file. (Money files have a .mny extension.)
3. Click **Open**.
4. If you set a password for Money, you'll need to sign in. Type in the **Password** box, and click **Sign In**. Money opens the home page for the file you selected.

INTRODUCTION

When you open Money, it assumes you want to open the last file you worked on. You can tell Money to open a different file by using the File menu.

HINT

Opening the File Fast
The last few files you worked on appear at the bottom of the File menu. To skip the Open dialog box, simply click a filename at the bottom of the menu to open that file.

TIP

Keyboard Shortcuts
As with most software systems, you'll find several shortcuts that apply to nearly all Microsoft products. For example, instead of using the File menu, you can press **Ctrl+O** to open a file.

Backing Up Your Files

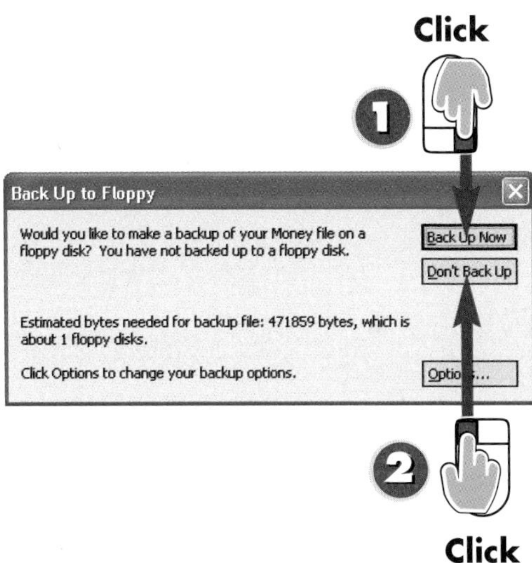
Click
1
Back Up to Floppy
Would you like to make a backup of your Money file on a floppy disk? You have not backed up to a floppy disk.
Back Up Now
Don't Back Up
Estimated bytes needed for backup file: 471859 bytes, which is about 1 floppy disks.
Click Options to change your backup options.
Options...
2
Click

1. When you see the message about backing up your file, and you want to do so, insert a blank disk in your disk drive and click **Back Up Now**.
2. If you don't want to back up your file, click **Don't Back Up**.

INTRODUCTION

Periodically, when you are working in Money—and especially when you exit Money—a message appears asking you if you want to back up your file; doing so is a good idea. In addition to backing up a copy, Money also saves the file you're working with to the location you specified when you set up the file.

TIP

Computing Pitfalls
All it takes is a good lightning strike, power surge, or other mishap for your hard drive to become disabled. That's why it's a good idea to back up. It could save you a lot of time and frustration in the long run.

Printing

Open the **File** menu and choose **Print**. A dialog box with various print options appears.

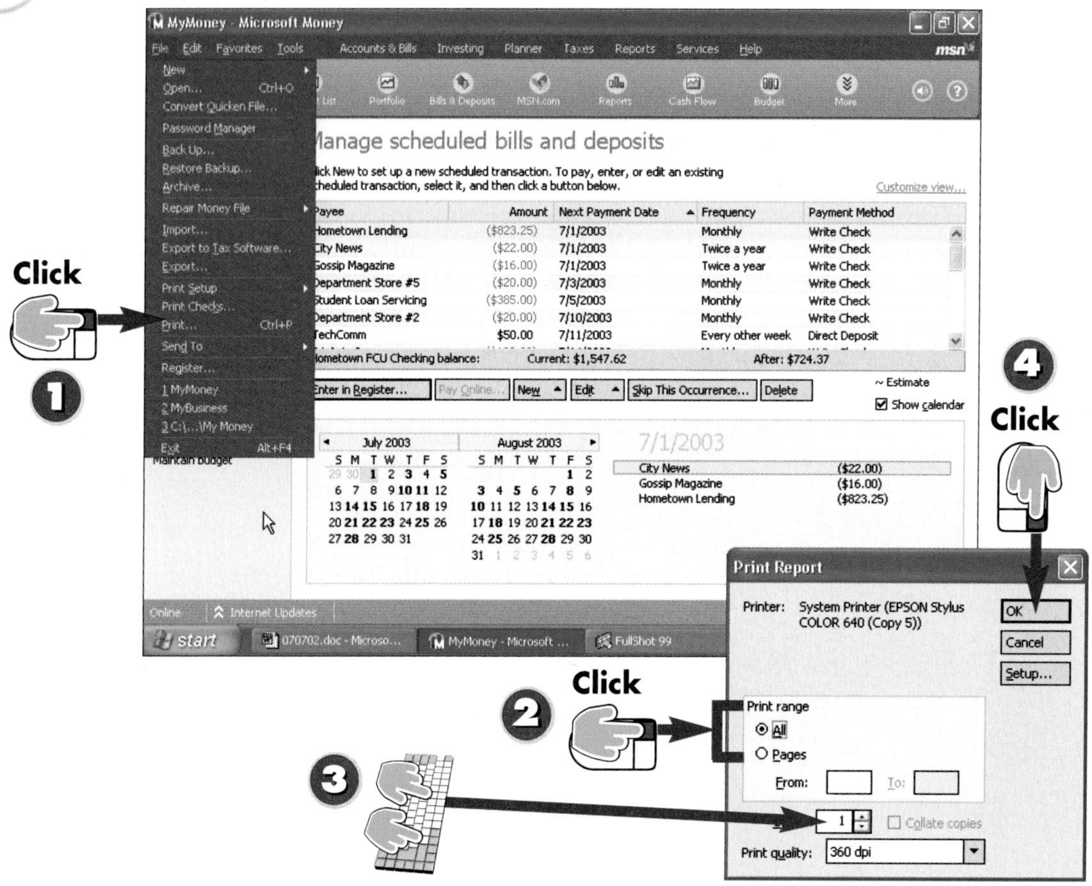

To print all information, select **All**. To print only certain pages, select **Pages**, and type the page you want to start on in **From** and the page you want to end on in **To**.

To specify how many copies you want to print, type the number in **Copies**.

When you are ready to print, click **OK**.

INTRODUCTION

When you start using various features in Money, such as reports or cash-flow outlooks, you might want to print some of your financial information. To do so, first open the item you want to print, such as a report, and then complete the steps in this task.

TIP

Adjusting Printer Settings
To adjust your printer settings, click **Setup** to access your printer information. To adjust the print quality, click the **Print quality** down arrow, and select a new setting.

TIP

Keyboard Shortcuts
You can also use the **Ctrl+P** keyboard shortcut to print. This shortcut does not open the Print dialog box, and instead sends the print job immediately to your printer.

Setting Up or Changing Your Password

Start

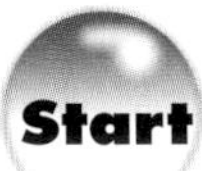

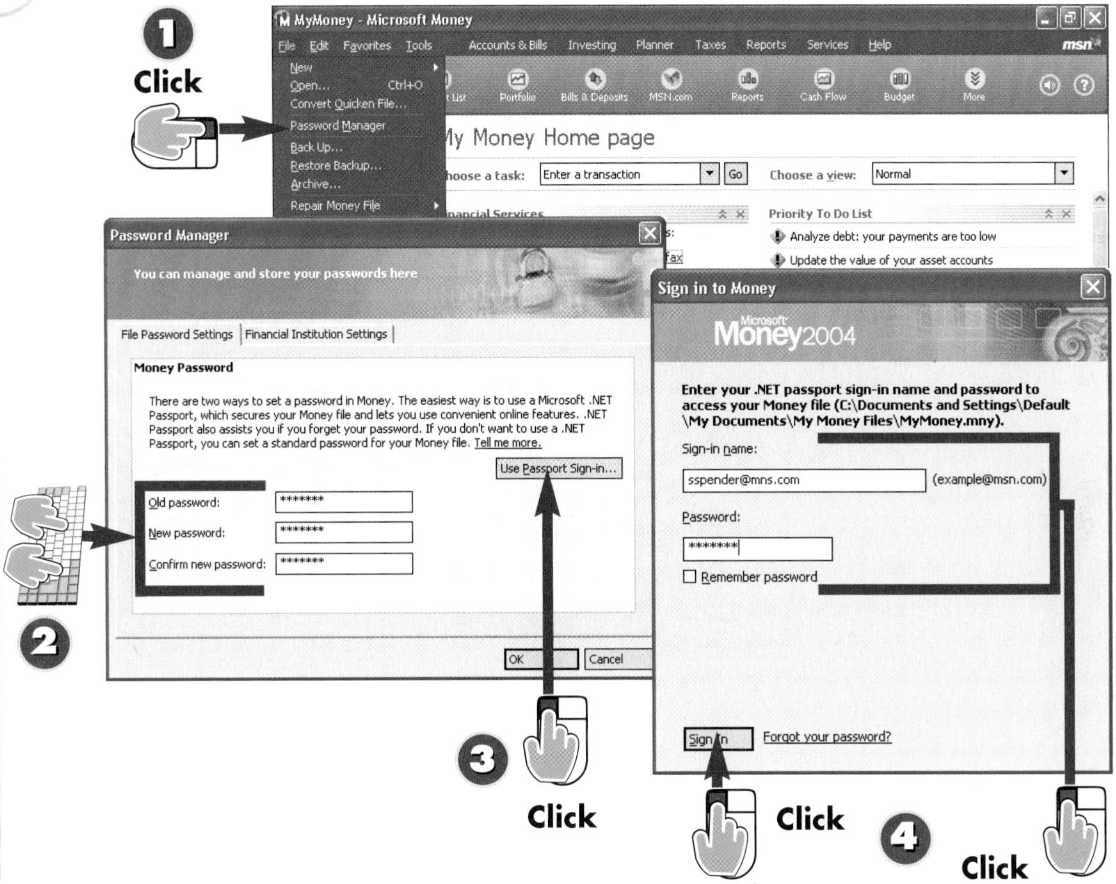

1. Open the **File** menu and choose **Password Manager**.
2. To change a password, type the current one in the **Old password** box, type the new one in both the **New password** box and the **Confirm new password** box.
3. To set up a .NET Passport password, or to use one you already have, click **Use Passport Sign-in**.
4. Type your user ID under **Sign-in name**, type your .NET password under **Password**, and then click **Sign In**.

End

INTRODUCTION

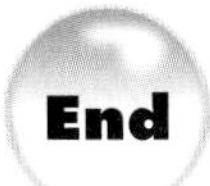

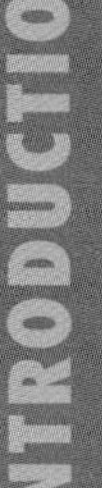

If you haven't yet set up a password for Money, or would like to change the one you already have, you can do so using Money's Password Manager. You access the Password Manager from the File menu once you're inside Money.

HINT

Setting Up a Standard Password
If you don't yet have a password, the **Old password** box shown in step 2 is grayed out. Use the **New password** and **Confirm new password** boxes to set up a new, standard password.

TIP

Remembering the Password
Be sure you remember the new password or write it down someplace so you don't forget it.

Getting Help

Start

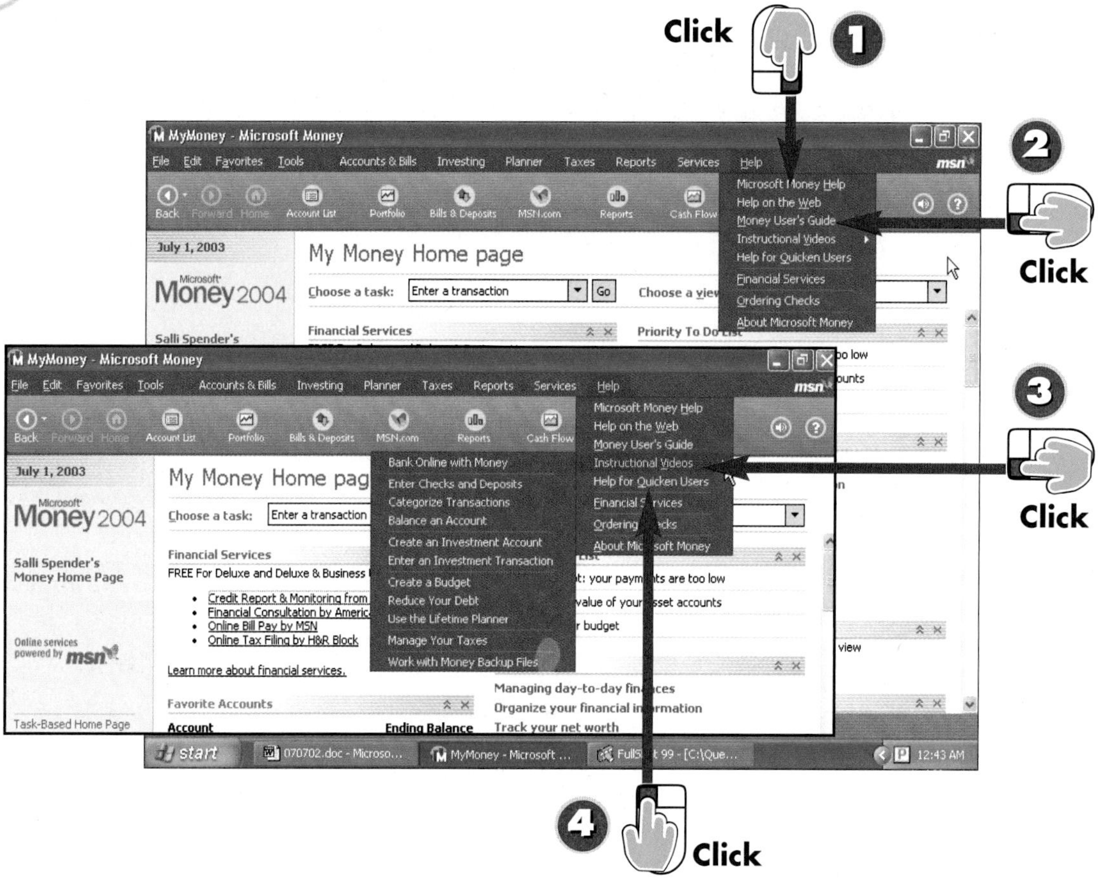

1. To access Microsoft Money Help, open the **Help** menu and choose **Microsoft Money Help**.
2. To view the online User's Guide, be sure you are connected to the Internet, then open the **Help** menu and choose **Money User's Guide**.
3. To view a help video, open the **Help** menu, select **Instructional Videos**, and then select a video topic from the submenu that appears.
4. If you're a former Quicken user, open the **Help** menu and choose **Help for Quicken Users** to get some customized help just for you.

INTRODUCTION

If you want more information about Money, you can get help in many ways: using Microsoft Money Help, viewing the Money User's Guide, or troubleshooting any problems you might have by using Help on the Web. You can also view mini videos that show you how features work.

TIP

Accessing Help on the Web

To view the Help on the Web to troubleshoot problems or get answers to questions you have about Microsoft Money, be sure you are connected to the Internet, then open the Help menu and select **Help on the Web**.

Getting the Latest Financial Updates

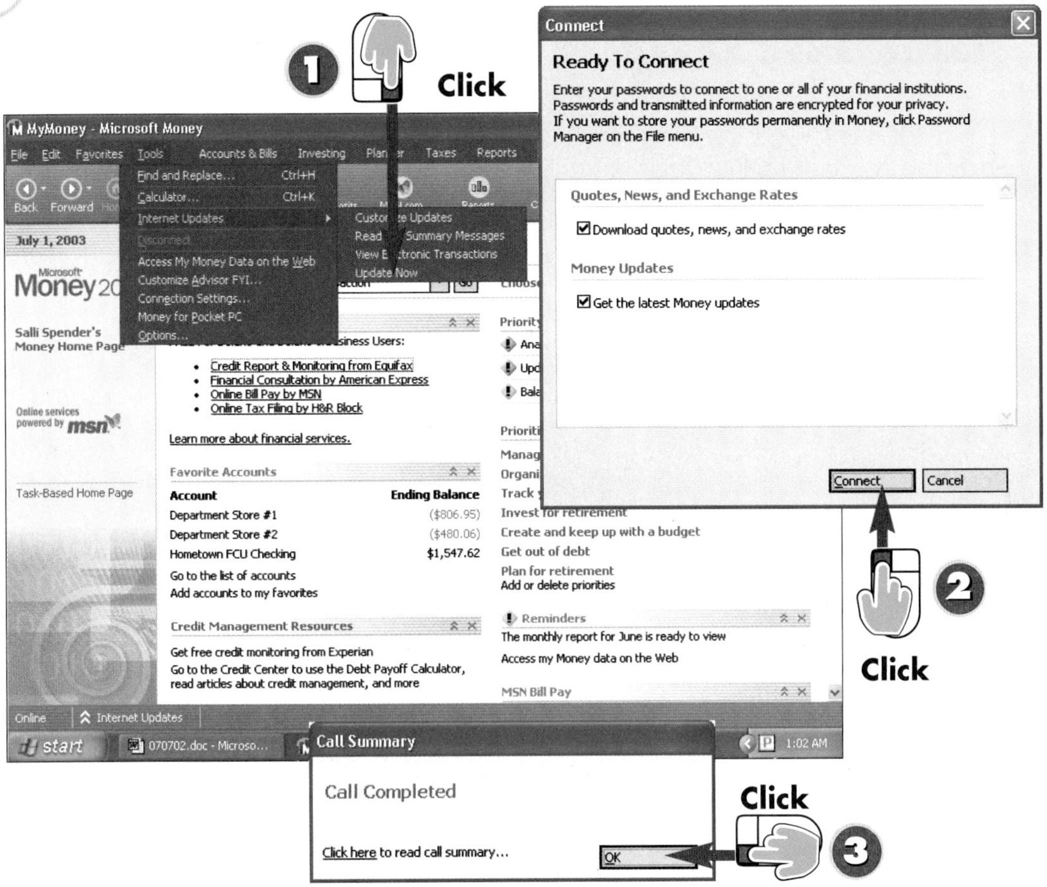

1 Connect to the Internet, open the **Tools** menu, choose **Internet Updates**, and then select **Update Now**.

2 Click the **Connect** button. Progress messages appear telling you that Money is processing updates, receiving information, and so on.

3 Click **OK** to complete the update.

INTRODUCTION

From time to time, you should update your Money files and any other financial information, such as stock quotes, interest rates, and so on. If you forget, Money will place an alert on your home page to remind you.

TIP

Updating Your Accounts
If you set up accounts in Money in order to get statements or other financial information online, you will get the latest information from those accounts when you update.

PART 3

Exploring Your Home Page

Now that you have completed the setup process and have learned some of the basics, let's get to the good stuff: working with your Microsoft Money home page. The results of all the time and effort you put into setting up your file appear on your home page. The priorities you chose, the information you entered, and additional financial goodies are initially broken down into categories in two columns. Each category appears as a block on your home page. You can browse through all the categories and information, open them to take a closer look, close them, remove them, rearrange them, add new categories, and access a host of other information to help you manage and meet your financial goals. You can even change the default page you see each time you enter Microsoft Money. Your home page is exactly what its name suggests: home base.

Money's Home Page

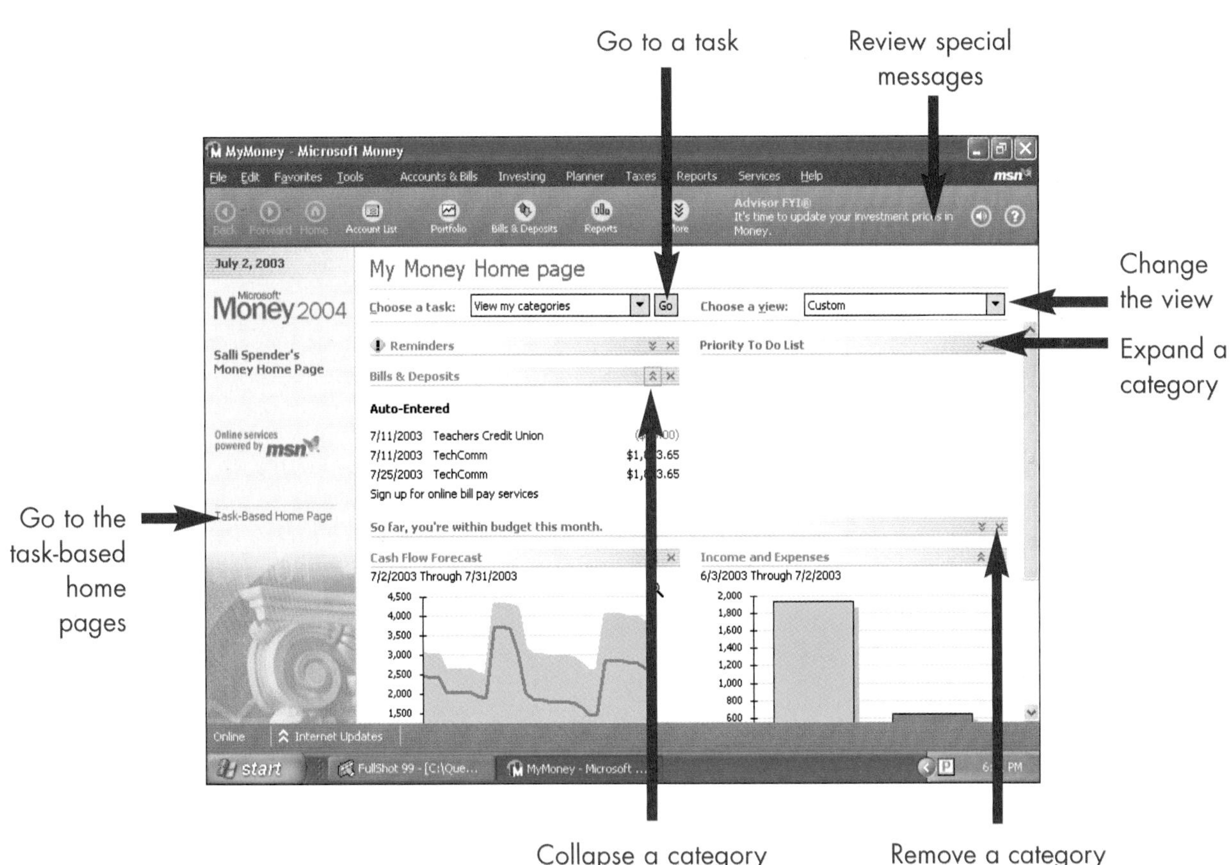

Using Alternative Views

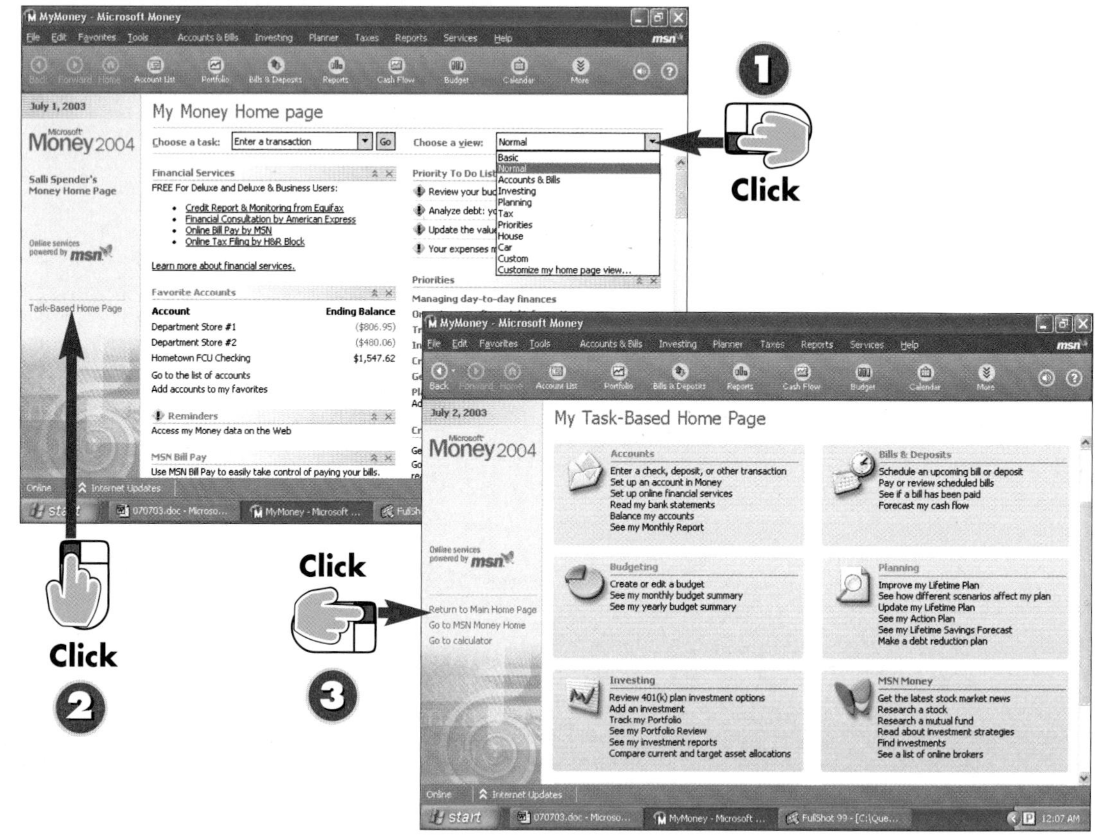

1. On your Microsoft Money home page, click the **Choose a view** down arrow and select an option to see a different view.

2. To see another view, click the **Task-Based Home Page** link.

3. To go back to the main home page, click the **Return to the Main Home Page** link.

INTRODUCTION

Before you change and rearrange the categories on your home page, take a look at the alternative views you can use to view the information on your home page. There are several alternative views from which you can choose, each with a unique purpose.

TIP

Using the Task-Based Home Page

The Task-Based home page is one of my favorite views. The same information that is accessible from the main home page is also accessible from the Task-Based home page, but the information is arranged by task, which makes finding what you need easier.

Customizing the Task List

Click 3

Click 1

Click 2

Click 4

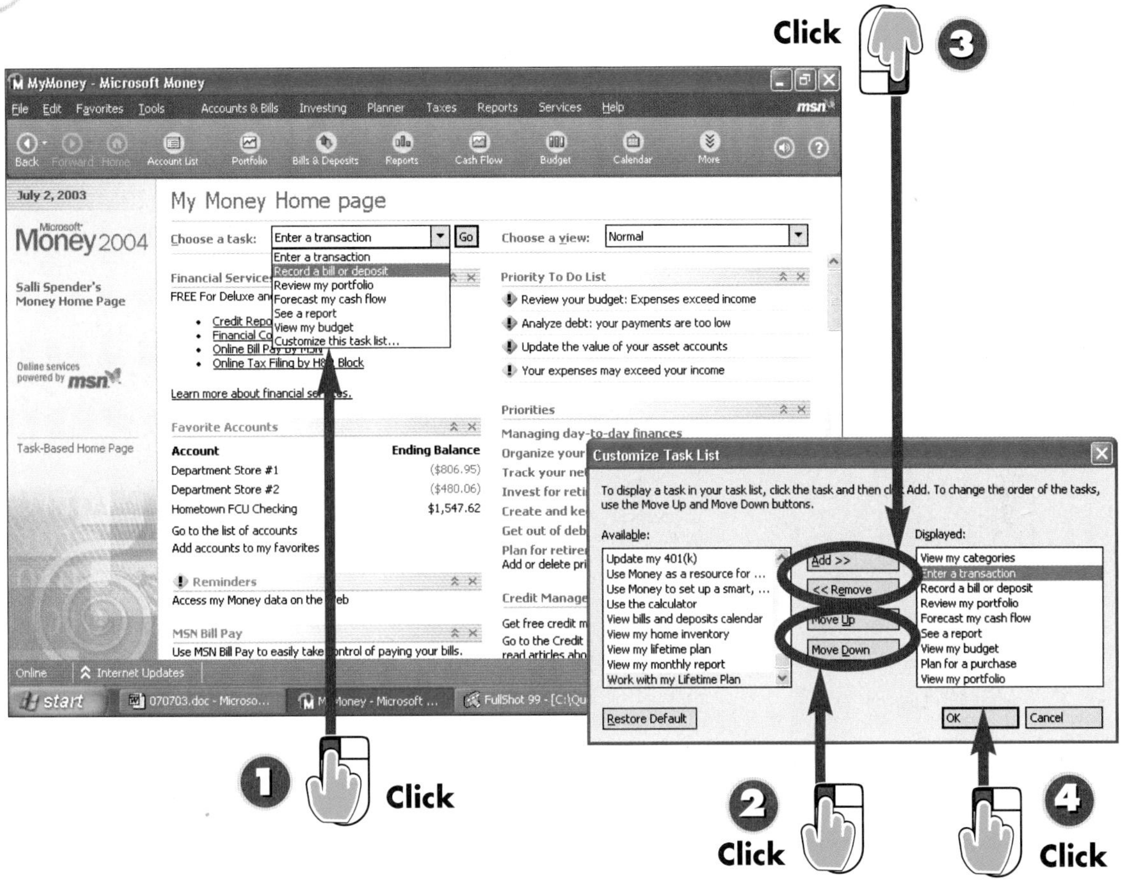

1. On your Microsoft Money home page, click the **Choose a task** down arrow, select **Customize this task list**, and click **Go**.

2. To add a task to the list, click a task in the **Available** list and click **Add**.

3. To remove a task from the list, click the task in the **Displayed** list and click **Remove**.

4. To move a task up or down on the list, click the task in the **Displayed** list.

INTRODUCTION

Now let's look at changing some things on your home page, such as customizing the task list located on the upper-left corner. The task list is used to select key functions to perform, such as maintaining your account information or running a report. You can customize the functions that appear on this list so that you can access them quickly.

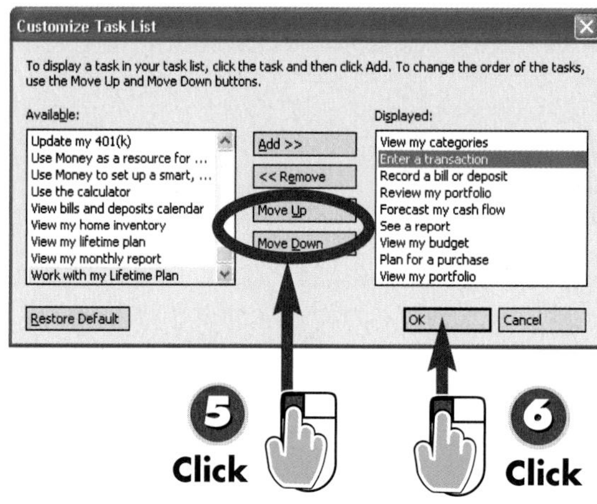

5. Click **Move Up** or **Move Down** as many times as necessary to move the task where you want it.

6. When you are finished arranging, adding, and removing tasks, click **OK**.

TIP

Adding Tasks
For easy access, you can add tasks to your list for your accounts. Adding tasks to your list is another way to quickly access tasks you use a lot.

Modifying the Order of Categories

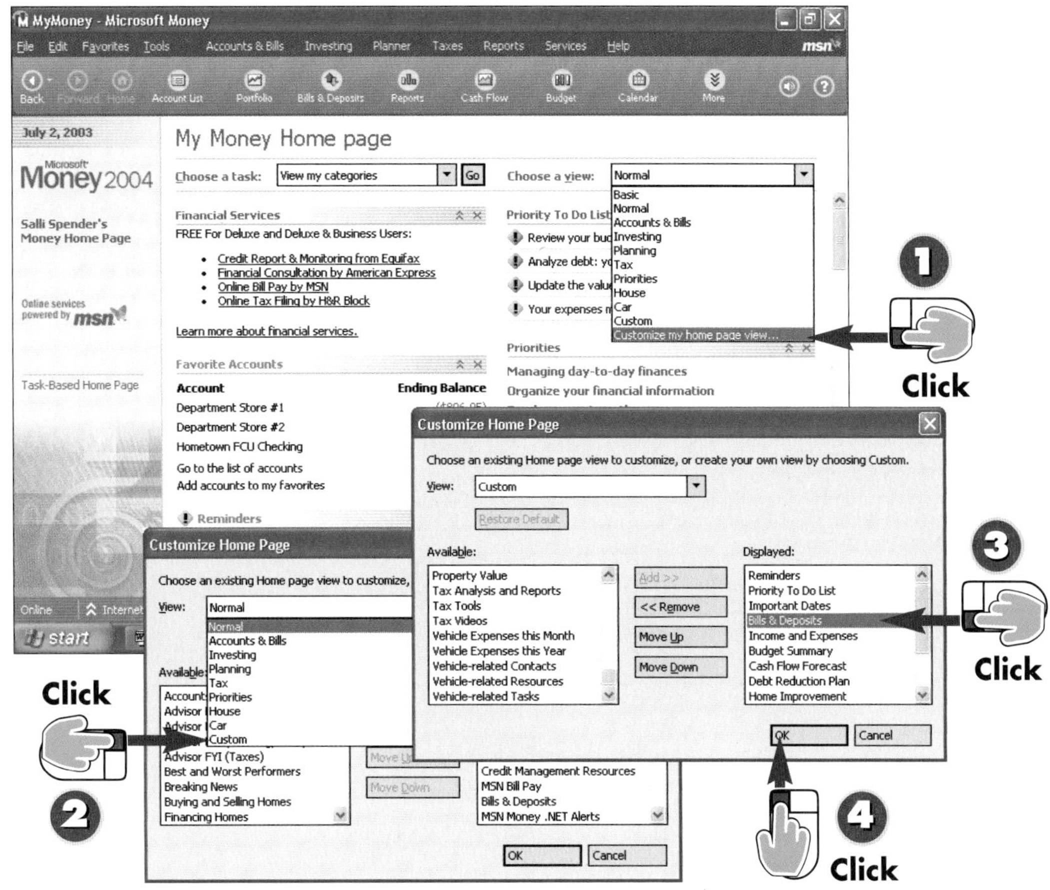

1. On your Microsoft Money home page, click the **Choose a view** down arrow and select **Customize my home page view**.
2. Click the **View** down arrow and select **Custom**. The changes you make to the categories will be saved under this view.
3. Add categories to the **Displayed** list and arrange them, moving them up or down, just as you did the tasks in your task list earlier in this part.
4. Click **OK** to apply the changes.

INTRODUCTION

You can change categories that appear on your home page just like you did tasks that appear in your task list. You can add a category, remove one, and arrange the order in which they appear.

TIP

Contemplating Categories
When considering what categories you want to appear on your home page, think about what categories are most important to you. Put the important categories high on the list, and those that are less important farther down.

TIP

Updating Categories
As you work in Money creating plans, budgets, and so on, you probably will want to come back to this task and update your categories as needed.

Collapsing or Expanding Categories

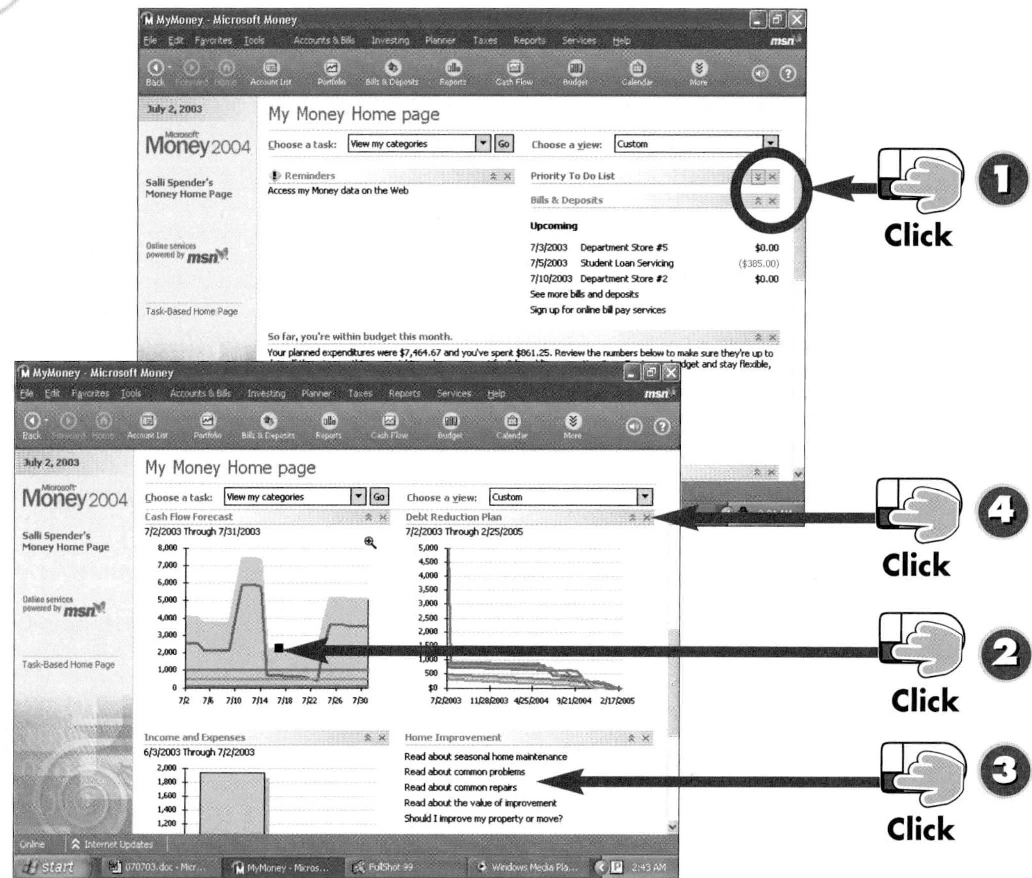

1. To collapse a category, click the double up arrows. To expand it, click the double down arrows.
2. To view pop-up information about a specific area of a flow or pie chart, place your mouse pointer over the area.
3. To view more detailed information about a category, click the links within that category.
4. To remove a category altogether, click the × button next to the category.

INTRODUCTION

Now that you have your categories in order, let's see how they work. You can open categories to view them in more detail, update information for a category, collapse the categories, or rem ove them.

TIP

Re-adding Removed Categories

You can always add a category back or find a new one to add by performing the steps in the preceding task.

Changing Your Default Home Page

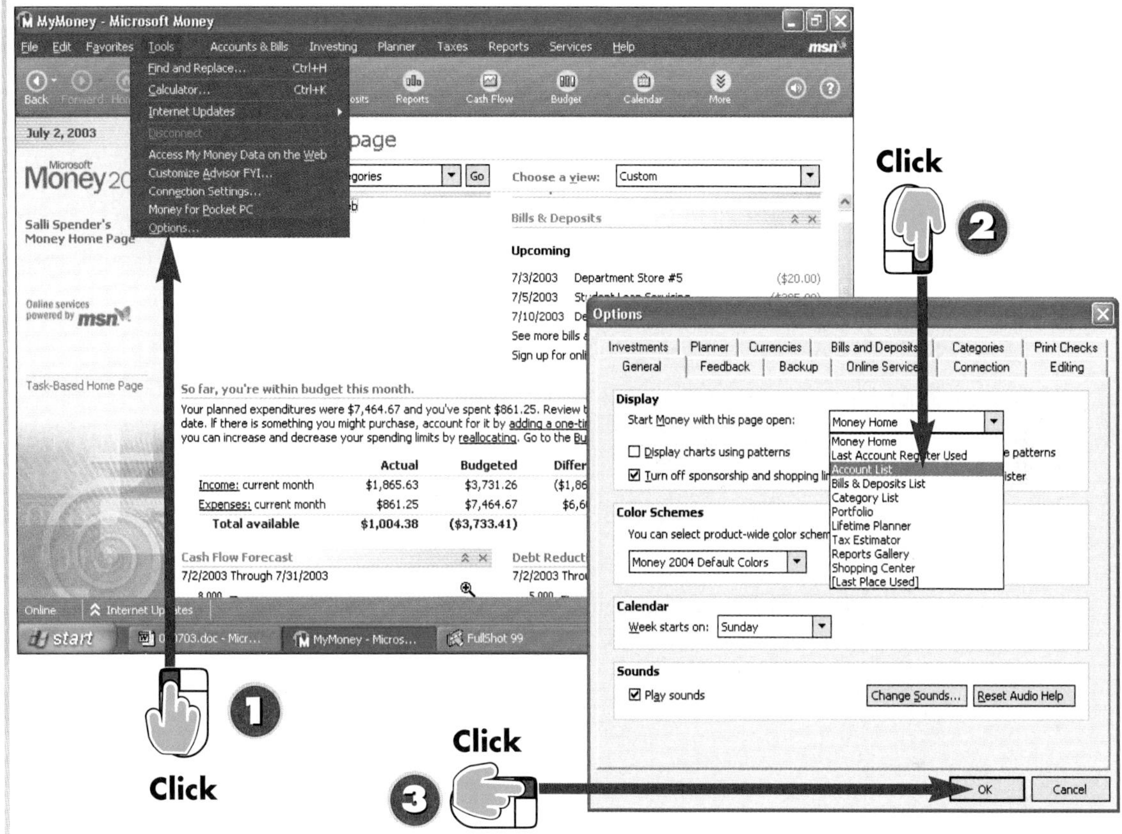

1. Open the **Tools** menu and choose **Options**.
2. Click the **Start Money with this page open** down arrow and select the desired option.
3. Click **OK**.

INTRODUCTION

Now that you know how to use and customize your home page, you can also change what page you see each time you open Money. If you like your home page the way it is, that's great; don't change a thing. If, however, you prefer to see a different view—for example, your accounts list—each time you enter Money, you can change the default page.

TIP

Viewing the Default Page
The default page doesn't take effect until you exit and re-enter Money.

PART 4

Working with Your Accounts

So far, you have set up your accounts, learned how to use the home page, and learned how to get around in Money. Now that you are feeling more comfortable with the program, it's time to find out how to set up new accounts, remove or change account information, set up accounts online, and organize and manage all those accounts.

The Accounts List

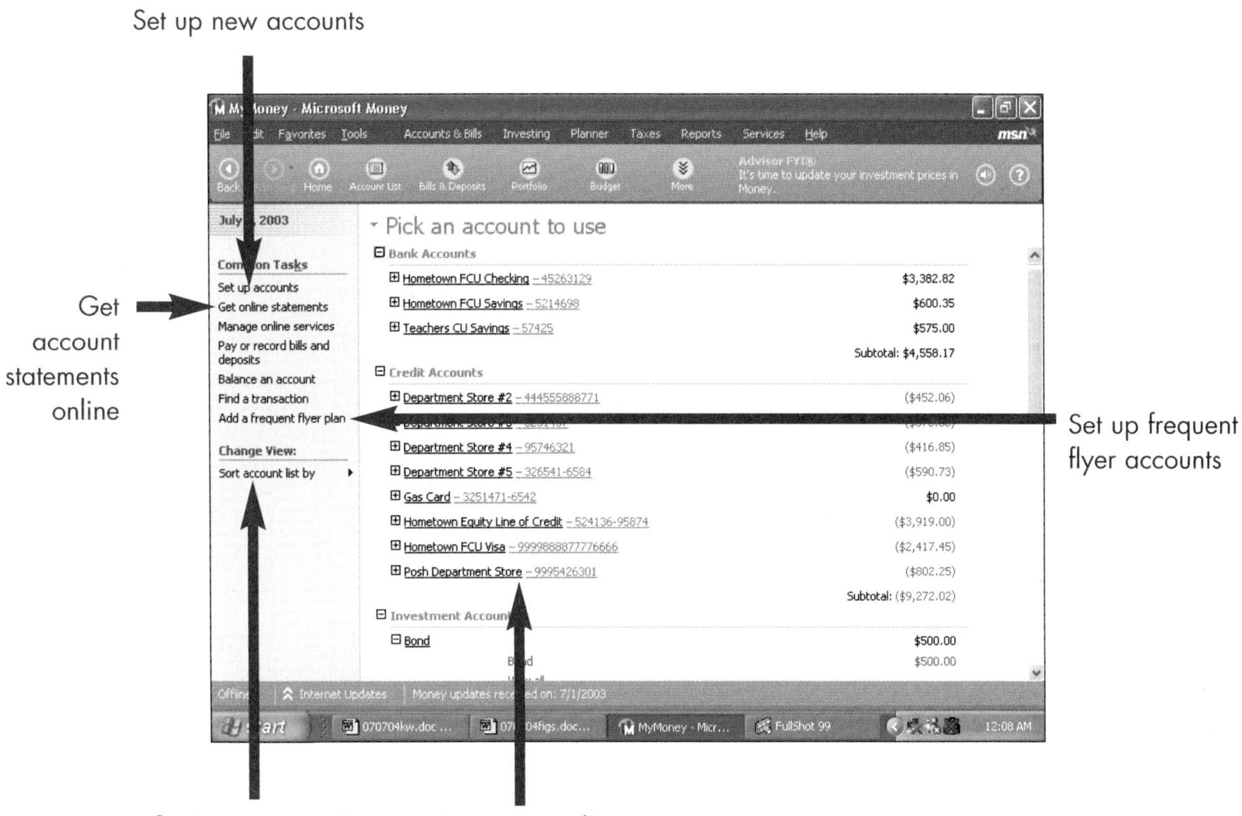

Reviewing and Updating Account Information

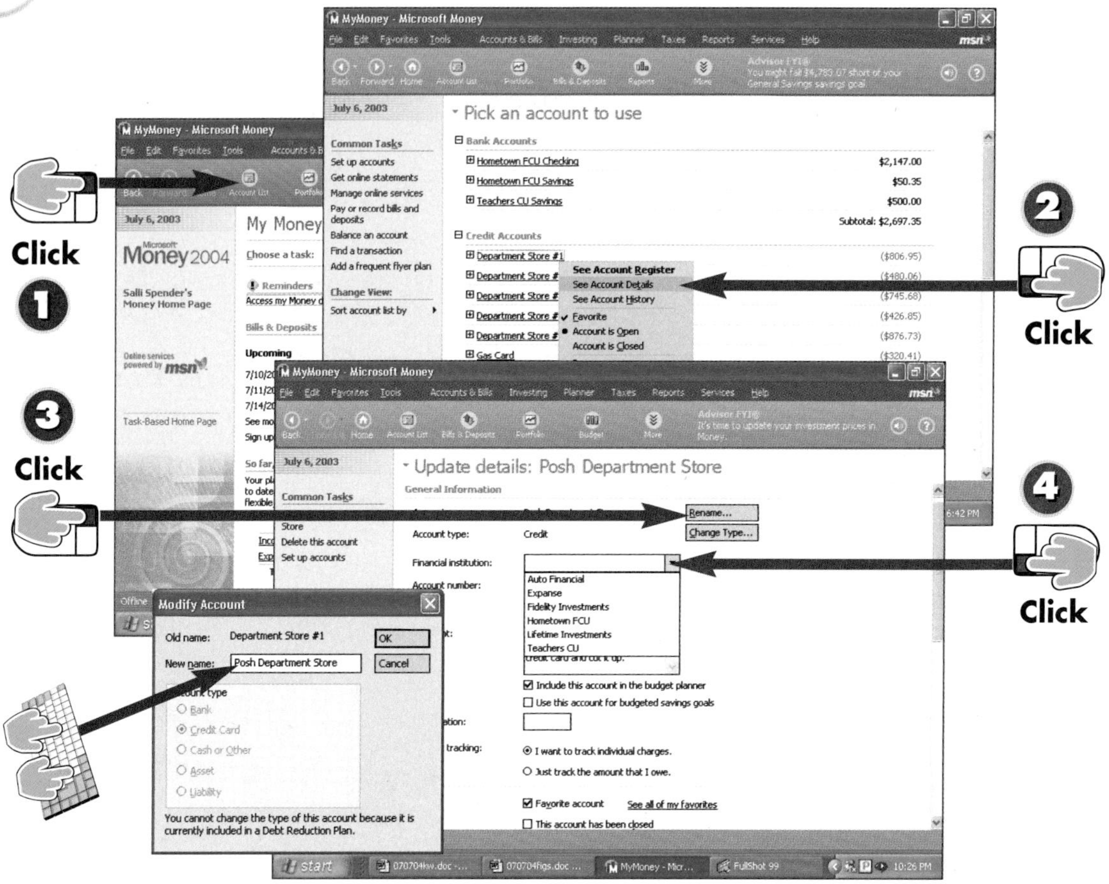

1. Click the **Account List** button in the Money toolbar.

2. To view information about a specific account, right-click on the account name and select **See Account Details**.

3. To change the name of the account, click the **Rename** button. In the dialog box that appears, type a new name for the account in the **New name** box, and click **OK**.

4. If the account is associated with a financial institution (for example, it's a bank card), click the **Financial institution** down arrow and select the name from the list.

INTRODUCTION

From time to time, you will probably want to review and update your accounts to ensure that the account information is accurate and up to date. You can view and update all the accounts you have entered so far from an area called the *account list*.

TIP

Viewing Account Balances

Money lists account balances, shown in step 2 to the right of the account name; below them are subtotals for each section. Red figures represent your debt, and black ones show your income and/or assets.

TIP

Changing the Account Type

To change the account type, click the **Change Type** button (beneath the Rename button), select a new account type, and click **OK**.

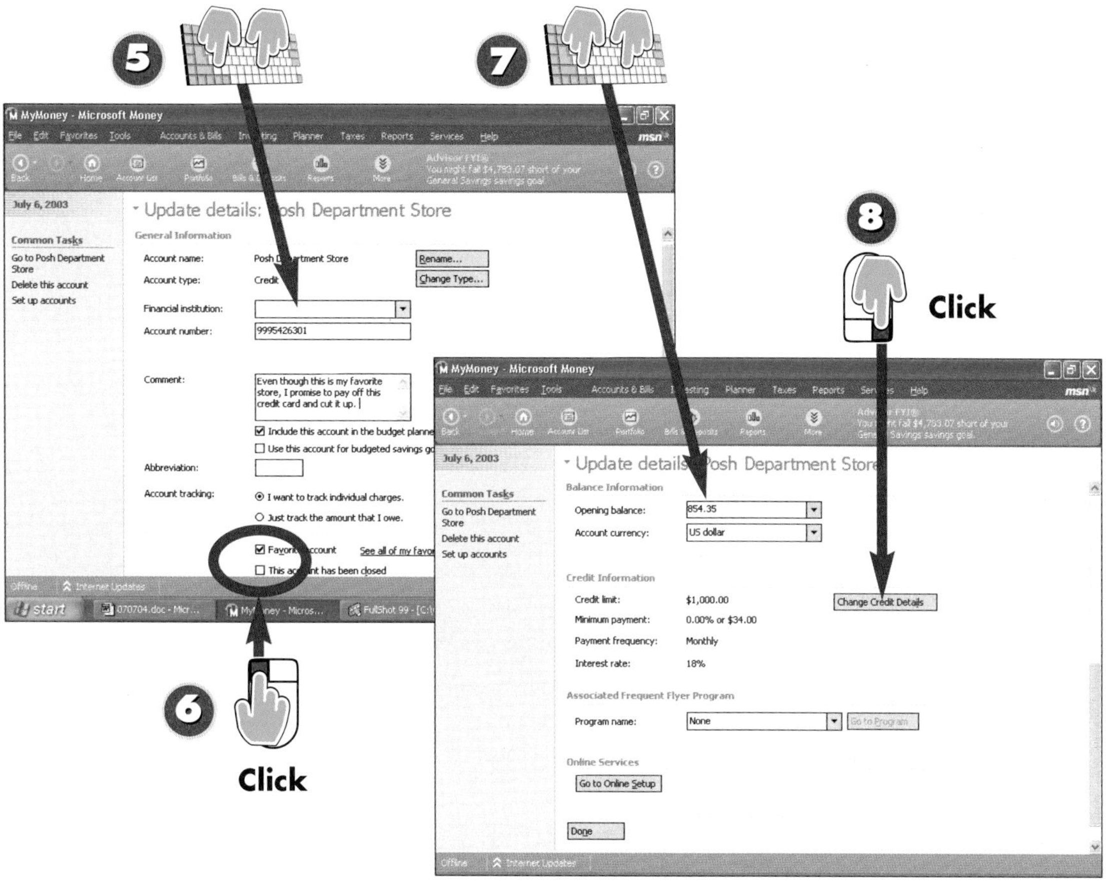

5 If the account number is not already displayed, type it in the **Account number** box.

6 In the **Account tracking** area, specify whether you want to track individual charges (useful when viewing reports or account summaries) or just the amount owed.

7 Scroll down to see the account's balance information. If the entry in the **Opening balance** box is incorrect, change it.

8 To change or update details about a credit card, click the **Change Credit Details** button.

See next page

HINT

Adding Comments
Use the **Comment** box to type notes about an account—for example, something important or unique about it. You'll learn about the budget check boxes under the Comment box in Part 6, "Managing Your Budget."

TIP

Adding an Abbreviation
For quick identification purposes, you can type a code or other short label in the **Abbreviation** box. You might then use this abbreviation when searching for information on this account.

TIP

Adding to Favorites
To add the account to your Favorites list, click the **Favorite account** check box to mark it. You can access all your favorite accounts from the Favorites menu.

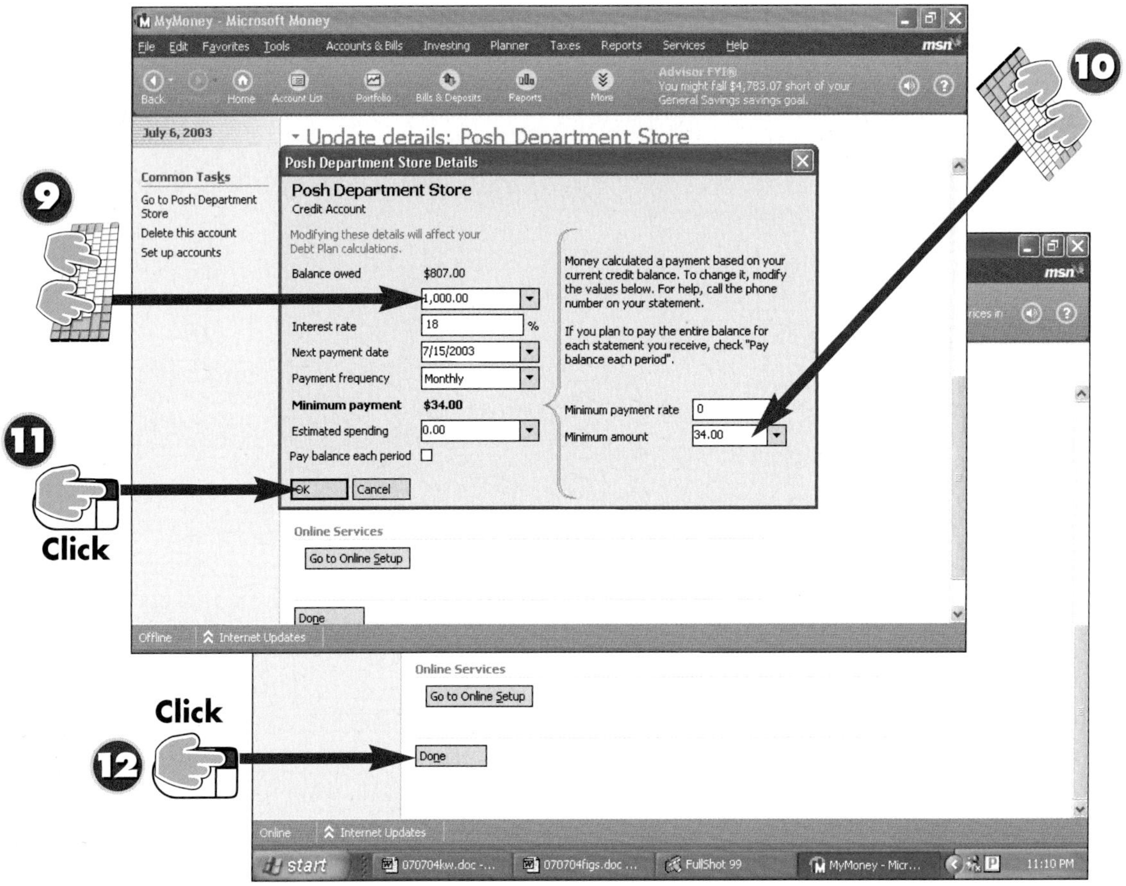

9 To specify the credit limit, interest rate, next payment due date, or payment frequency, type the desired value in the appropriate boxes.

10 Click **Minimum payment** to reveal minimum payment information. Type the amount due for each payment in the **Minimum amount** box.

11 Click **OK**.

12 Click **Done**.

TIP

Entering the Minimum Payment

If you know the percentage of the total that is required as a minimum payment, type that value in the **Minimum payment rate** box in the dialog box shown in steps 9–11.

Sorting Accounts

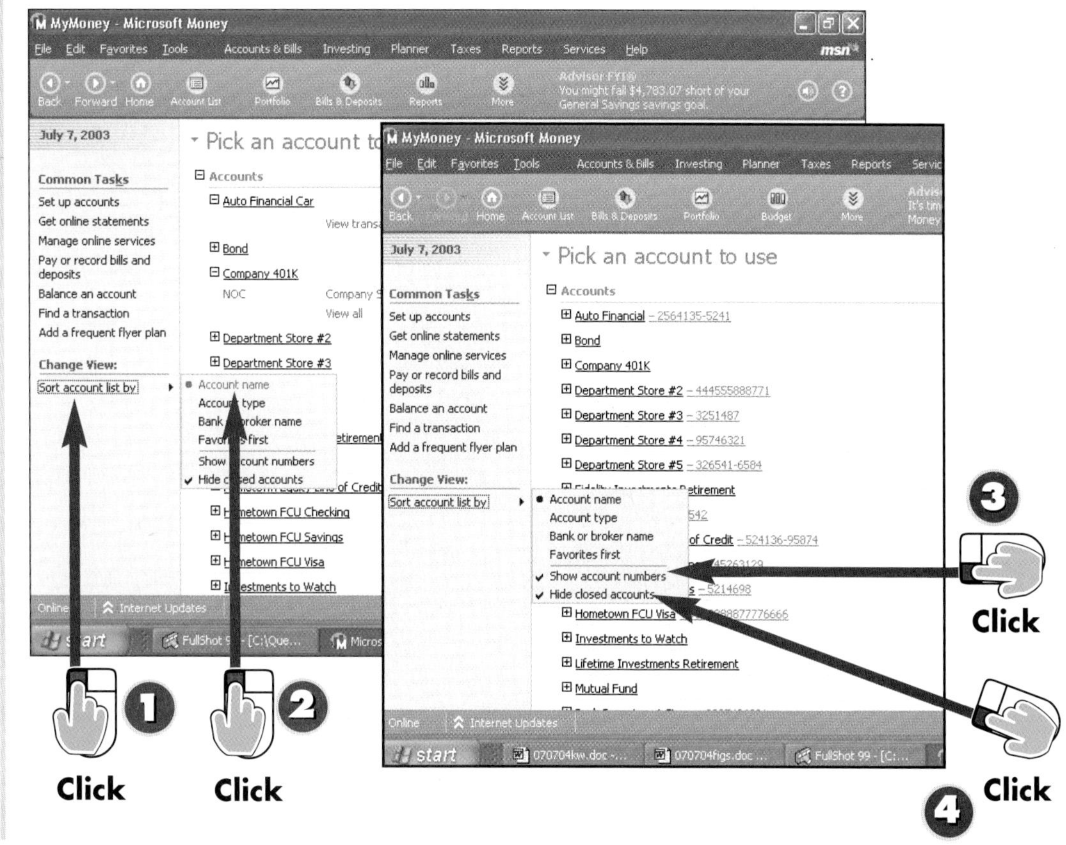

1 After clicking the **Accounts List** button on the Money toolbar, click the **Sort account list by** link in the Pick an account to use window.

2 Select a sort type from the submenu that appears (the current sort type is highlighted). Your accounts are sorted according to the sort type you selected.

3 To view account numbers for all your accounts, click the **Sort account list by** link and choose **Show account numbers**. A check mark appears once selected.

4 To view only open accounts, click the **Sort account list by** link and choose **Hide closed accounts**. A check mark appears to indicate that the option is selected.

INTRODUCTION

There are several ways to sort your accounts. The default is to list all accounts by type, but you can also sort by name, or even configure Money to show your favorite accounts first.

TIP

Experimenting with Sort Options

Play around with the various sort options to see which one you like best.

Tracking Frequent-Flyer Information

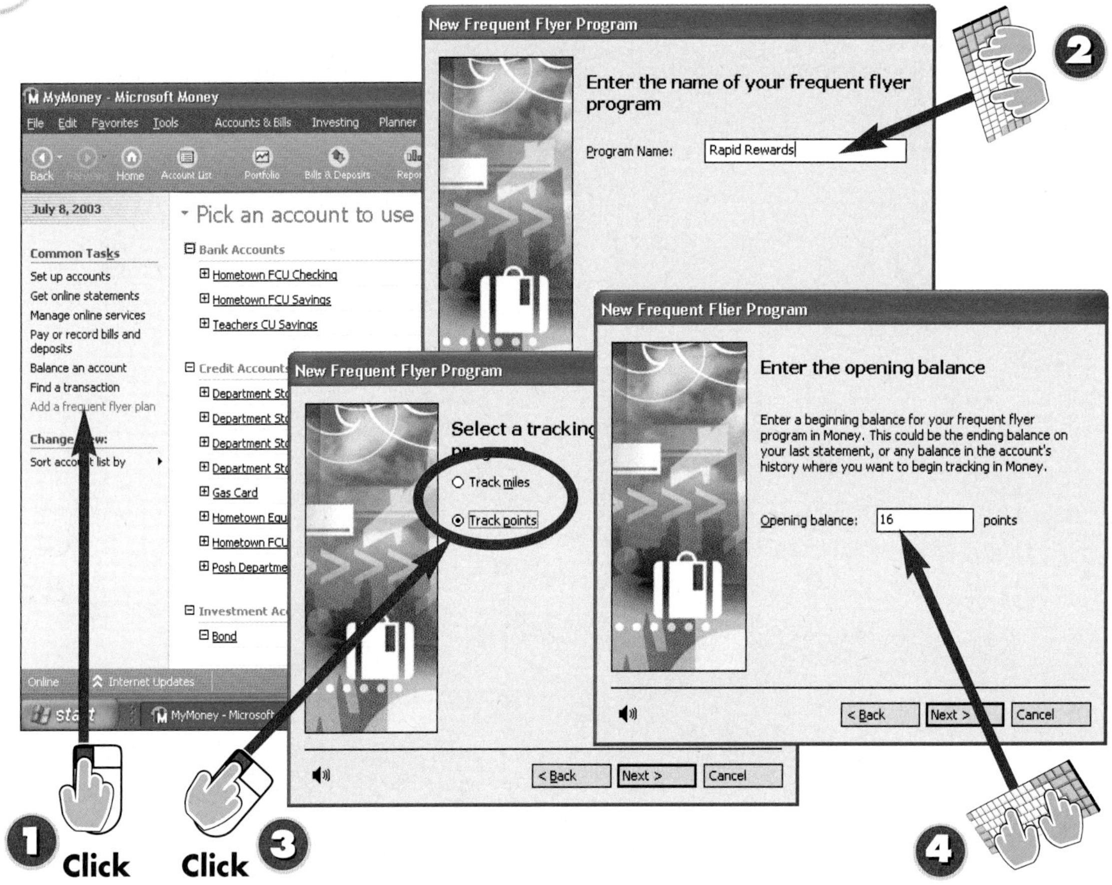

1. After clicking the **Accounts List** button on the Money toolbar, click the **Add a frequent flyer plan** link in the Pick an account to use window.
2. Type the name of your frequent-flyer plan in the **Program Name** box and click **Next**.
3. Depending on how your frequent-flyer program works, click either **Track miles** or **Track points**. Then click **Next**.
4. In the **Opening balance** box, type the number of points or miles you have accumulated thus far, and then click **Next**.

INTRODUCTION

If you have a frequent-flyer account that you use to gain miles or points, you can use Money to keep track of that account. In this task, you learn how to set up a frequent-flyer account, and how to edit it as needed.

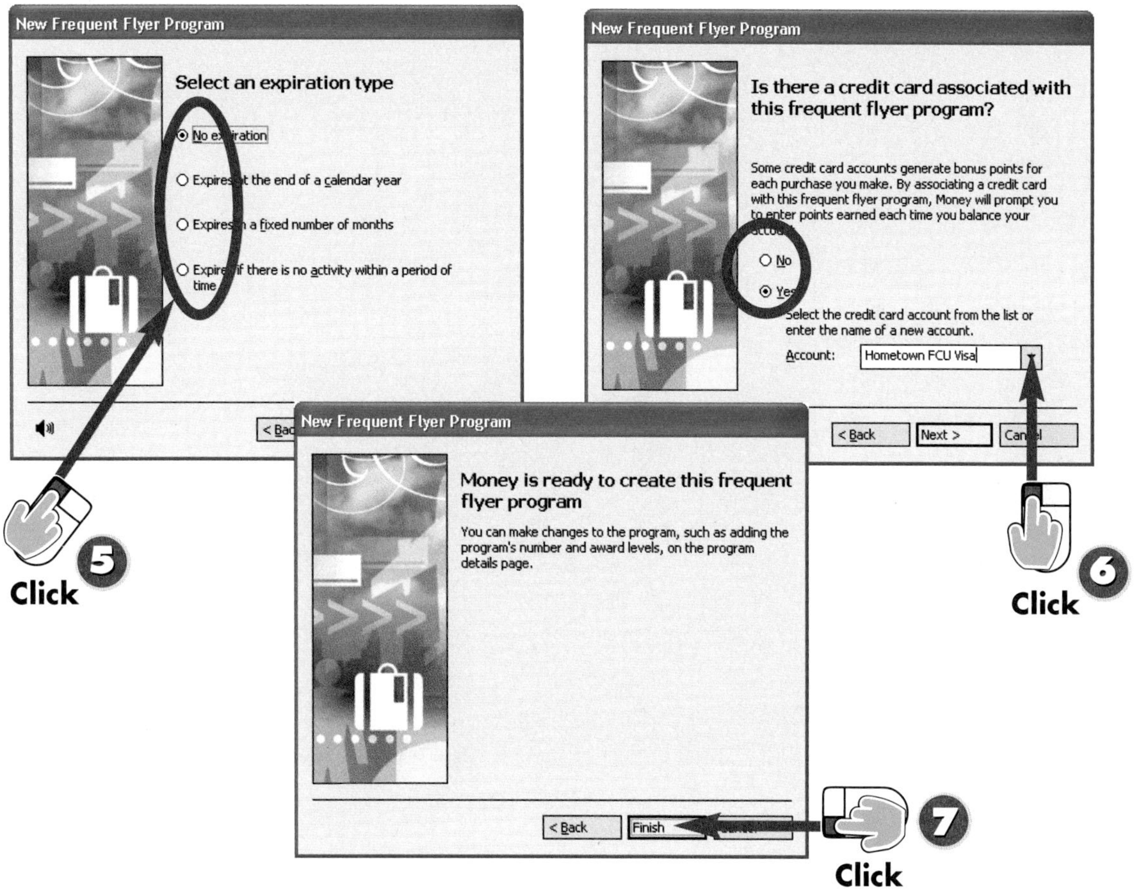

5. Under **Select an expiration type**, click the option button that best describes when/if your plan expires, and click **Next**.
6. If you have a credit-card account that accrues points or mileage, click **Yes** and type the account name in the **Account** box; if not, click **No**. Then click **Next**.
7. Click **Finish**.

TIP

Changing an Existing Account
To make changes to an existing frequent-flyer account, click the account name in the screen shown in step 1. Then, under **Common Tasks**, click the **Change Program Details** link, make your changes, and click **Done**.

TIP

Adding Points or Miles
To add points or miles to an existing frequent-flyer account, click the account name in the screen shown in step 1. Then, click the **New** button, enter your points or miles information, and click **OK**.

Adding a New Account

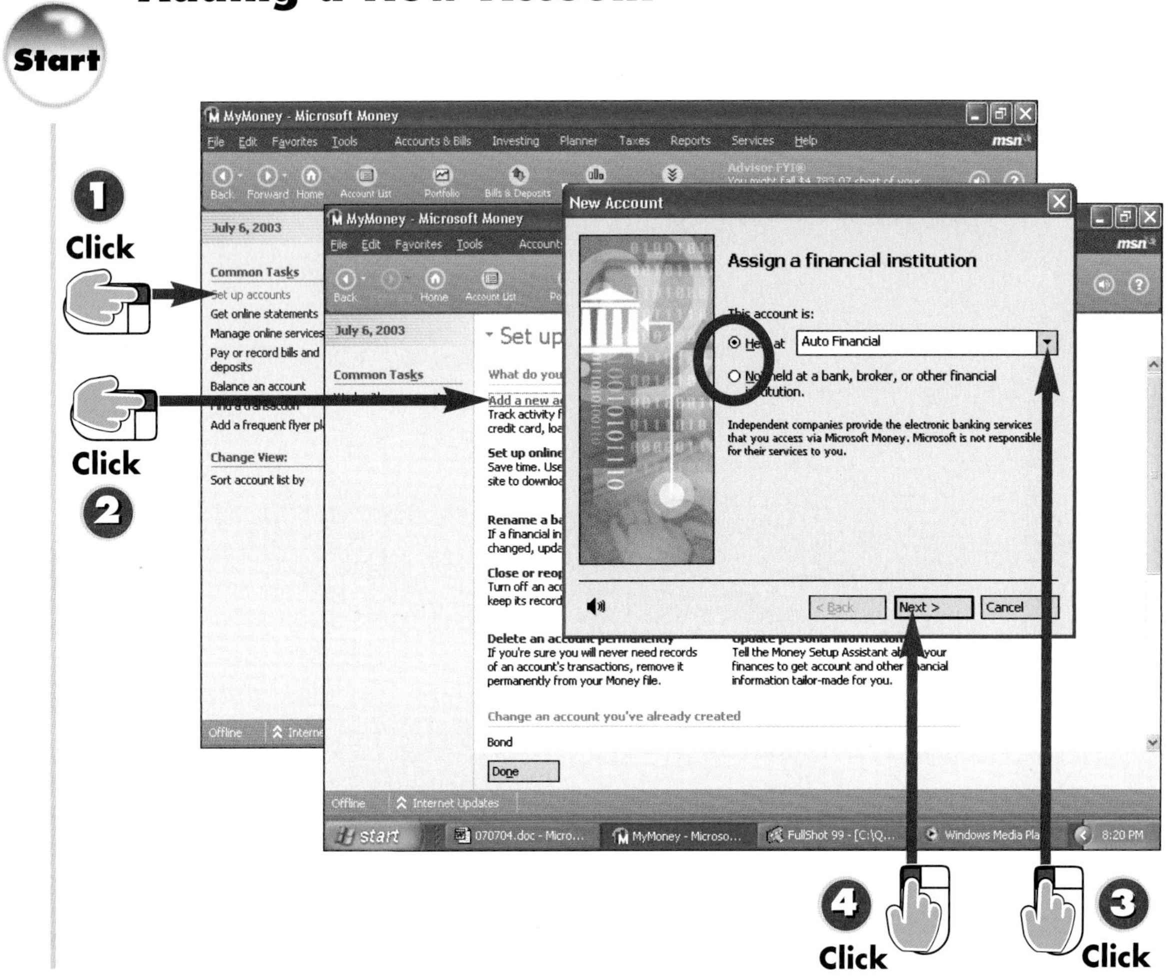

Start

Click 1 · Click 2 · Click 3 · Click 4

1. After clicking the **Accounts List** button on the Money toolbar, click the **Set up accounts** link in the Pick an account to use window.
2. Click the **Add a new account** link.
3. Specify whether the account is held at a financial institution and, if so, type the name of that financial institution in the **Held at** box. Otherwise, click **Not held at**.
4. Click **Next**.

INTRODUCTION

Over time, you will undoubtedly acquire new accounts, such as new credit cards, that you want to track with Money. In this task, you'll learn how to add a new account to Money.

TIP

Questions May Vary

The questions that the wizard asks may vary depending on what kind of account you add. As a result, you may not see on your wizard exactly what you see here when you add your own account.

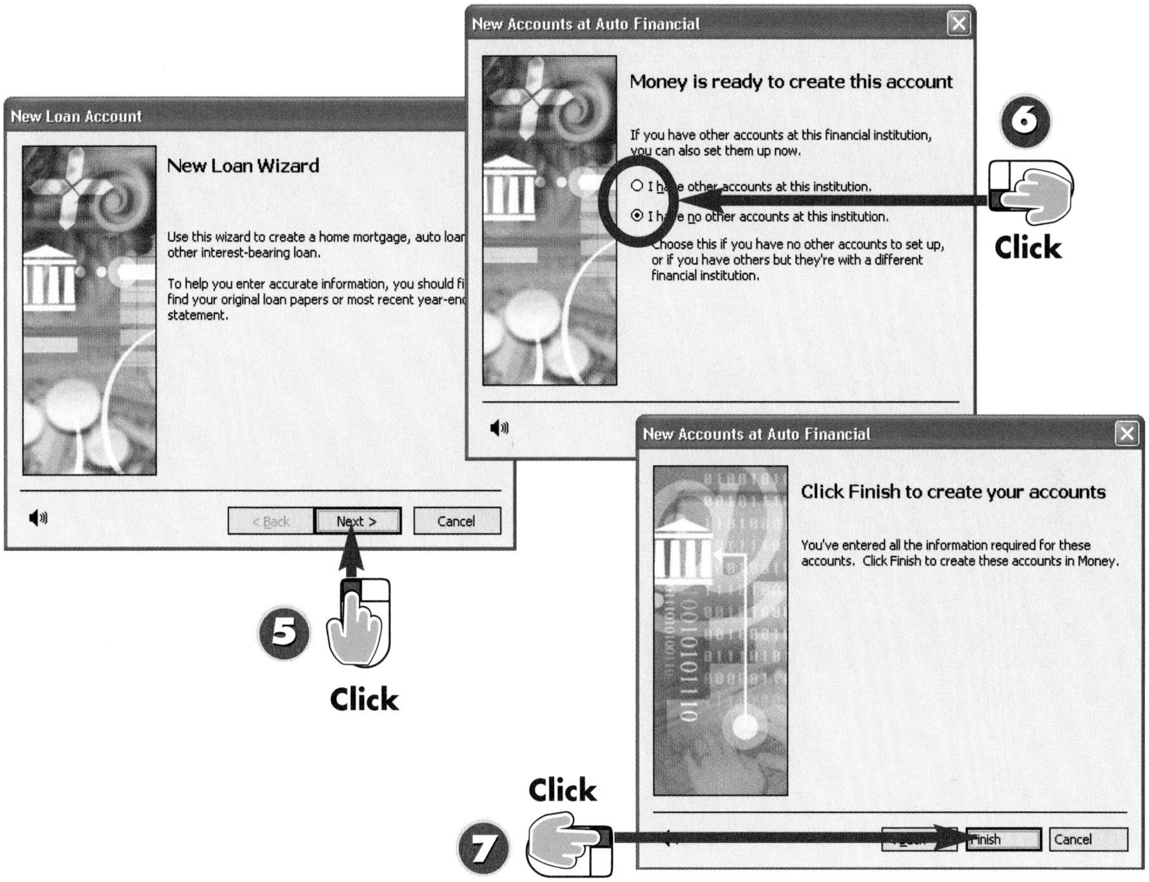

5. Continue answering each question the wizard asks about your account, clicking **Next** to move to the next set of questions.

6. Specify whether you have other accounts with the same financial institution that you'd like to set up in Money. Then click **Next**.

7. If you chose not to set up other accounts in step 6, click **Finish**.

8. If you chose to set up other accounts in step 6, repeat steps 3–6 for each account you want to set up.

TIP

Changing the Information
If you need to go back and change information you already entered, click the **Back** button until you reach the desired area, make the changes, and click **Next** until you return to where you left off.

Closing and Reopening Accounts

Start

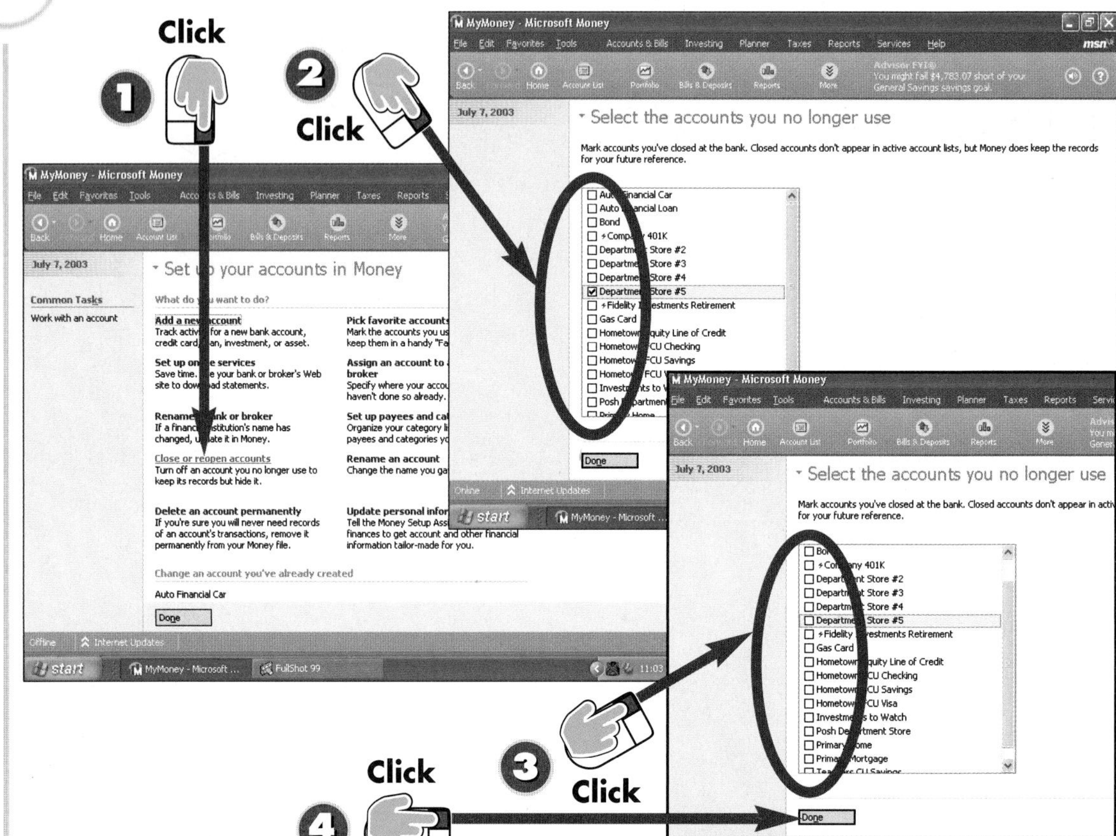

1. After clicking the **Accounts List** button on the Money toolbar, click **Set up accounts**, and then click the **Close or reopen accounts** link.
2. Click the check box next to the account(s) you want to close.
3. To reopen an account that is closed, click in the check box next to the closed account to remove the check mark.
4. Click **Done**.

INTRODUCTION

When you close an account—for example, after paying it off or if you just don't use it much—you can update the account information to let Money know that the account is closed. You should do this so that all of your account information is accurate. You may also re-open an account that once was closed.

TIP

Closing Accounts

You can also close an account from within the account list by right-clicking the account name and selecting **Account is closed** from the pop-up menu. Then follow steps 2–3.

HINT

Closing Credit Cards

In the case of a credit card, telling Money you closed the account is important. Money tracks the interest you pay and also how that account affects your debt-to-income ratio.

Deleting an Account

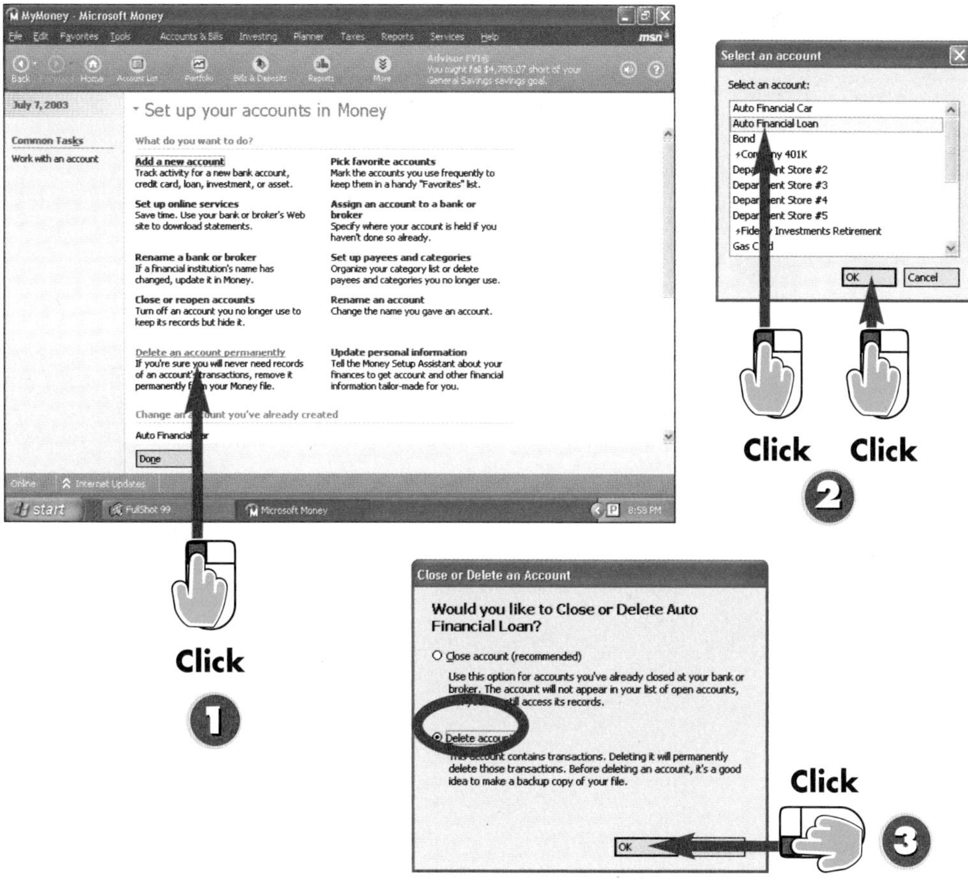

1. After clicking the **Accounts List** button on the Money toolbar, click **Set up accounts**, and then click the **Delete an account permanently** link.
2. In the Select an account dialog box, click the account you want to delete, and click **OK**.
3. Click the **Delete Account** option and click **OK**.

INTRODUCTION

You can add new accounts, rename them, and edit their information, so of course you can also delete them. But be very careful with this kind of power because it could come back to bite you. If you are sure this is what you want to do, follow these steps.

TIP

Second Thoughts

If the account you are deleting is involved in some way with your debt/income, or included in a budget or other plan, Money will display a message telling you that there is a problem before it deletes the account. You can then decide whether you want to proceed or cancel the action.

Adding Spouse/Partner Accounts

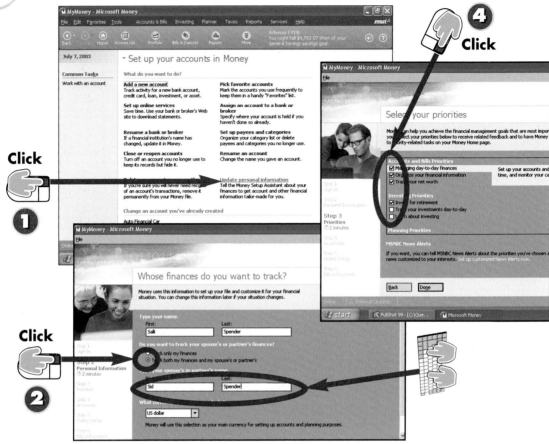

1. After clicking the **Accounts List** button on the Money toolbar, click **Set up accounts**, and then click the **Update personal information** link.
2. Click the **Track both my finances and my spouse's or partner's** option.
3. Type your spouse's or partner's first and last name and click **Next**.
4. Select your goals or financial preferences by clicking in the desired check box(es) under each category. (Use the scrollbar to see all the options.) Then click **Done**.

INTRODUCTION

If you didn't combine your spouse's or partner's financial information with your own when you set up your Money file, it's not too late. You can do so at any time.

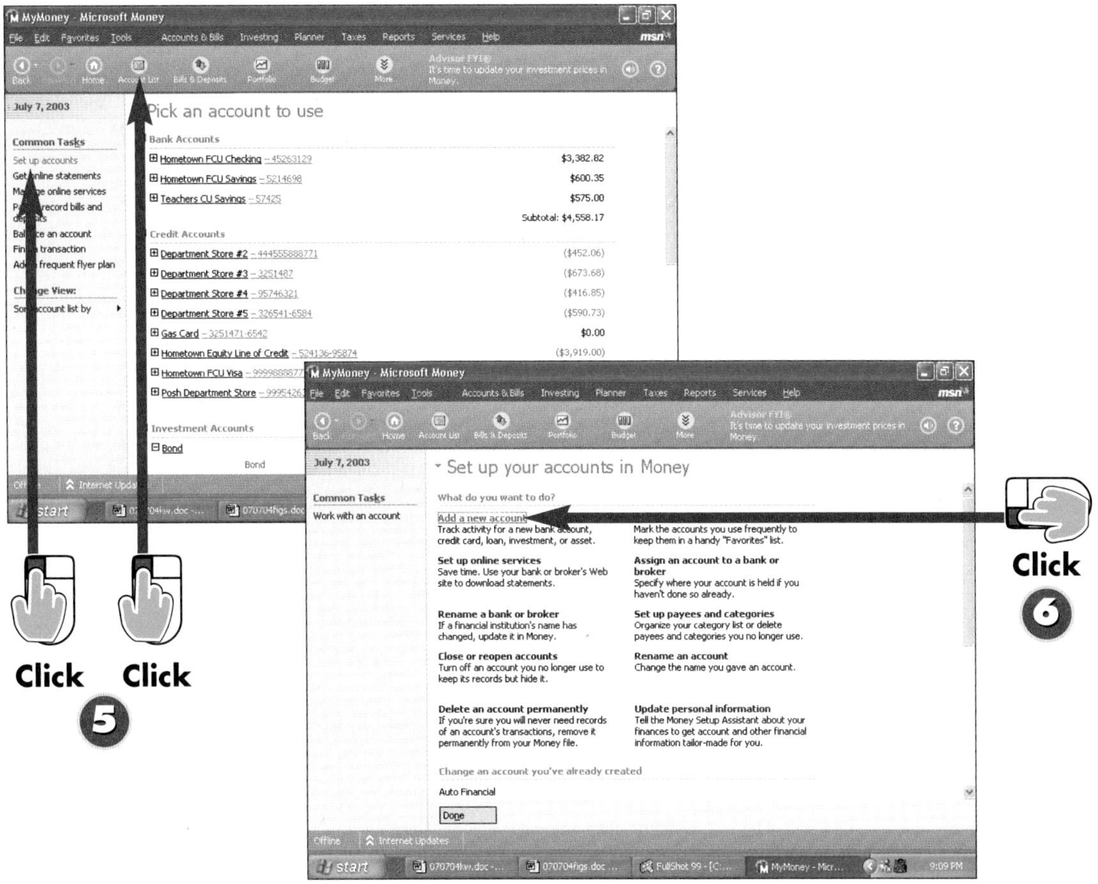

Click Click 5

Click 6

5 To add new accounts for your spouse or partner, click the **Accounts List** button on the Money toolbar, and click the **Set up accounts** link.

6 From the Set up your accounts in Money window, click the **Add a new account** link.

7 Follow the steps 3–8 in the task "Adding a New Account" earlier in this part for each account you are setting up.

TIP

Tracking Your Own Accounts
If you decide later that you want to track only your own accounts, return to the screen shown in step 2 and click the **Track only my finances** option button.

Viewing and Organizing Account Categories

Start

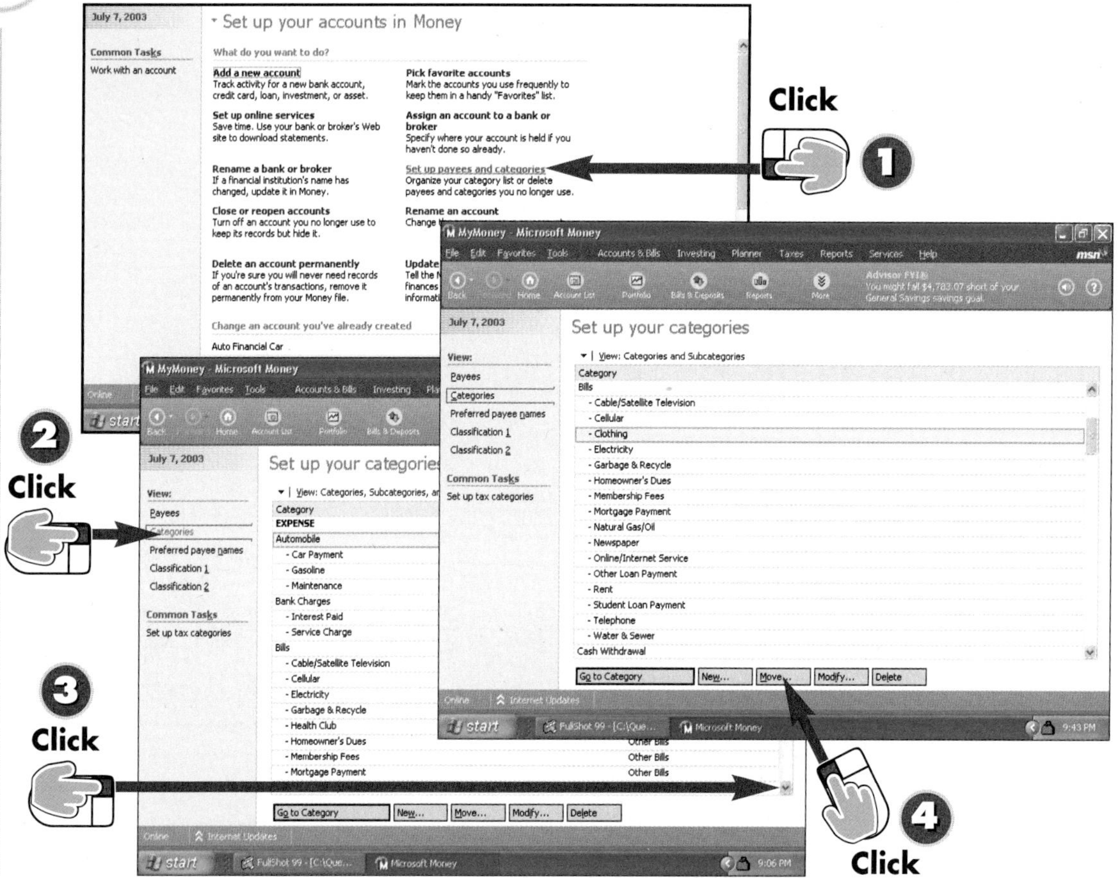

1. After clicking the **Accounts List** button on the Money toolbar, click **Set up accounts**, and then click the **Set up payees and categories** link.

2. In the Set up your categories window, under **View**, click the **Categories** link.

3. Scroll through the list of categories to familiarize yourself with them.

4. To move a sub-category to another category, select the sub-category and click **Move**.

INTRODUCTION

Money provides standard groups, categories, and sub-categories, in that order, to help organize and track your account expenses and income. In the Set up your categories window, groups are listed to the right of the categories and the sub-categories appear beneath the categories.

TIP

Changing the View
You can change how categories are listed by clicking the down arrow next to the current view (see the top of the category list) and selecting another view.

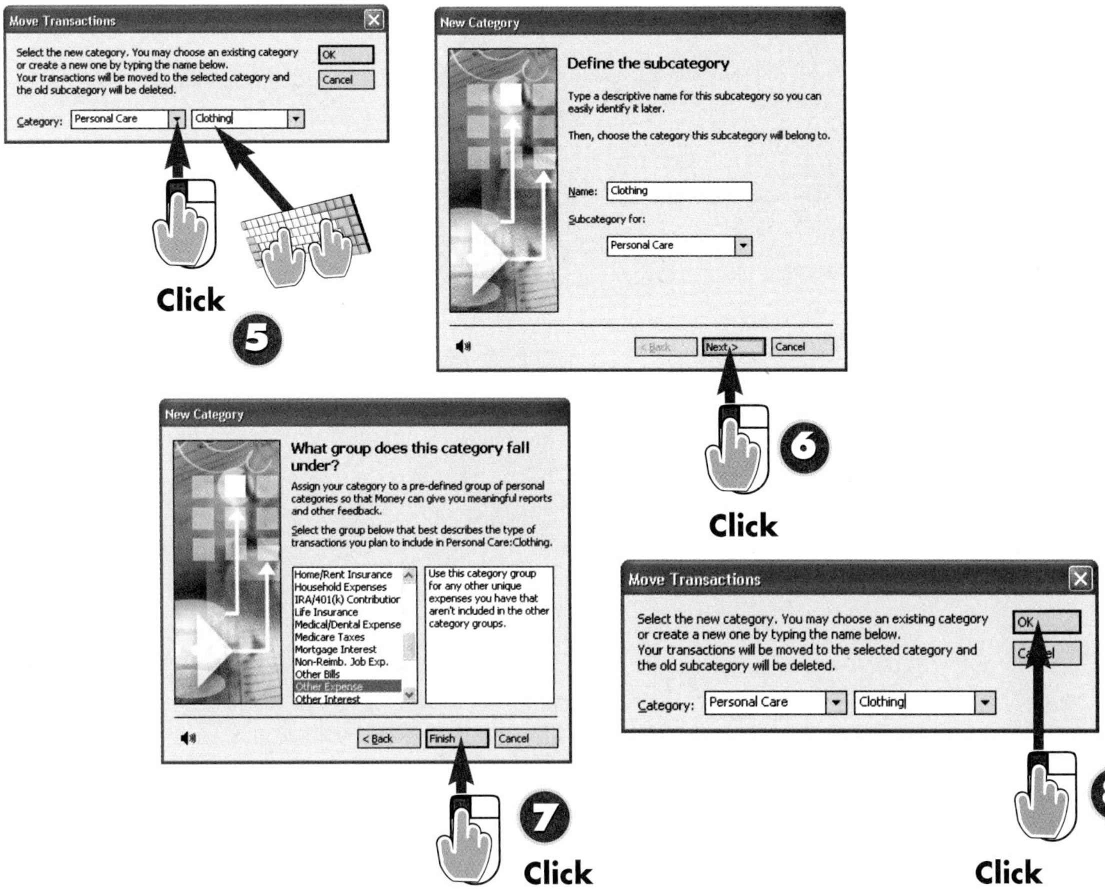

Click

5

6

Click

7

Click

8

Click

5 Click the **Category** down arrow and select the category to which the sub-category should be moved, type the name of the sub-category, and click **OK**.

6 If the sub-category name in step 5 is new, the New Category dialog box opens and asks you to verify the sub-category and category names. Do so, and click **Next**.

7 Accept the default group (unless you see another one that better describes the transactions you plan to include in the category) and click **Finish**.

8 Click **OK**.

TIP

Moving Categories
You can move a category the same way you move a sub-category. Be aware, however, that if you move a category, all its sub-categories will be deleted. For this reason, it is better to move the sub-categories around and add or delete categories as needed.

TIP

Viewing Category Details
To see more detailed information about a category and what accounts are connected to it, select the category and click the **Go to Category** button. In the category window you'll see account transactions that are associated with the category.

Adding a New Account Category

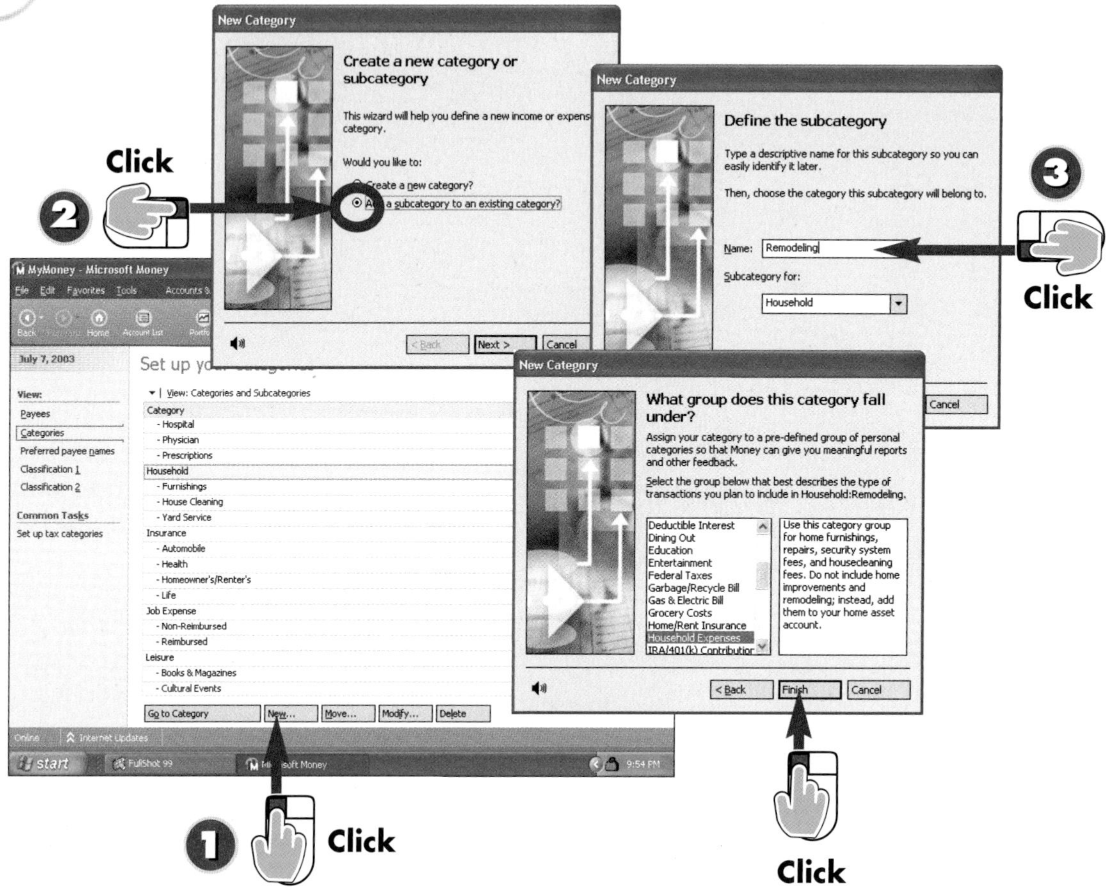

1. In the Set up your Categories window, click the category under which the sub-category should appear, and then click the **New** button.
2. Click the **Add a subcategory to an existing category** option and click **Next**.
3. In the **Name** box, type a name for the new sub-category. Then click **Next**.
4. Accept the existing group for the new sub-category, and click **Finish**.

INTRODUCTION

If, in its set group of account categories and sub-categories, Money doesn't offer a particular category or sub-category that you need in order to track your expenses or income, you can add your own. The steps here demonstrate how to add a sub-category; see the tip on this page to learn how to add a new category.

TIP

Adding a New Category
If you want to add a new category, click **Create a new category** in the wizard dialog box shown in step 2 and answer the remaining questions the same way you did for adding a sub-category.

Renaming or Deleting an Account Category

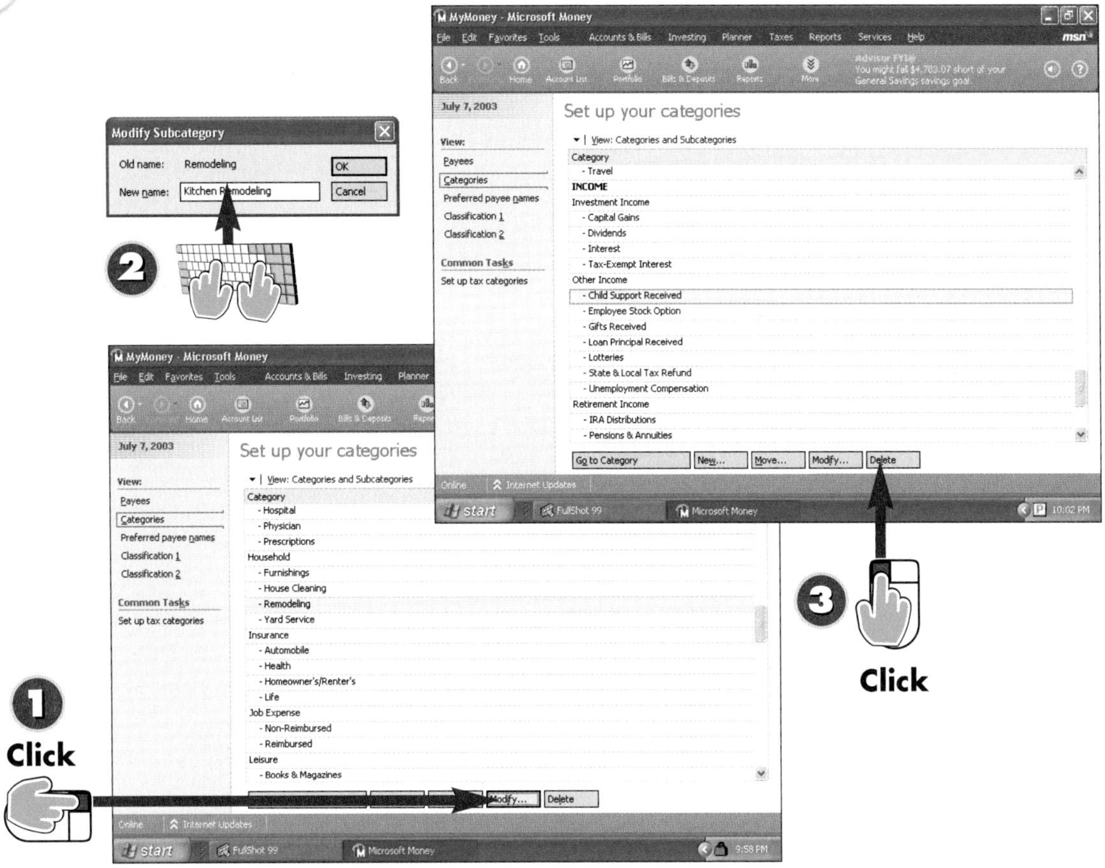

1. To change the name of a category or sub-category, on the Set up your categories window, click its name in the category list, and then click the **Modify** button.

2. Type the new name and click **OK**.

3. To delete a category or sub-category, select its name in the category list, and then click the **Delete** button.

INTRODUCTION

As with accounts, you can change the names of categories and sub-categories or delete them altogether if you know you won't use them.

TIP

Organizing Categories
Give some thought as to how you want to track your finances; that will guide how you organize and name your account groups, categories, and sub-categories.

Creating Account Classifications

Click

Click

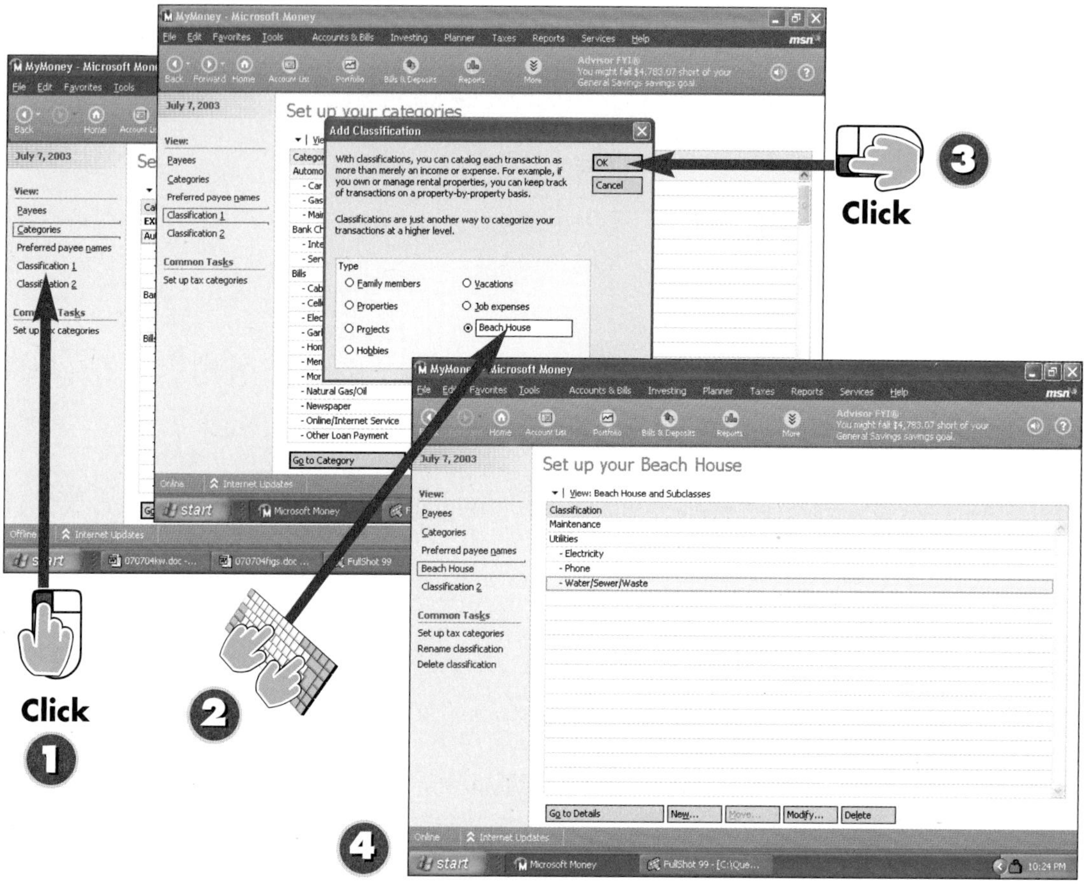

1. In the Set up your categories window, under **View**, click the **Classification 1** link.

2. In the **Type** area, click the classification type that best meets your needs, or type one of your own in the box at the end of the list.

3. Click **OK**.

4. Follow the steps in the task "Adding a New Account Category" earlier in this part to add categories and sub-categories to your new classification.

INTRODUCTION

To further manage your accounts, you can employ an additional level of tracking by creating classifications. *Classifications* can be used to track accounts that you want to separate from the rest of your bills and accounts.

TIP

Using Classifications
Defining and using classifications can be a great way of tracking an account you want to keep separate without having to create a new Money file.

Entering Payee Information

Click
1
Click
2
3
4
Click

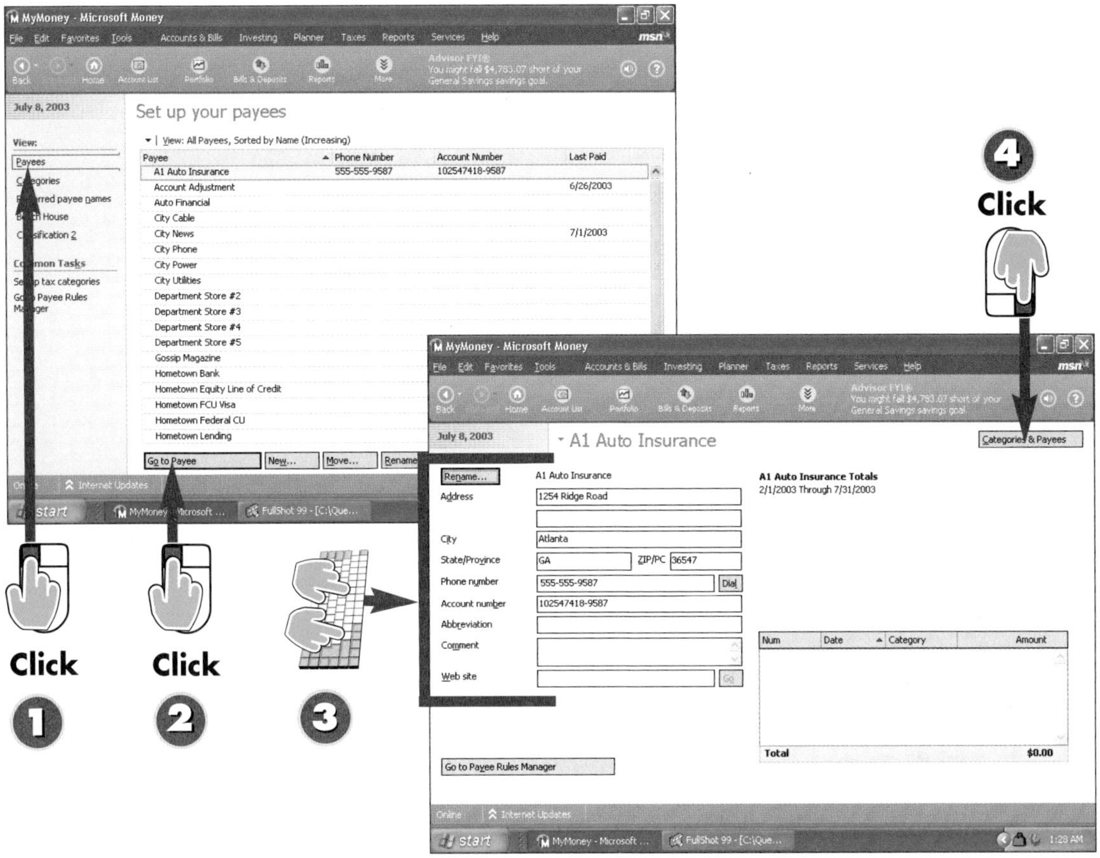

1. In the Set up your categories window, click the **Payees** link.

2. Click the account you want to review or update to select it, and then click the **Go to Payee** button.

3. Enter or change the payee information as needed. If there is a Web site for the account, type it in the **Web site** box.

4. Click **Categories & Payees** to return to the list of payees.

INTRODUCTION

When you set up an account, Money automatically creates a list of payees, or the people or companies you pay. You can review these lists and update the contact information as needed.

TIP

Renaming Payees
To change the name of the payee, click the **Rename** button on payee window, shown in steps 3 and 4, and type the new name.

HINT

Viewing Transactions
When you start recording payments, deposits, and so on for your accounts, those transactions will appear in the box on the right side of the payee window, shown in steps 3 and 4.

Adding a New Payee

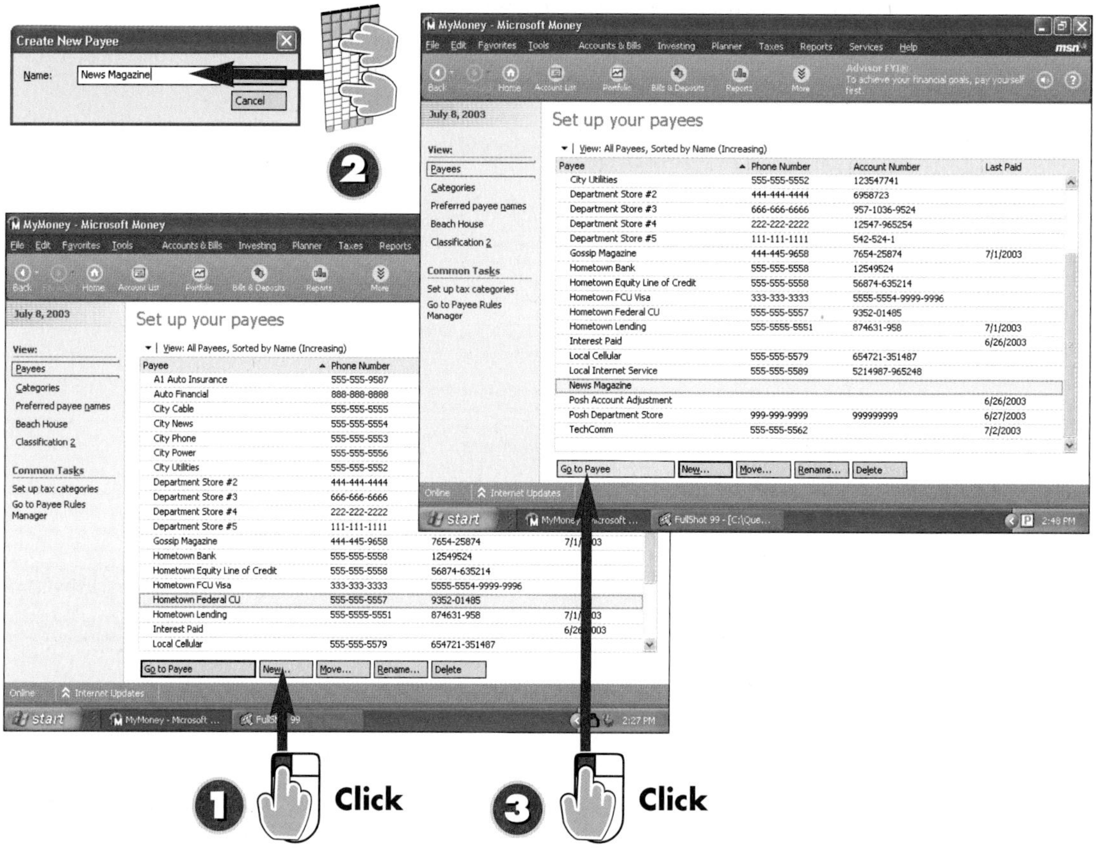

1. In the Set up your payees window, click the **New** button.
2. Type a name for the new payee in the **Name** box and click **OK**.
3. Click the new payee in the list, and then click the **Go to Payee** button to enter the payee information as shown in the preceding task.

End

INTRODUCTION

If you want to add a new payee, you can do so from the screen shown here or when you create a new account.

TIP

Changing Views

As with categories, you can change how payees are listed by clicking the down arrow next to the current view (see the top of the payee list) and selecting another view.

Deleting a Payee

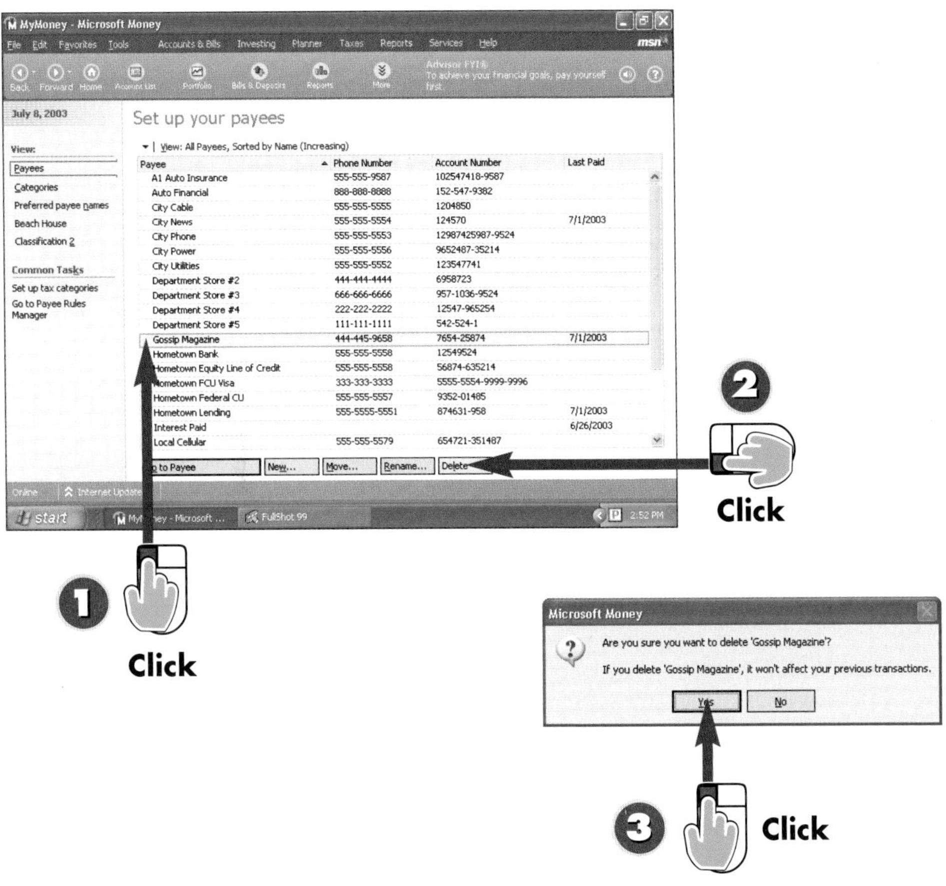

1. In the Set up your Payees window, click the payee you want to remove to select it.
2. Click **Delete**.
3. Money asks whether you are sure you want to delete the payee, and notes whether the deletion will affect other transactions. To proceed with the deletion, click **Yes**; otherwise, click **No**.

End

INTRODUCTION

Payees you no longer need can be removed just like all other account information. Just be sure that deleting a payee will not negatively affect other accounts—for example, ones that contain the same information.

Setting Up Accounts Online

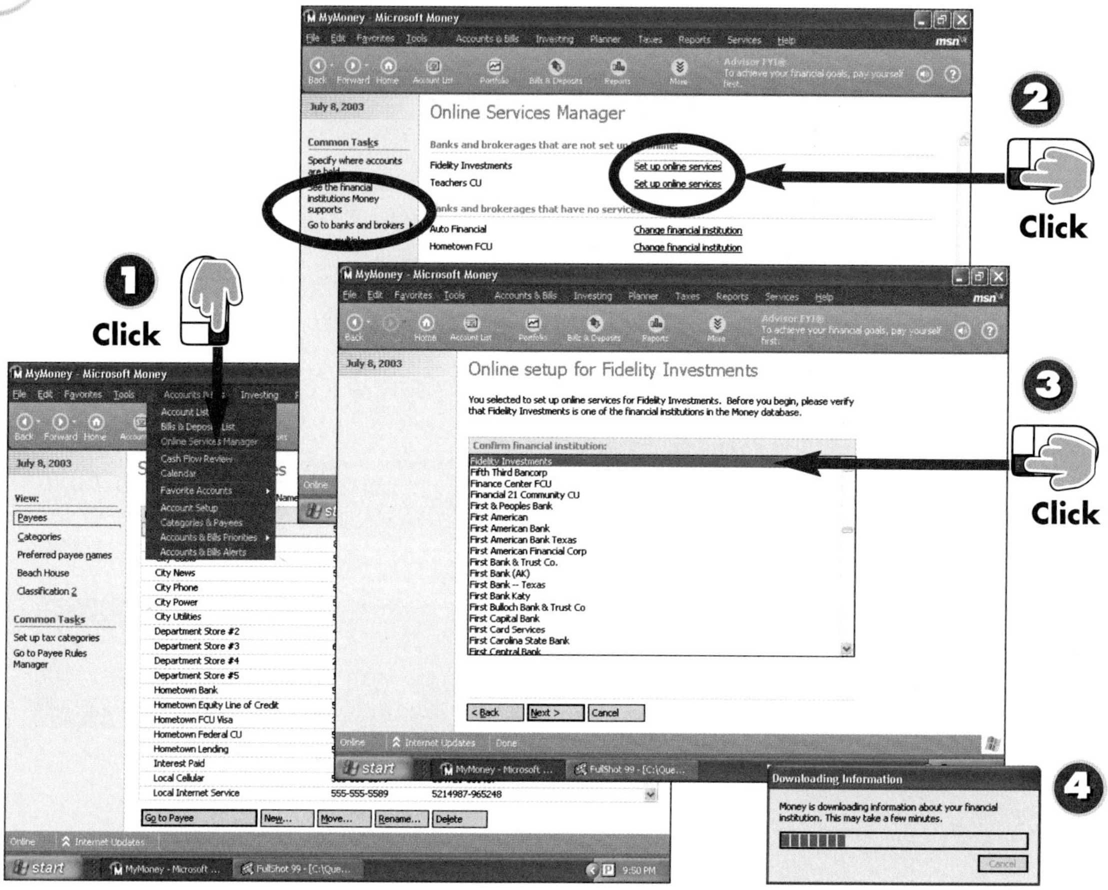

1 Open the **Accounts & Bills** menu and choose **Online Services Manager**.

2 Click the **Set up online services** link next to the account you want to set up.

3 Verify the account name by selecting it from the **Confirm financial institution** list and click **Next**. Money downloads information from the financial institution.

4 If necessary, enter your user ID and password. Then click **Next**. Money updates your account information; follow the prompts to complete the online setup.

INTRODUCTION

You can set up certain accounts in Money to use online services, enabling those accounts to download information directly from the holding company's Web site. Check with your account's company to arrange for online access, if it is available, and to obtain your access information before performing this task.

TIP

Steps May Vary

The exact process of setting up accounts for online services may vary depending on the type of account and the financial institution that holds it.

HINT

Seeing the List

To see which financial institutions work with Money for online services, click **See the financial institutions Money supports** on the screen shown in step 2. (You must be online to access the list.)

Getting Online Statements

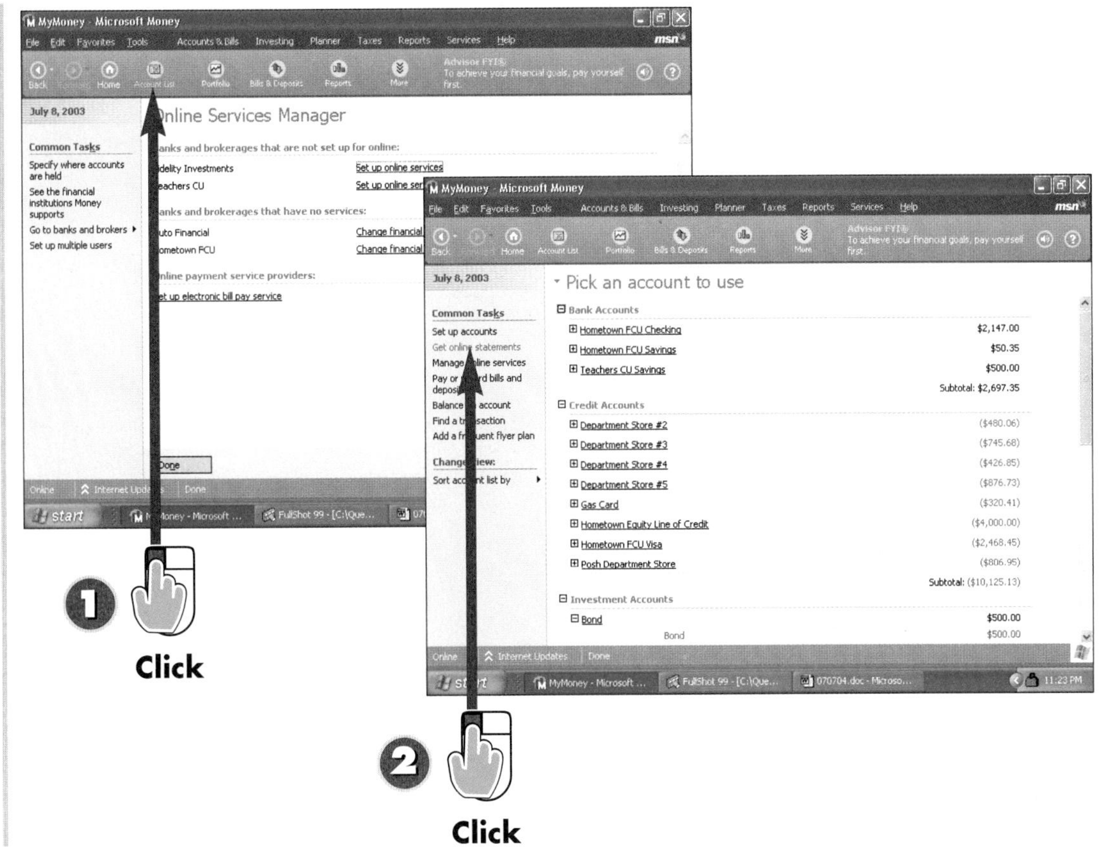

1. Click the **Account List** button on the Money toolbar.

2. Click the **Get online statements** link on the left side of the screen.

3. Select the account for which you want to download a statement. A message appears to let you know Money is downloading information from the financial institution.

4. Follow the prompts for the download, responding as needed.

INTRODUCTION

If you have set up an account for online services, you can download statements for that account from the holding company's Web site to Money, which means you don't have to update the account information by hand. However, you must have online services set up for that account and be connected to the Internet.

TIP

Steps May Vary
The exact process of downloading statements may vary depending on the type of account and the financial institution that holds it.

HINT

Viewing Balances
You can view balances for statements you've already downloaded by clicking the **View downloaded statements** link in the window shown in step 3.

PART 5

Managing Your Account Activity

You've learned how to add, modify, and delete accounts within Money; this part focuses on entering, modifying, and deleting transactions within your accounts, such as payments, deposits, and so on. You'll also learn about paying bills and transferring funds, searching for account information, balancing your accounts, and setting up reminders for yourself so that you can pay your bills on time. Lastly, you'll take a look at cash-flow projections to help you see into your financial future.

Manage Scheduled Bills and Deposits

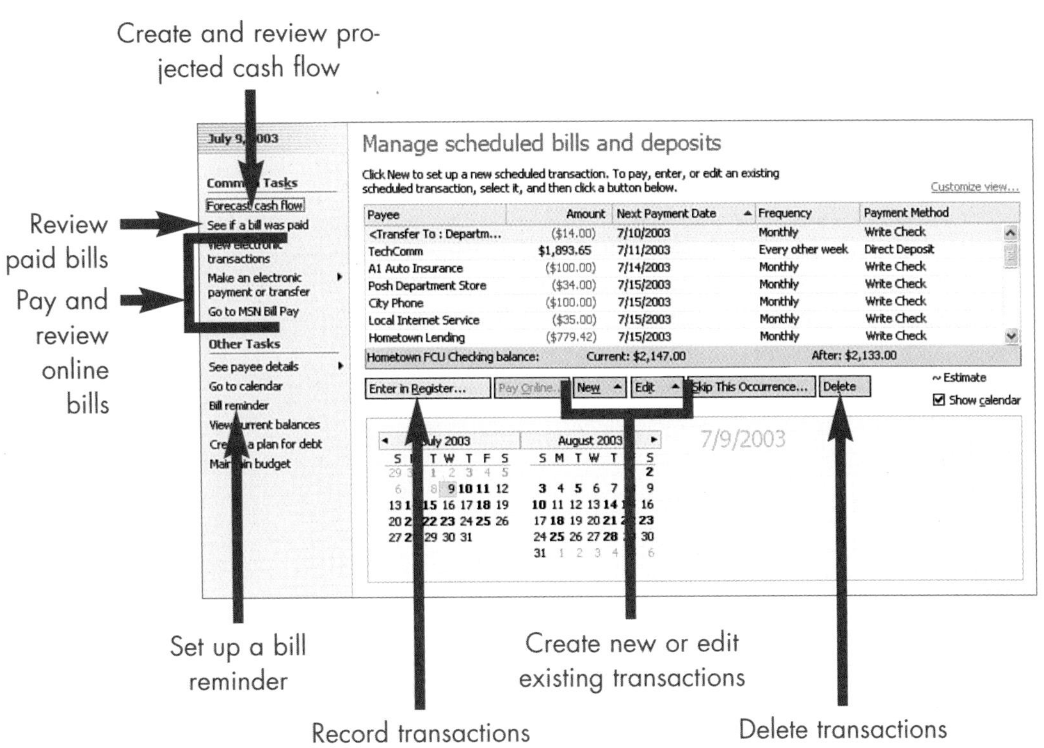

Recording Account Transactions

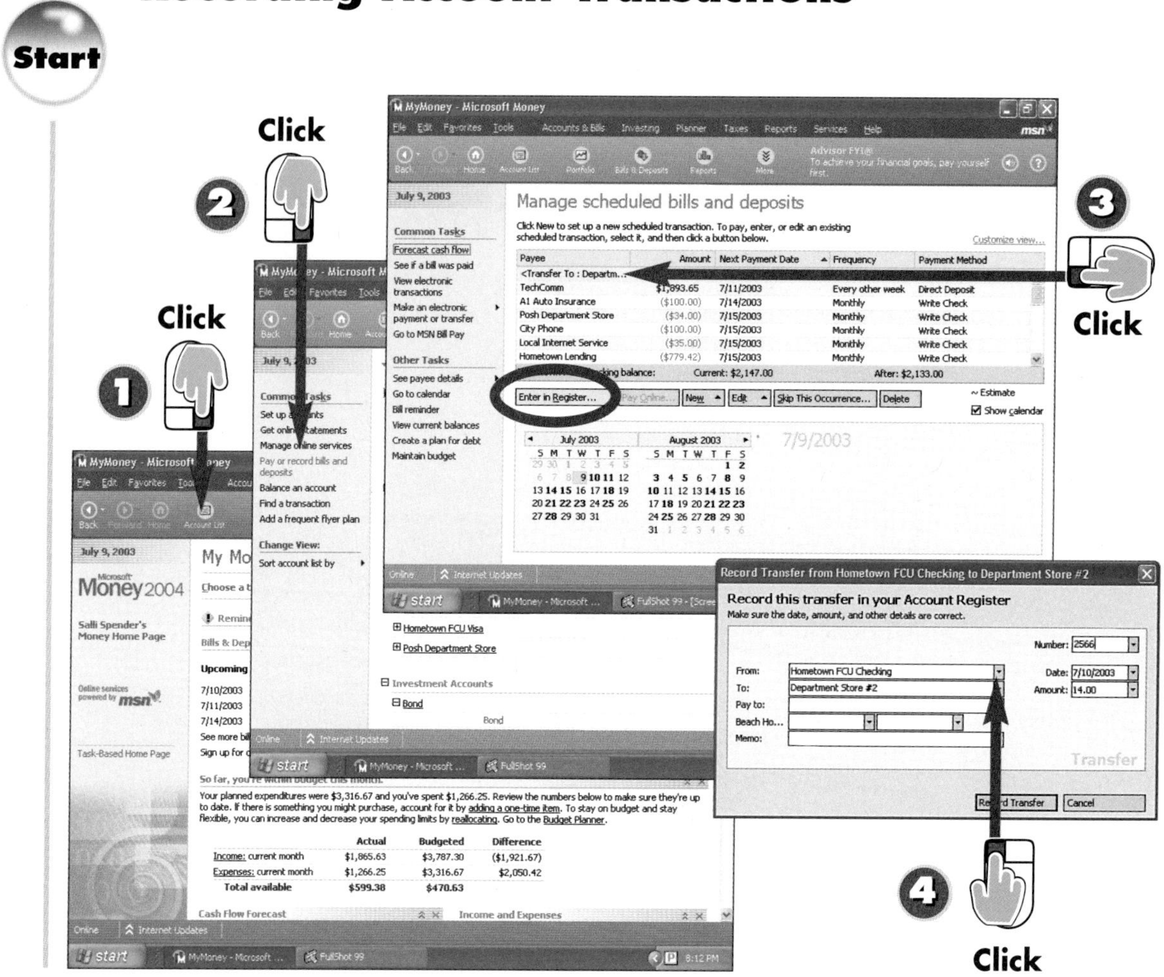

1. On the Money toolbar, click the **Account List** button.

2. In the Pick an account to use window, under **Common Tasks**, click the **Pay Record Bills and Deposits** link.

3. In the Manage scheduled bills and deposits window, click the transaction to record and click **Enter in Register**. Some of the information may already be entered.

4. To change or enter the account from which funds should be drawn or to whom the funds are paid, click the **From** and **To** down arrows and select the account names.

INTRODUCTION

When you pay a bill, make a deposit, or transfer funds, record the transaction in Money to keep your account information up to date. Transaction information for accounts set up for online services is downloaded and updated automatically, but chances are you have at least some accounts you'll need to update yourself.

TIP

Viewing the Calendar Months

To view the calendar months in the Manage scheduled bills and deposits screen (see step 3), click the **Show calendar** check box to mark it. (To hide the calendar, click the check box again to deselect it.) The days in bold are days on which a bill is due or a deposit is to occur. To see details about those days, click the **Go to calendar** link under Other Tasks.

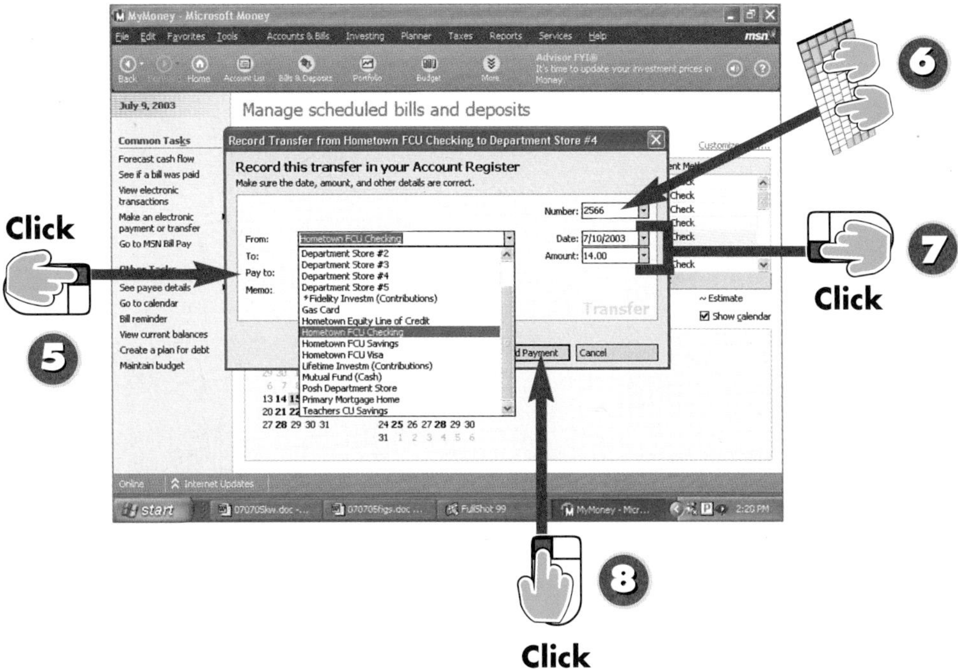

5 In the **Pay to** field, type or change the name of the person or company to whom the bill is being paid, if applicable.

6 In the **Number** field, change or type the check number, if you are paying by check, or click the down arrow to select another method of payment.

7 Type the date of payment in the **Date** box and the amount being paid in the **Amount** box.

8 Click the **Record Transfer** or **Payment** button.

TIP

Categorizing Transactions

If you set up a classification for this account in Part 4, the name of that classification appears beneath the **Pay to** field. You can use the boxes to the right of the classification name to select a category and sub-category to track your expenses for the classification. In addition, you can use the **Memo** box to type any notes about the transaction you are recording.

TIP

Tracking Checks

As you enter transactions in Money, the program will keep track of your check numbers and fill them in automatically. If you skipped a check, you can change the number by typing the correct number in the **Number** box.

Adding a New Bill

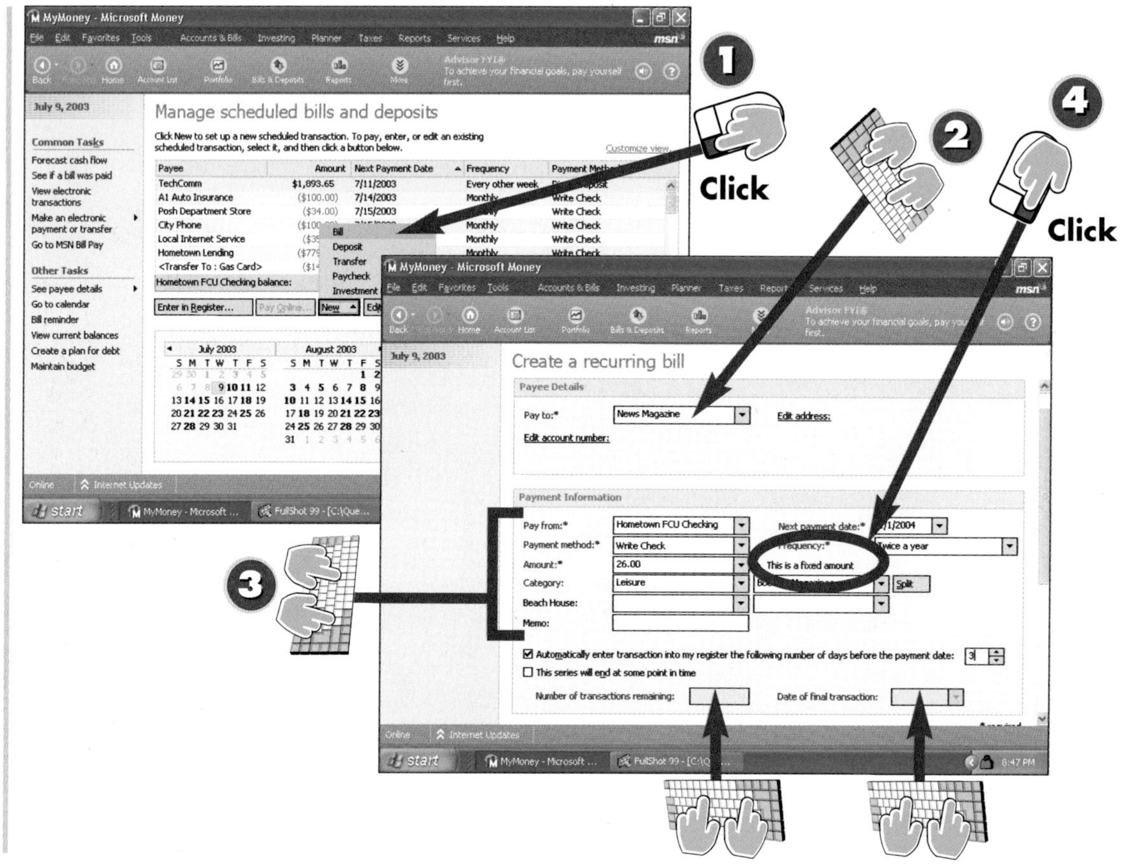

1. In the Manage scheduled bills and deposits window, click the **New** button and choose **Bill** from the menu that appears.

2. Type the name of the payee in the **Pay to** box.

3. Select or enter the payment information just as you did in the preceding task.

4. If the payment amount always differs, click the **Amount** box up arrow and select **Estimate because the amount varies**. Otherwise, select **This is a fixed amount**.

INTRODUCTION

When you add a new account to Money, the program automatically includes that account in your list of payees. If the account involves paying a bill, however, you still need to add the bill information.

TIP

Changing the Account Number

You can review and/or change the account number by clicking the **Edit account number** link below the Pay to box. To review and/or change the address, click the **Edit address** link.

TIP

Handling Fluctuating Amounts

If payment amounts change for a bill each month, enter the amount each time you pay the bill. This allows Money to create an average payment and adjust your cash-flow outlook accordingly.

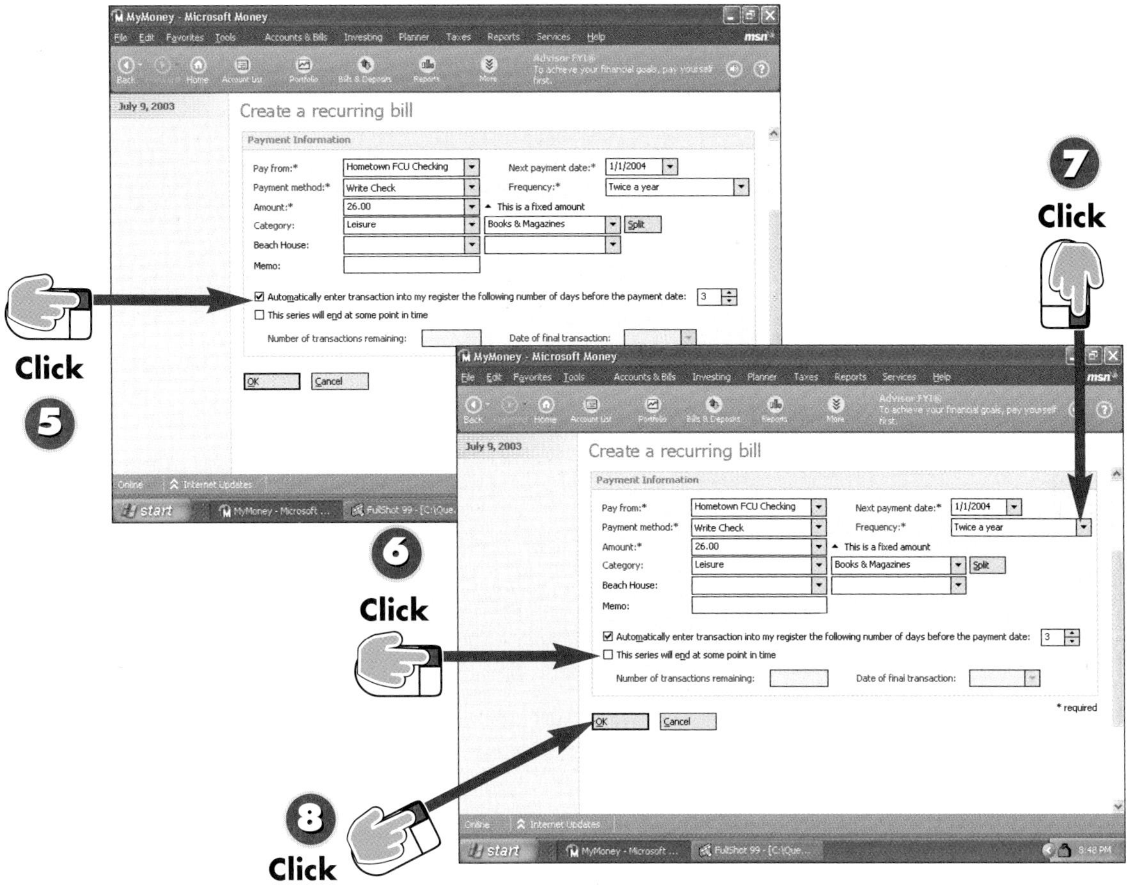

Click 7

Click 5

Click 6

Click 8

5 To automatically enter this bill in your register, click the **Automatically enter transaction...** check box, and specify when you want Money to register the bill.

6 If payments on this bill will end at some point, click the **This series will end...** check box, type the number of transactions left, and the date they will end.

7 If the date in the **Next payment date** box or the frequency of payment in the **Frequency** box are incorrect, click the down arrows to change them.

8 Click **OK**.

TIP

Selecting the Bill

When you add a bill, Money lists it with the rest of your bills and deposits. That way, each time you pay the bill, you can select the bill from the list, click **Enter in register**, and update the payment information.

Adding a New Deposit or Paycheck

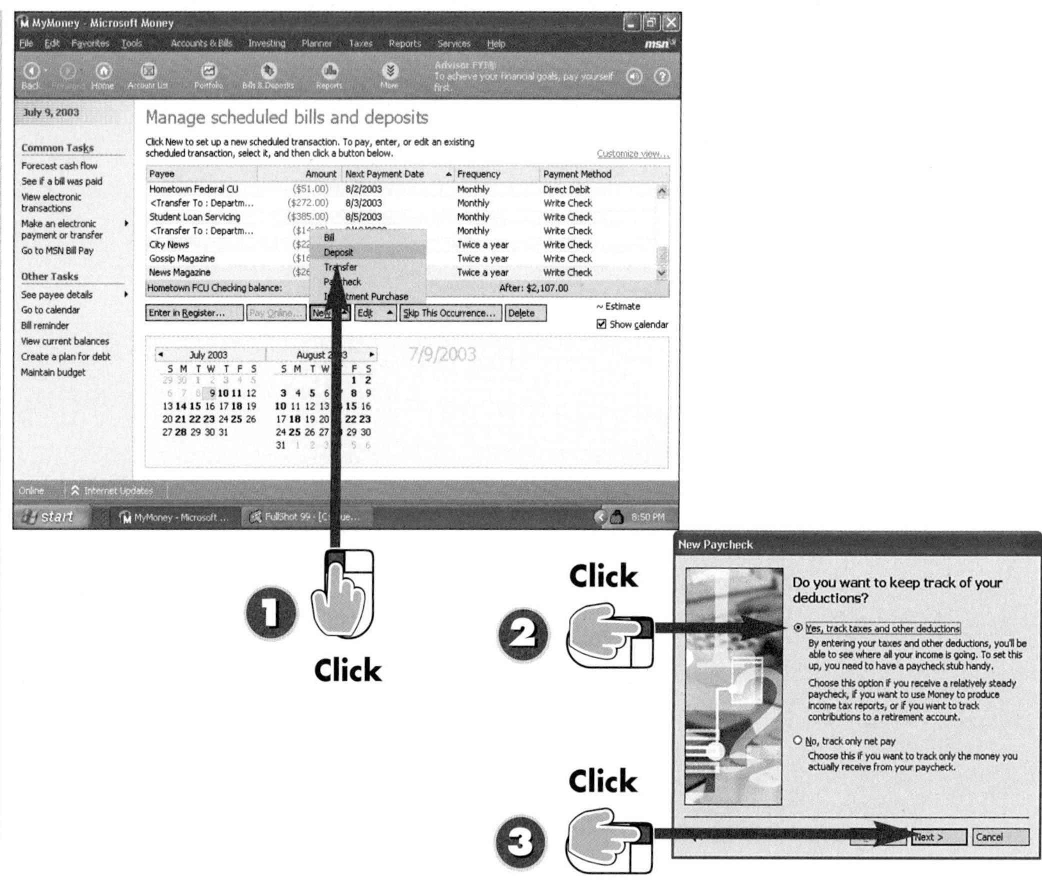

1. In the Manage scheduled bills and deposits window, click the **New** button and choose **Deposit** or **Paycheck**. If you select deposit, go to step 5.
2. If you are entering a paycheck, a wizard opens and asks whether you want to keep track of your deductions. If you select **No**, click **Finish** and go to step 5.
3. If you select **Yes** in step 2, click **Next**. Money asks if the paycheck makes contributions to a retirement account.

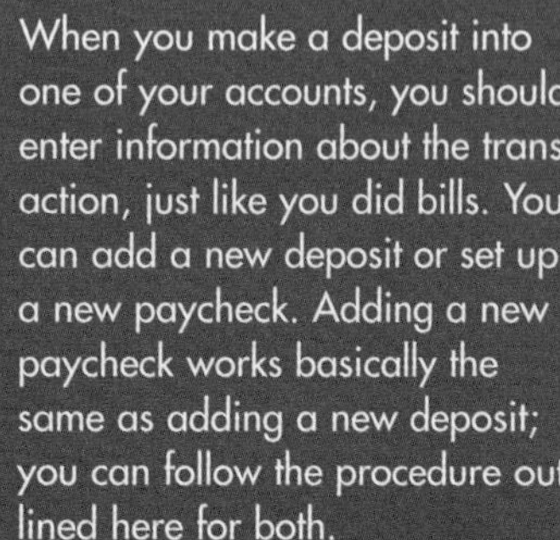

INTRODUCTION

When you make a deposit into one of your accounts, you should enter information about the transaction, just like you did bills. You can add a new deposit or set up a new paycheck. Adding a new paycheck works basically the same as adding a new deposit; you can follow the procedure outlined here for both.

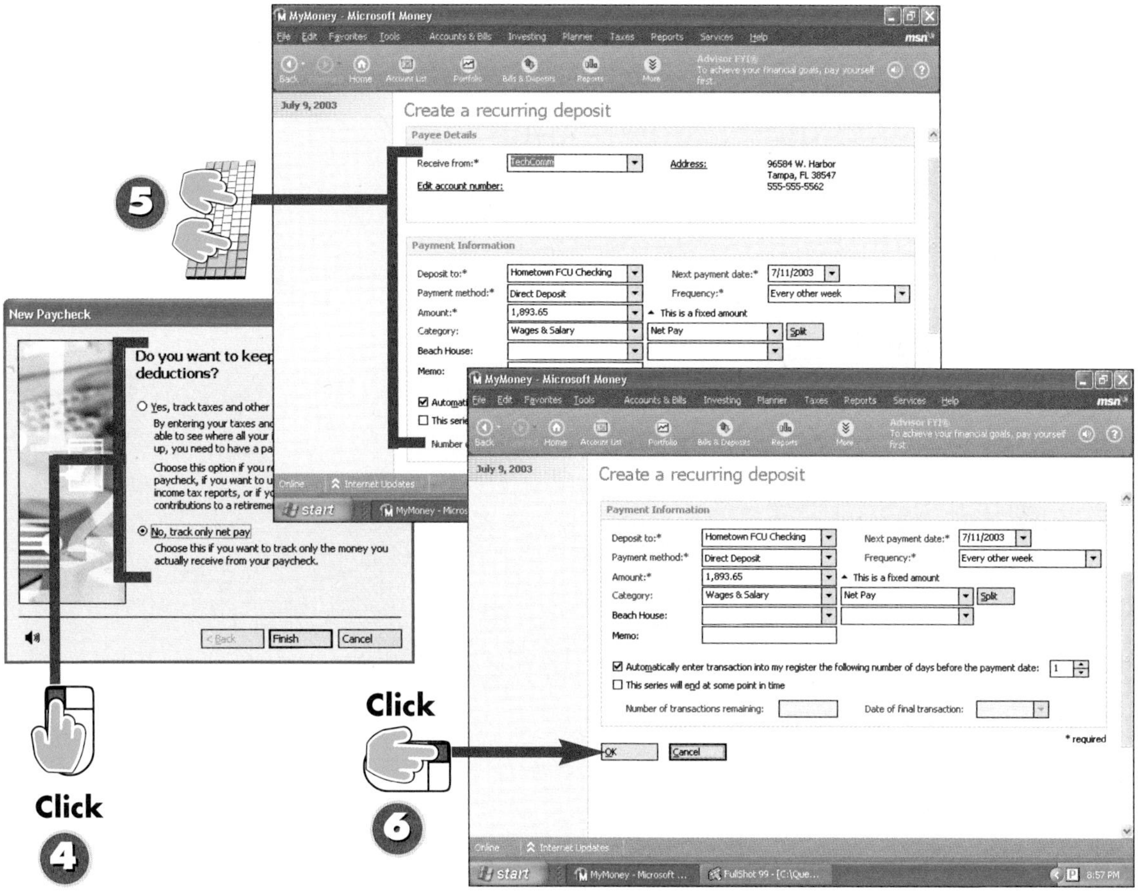

Click

4

Click

6

5

4 Click the **Yes** or **No** option, then click **Next**. Answer all remaining questions, clicking **Next** after you answer each one to move through the wizard. Then click **Finish**.

5 Select or enter the payment information just as you did in the task "Recording Account Transactions" earlier in this part.

6 Click **OK**.

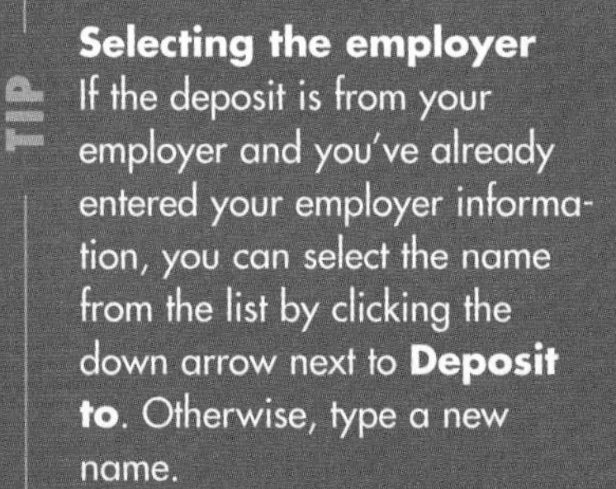

TIP

Selecting the employer
If the deposit is from your employer and you've already entered your employer information, you can select the name from the list by clicking the down arrow next to **Deposit to**. Otherwise, type a new name.

Adding a New Transfer

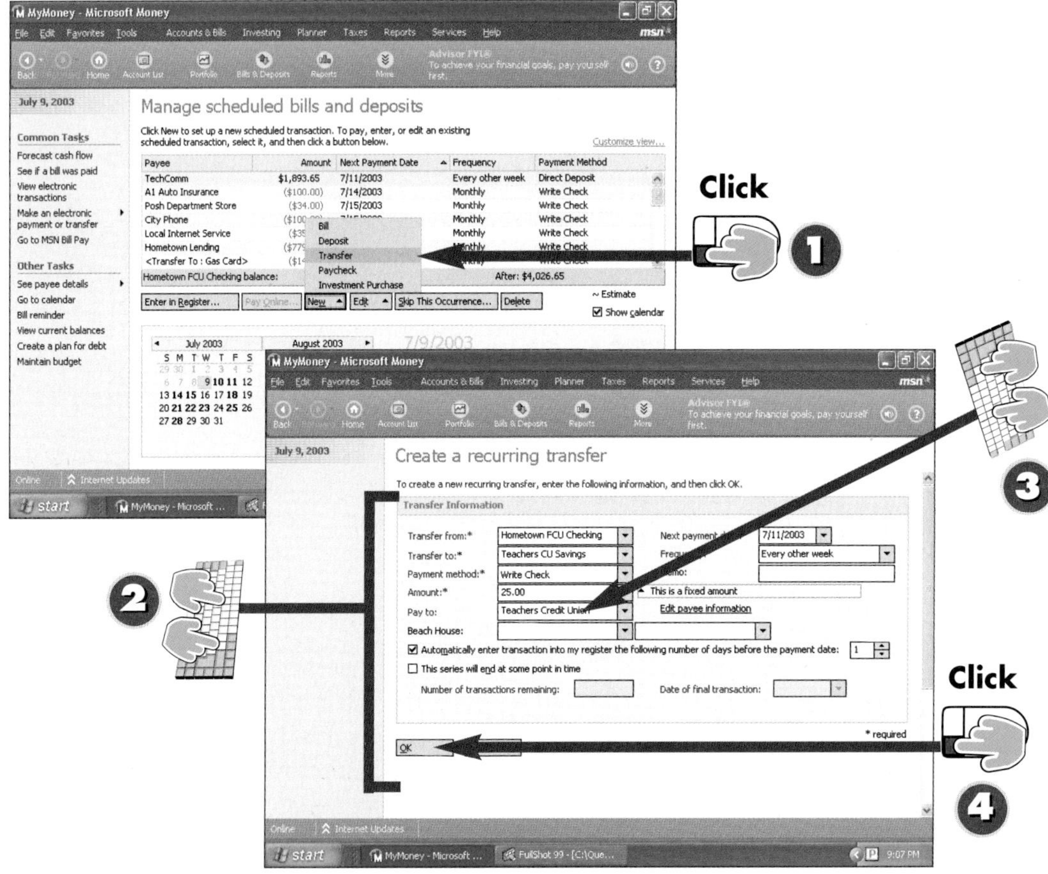

1. In the Manage scheduled bills and deposits window, click the **New** button and choose **Transfer**.
2. Select or enter the transfer information just as you did in the task "Recording Account Transactions" earlier in this part.
3. If you are writing a check for the transfer, type the payee's name in the **Pay to** box or select it from the drop-down menu.
4. Click **OK**.

INTRODUCTION

If you transfer money between accounts, this procedure is for you. Entering a transfer works just like adding a bill or deposit; much of the information is the same.

TIP

Editing Payee Information

If you want to view or change the payee information, click the **Edit payee information** link to the right of the Pay to box in the window shown in steps 2–4.

HINT

Entering the Category

If the transfer relates to a classification (here, Beach House), enter the category and subcategory in the corresponding boxes. If you don't have classifications or they don't apply, leave the boxes blank.

Adding a New Investment Purchase

Click

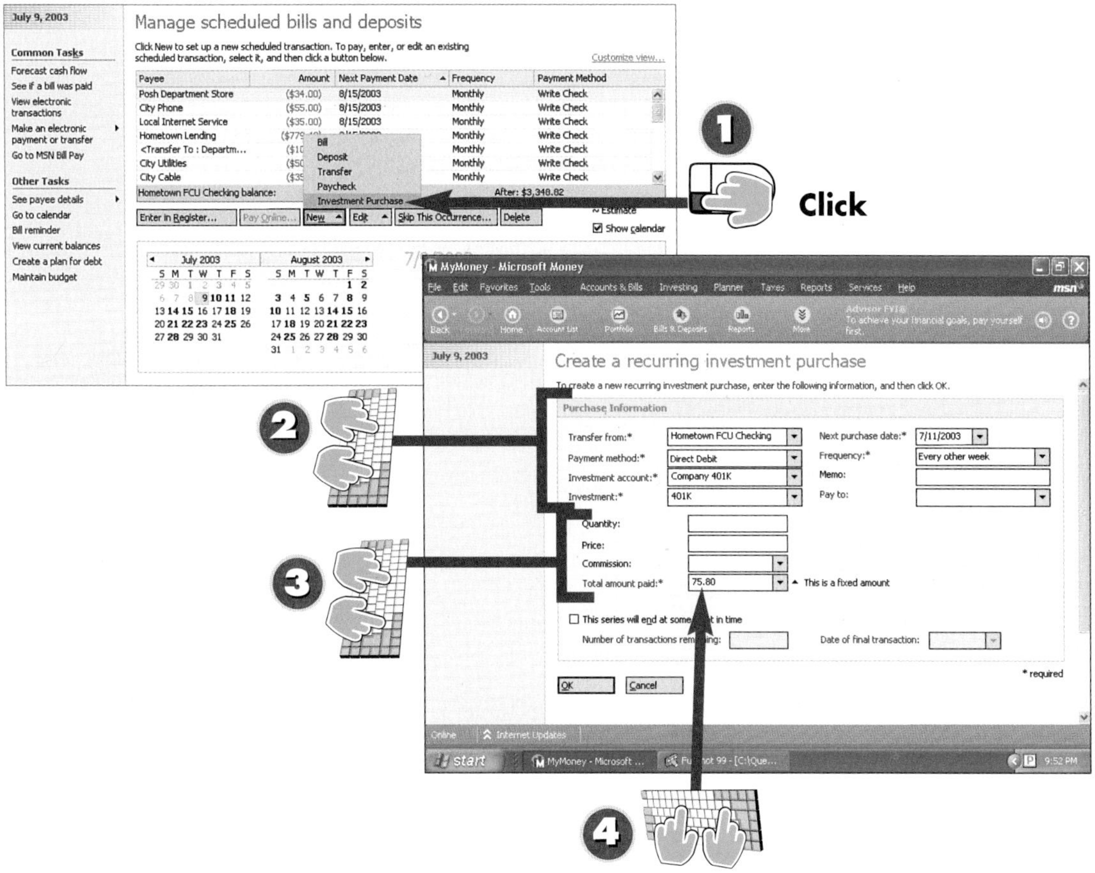

1. In the Manage scheduled bills and deposits window, click the **New** button and choose **Investment Purchase**.
2. Select or enter the purchase information as you did the in the task "Recording Account Transactions" earlier in this part.
3. Type the requested information in the **Quantity**, **Price**, and **Commission** fields, if applicable.
4. Type the amount of the investment purchase in the **Total amount paid** box. Then, click **OK**.

INTRODUCTION

You can add one more type of account from the Manage scheduled bills and deposits window: accounts for investment purchases.

TIP

Required Information

Note that the boxes with the asterisks (*) next to them require that you enter or select information to complete the investment purchase.

Modifying Bill or Deposit Information

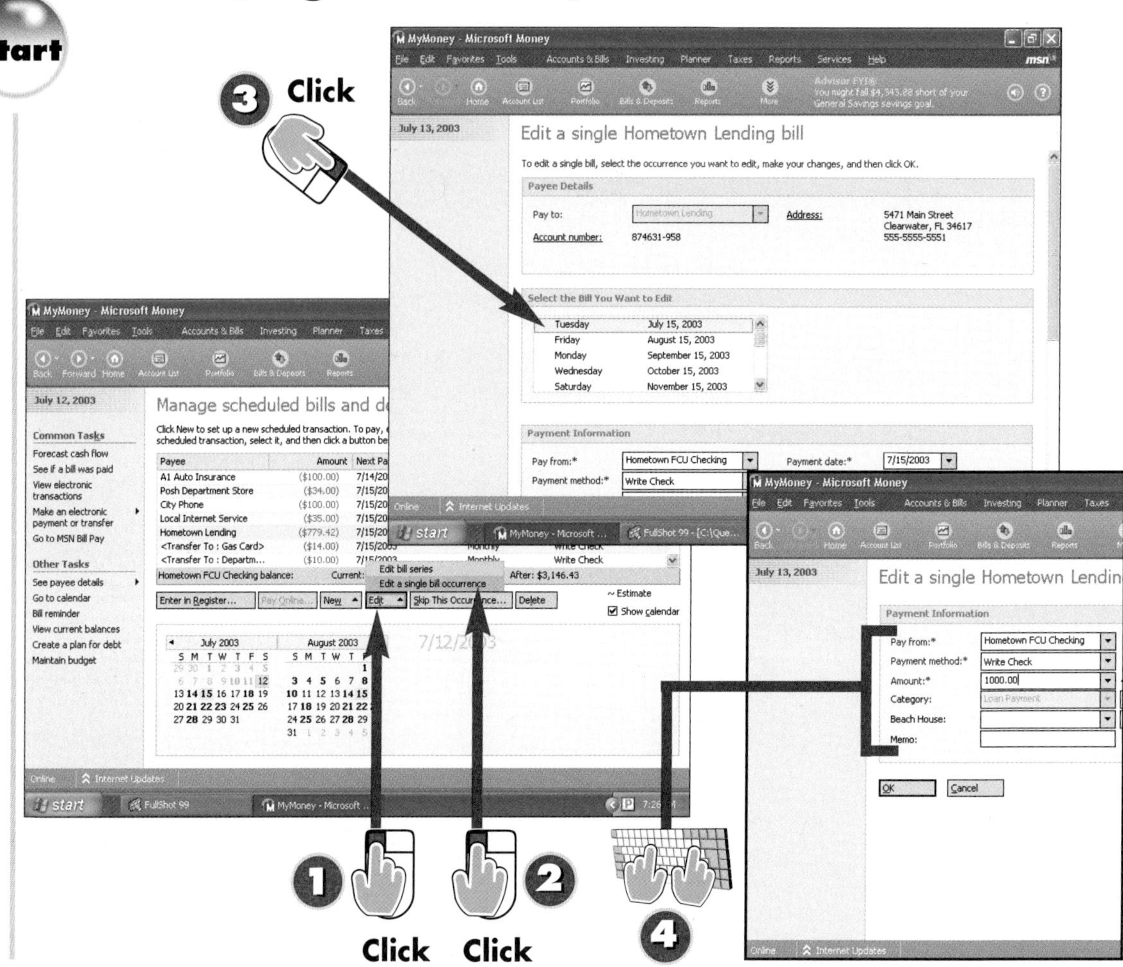

1. In the Manage scheduled bills and deposits window, click the bill or deposit you want to modify, and click the **Edit** button.
2. Choose **Edit bill series** or **Edit a single bill occurrence** for bills; or choose **Edit deposit series** or **Edit a single deposit occurrence** for deposits.
3. Under **Select the Bill You Want to Edit**, click the bill that you want to update. (For deposits, under **Select the Deposit You Want to Edit**, click the desired deposit.)
4. Under **Payment Information**, make payment changes as needed—for example, changing the value in the **Amount** field. Then, click **OK**.

INTRODUCTION

If a recurring bill or deposit changes, you should update Money to reflect that change. When modifying a bill or deposit, you can either change the entire billing series or make a one-time change—for example, to pay extra one month on a bill.

TIP

Making Permanent Changes
In step 1, select **Edit bill/deposit series** to make permanent changes to all bills or deposits for a specific account. Select **Edit a single bill/deposit occurrence** to make a one-time change to a bill or deposit for a specific account.

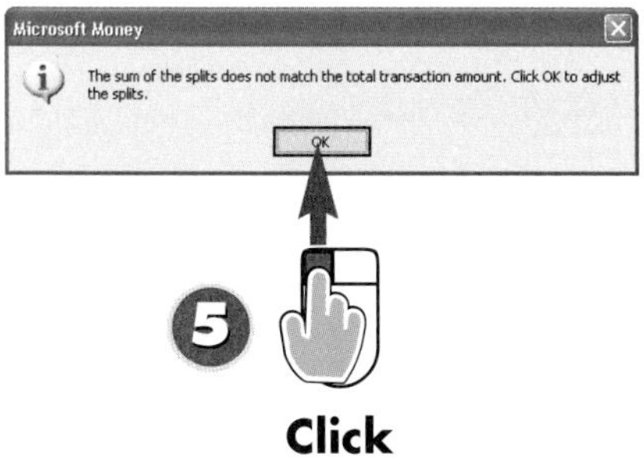

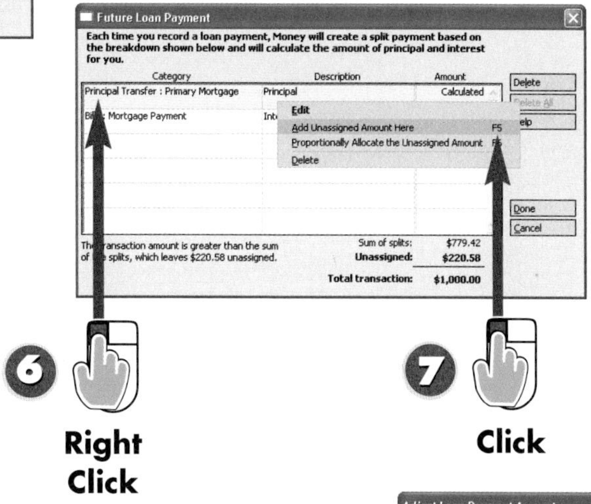

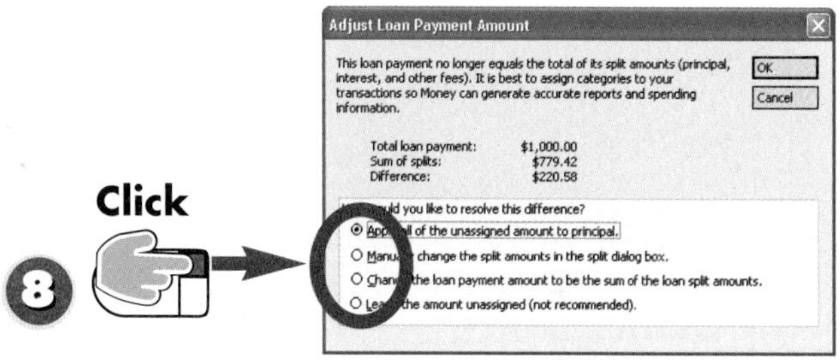

Click

Right Click

Click

Click

5 If you are paying extra on a loan account, Money needs to know how much of the extra amount you want to split between the principal and the interest. Click **OK**.

6 To apply the entire extra amount to either the principal or the interest, right-click either the principal or the interest row in the Future Loan Payment dialog box.

7 From the pop-up menu, select **Add unassigned amount here**, then click **Done**.

8 In the Adjust Loan Payment Amount dialog box, click the option to resolve the difference, and click **OK**. Then click **Done** in the Future Loan Payment dialog box.

TIP

Understanding Terms
At the bottom of the Future Loan Payment dialog box, next to **Sum of splits**, is how much you normally pay. Next to **Unassigned** is the total extra amount you have to apply to either the principal or the interest, or to split between both. The total amount you are paying is next to **Total transaction**.

Deleting Bill or Deposit Information

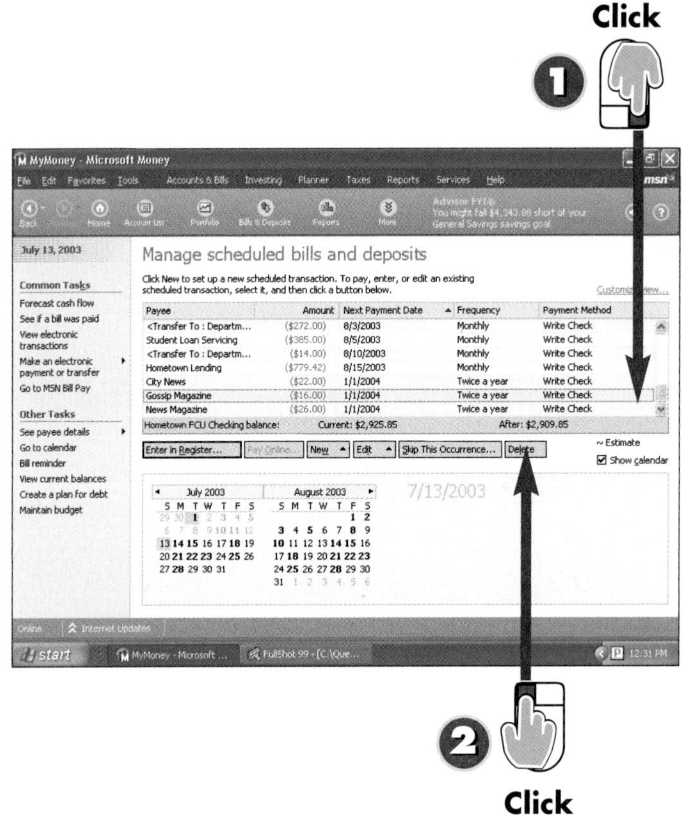

1. In the Manage scheduled bills and deposits window, click the bill or deposit you want to remove to select it.

2. Click **Delete**.

INTRODUCTION

If you no longer pay a certain bill or make a particular deposit, you can delete it from your bills and deposits list. Just be sure you really want to remove it, because deleting it will remove it from Money permanently.

Setting Up Accounts for Electronic Pay

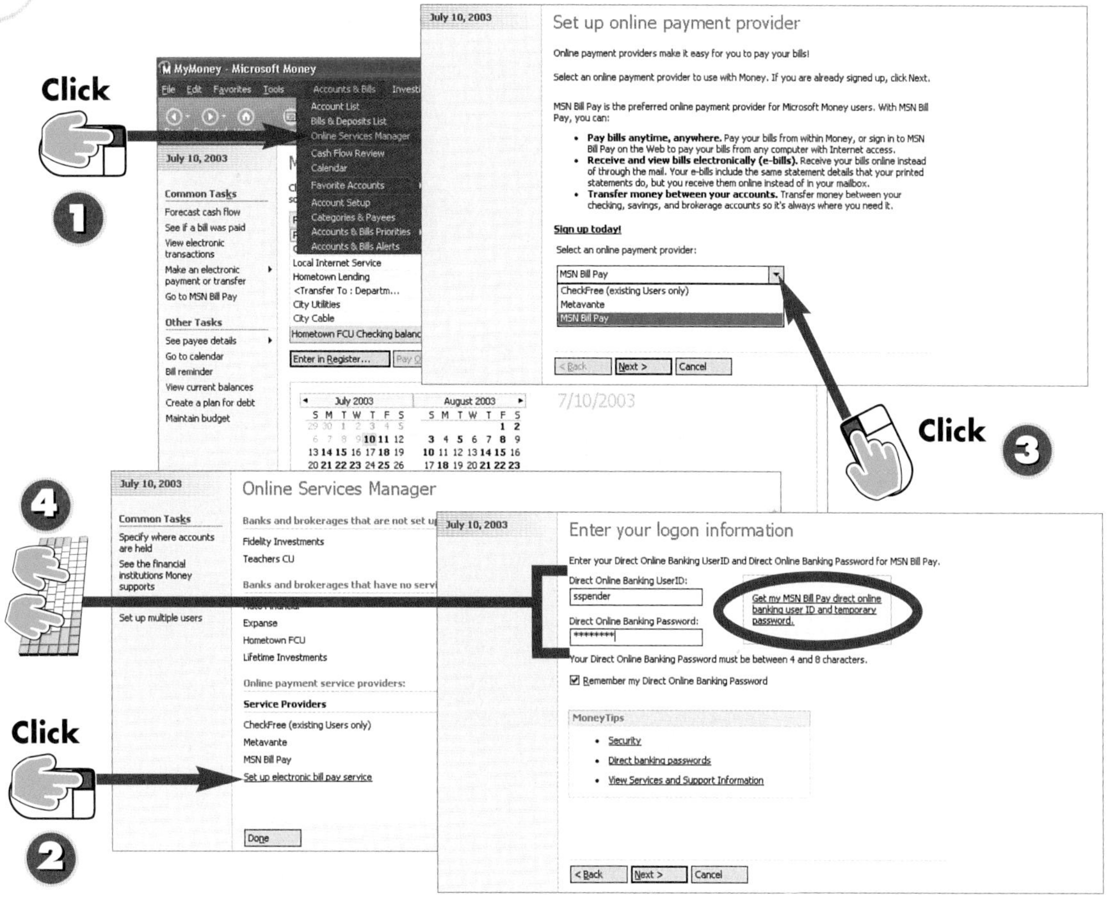

1. To set up online payment service through Money, click **Accounts & Bills** in the Money toolbar and select **Online Services Manager**.
2. In the Online Services Manager window, under **Online payment service providers**, click the **Set up electronic bill pay service** link.
3. On the Set up online payment provider window, click the down arrow under **Select an online payment provider**, choose the provider you want, and click **Next**.
4. Enter your user ID and password, and click **Next**. Follow and complete the instructions for the online service provider setup.

INTRODUCTION

If you have not already set up your accounts for online services, you can do so now to pay bills or transfer funds at the touch of a button. First, however, you must have an online bill-paying service set up. You can use the online service providers offered through Money, such as MSN Bill Pay, to pay bills or transfer funds through Money. Be sure to connect to the Internet before you begin this task.

TIP

Getting Your ID and Password

If you don't know your user ID and password, click the link inside the shaded box next to the user ID and password boxes to find out how to obtain them.

Paying Bills or Transferring Funds Online

Start

Click

Click

Click

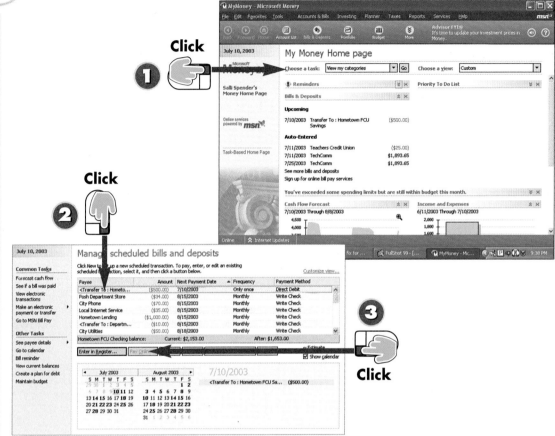

1 After connecting to the Internet, click **Bills & Deposits** on the Money toolbar.

2 In the Manage bills and deposits window, click the desired bill or transaction.

3 Click the **Pay Online** button, verify your payment/transfer information, and click **Submit Payment**.

End

INTRODUCTION

If you set up an account for online services, you can use Money to pay bills or transfer funds. If you have online services set up outside of Money, use the Internet to pay your bills or transfer funds and keep your account information up to date in Money by manually updating it or downloading your statements into Money.

TIP

Getting Help
For additional help, click the question mark in the Money toolbar. Then, under Ask Money, type **electronic payment or transfer** and click **Search**. All topics related to the search appear as clickable links.

TIP

Setting Payee Info
If you are paying a bill or transferring funds for the first time, you may be required to enter information about the payee so that the online service provider knows where to send your payment or transfer your funds.

Writing and Printing Checks

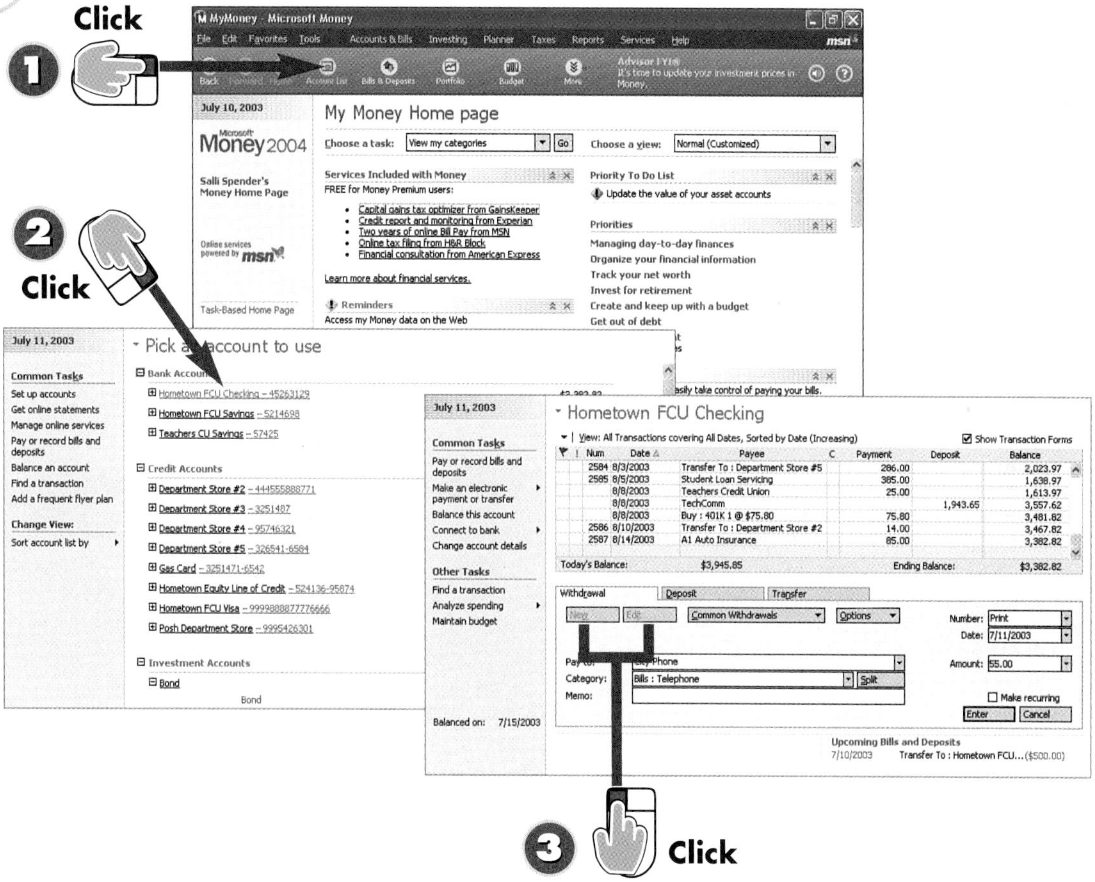

1 Once you receive your checks, be sure the paper is loaded in your printer and your printer is turned on. Then, on the Money toolbar, click **Account List**.

2 In the Pick an account to use window, click the account from which you are writing the check—for example, your checking account.

3 If you already have a transaction listed that you want to use to write the check, select it and, in the Withdrawal tab, click the **Edit** button. To create a new transaction, click **New**.

See next page

INTRODUCTION

Money provides you with the option to purchase and set up computer checks. These checks can be set up and printed from Money and used just like regular checks. Before you can set up and print checks through Money, you must order them first. For information about the checks and how to order them, visit the Microsoft Money 2004 Web site at www.microsoft.com/money/support/supplies/.

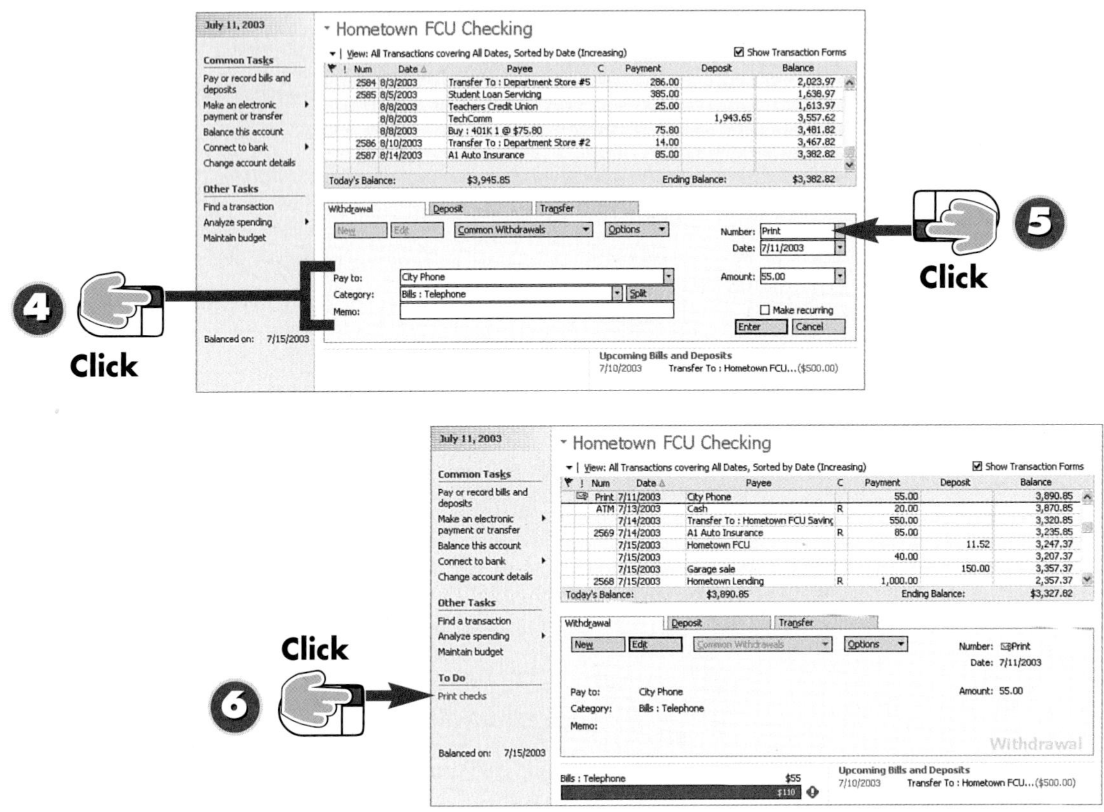

4. In the Withdrawal tab, enter or change all the information for the transaction as described in Part 4.
5. Click the **Number** down arrow and select **Print this transaction**. When you are finished entering or changing the transaction information, click **Enter**.
6. In the To Do area on the left side of the screen, click the **Print checks** link.

TIP

Testing the Print Job

To see how the check will look before you actually print the information on the check, put a regular piece of printer paper in your printer. Then, in the Print Checks dialog box, click **Test Print**.

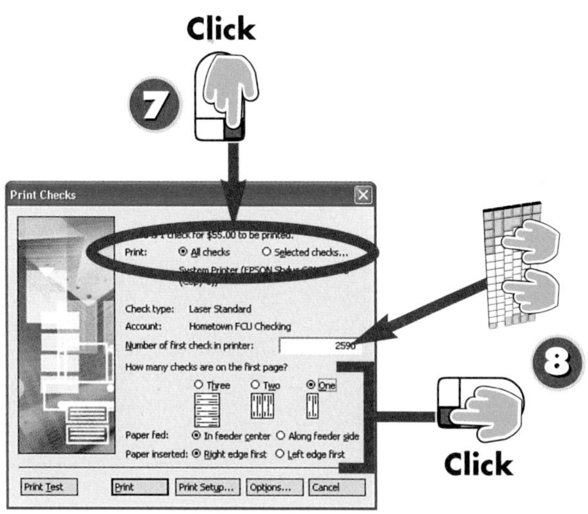

7. In the Print Checks dialog box, next to **Print**, click either **All checks** or **Selected checks**, depending on your needs.
8. In the **Number of first check in printer** box, type the check number.
9. Select any additional print options, and click the **Print** button.

TIP

Changing Print Options
To change check-printing options, such as how you want the printed information to appear on the check, click the **Options** button in the Print Checks dialog box and make your selections. Click **OK** when you are finished.

HINT

Changing Setup Options
To change check-setup options, such as the printer, font, or check type, click the **Print Setup** button in the Print Checks dialog box and make your selections. Click **OK** when you are finished.

Reviewing Paid Bills

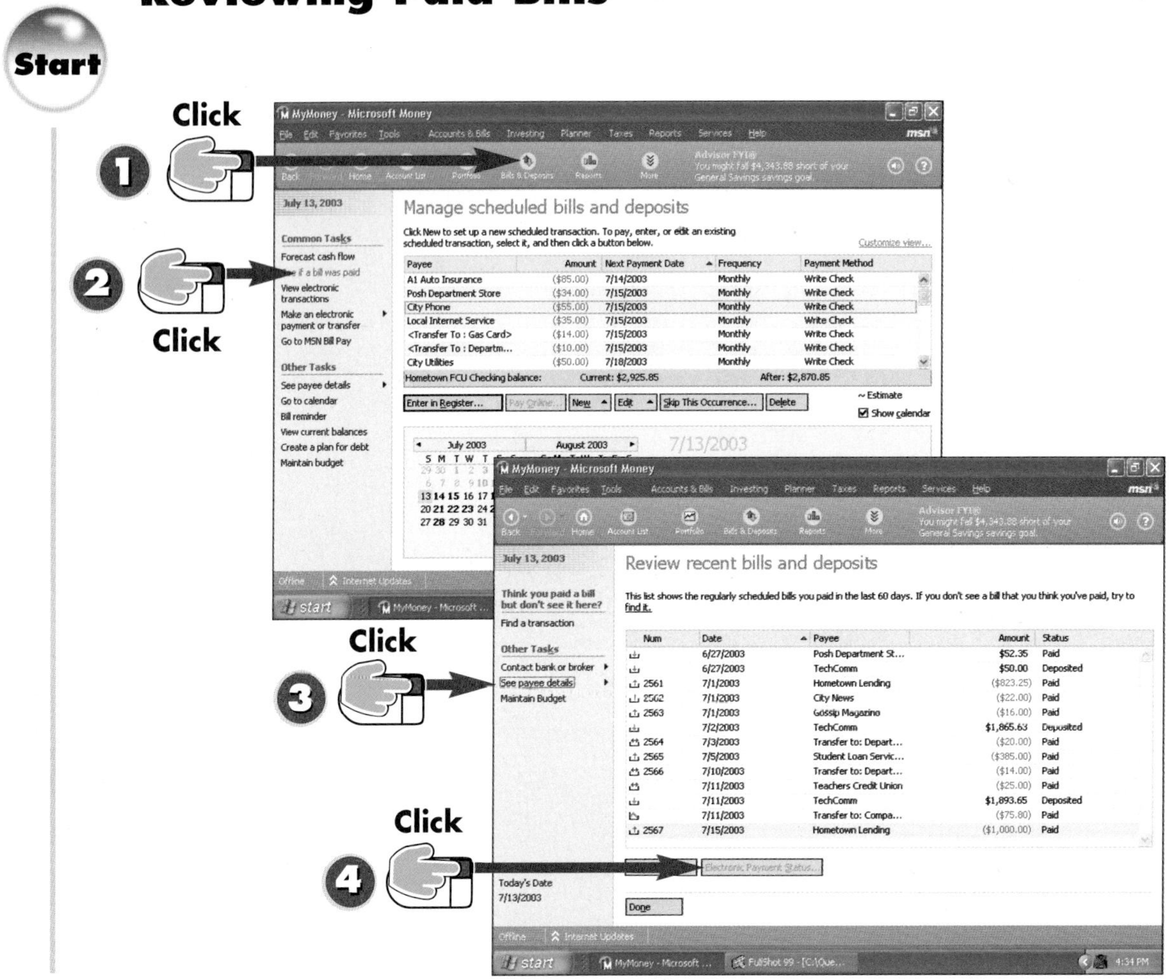

Start

1 Click

2 Click

3 Click

4 Click

1. On the Money toolbar, click **Bills & Deposits**.

2. In the Manage scheduled bills and deposits window, under **Common Tasks**, click **See if a bill was paid**.

3. To see details about a particular bill, click the bill in the list, and then click the **See payee details** link on the left side of the screen.

4. If a bill was paid electronically and you want to see the status, click the bill to select it and then click **Electronic Payment Status**.

INTRODUCTION

Now that you have paid some bills and entered transactions in the Money register, you can take a look at what bills have been paid.

TIP

Editing Account Information
If you want to edit the account information, click the bill to select it and then click **Edit**, make your changes, and click **OK** when you are finished.

TIP

Researching Banks and Brokers
To view information about a financial institution or account, click the **Contact bank or broker** link in the Review recent bills and deposits window. Then select the desired financial institution.

Searching for Account Transactions

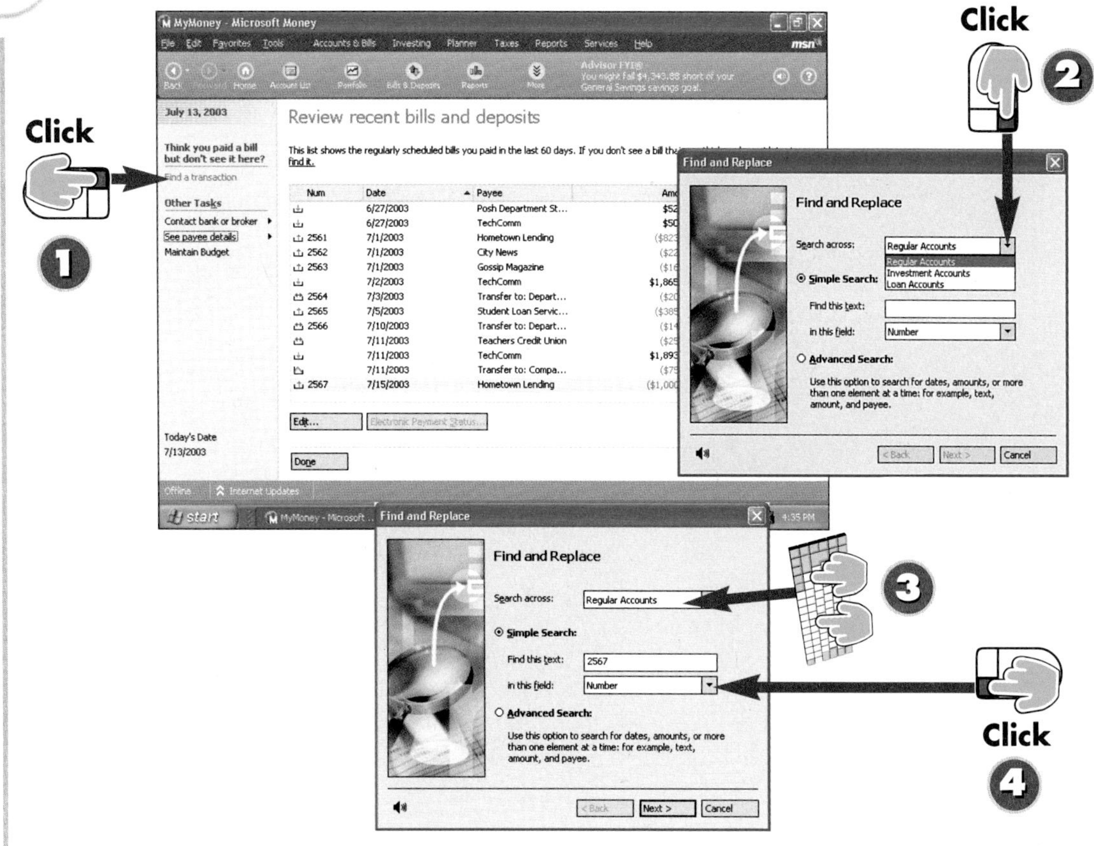

1. In the Review recent bills and deposits window, under **Think you paid a bill but don't see it here?**, click the **Find a transaction** link.

2. Click the **Search across** down arrow and select the accounts you want to search.

3. Enter the text you are searching for. For example, if you are searching for a specific check number, type that number in the **Find this text** box.

4. Click the **in this field** down arrow and select the area you want to search (this pertains to the boxes you filled in when you set up the account transaction).

See next page

INTRODUCTION

If you entered the wrong check number for a bill you paid (as the example shows here), or if you wrote a check but forgot to record the payee, you can use Money's Find and Replace wizard to locate the transaction and then make the correction.

TIP

The Advanced Search Tool

The Advanced Search tool can be used to search for more than one thing—for example, a payee on a specific date or something even more detailed.

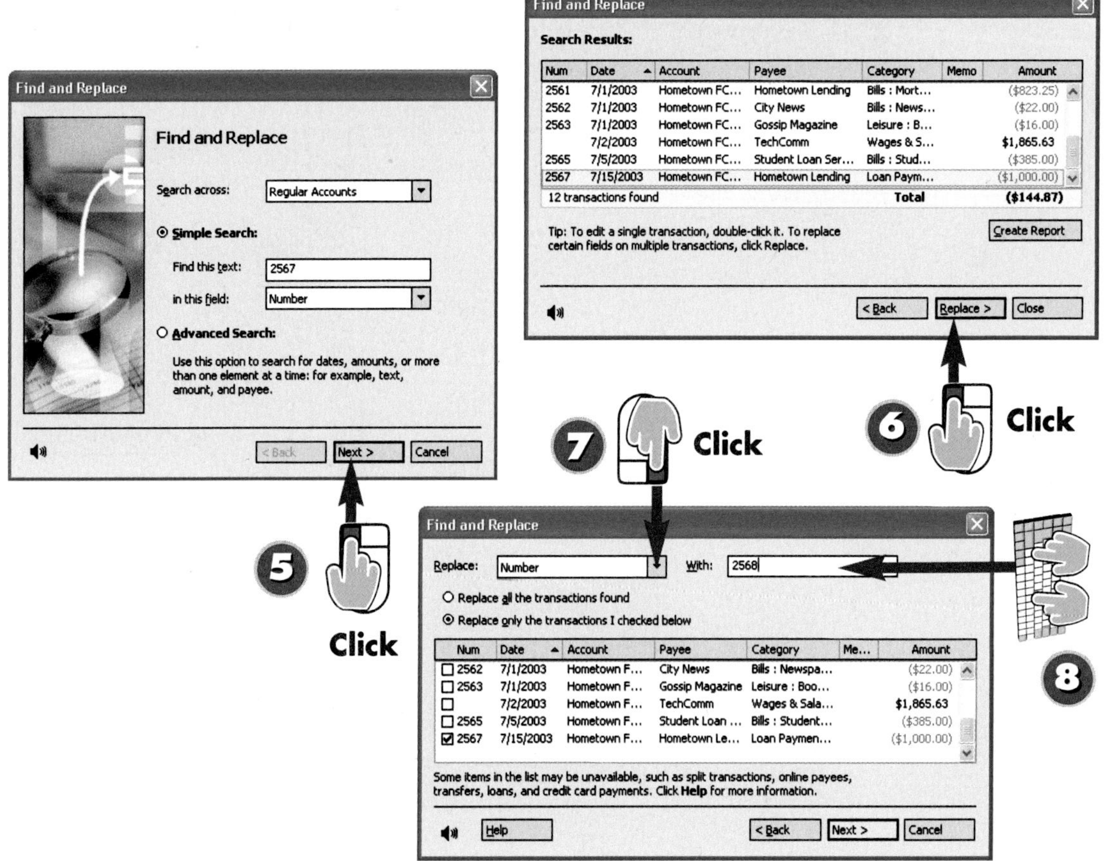

5 Click **Next**.

6 If Money located the transaction you're looking for, click it in the **Search Results** list, and then click **Replace**.

7 Click the **Replace** down arrow and select what aspect of the transaction you want to replace (the example shown here is **Number**, meaning the check number).

8 Type the correct check number in the **With** box.

TIP

Viewing Reports

In step 6, if you want to see a report about transactions you are searching, select the transaction you want by clicking it in the Find and Replace dialog box. If there are multiple transactions you want to see, hold down the **Shift** key and click each one you want. Then click **Create Report**.

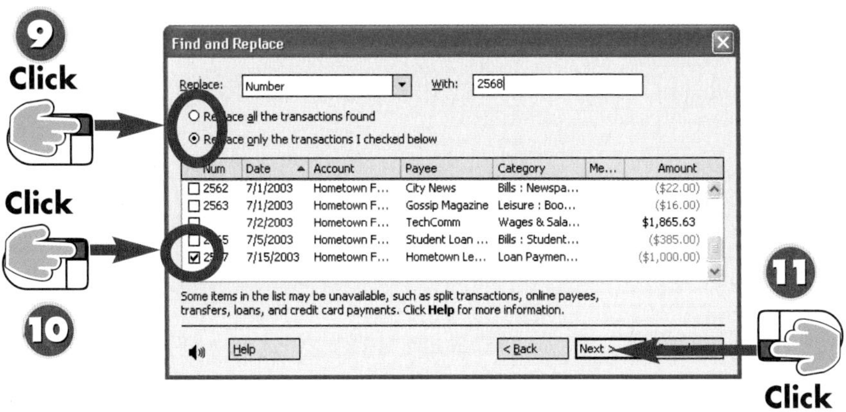

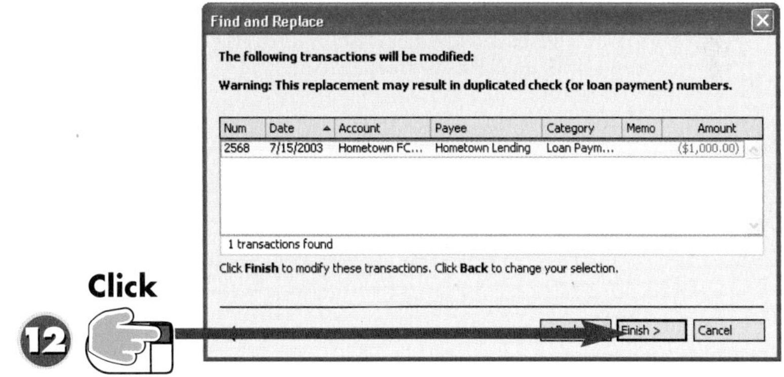

9. Click the **Replace only the transactions I checked below** option button to select it.
10. Click the check box next to the check number you want to replace.
11. Click **Next**.
12. Click **Finish**.

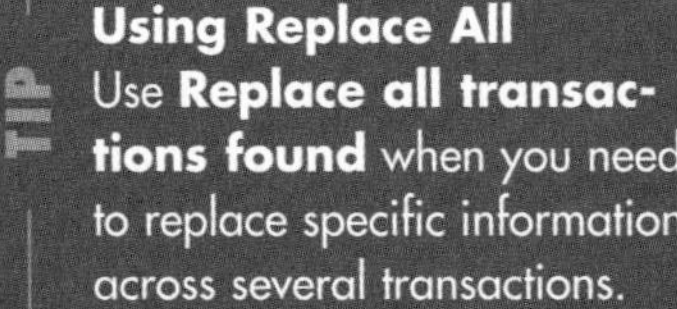

Using Replace All
TIP
Use **Replace all transactions found** when you need to replace specific information across several transactions.

Setting Up or Changing Bill Reminders

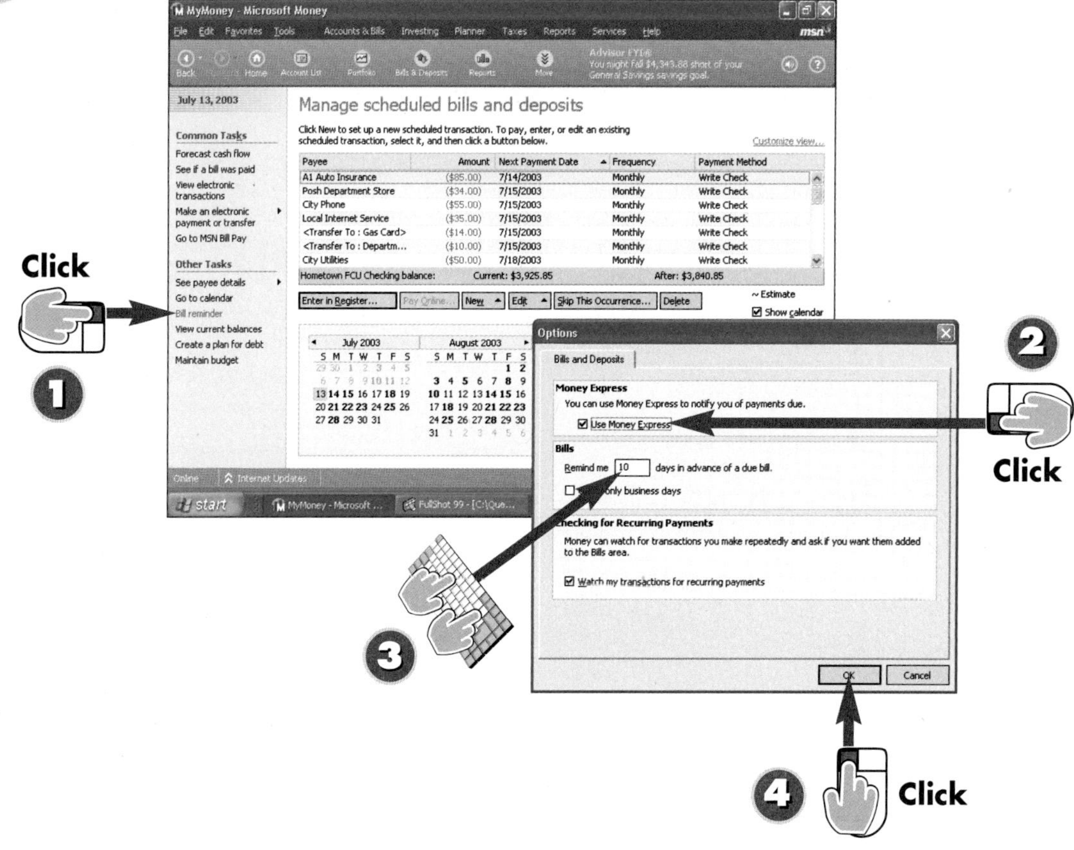

1. In the Manage scheduled bills and deposits window, click the **Bill reminder** link on the left side of the page.
2. Click the **Use Money Express** check box to select it; this enables Money to notify you when it's time to pay your bills.
3. Under **Bills**, in the **Remind me** box, specify when you want to be reminded (in number of days).
4. Click **OK**.

INTRODUCTION

You can set up Money to remind you when it's time to pay your bills. This will keep you in line and on the financial ball. The reminders appear on your home page.

TIP

Business Days

If you want the number you enter in step 3 to be counted in business days, click the **Count only business days** check box to select it.

TIP

Disabling Tracking

If you don't want Money to track the transactions you use most and ask you if you want them added to your list of bills, click the **Watch my transactions for recurring payments** check box to remove the check.

Balancing Accounts

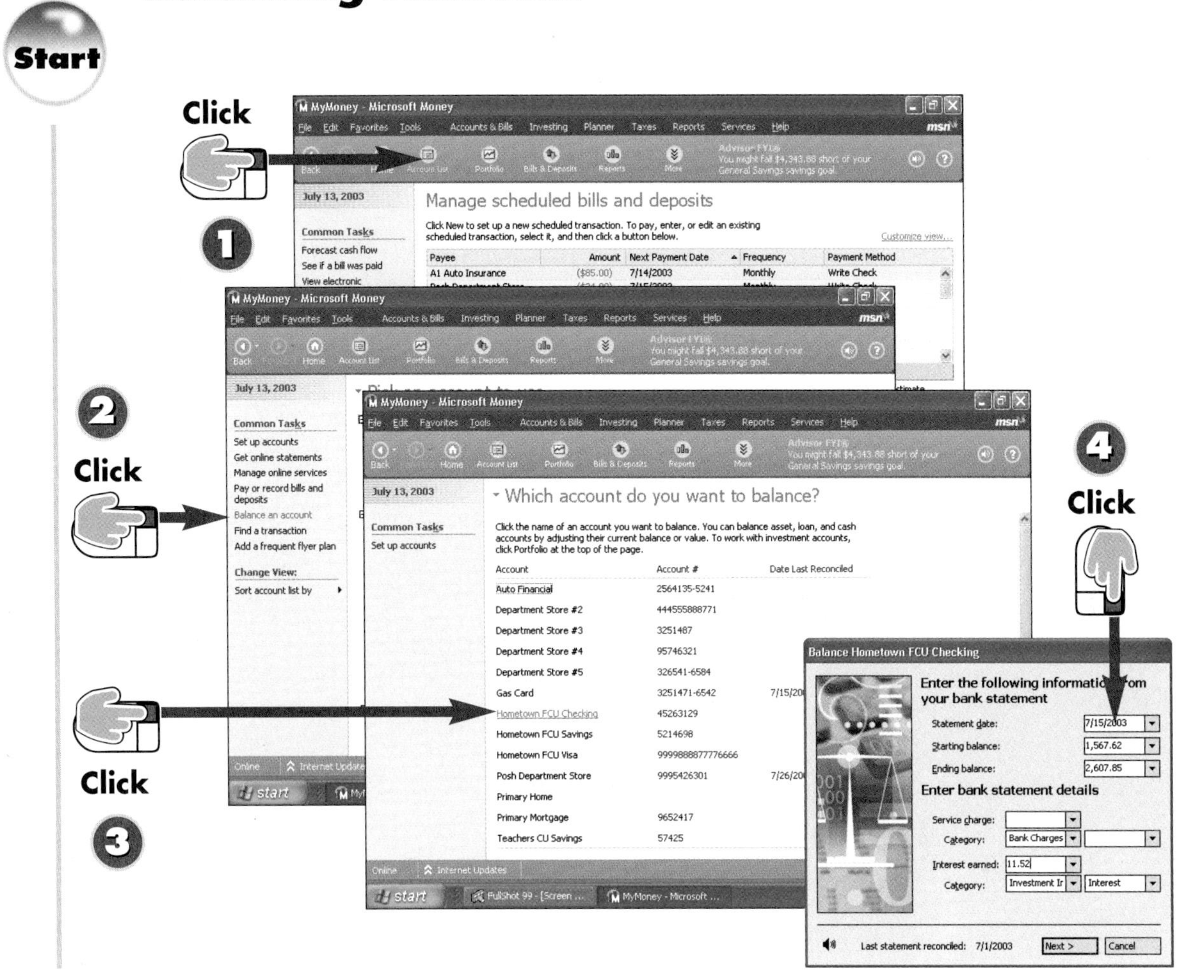

1. On the Money toolbar, click the **Account List** button.
2. In the Pick an account to use window, under **Common Tasks**, click the **Balance an Account** link.
3. In the Which account do you want to balance? window, click the account you want to balance.
4. Type or select the statement date in the **Statement date** box.

INTRODUCTION

To keep your accounts in Money in sync with your statements, you should balance your accounts. As with most features in Money, a wizard takes you through the process of balancing your accounts. Make sure you have your latest statement handy because you will need information from it.

TIP

Sorting the Account List
To change how the account list is sorted, click the **View** down arrow at the top of the window, just as you did with other account lists.

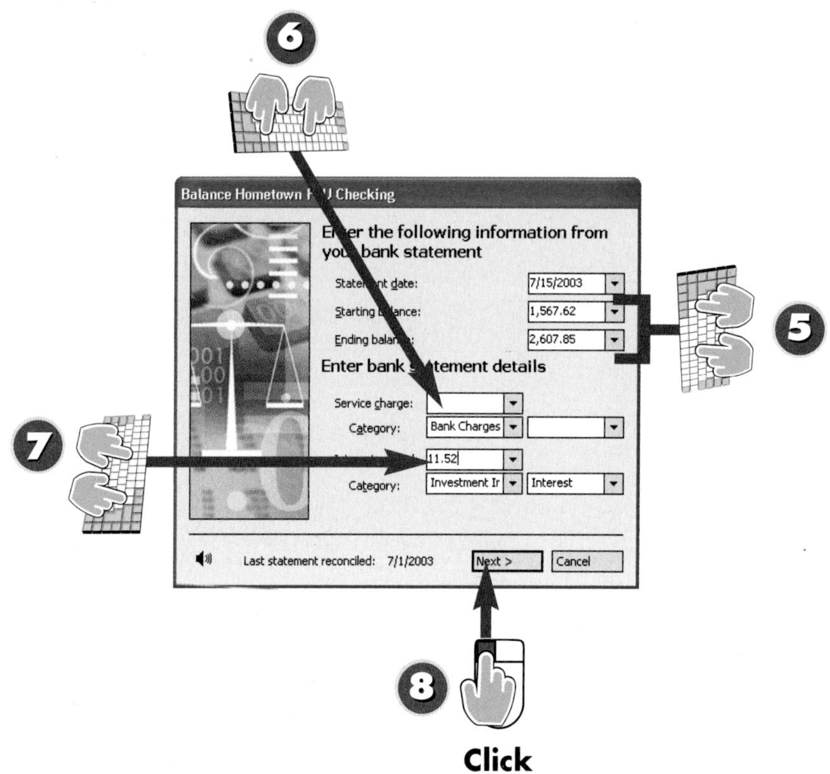

5 Type the requested information in the **Starting balance** and **Ending balance** fields.

6 Enter any service charges—for example, monthly charges—in the **Service charge** box. Then, select the category and subcategory for the charges.

7 If applicable, type the interest earned for the statement period, and then select a category and subcategory for that data.

8 Click **Next**.

TIP

Downloading Statements

If you have accounts set up for online services and you want to balance one of those accounts, you should download the statement before balancing. Although the information you need to balance an account is different depending on the type of account, the process is basically the same for all account types.

TIP

Handling Discrepancies

If there is a discrepancy between what Money thinks is your beginning and ending balance and what you entered, a message appears telling how much that discrepancy is and enabling you to enter the correct figures.

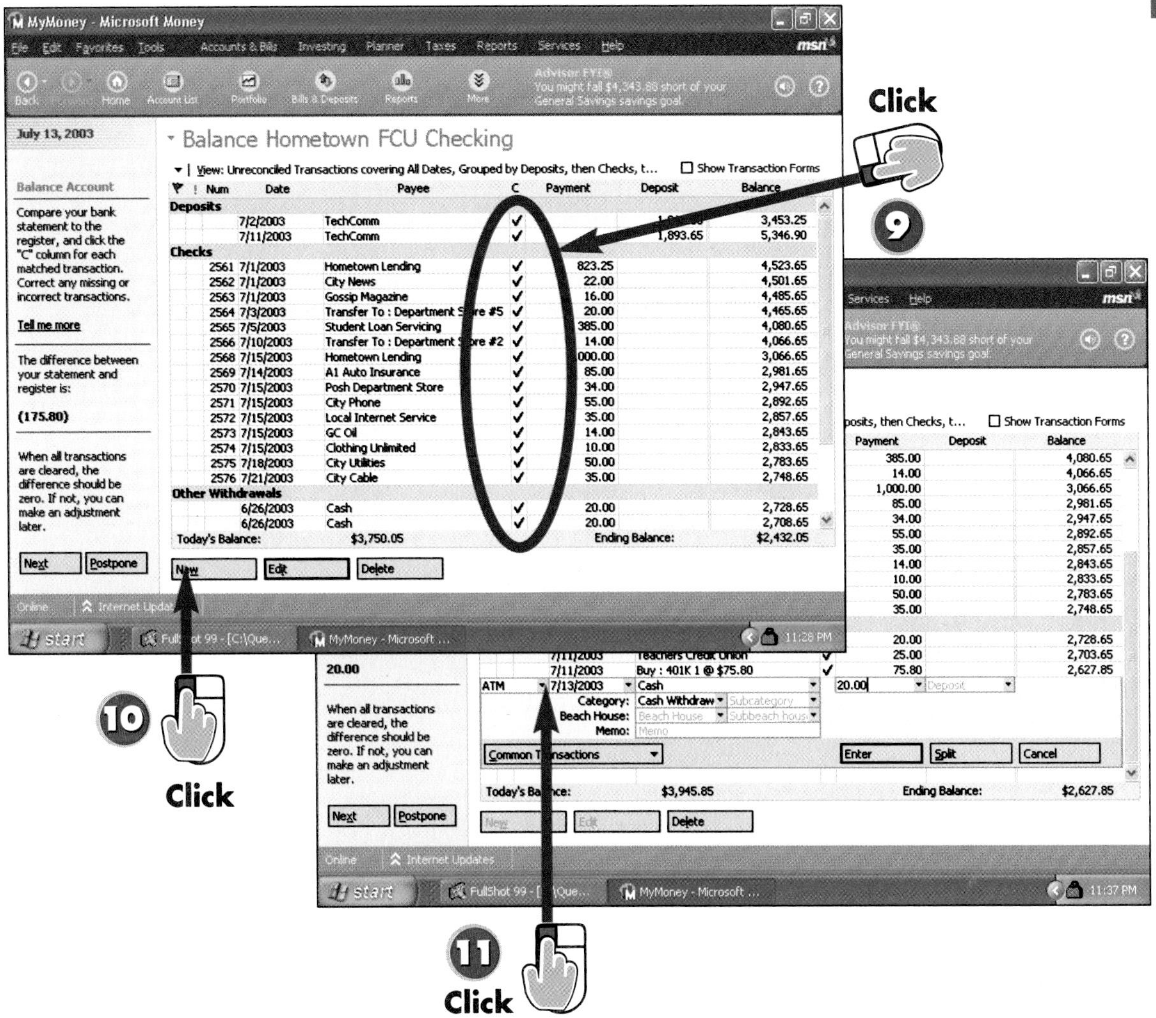

MyMoney - Microsoft Money

July 13, 2003

Balance Account

Compare your bank statement to the register, and click the "C" column for each matched transaction. Correct any missing or incorrect transactions.

Tell me more

The difference between your statement and register is:

(175.80)

When all transactions are cleared, the difference should be zero. If not, you can make an adjustment later.

Balance Hometown FCU Checking

View: Unreconciled Transactions covering All Dates, Grouped by Deposits, then Checks, t... ☐ Show Transaction Forms

Num	Date	Payee	C	Payment	Deposit	Balance
Deposits						
	7/2/2003	TechComm	✓			3,453.25
	7/11/2003	TechComm	✓		1,893.65	5,346.90
Checks						
2561	7/1/2003	Hometown Lending	✓	823.25		4,523.65
2562	7/1/2003	City News	✓	22.00		4,501.65
2563	7/1/2003	Gossip Magazine	✓	16.00		4,485.65
2564	7/3/2003	Transfer To : Department Store #5	✓	20.00		4,465.65
2565	7/5/2003	Student Loan Servicing	✓	385.00		4,080.65
2566	7/10/2003	Transfer To : Department Store #2	✓	14.00		4,066.65
2568	7/15/2003	Hometown Lending	✓	1,000.00		3,066.65
2569	7/14/2003	A1 Auto Insurance	✓	85.00		2,981.65
2570	7/15/2003	Posh Department Store	✓	34.00		2,947.65
2571	7/15/2003	City Phone	✓	55.00		2,892.65
2572	7/15/2003	Local Internet Service	✓	35.00		2,857.65
2573	7/15/2003	GC Oil	✓	14.00		2,843.65
2574	7/15/2003	Clothing Unlimited	✓	10.00		2,833.65
2575	7/18/2003	City Utilities	✓	50.00		2,783.65
2576	7/21/2003	City Cable	✓	35.00		2,748.65
Other Withdrawals						
	6/26/2003	Cash	✓	20.00		2,728.65
	6/26/2003	Cash	✓	20.00		2,708.65

Today's Balance: $3,750.05 Ending Balance: $2,432.05

Next Postpone New Edit Delete

Click

9

10

Click

ATM 7/13/2003 Cash 20.00

Category: Cash Withdraw

Memo:

Common Transactions Enter Split Cancel

Today's Balance: $3,945.85 Ending Balance: $2,627.85

11

Click

9. Using your statement, compare the deposits and withdrawals. For each transaction that matches or has cleared, mark the corresponding check mark in the **C** column.

10. To add a transaction, click **New**.

11. Click the first down arrow (as shown for this step) and choose a transaction type.

See next page

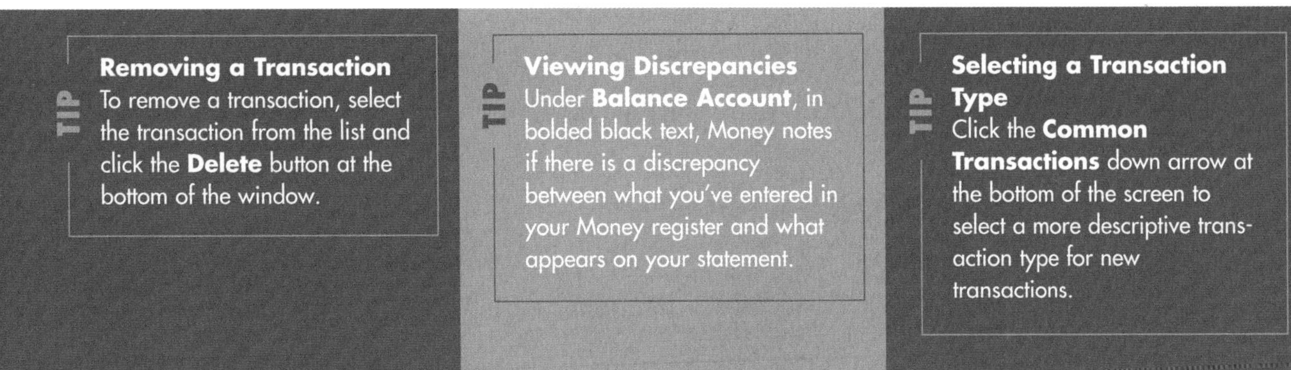

TIP

Removing a Transaction
To remove a transaction, select the transaction from the list and click the **Delete** button at the bottom of the window.

TIP

Viewing Discrepancies
Under **Balance Account**, in bolded black text, Money notes if there is a discrepancy between what you've entered in your Money register and what appears on your statement.

TIP

Selecting a Transaction Type
Click the **Common Transactions** down arrow at the bottom of the screen to select a more descriptive transaction type for new transactions.

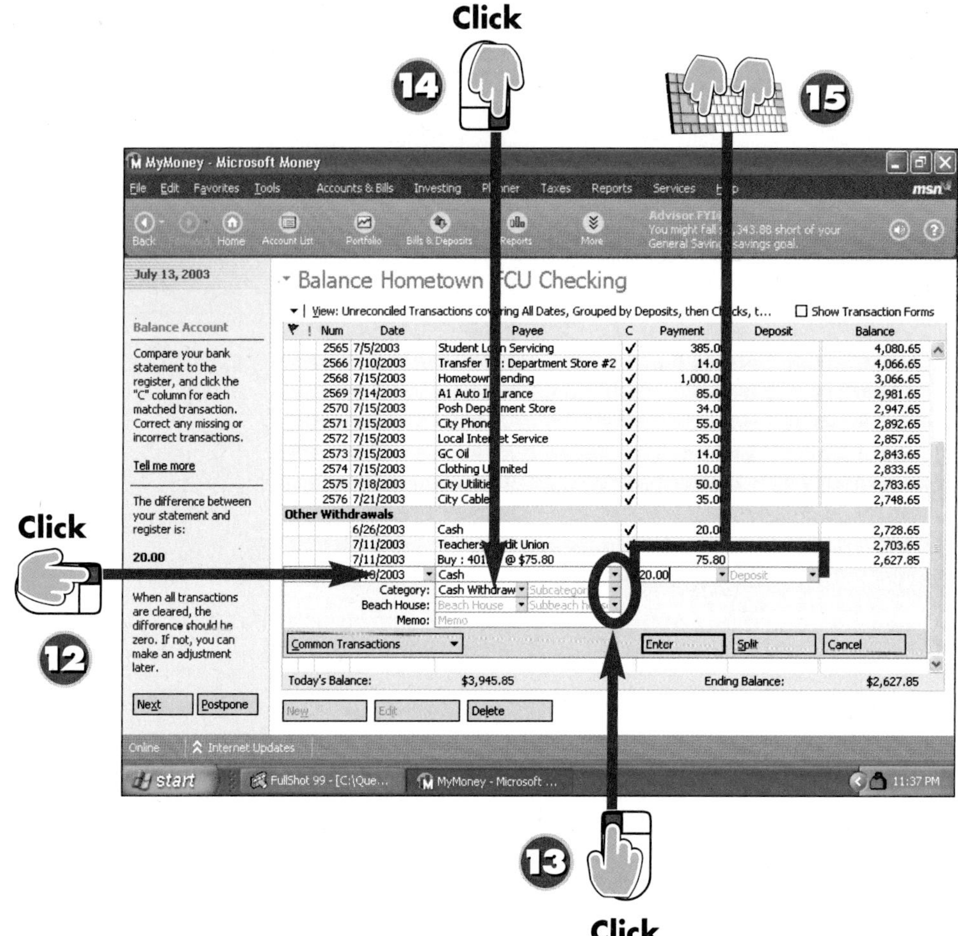

12 In the empty field at the bottom of the **Date** column, type the date on which the transaction took place.

13 Change or enter the payee by clicking the down arrow on the box at the bottom of the **Payee** column and selecting the name from the menu that appears.

14 Using the two drop-down lists next to **Category**, click the down arrow(s) and select a category and subcategory (if applicable) from the menu that appears.

15 Type the transaction amount in the empty box at the bottom of the **Payment** column (or **Deposit** column, if the transaction is a deposit). Then, click **Enter**.

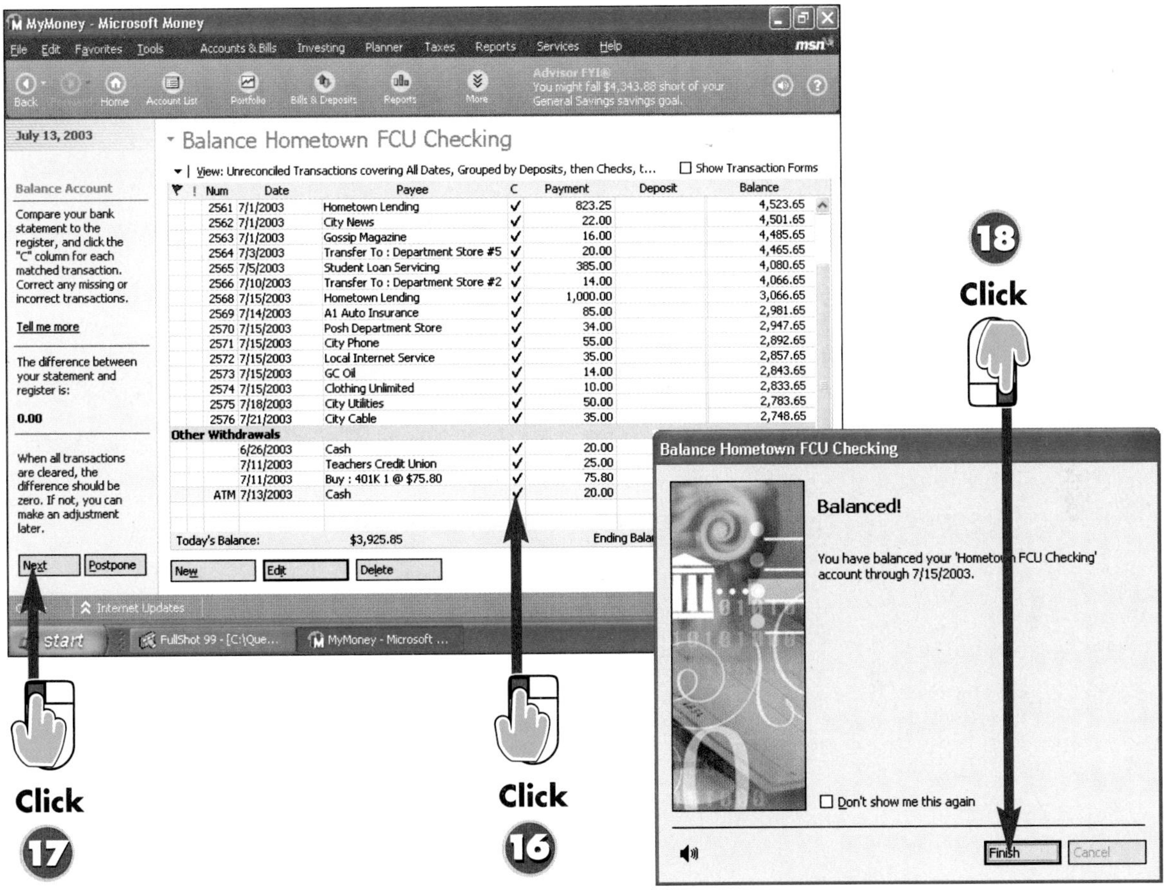

16 Click in the **C** column in the new transaction row you just added to add a check mark (this indicates that the transaction has cleared your account).

17 If all transactions are reconciled or balanced and there is no discrepancy, click **Next**.

18 In the Balance dialog box, click **Finish**. All accounts marked C (cleared) are now marked R (reconciled).

TIP

Postponing

If Money continues to find discrepancies, and you are not sure where the hole is, click the **Postpone** button to continue using Money without balancing the account. You can then go back and balance the account at a later time.

Reviewing Projected Cash Flow

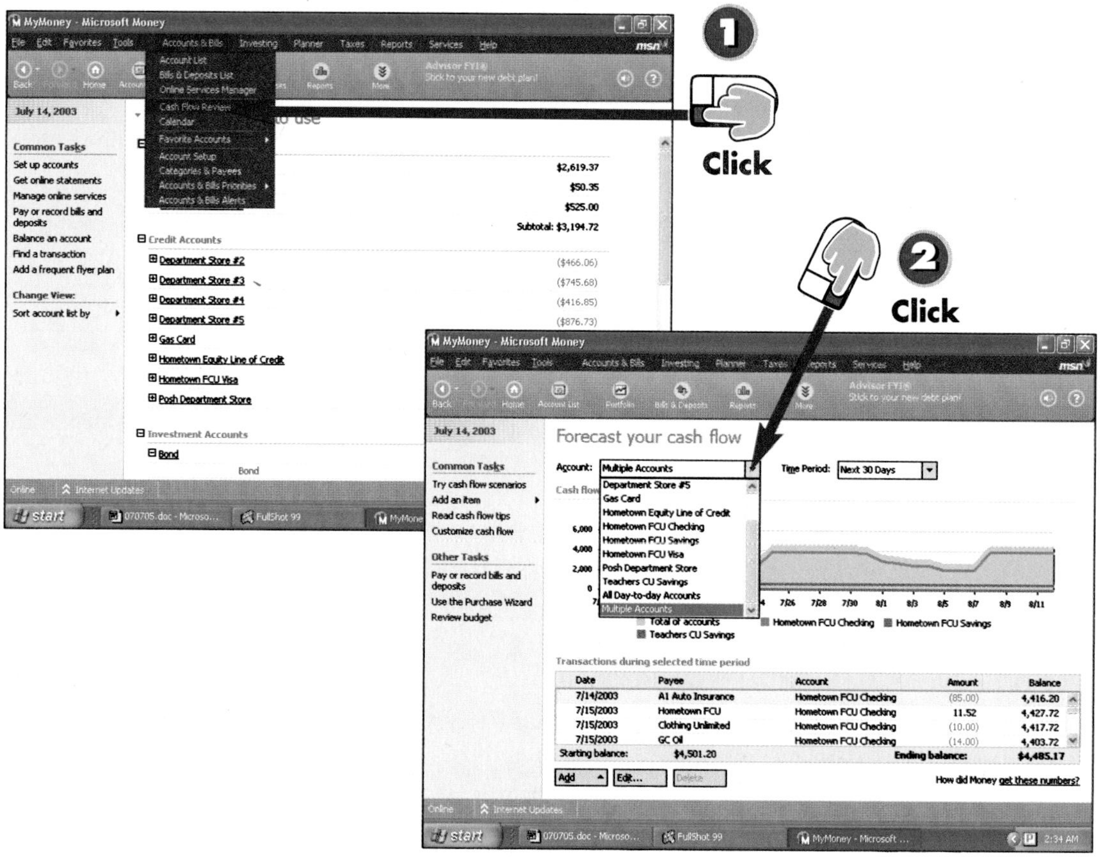

1 Open the **Accounts & Bills** menu and choose **Cash Flow Review**.

2 Click the **Account** down arrow and choose the account you want to review. To view more than one, choose **Multiple Accounts**. The Multiple Accounts dialog box opens.

INTRODUCTION

With cash-flow projections, you can see how your financial situation looks now, and how it will look all the way through the next year. Money uses the information you've entered, including deposits, monthly bills, and so on, to create an outlook for you.

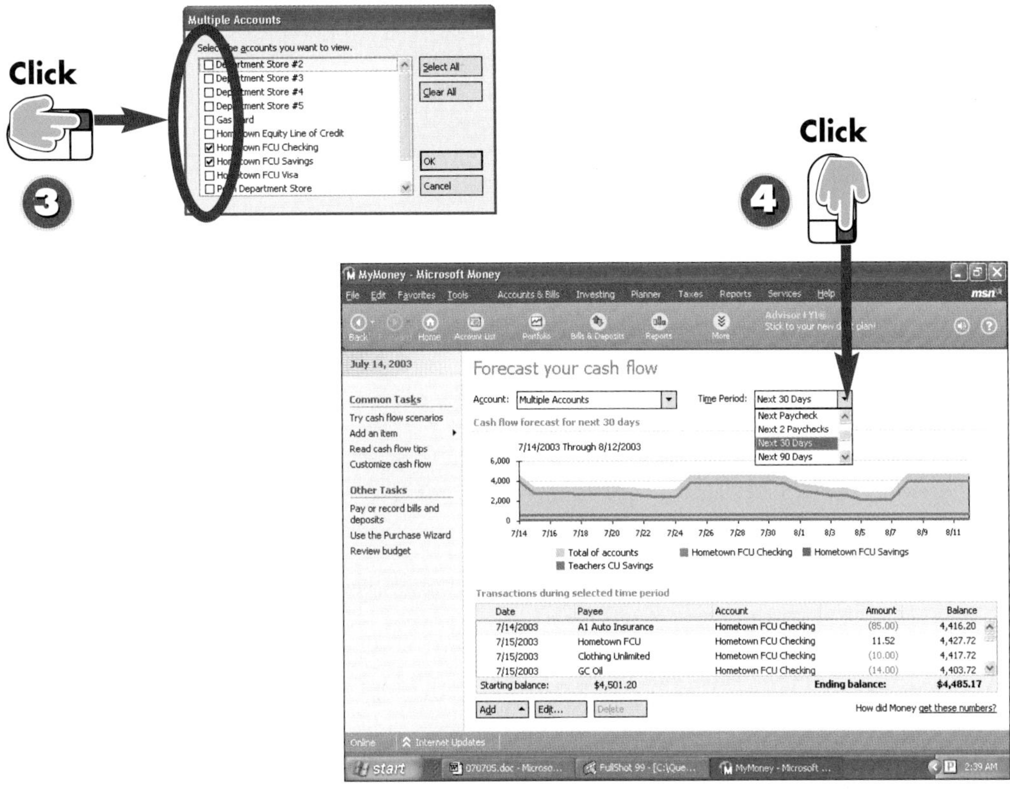

3. If you chose **Multiple Accounts** in step 2, click the check box next to each account you want to review, and click **OK**. Money adjusts the line graph accordingly.
4. To view a different time frame, click the **Time Period** down arrow and choose the desired period from the list.

TIP

Getting Advice
For a little friendly advice, click the **Read cash flow tips** link under **Common Tasks**.

Adding to the Cash Flow

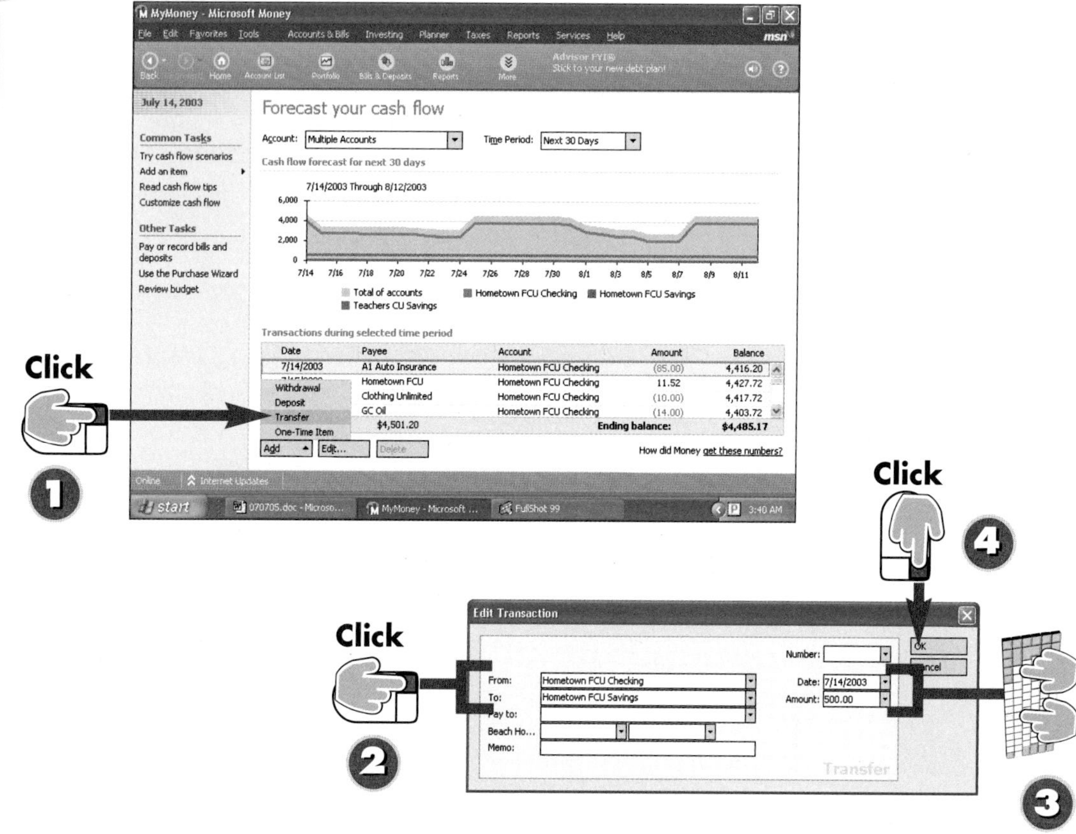

1. On the bottom of the Forecast your cash flow window, click the **Add** up arrow and choose **Transfer** from the menu that appears.
2. Using the **From** and **To** drop-down lists, select the account from which the transfer will originate, and the account into which the funds will be deposited.
3. Using the **Date** and **Amount** boxes, enter the date and amount of the transfer.
4. Click **OK**.

End

INTRODUCTION

Should you need to adjust your cash-flow outlook by adding a withdrawal, deposit, transfer, or one-time item, you can easily do so. The process is very similar to the procedures you performed earlier in the book with bills, transactions, and accounts. This task covers adding a transfer, but the steps for each procedure are quite similar.

TIP

Adjusting the Projection

As you make changes, Money adjusts the projection accordingly and displays it after you are finished so you can see how your changes affect your cash flow.

Editing the Cash Flow

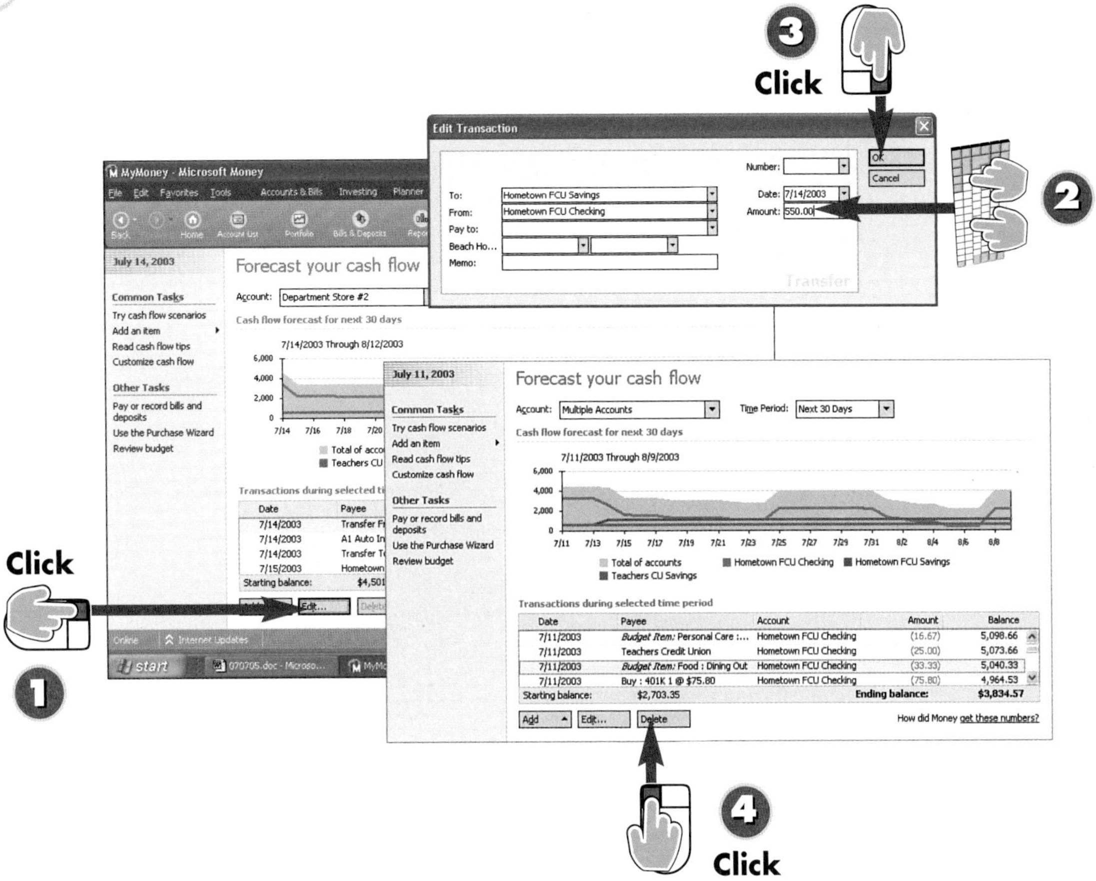

1. To change a transaction, click it in the Forecast your cash flow window, and click the **Edit** button. The Edit Transaction dialog box opens.
2. Make the desired changes—for example, changing the transaction amount, as shown here.
3. Click **OK**.
4. To remove or skip a transaction, click the transaction in the list under **Transactions during selected time period**, and then either click **Delete** or **Skip**.

INTRODUCTION

You can adjust transactions by editing or removing transactions to see how your cash-flow projection is affected. If the outcome is favorable, you don't have to do a thing. If you want to change it back, however, you can edit the transaction to restore its original information.

TIP

Viewing Account Details

To take a closer look at a specific area of the chart, place your mouse pointer over one of the colored lines in the chart, but don't click. A pop-up appears with details about the account.

Experimenting with Cash-Flow Scenarios

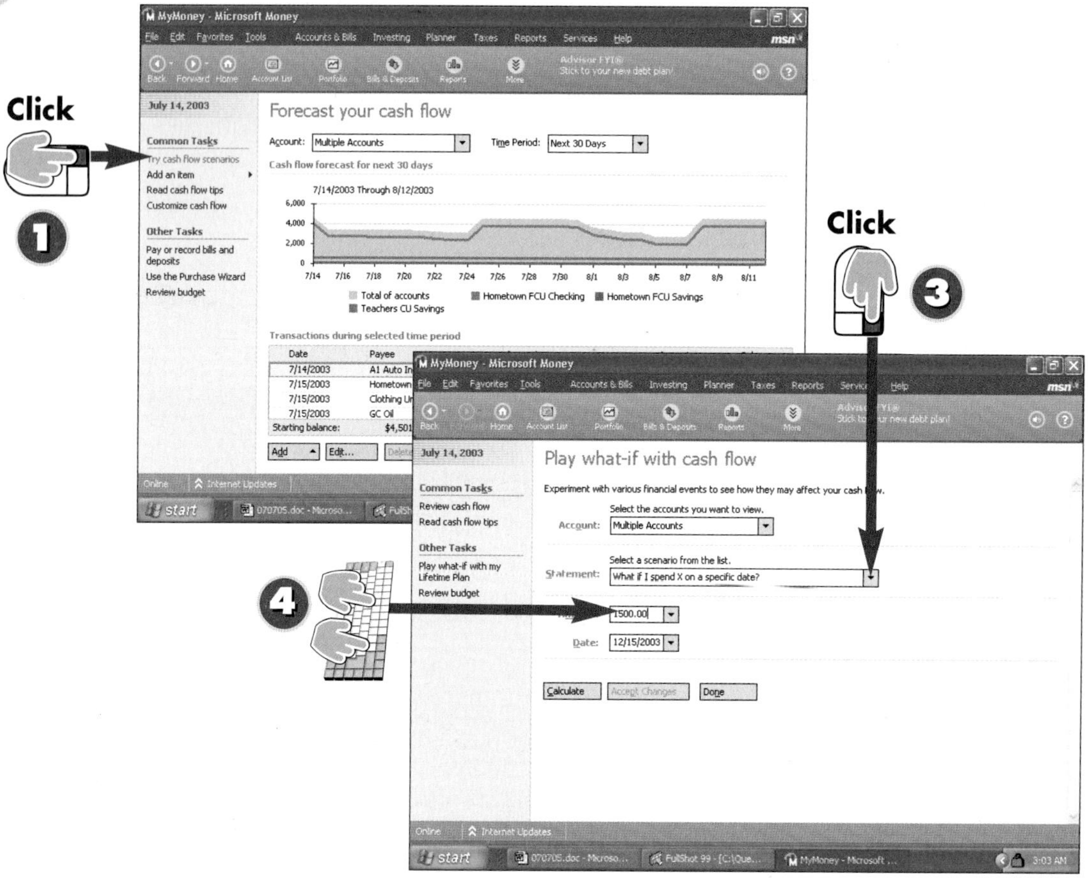

1. In the Forecast your cash flow window, under **Common Tasks**, click the **Try cash flow scenarios** link.
2. In the Play what-if with cash flow window, click the **Account** down arrow and select an account. To play with multiple accounts, click **Multiple Accounts**.
3. Click the **Statement** down arrow and select a scenario from the list that appears.
4. In the **Amount** box, type the amount of money you'd like to play with.

INTRODUCTION

Suppose you want to find out how your finances would be affected if you bought an expensive new item or went on vacation, or how much you could accumulate if you saved more money over a specific period of time. In any of these instances, you can use Money's Cash Flow Scenarios feature to play "what if" with your finances.

TIP

Customizing Cash Flow
To change how Money calculates and estimates your cash-flow projections, click the **Customize Cash Flow** link under **Common Tasks** in the Forecast your cash flow window and make the desired changes.

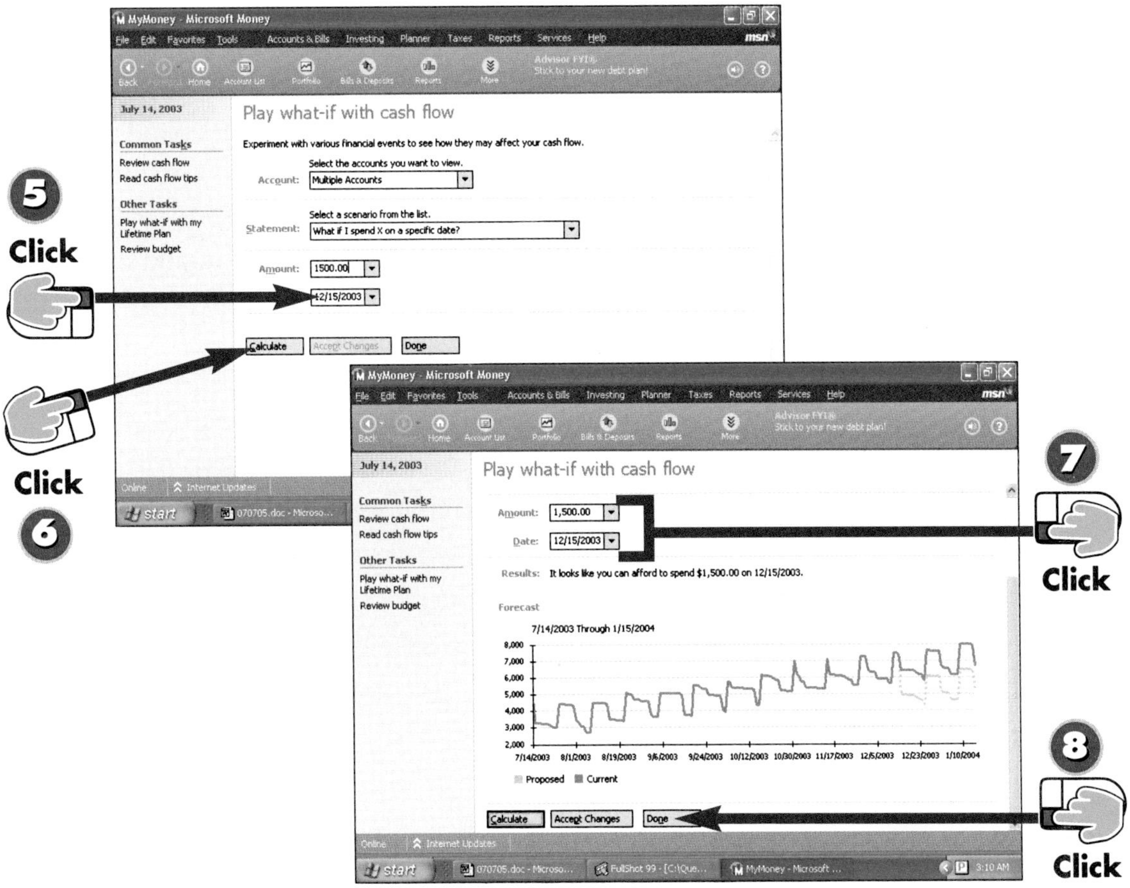

5 Click

6 Click

7 Click

8 Click

5 Click the **Date** down arrow and select the date or frequency (if applicable) on which you would like to base the scenario.

6 Click **Calculate**.

7 Try different scenarios by changing the values in the **Amount** and **Date** fields if you like to find out "what if."

8 Click **Done** when you are finished.

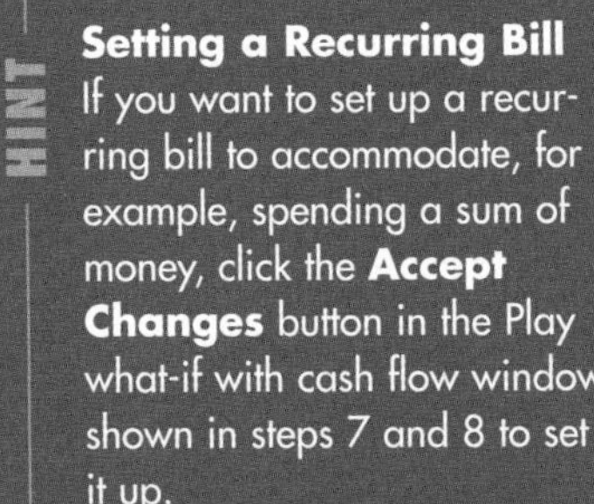

HINT

Setting a Recurring Bill

If you want to set up a recurring bill to accommodate, for example, spending a sum of money, click the **Accept Changes** button in the Play what-if with cash flow window shown in steps 7 and 8 to set it up.

PART 6

Managing Your Budget

You've set up all your accounts, entered all your bills and deposits, and determined what your cash-flow projection looks like. By now, you should have a really good idea of how your finances look and where you need some help. Now would be a good time, then, to talk about creating and maintaining a budget.

Setting up a budget helps you control your income, bills, and expenses. You can allocate funds for everything from paying bills and planning for a family vacation to paying for school lunches and everything in between. Microsoft Money allows you to update income or account categories, add new income, and update or create categories and sub-categories with the costs of your living expenses. The categories and sub-categories appear beneath the budget groups that Money uses to organize all your financial information.

The Budget Planner

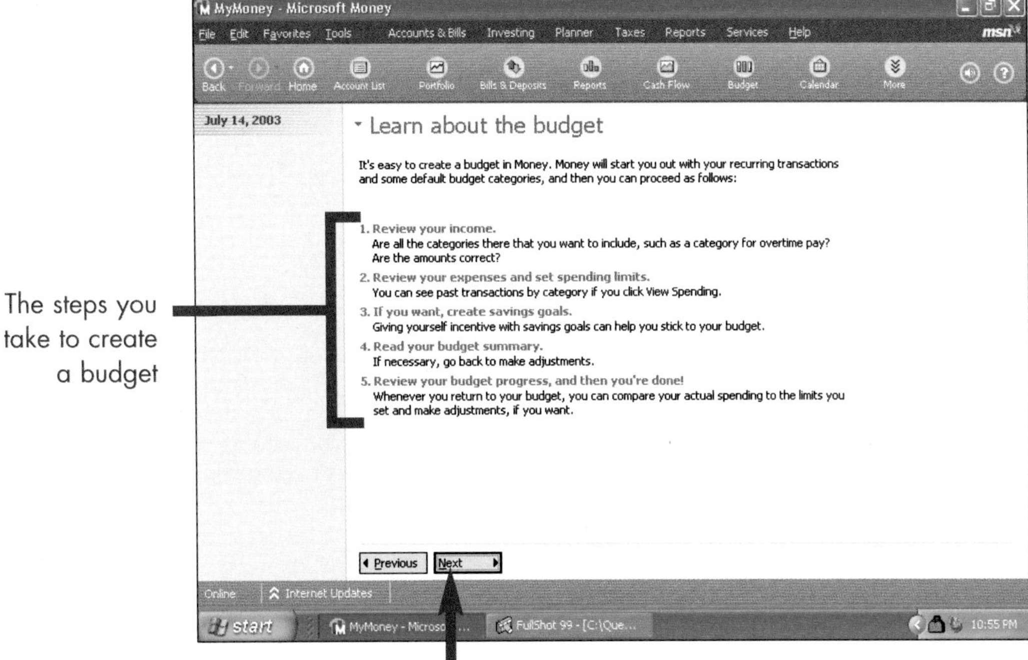

Creating a New Budget

Start

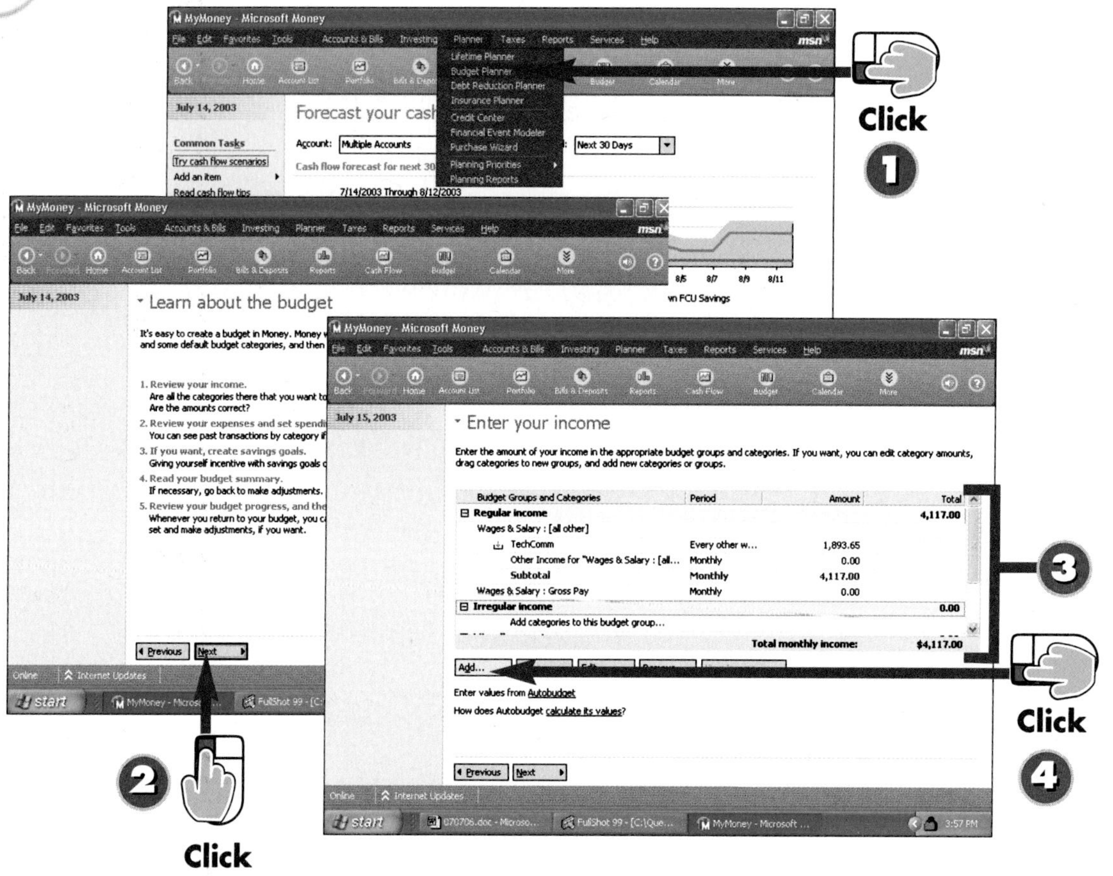

1. Open the **Planner** menu and choose **Budget Planner**.
2. Read and/or listen to the overview, and then click **Next**.
3. Review your income information to make sure it is accurate, and determine whether there are areas you need to update.
4. To add a new sub-category, click the category or group you want to add the sub-category to (in this example, **Irregular income**) and click **Add**.

INTRODUCTION

After you review, add, and/or update all your income and debt information, Microsoft Money compares your income to your debt and tells you if you have anything extra left over to apply toward a financial goal. You can use this information to adjust your budget if needed and create financial goals for yourself.

TIP

Deleting a Category
To delete an income category or sub-category, click it to select it and then click **Remove**.

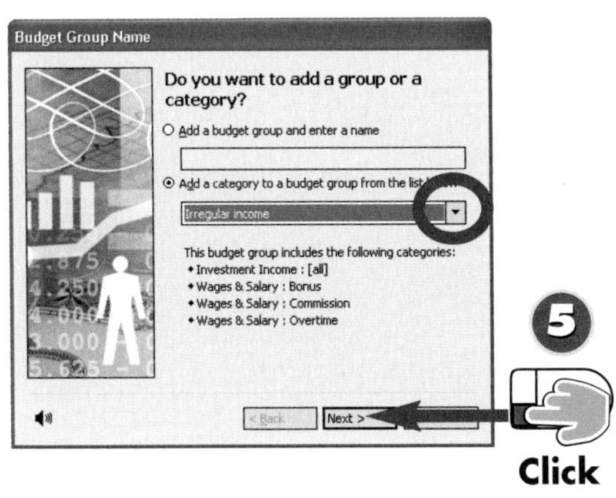

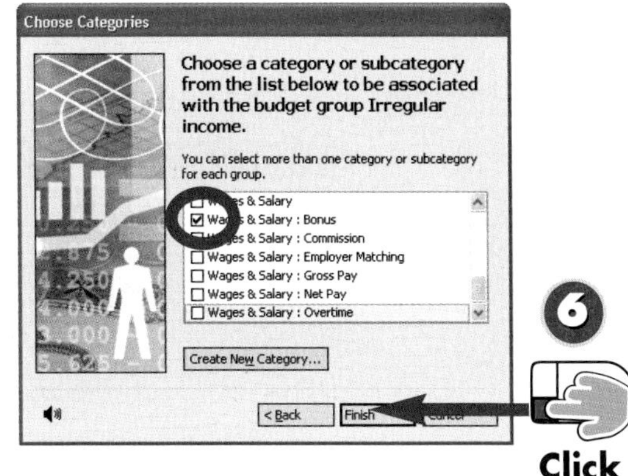

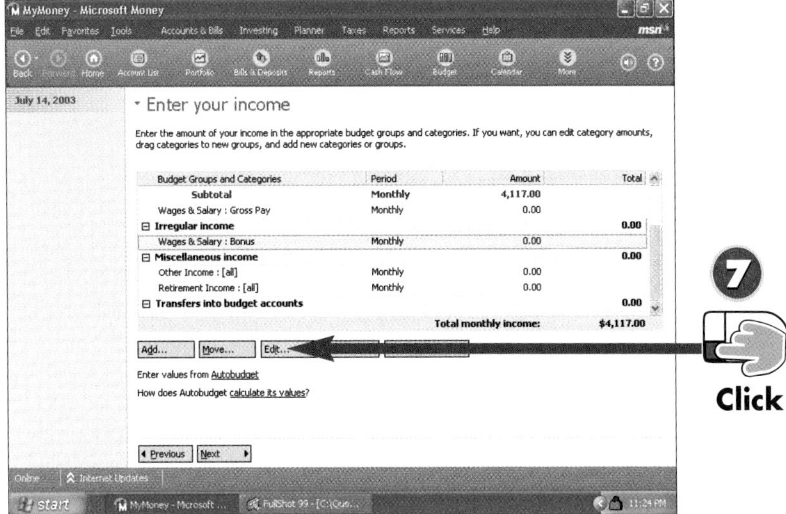

5 Click the down arrow below the **Add a category** option button and select the category you want to add. Then, click **Next**.

6 To select sub-categories, click the check boxes next to them. (To deselect a sub-category, click the checked box again.) Then click **Finish**.

7 Click the sub-category you just added (in this example, **Wages & Salary : Bonus**) to select it, and click **Edit**.

See next page

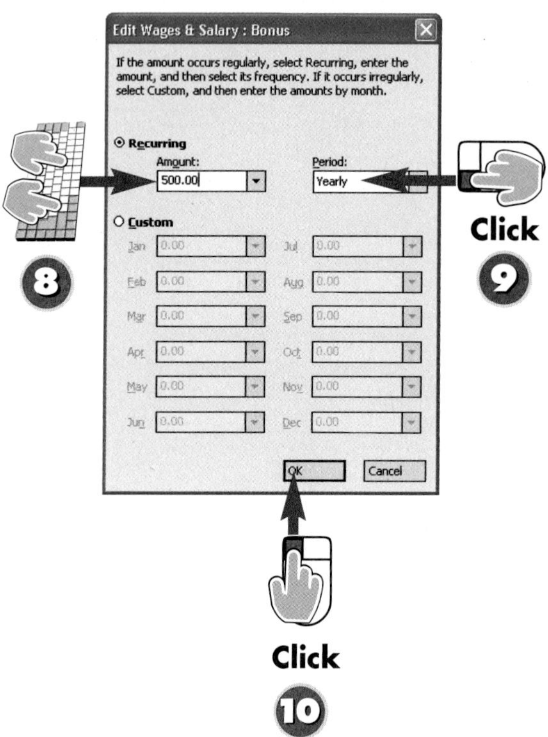

8. If you receive the amount you're entering on a consistent basis, click the **Recurring** option button and enter the amount.
9. Click the **Period** down arrow and select the frequency with which you expect the amount to affect your budget.
10. Click **OK**.

TIP

Adding Sporadic Income

If you are adding or editing income or an expense that is scattered throughout the year, click the **Custom** option button in the sub-category's Edit dialog box and enter the amounts in the appropriate months.

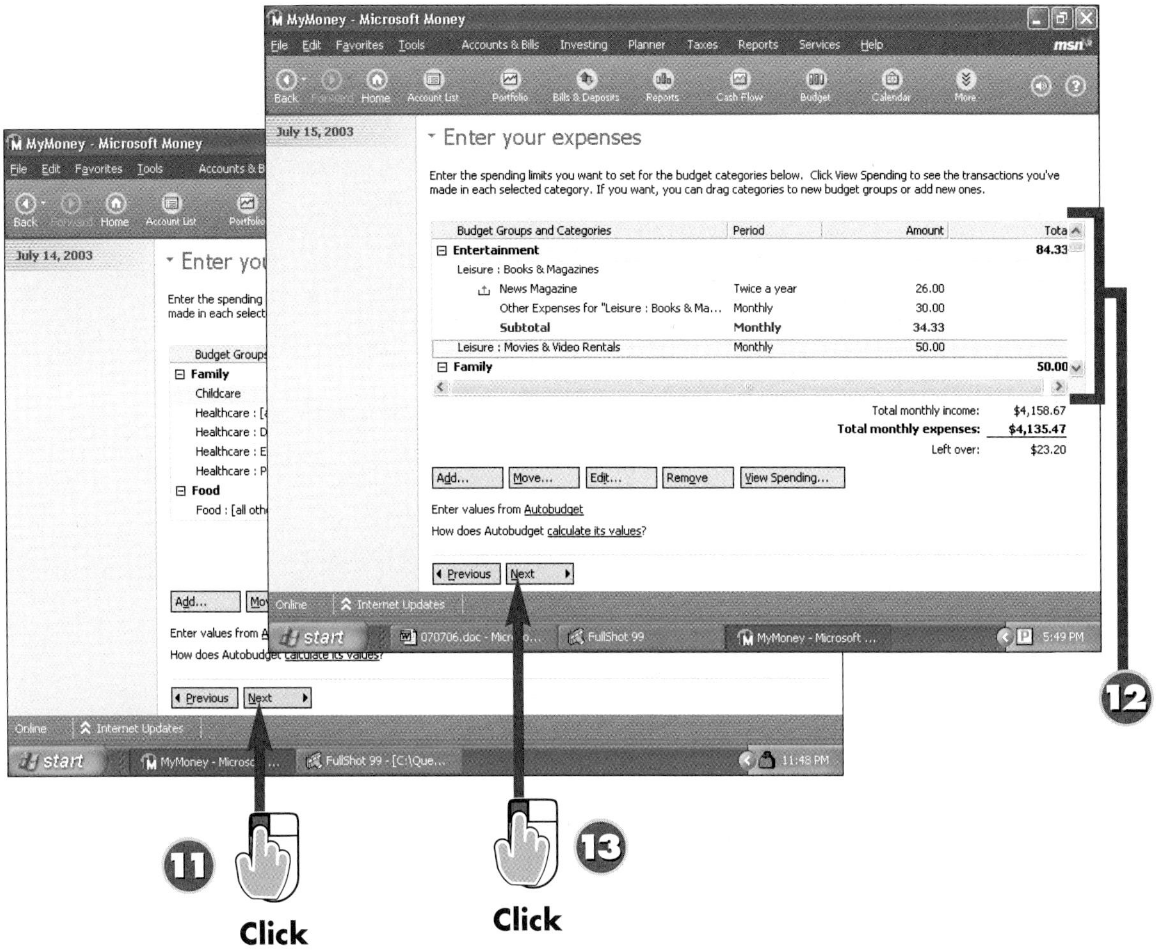

11 Repeat steps 4–10 as many times as needed to update all your income information. When you're finished, click **Next**.

12 Review all your expenses, and then add to and edit categories and groups just as you did with your income information.

13 When you are finished updating all your expenses, click **Next**.

See next page

HINT

Viewing Spending and Income

To view spending or income history or transactions for a specific area, select the category or sub-category and click **View Spending** or **View Income**.

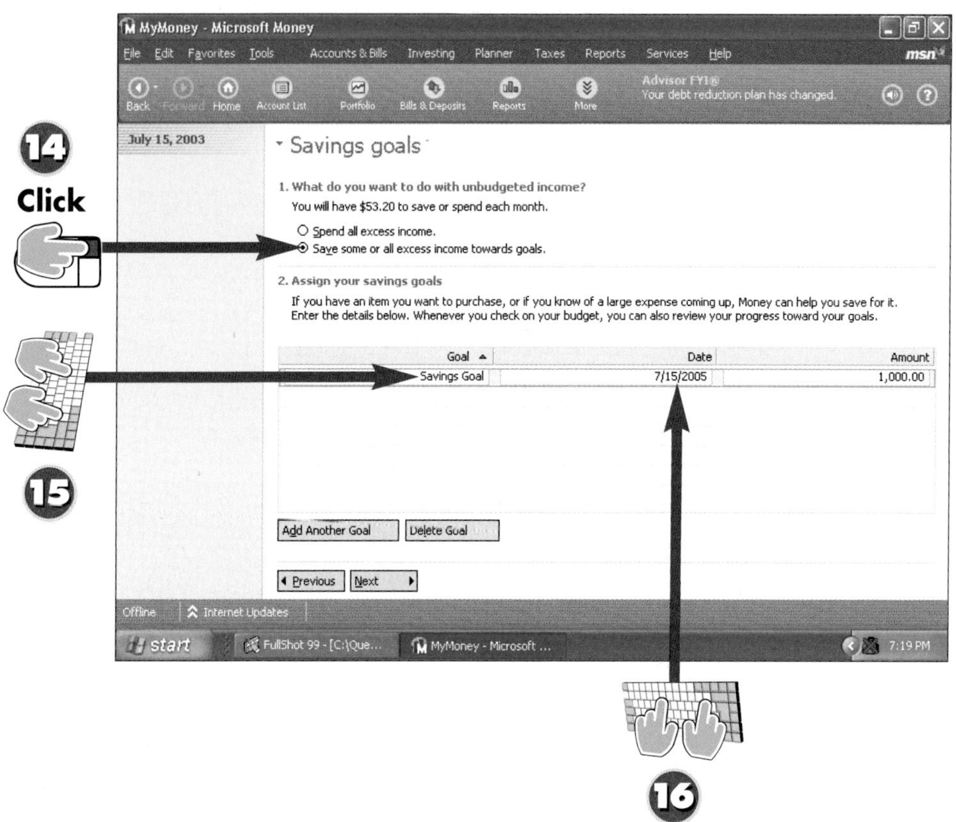

14 Select the option button that reflects how you want to use excess funds (in this example, **Save some or all excess income towards goals** is selected).

15 To set up a goal, such as savings, click in the **Goal** box and type a name for your goal.

16 In the **Date** box, type the date by which you want to reach the goal.

TIP

Adding More Goals

If you want to add another goal, click **Add Another Goal**. To remove a goal, select the goal and click **Delete Goal**.

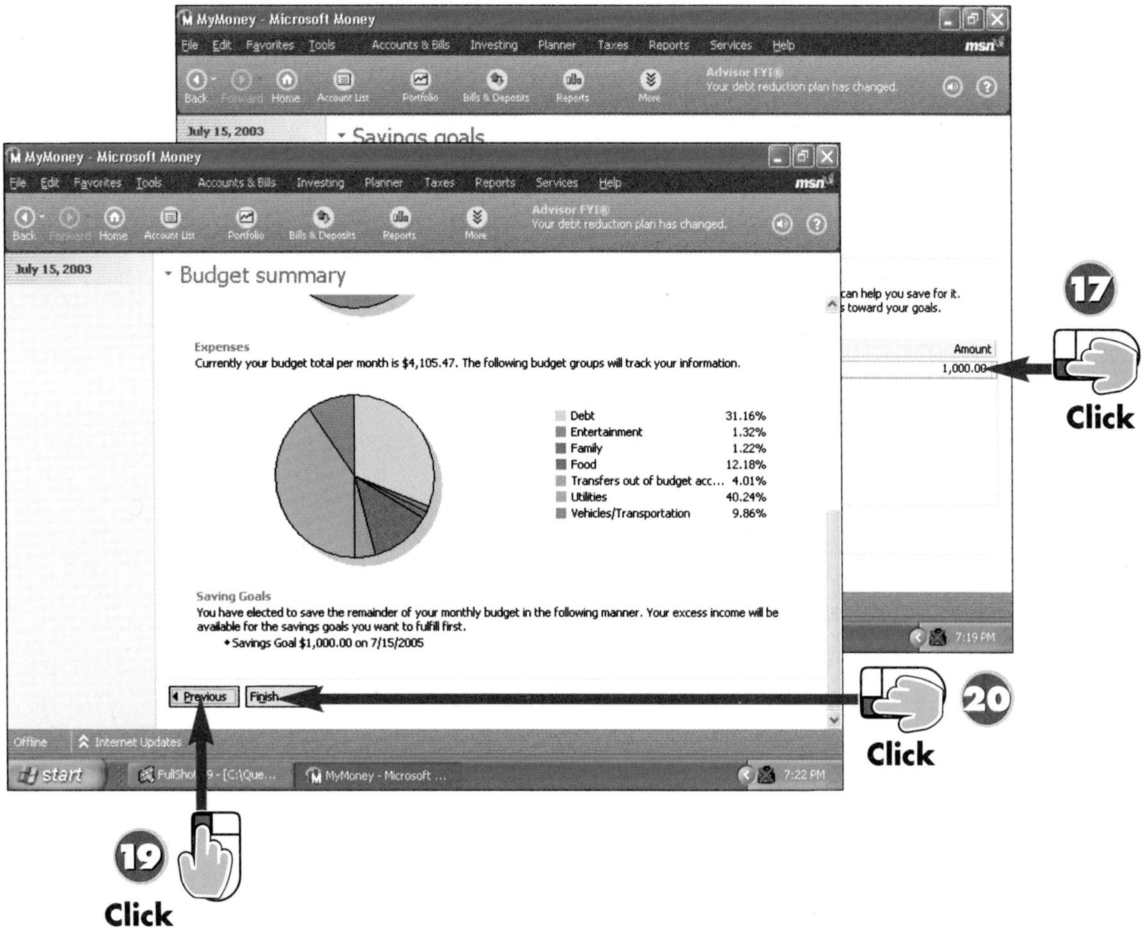

17 In the **Amount** box, type the amount you want to set as your goal.

18 Click **Next**.

19 Review your budget summary by scrolling down to see all the information. If you need to make changes, click **Previous**.

20 When you are satisfied with your budget click **Finish**.

Viewing Budget Reports

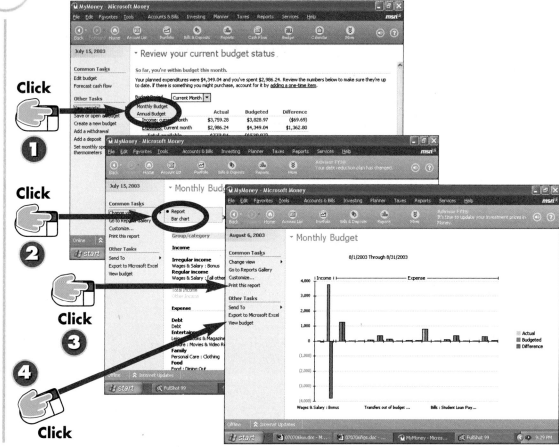

Start

1. Under **Other Tasks**, click **View reports** and select either **Monthly Budget** or **Annual Budget**. The selected budget report appears.

2. To view the report as a bar chart, click **Change view** and choose **Bar chart**.

3. To print the report, click **Print this report**.

4. To return to your budget, click **View budget**.

INTRODUCTION

Budget reports can provide a bird's-eye view of how your budget is doing on a monthly or yearly basis. You can print these reports, export them, or attach them to an email message to send off.

TIP

Customizing the Layout

You can customize the report by clicking **Customize** and changing the layout, content, or appearance of the report.

HINT

Exporting to Excel and Email

To create an Excel spreadsheet for the report, click **Export to Microsoft Excel**, type a name for the report, and click **OK**. To attach a report to an email message, click **Send to** and select **Mail recipient**.

Start

Adding Withdrawals or Deposits to Your Budget

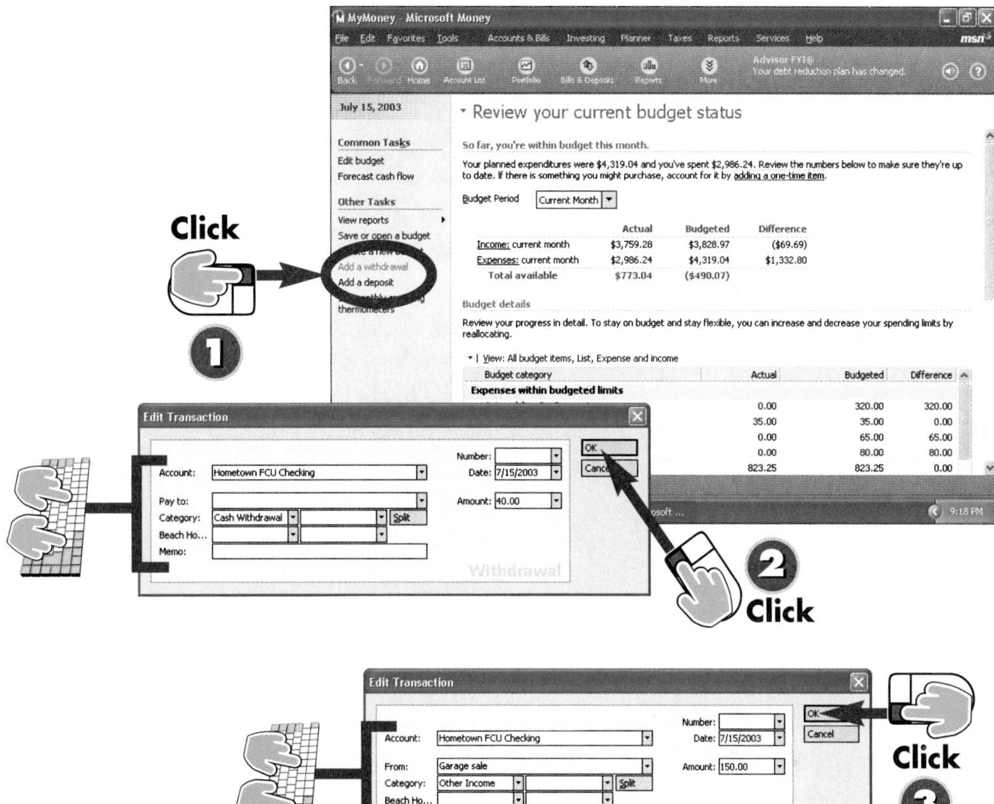

1. Under **Other Tasks**, click **Add a deposit** or **Add a withdrawal**.

2. If you chose **Add a withdrawal**, enter the transaction information—the account, date, amount, and so on—and click **OK**.

3. If you chose **Add a deposit**, enter the transaction information—the account, date, amount, and so on—and click **OK**.

End

INTRODUCTION

As you record transactions, such as withdrawals and deposits, for your accounts, Money automatically keeps track of those debits and credits in your budget. However, you can add withdrawals and deposits from within your budget as well.

Reallocating Funds

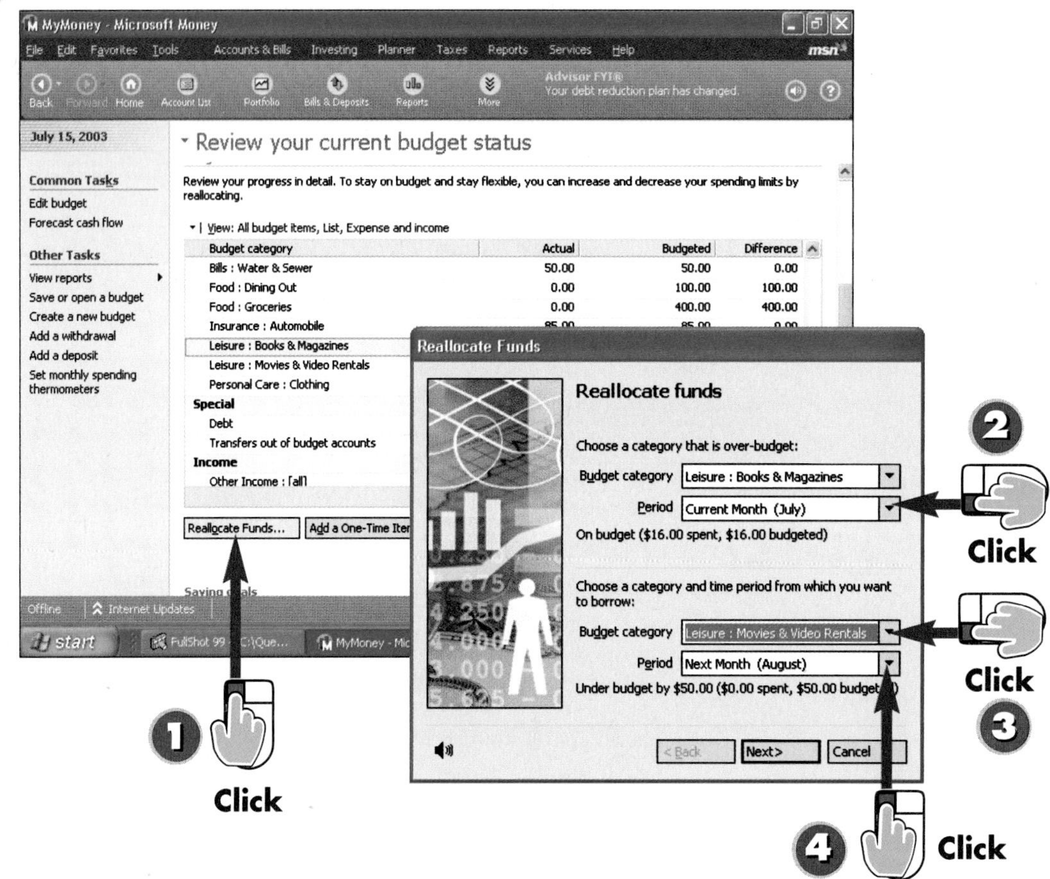

1. Select the category from which you want to reallocate funds (in this example, **Leisure : Books & Magazines**) and click **Reallocate Funds**.
2. Under **Choose a category that is under budget**, click the **Period** down arrow and select the time period for which you want the funds reallocated.
3. Under **Choose a category and time period from which you want to borrow**, click the **Budget category** down arrow and select a category.
4. Click the **Period** down arrow and select the time period for which you want the funds allocated.

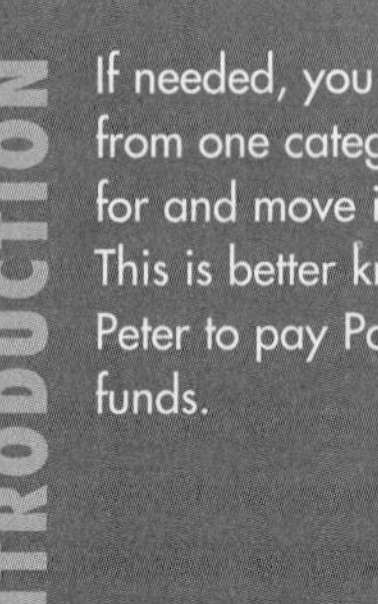

INTRODUCTION

If needed, you can take money from one category you budgeted for and move it to another area. This is better known as robbing Peter to pay Paul, or reallocating funds.

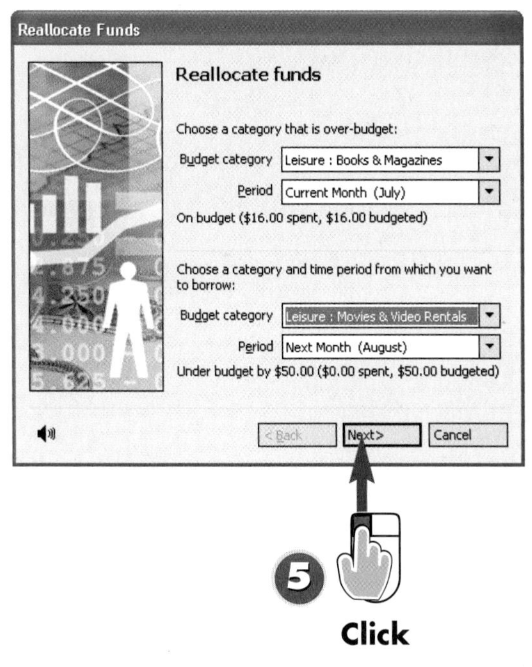

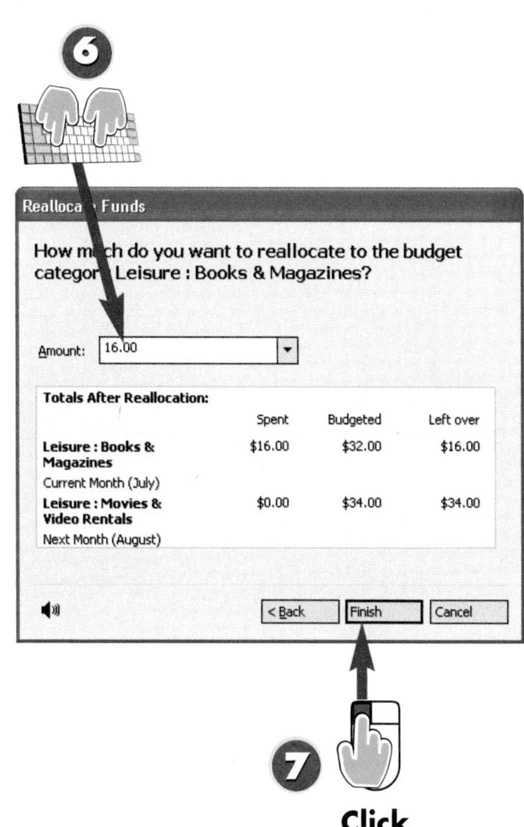

5 Click **Next**.

6 In the **Amount** field, enter the amount you want to take from the first category and apply to the second category.

7 Click **Finish**.

Updating Budget Information

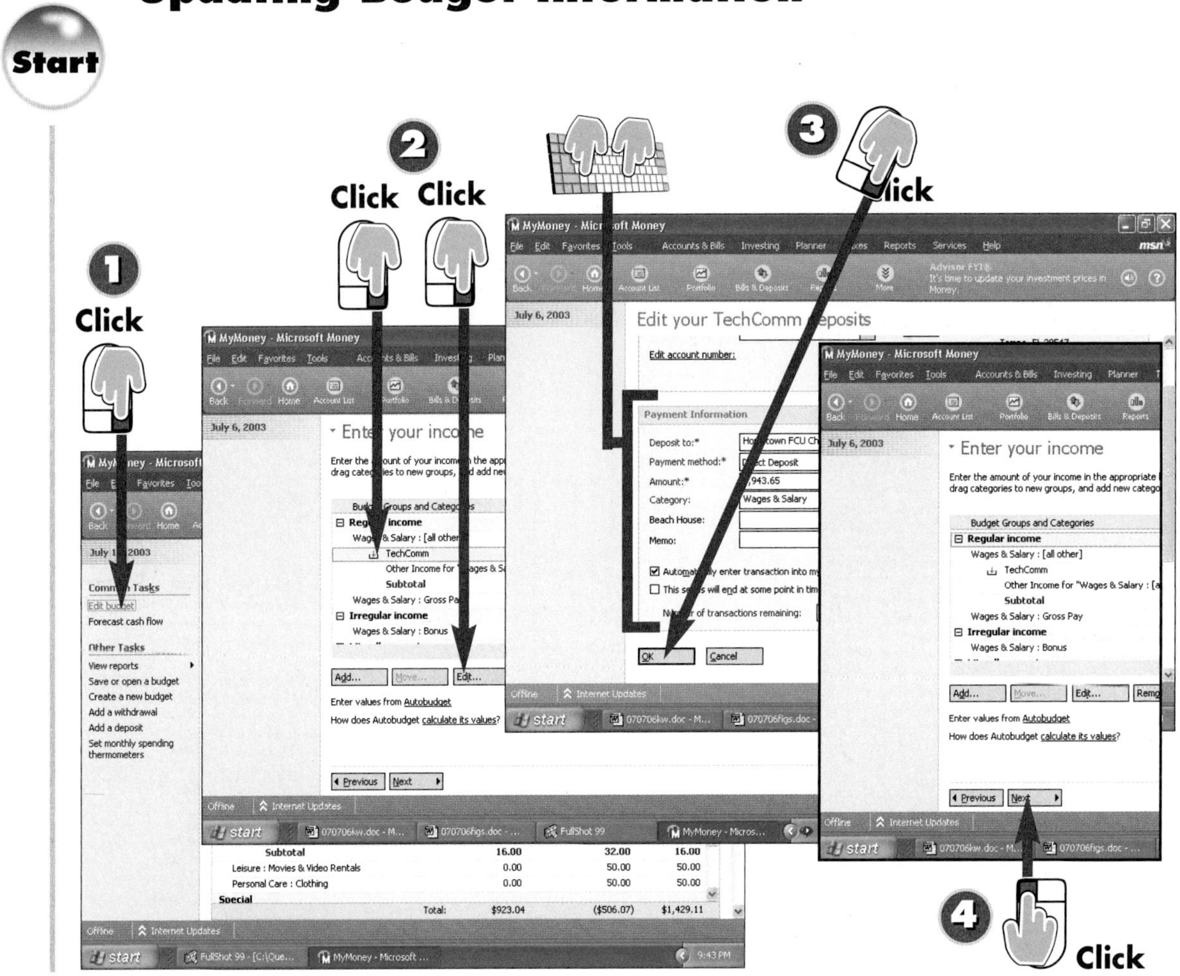

Click
Click Click
Click
Click

1. Under **Common Tasks**, click **Edit budget**.
2. To change your income information, select the category you want to change (here, **TechComm**) and click **Edit**.
3. Change the income information by clicking in the desired box and typing the new information. When you are finished, click **OK**.
4. Click **Next**.

INTRODUCTION

As you work with your budget, you will likely need to adjust it to keep it working for you. You can update any information just as you did when you set up the budget.

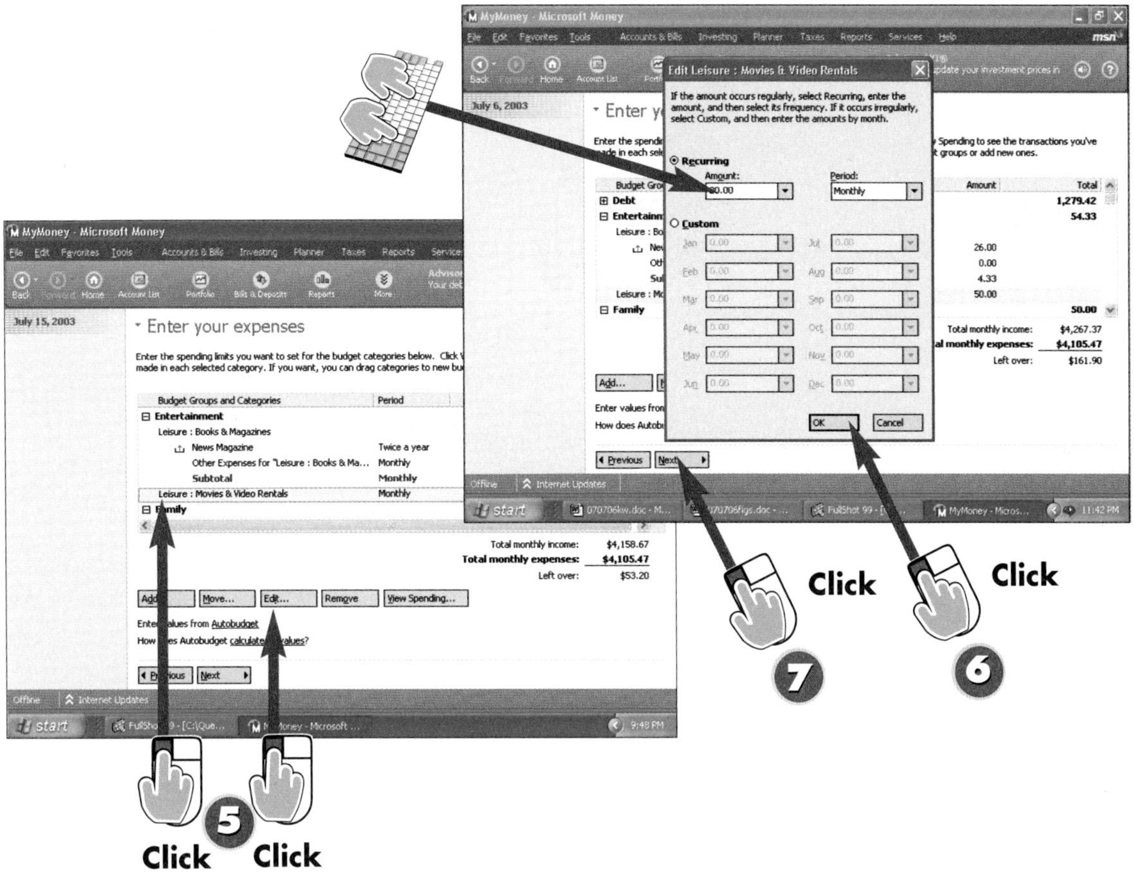

5 To change your expenses information, select the category you want to change (here, **Leisure : Movies & Video Rentals**) and click **Edit**.

6 Change the expense information by clicking in the desired box and typing the new information. When you are finished, click **OK**.

7 Click **Next**.

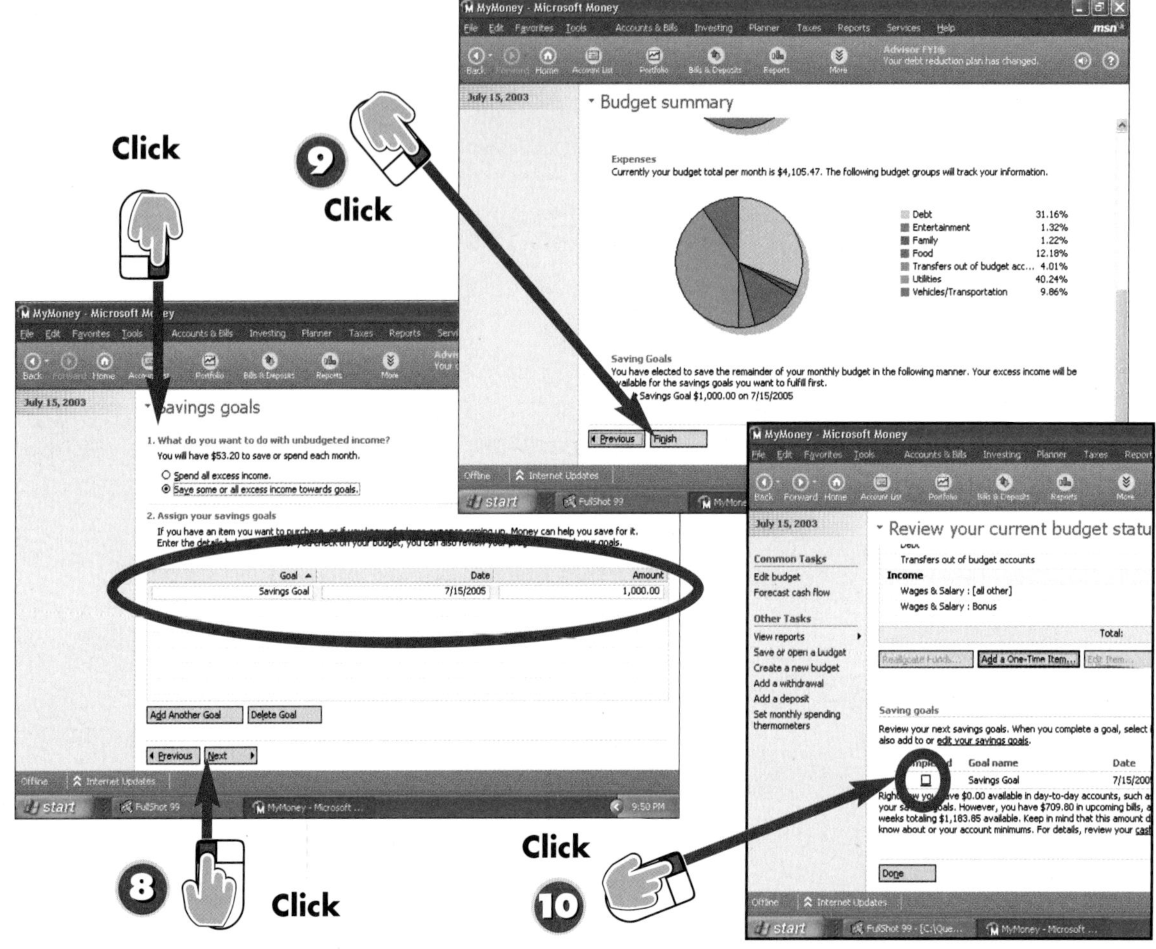

8 Update your financial goals—for example, by typing a new goal name, date, or amount—and then click **Next**.

9 Review your budget summary and click **Finish**.

10 When you reach a financial goal, click the box under **Completed**; Money removes the goal from your budget status.

TIP

Creating and Opening Budgets
You can create a new budget—for example, if you have two properties you want to keep separate—by clicking **Create a new budget** on the left side of the Budget Planner screen. To open a saved budget, click **Save or open a budget** and locate the budget you want to open.

Viewing Different Budget Periods

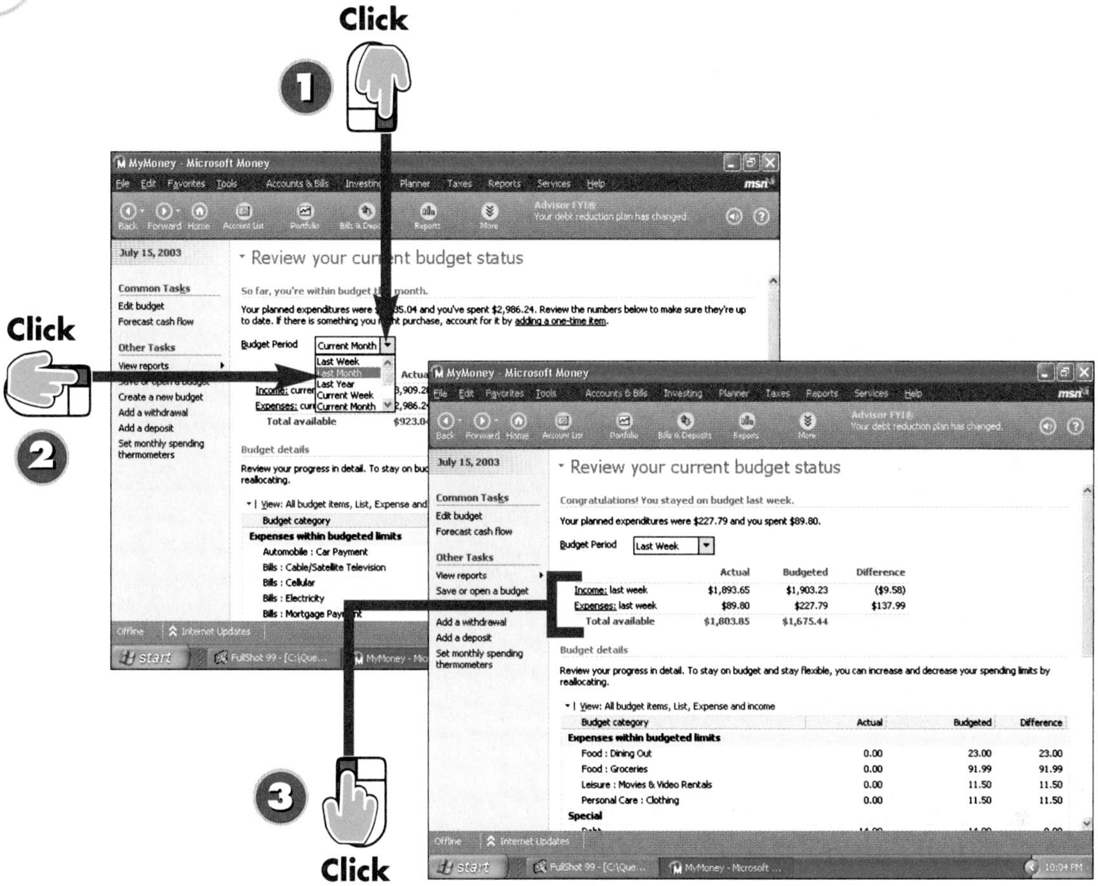

1. In the Review your current budget status window, click the **Budget Period** down arrow.
2. Select a time period.
3. To go straight to your income or expenses information for the selected time period, click either the **Income** or **Expenses** link.

INTRODUCTION

To view your budget from each and every angle, you can select different periods of time to pinpoint certain areas or broaden your scope. Each view gives you a different perspective on your budget.

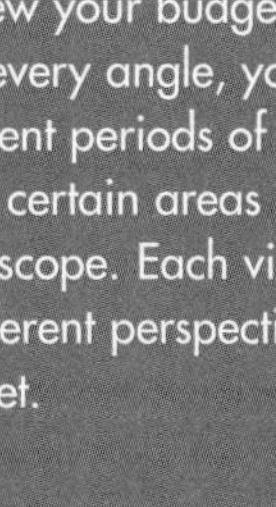

Setting Up Reminders to Keep You on Budget

Start

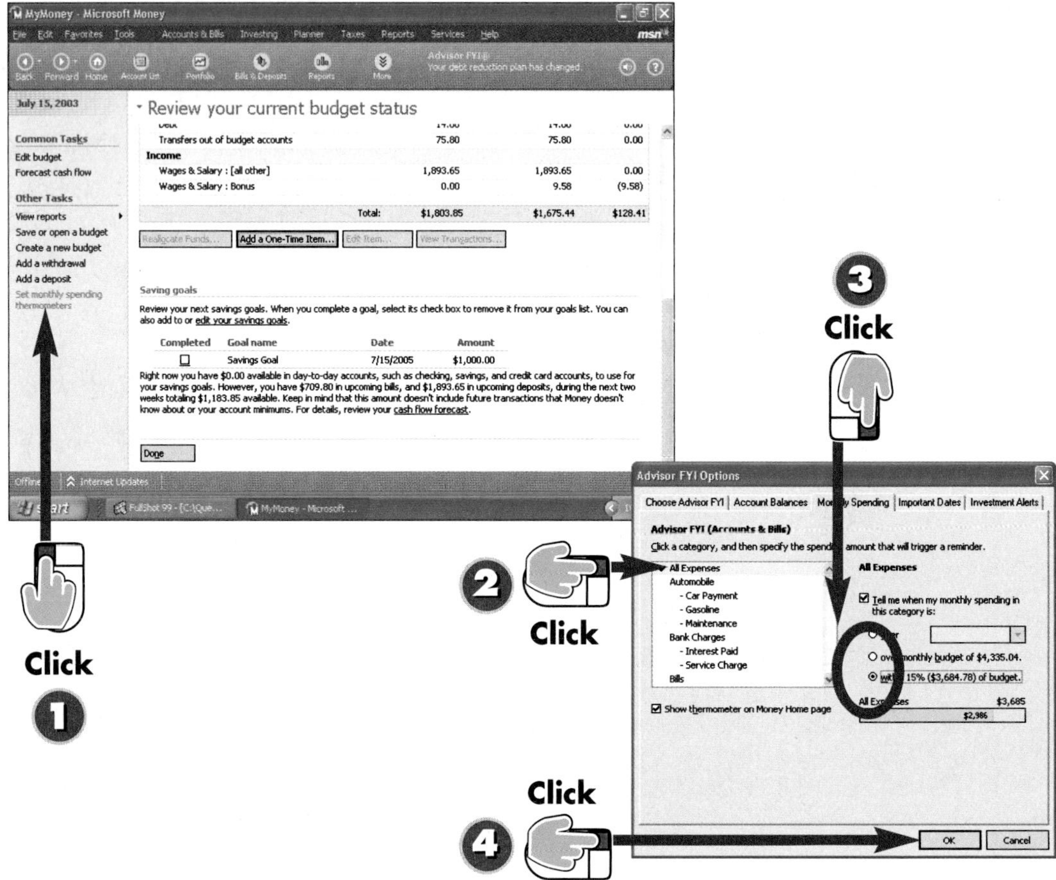

1 Under **Other Tasks**, click **Set monthly spending thermometers**.

2 Click the categories you want to monitor. If you want to monitor all categories, click **All Expenses**.

3 Click an option button under **Tell me when my monthly spending in this category is** to specify how closely monitored you want your budget categories.

4 Click **OK**.

End

INTRODUCTION

You can set up reminders to get on your case when you are getting close to or over your budget. It's sort of like a nag-o-meter, similar to the reminders you set up to remind yourself to pay your bills.

TIP

Displaying the Thermometer

If you want the thermometer to be included with your other categories on your home page, click the **Show thermometer on Money Home page** check box to select it.

Revisiting the Cash-Flow Forecast

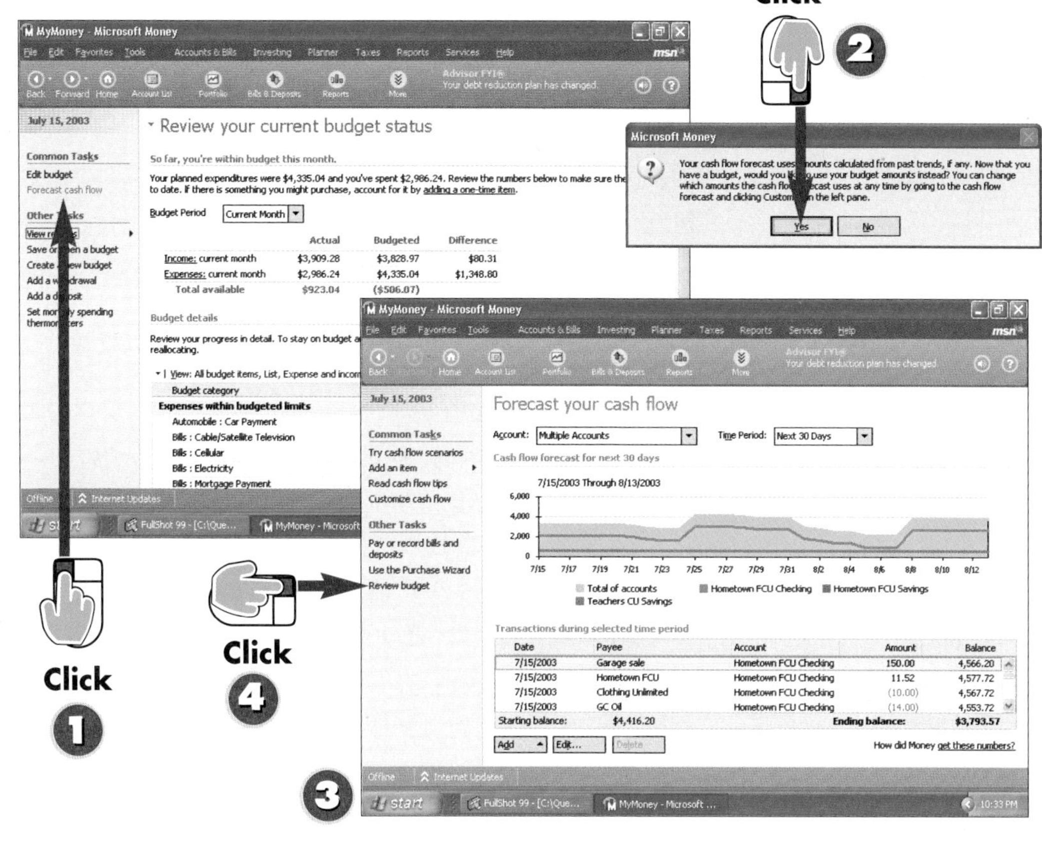

1. Under **Common Tasks**, click **Forecast cash flow**.
2. Money asks whether you want to use the budget amounts you entered to forecast your cash flow. Click **Yes**.
3. Take a gander at your new cash-flow projections and play around with them like you did in Part 5.
4. When you are finished, under **Other tasks**, click **Review budget** to return to your budget.

INTRODUCTION

In Part 5, you looked at your cash-flow projections. Now it's time to revisit the cash-flow forecast because when you set up a budget, the dynamics of your financial situation change. Revisiting the cash-flow forecast forces Money to update the forecast.

PART 7

Creating a Debt-Reduction Plan

Now that you have a budget set up and have some control over expenses and bills, you're ready to take that financial control a step further: creating a debt reduction plan. Of course, there are several different ways to help you manage your debt, such as the budget you just created. But Microsoft Money's Debt Reduction Planner can help you reduce your debt so you can reach your financial goals—maybe even a little faster than you originally thought. Microsoft Money takes the information you've already entered about all of your accounts and allows you to select the accounts you want to pay off more quickly, add new accounts, and set up a plan that works with your budget. You'll be surprised at how much money you can save just in interest by reducing your debt a little each month. And of course, as with your budget, you can change your plan if your financial situation changes by returning to the Debt Reduction Planner.

The Debt Reduction Planner

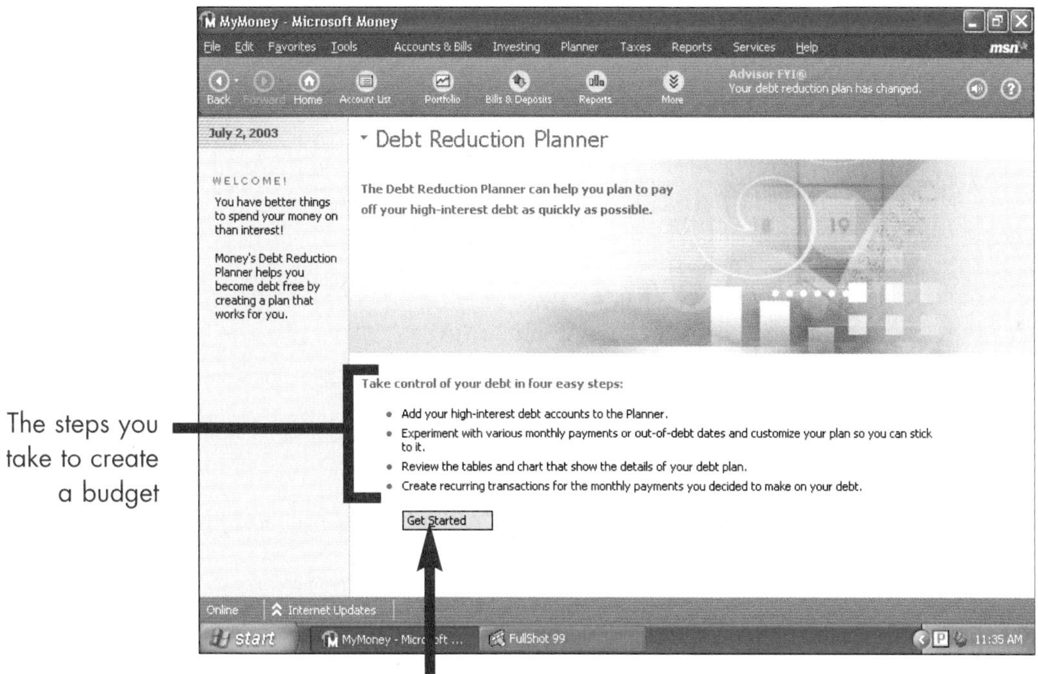

Specifying Which Accounts to Pay Off

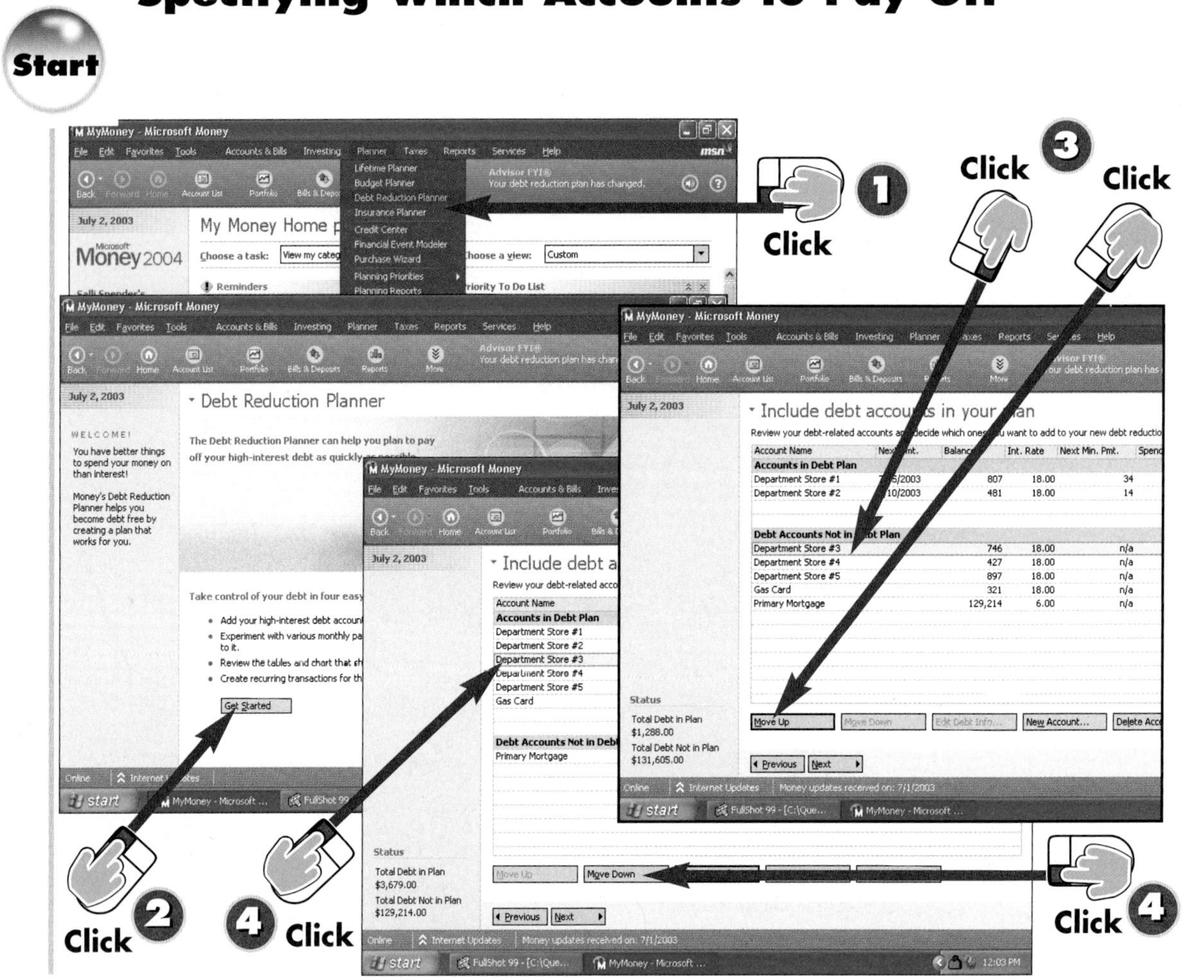

Click 1

Click 2

Click 3

Click 4

1. Open the **Planner** menu and choose **Debt Reduction Planner**.

2. Click **Get Started**. You'll see a list of the accounts you've entered into Money.

3. Under **Debt Accounts Not in Debt Plan**, click the first account you want to include in your plan; click **Move Up**. Repeat for each account you want to pay off.

4. If you want to remove an account from the plan, click the account under **Accounts in Debt Plan** and click **Move Down**.

INTRODUCTION

When creating a debt-reduction plan, first decide which accounts you want to pay off (start with high-interest ones, such as credit cards). Then, check your budget to see how much extra money you have each month to put toward reducing your debt. You'll need all this information to create your plan.

TIP

Disabling the Audio Help

If your PC has sound, you may hear helpful information about the Debt Reduction Planner. You can turn it off by clicking the sound icon in the upper-right corner of the window and selecting **Turn All Audio Help Off**.

TIP

Calculating Debt

Notice that Money calculates both the total debt in your plan as well as the total debt *not* currently in your plan in the lower-left corner of the window.

Editing Account Information

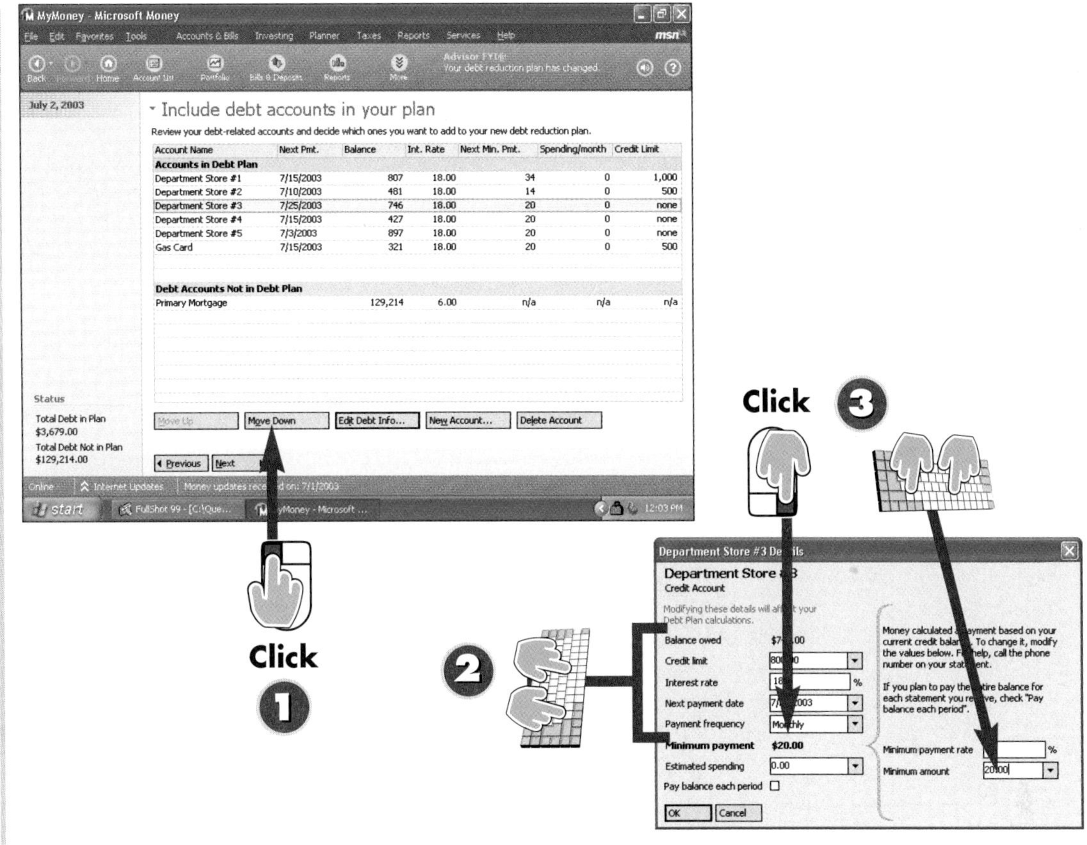

1. Select the account you want to check and click **Edit Debt Info.**
2. Enter, review, or change any of the account information by clicking in the appropriate box and typing the correct information.
3. To enter the minimum payment, click **Minimum payment**, and then type the minimum payment in the **Minimum amount** box.
4. When you are finished, click **OK**.

INTRODUCTION

After you finish selecting the accounts you want to include in your plan, you should make sure the information contained in each account is accurate—especially the balance, interest rate, and monthly payment amount.

TIP

Entering Your Minimum Payment
If you know it, enter the minimum percentage of your balance that you are required to pay each month in the **Minimum payment rate** area, above the **Minimum amount** box.

TIP

Estimating Spending
If you know you will be adding to the debt on an account—for example, using a credit card—type what you think you will be adding to the account each month in the **Estimated spending** box.

Creating or Deleting an Account

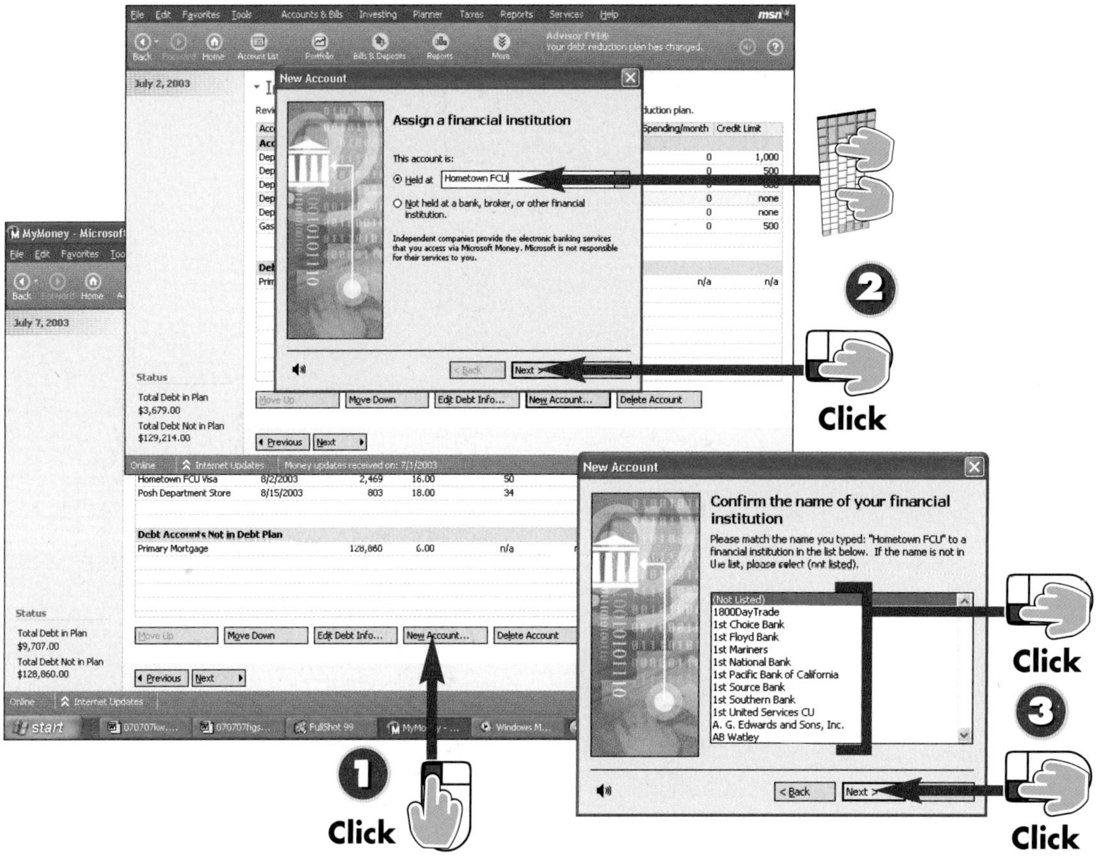

1. Click **New Account**. Money launches the New Account wizard.

2. Click in the **Held at** box and type the name of the financial institution. If the account is not held at a financial institution, click the **Not held at** option. Then click **Next**.

3. If you entered the name of a financial institution in step 2, confirm the name by selecting it from the list. (If you did not enter a name, you won't see this window.) Then click **Next**.

INTRODUCTION

If, after selecting and editing the accounts you want to include in your plan, you discover that you have an account you haven't entered but want to include, you can do so now. Alternatively, if you're absolutely certain that you want to remove the account entirely you can do that as well.

TIP

Adding New Accounts

Adding a new account here works just like it did when you learned about creating new accounts in Part 4. The questions posed by the wizard will vary depending on what type of account you are adding. This task shows you how to add an account that is held at a financial institution.

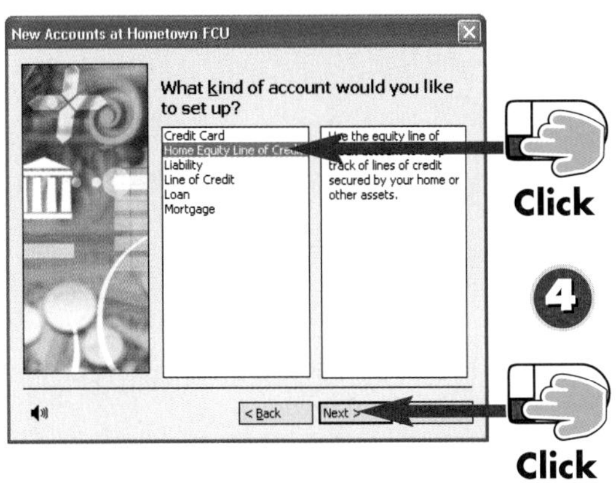

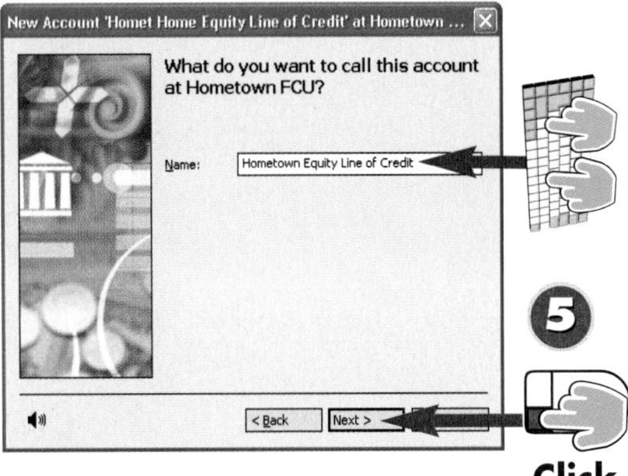

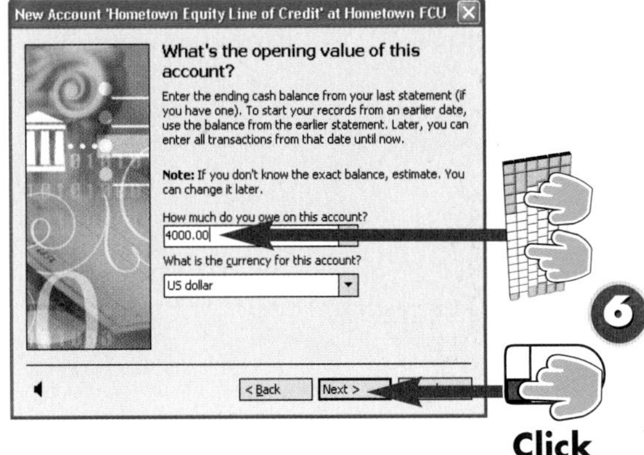

4. In the left pane, click the type of account you want to add (you'll see a description of the selected option on the right). Then click **Next**.
5. In the **Name** box, type the name you want to use within Money to identify the account you are adding. Then click **Next**.
6. In the **How much do you owe on this account?** box, type the account's current balance. Then click **Next**.

See next page

HINT

Selecting a Currency
If you use a currency other than the U.S. dollar, click the **What is the currency for this account** down arrow shown in step 6 and select the appropriate currency from the list that appears.

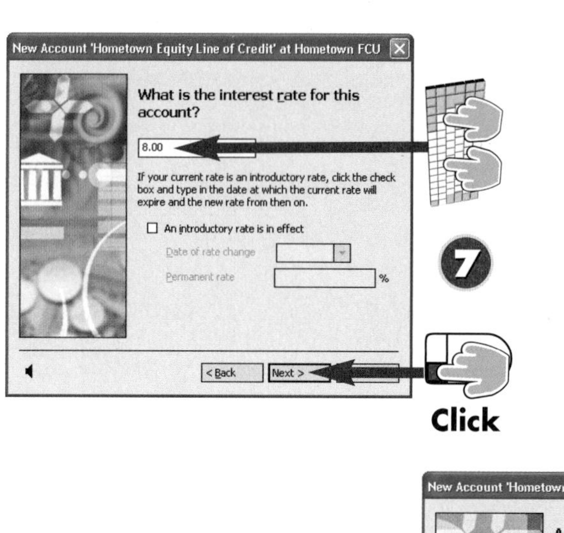

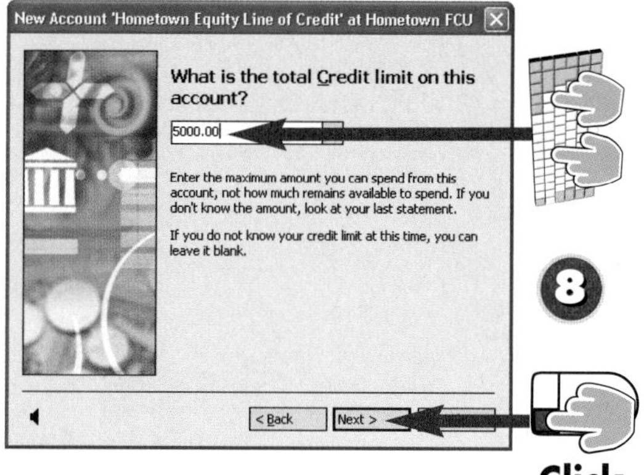

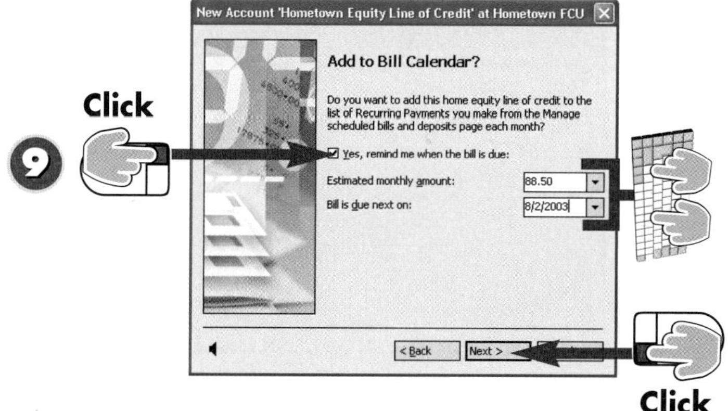

7. Type the account's current interest rate. Then click **Next**.

8. Type the account's credit limit, and then click **Next**.

9. To set up a monthly bill reminder, click the **Yes** box, type the amount due in **Estimated monthly amount**, and enter the due date in **Bill is due next on**. Then click **Next**.

HINT

Handling Introductory Rates

If the interest rate you typed in step 7 is an introductory rate, click the **An introductory rate is in effect** check box. Then type the permanent rate and the date on which that rate will take effect.

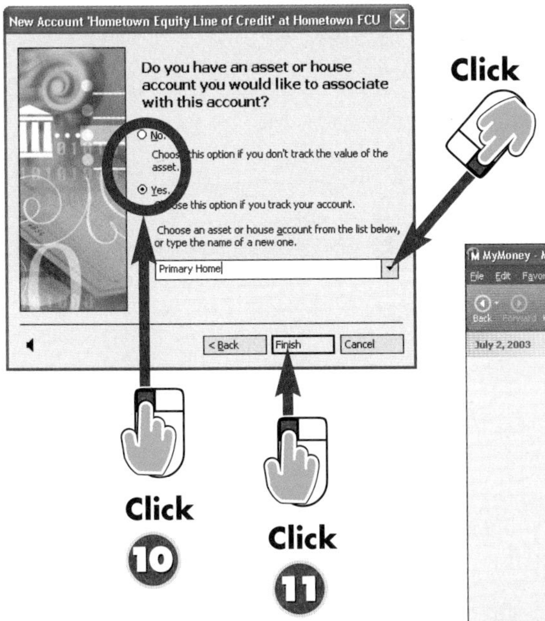

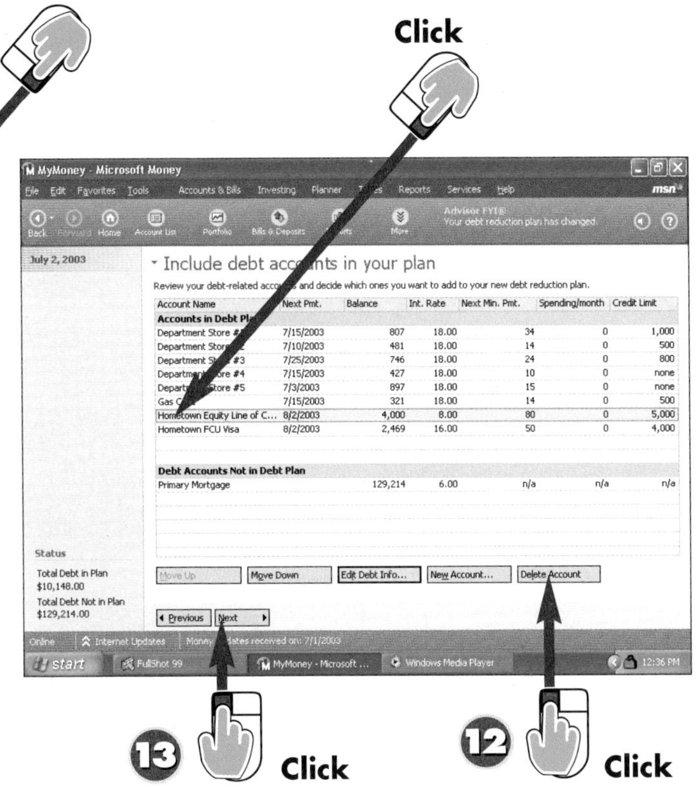

10 If you wish to associate the account with an asset or house account, click **Yes**, and choose the asset or house account from the drop-down list. If not, click **No**.

11 Click **Finish**. The account is added to your plan.

12 To remove an account, click the account in the list, and then click **Delete Account**.

13 When you are finished adding and/or deleting accounts, click **Next**.

TIP

Adding the Account to Your Budget

Adding a new account here also adds it to your comprehensive account list, which affects your income/expense ratio. You may want to add the account to your budget as well (see Part 6 if you need help).

CAUTION

Deleting an account completely removes that account from Money, and can adversely affect other areas, such as your budget. Double-check your information and the plans you have in place before you remove an account.

Putting More Toward Your Debt

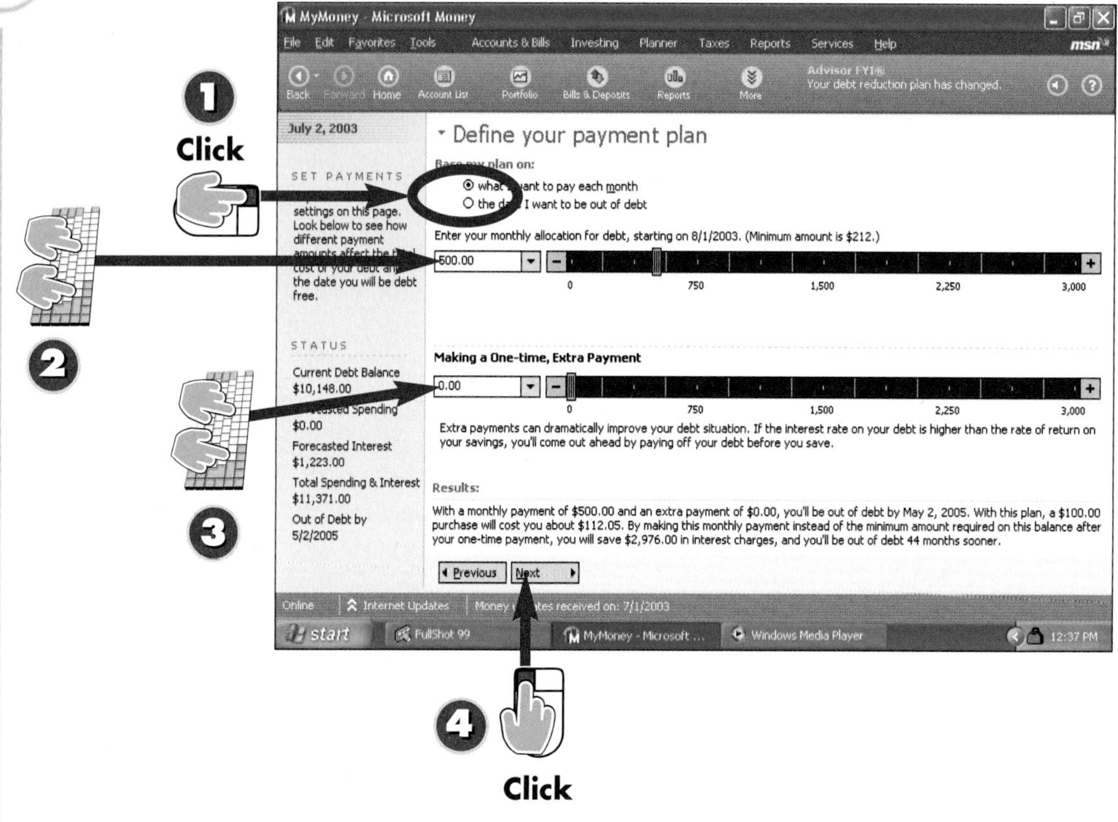

1. Specify whether you want your plan to be based on what you want to pay each month (as shown here), or the date you want to be out of debt.
2. Type the total dollar amount that you can apply each month toward your debt. (You can also use the slider to set the dollar amount.)
3. If you want to make a one-time extra payment, type that total dollar amount (or use the slider) under **Making a One-time, Extra Payment**.
4. Click **Next**.

INTRODUCTION

You're almost finished with your plan; now you need to look at your budget and decide how much money you can put toward paying off your debt each month. Money tells you the minimum amount of money you will need in order to stick to your plan. You can also consider making a one-time extra payment on one or more of your accounts, which can make a big difference in your debt. The last thing to consider is whether you have a date by which you want to be out of debt, no matter what it takes. So, think about your financial options, and plug those figures in. You can always come back to this plan to change them later if it doesn't work for you.

TIP

Summarizing Your Debt
In the lower-left corner of the window, Money summarizes how much debt and interest you will be paying, how much you will be spending (if applicable), and the approximate date when you will be out of debt.

Viewing Your Debt Reduction Plan Results

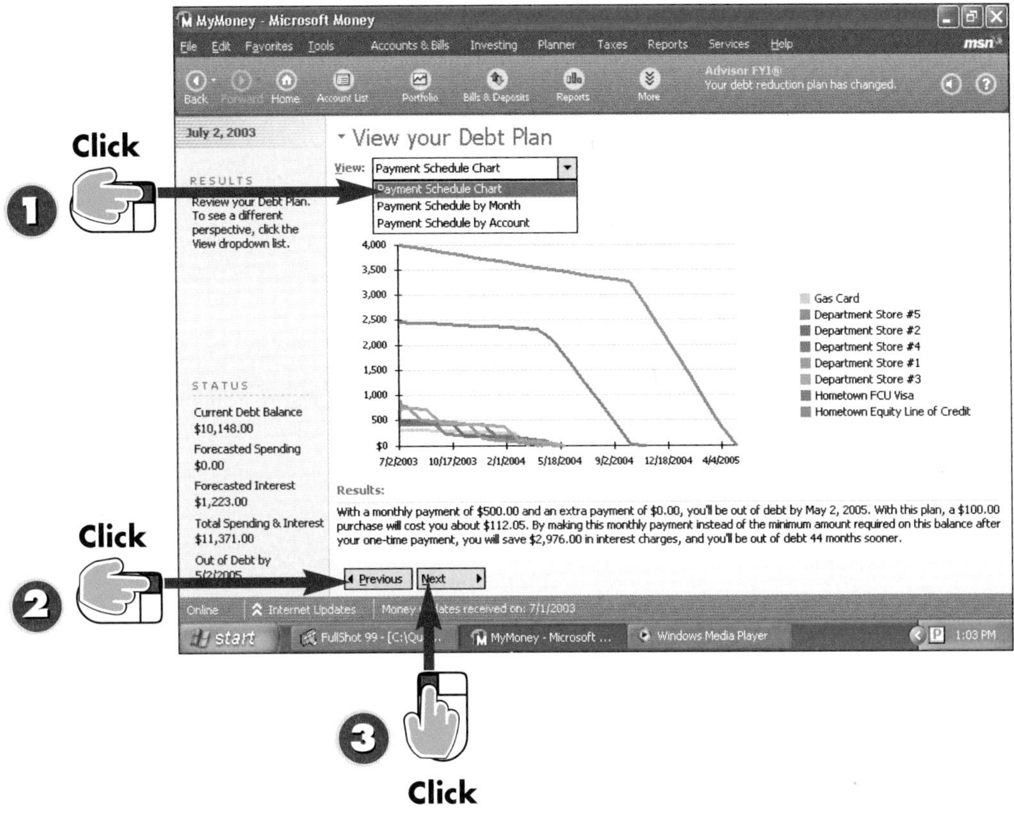

1. To see a different view of your plan, click the **View** down arrow and select another view.
2. To make changes to your plan, click the **Previous** button, make the desired changes, and click **Next** to return to the Results window.
3. When you are satisfied with the results, click **Next** to finalize your plan and put it into action.

INTRODUCTION

Now let's see how much paying that extra amount per month will reduce your debt, how much you will save in interest, and how long it will take to get out of debt. By default, your debt plan results appear in a bar chart by date and debt amount. A key on the right tells you which color represents which account. The Results area at the bottom tells you what you can save and what it will cost you to put this plan into action.

TIP

Making Changes Later
This debt reduction plan is not set in stone. You can return to the Debt Reduction Planner any time you need to in order to make changes by opening the **Planner** menu and clicking **Debt Reduction Planner**.

Putting Your Debt Reduction Plan Into Action

Start

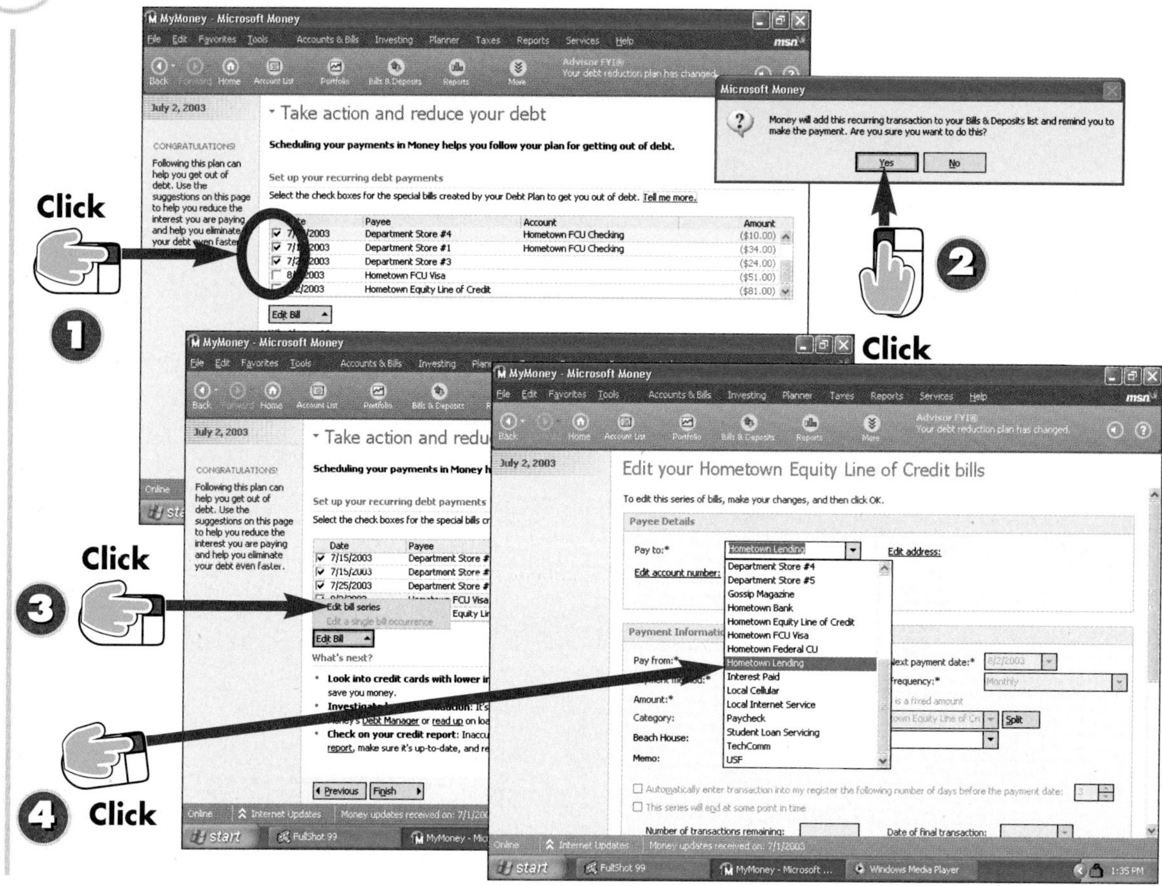

1. To accept the changes to your accounts and put your plan into action, click in each check box next to the accounts listed.

2. Click **Yes** to allow Money to update your bills.

3. To make changes to a bill, click the bill in the list to select it, click **Edit Bill**, and select **Edit bill series**.

4. To change the payee, click the **Pay to** down arrow and select the desired name. Alternatively, type the payee's name in the **Pay to** box.

INTRODUCTION

The final step in creating your debt reduction plan is to authorize Microsoft Money to make the needed changes to accounts and to your budget. That way, the payments you make for your bills reflect the amounts needed to reduce your debt.

TIP

Selecting Accounts
To take full advantage of your debt reduction plan, select all your accounts in step 1.

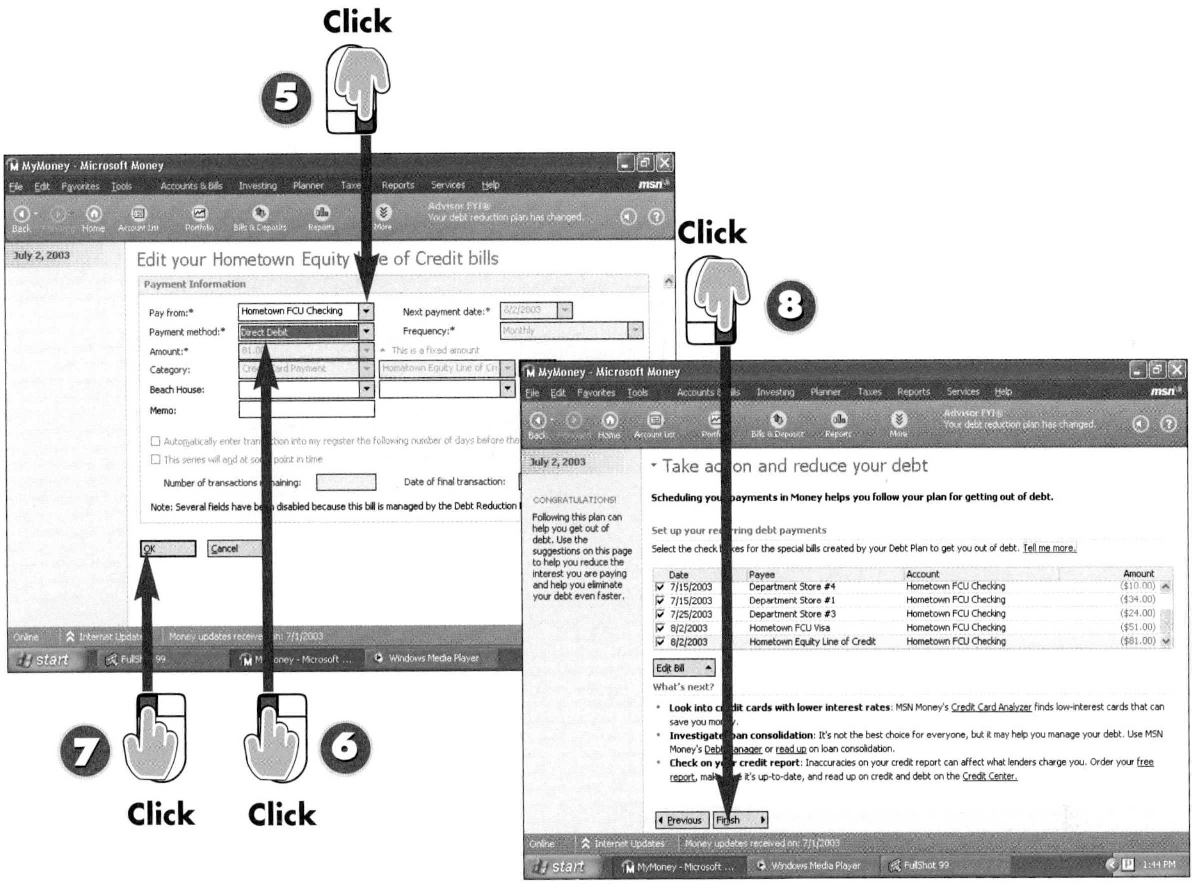

5 If the **Pay from** box is empty, click its down arrow and select the name of the account from which this bill will be paid.

6 Select how the bill will be paid from the **Payment method** list.

7 If applicable, select the payment date from the **Next payment date** list and how often the bill will be paid from the **Frequency** list. Click **OK** when finished.

8 Click **Finish**.

TIP

Learning More
To read about other debt reduction tips and advice, check out the links at the bottom of the Debt Reduction Planner window.

PART 8

Managing Your Investments

Whether you just have a 401K or you play the stock market like a pro, this is your stop to learn how to manage all your investment information. You can also add new investments, update existing ones, get the latest quotes for your investments, research, and read up on the latest market trends. You've already learned a bit about adding and updating your investment accounts. Now let's get into more detail using the Portfolio page that Money has set up for you.

Your Portfolio

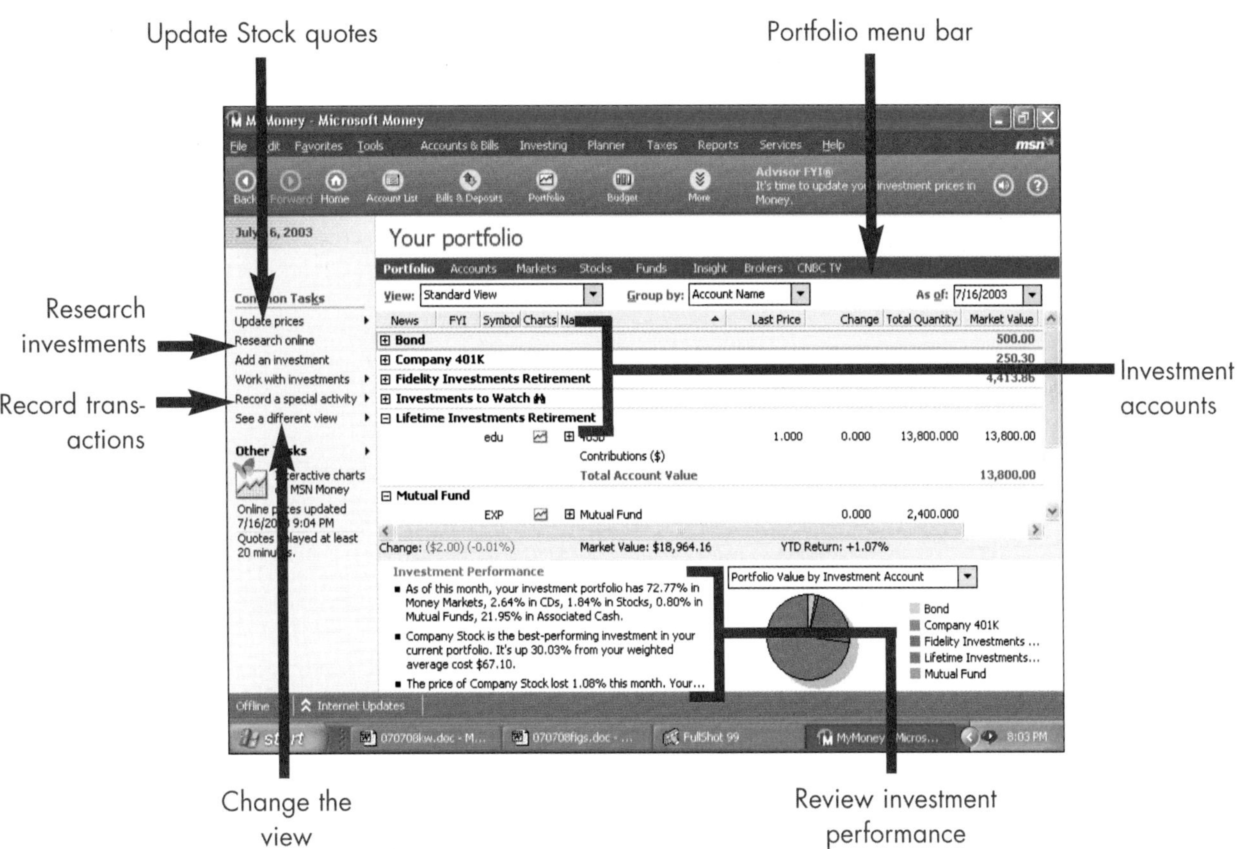

Update Stock quotes
Portfolio menu bar
Research investments
Record trans-actions
Investment accounts
Change the view
Review investment performance

Reviewing Existing Investments

Click the **Portfolio** button on the Money toolbar.

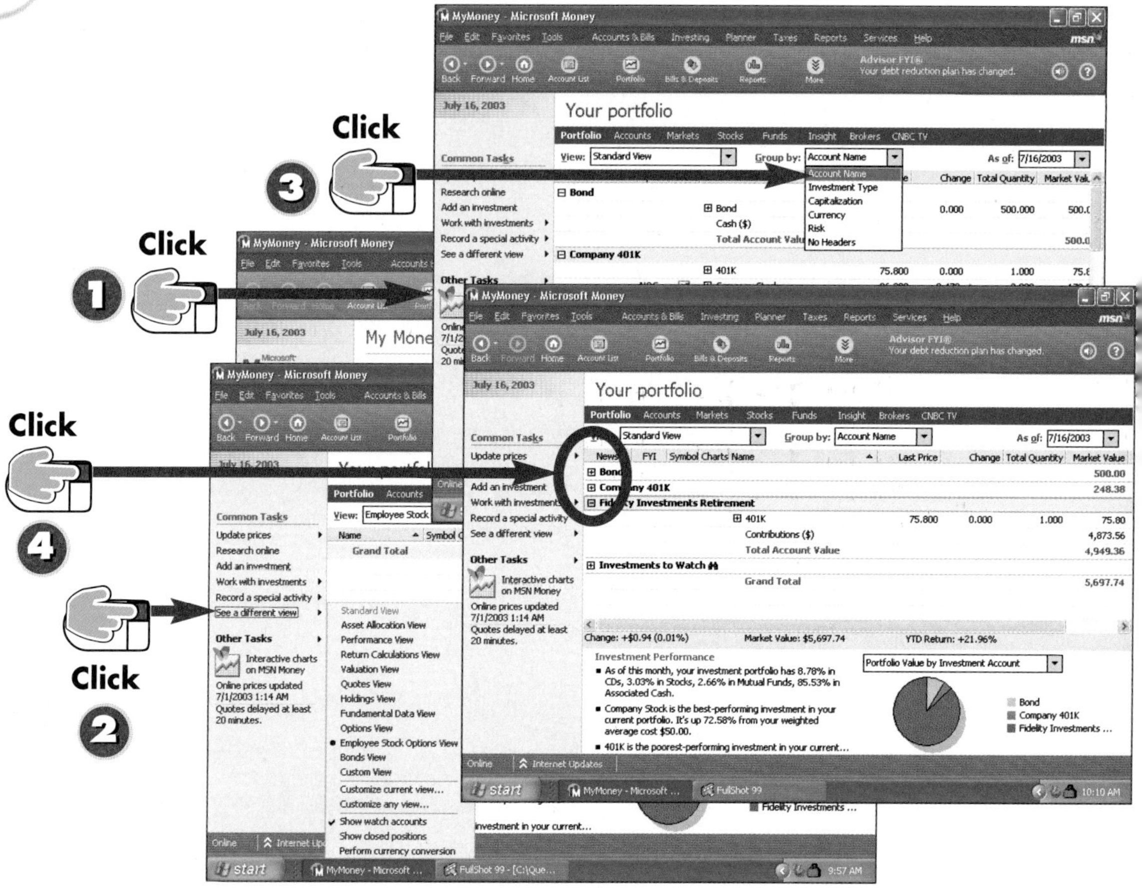

To change the view, under **Common Tasks**, click **See a different view** and select an option from the menu that appears.

To change how your investments are grouped, click the **Group by** down arrow and select an option from the list that appears.

Click the minus sign (**–**) to collapse or the plus sign (**+**) to expand the list of investments.

INTRODUCTION

Chances are, you set up your investment accounts when you set up all the rest of your accounts in Part 1. This task shows you how to review those investment accounts. For each investment, you can see how much money you have invested, the latest quotes, and how all your interests are performing.

TIP

Accessing Investments
Another way to access your investments is to open the **Investments** menu and select **Portfolio**.

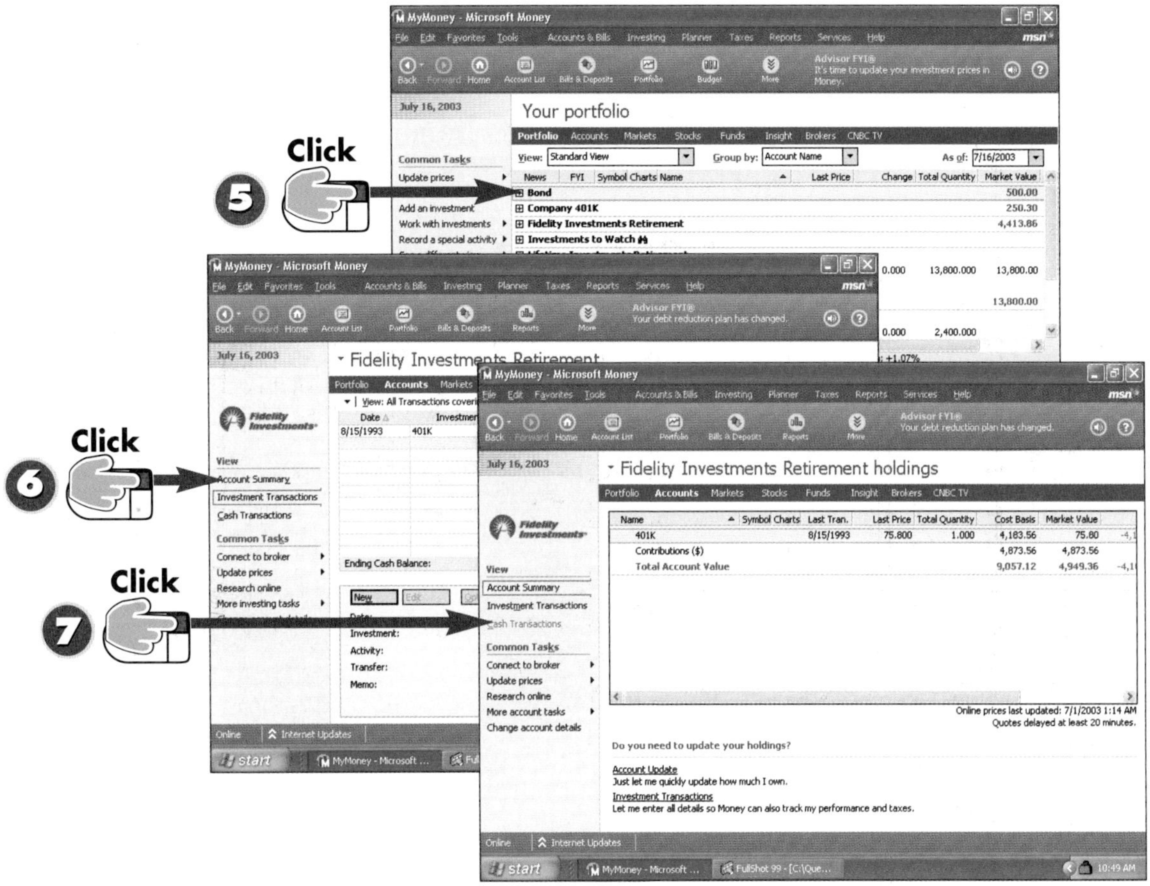

Click

5

Click

6

Click

7

5 To review detailed investment information, click the name of the investment you want to review.

6 To see an investment summary for the investment account you are reviewing, click **Account Summary** under **View**.

7 To view all cash transactions for the investment account you are reviewing, click **Cash Transactions** under **View**.

HINT

Performing Common Tasks

Under **Common Tasks** are several investment-related tasks that you can explore (most require you to connect to the Internet). **Connect to broker** provides links to one of your investment companies; **Update prices** downloads the latest stock quotes; **Research online** provides links to a host of investment information; **More account tasks** (also known as **More investing tasks**) and **Change account details** provide lots of other account options.

Recording Cash Transactions for Investment Accounts

Start

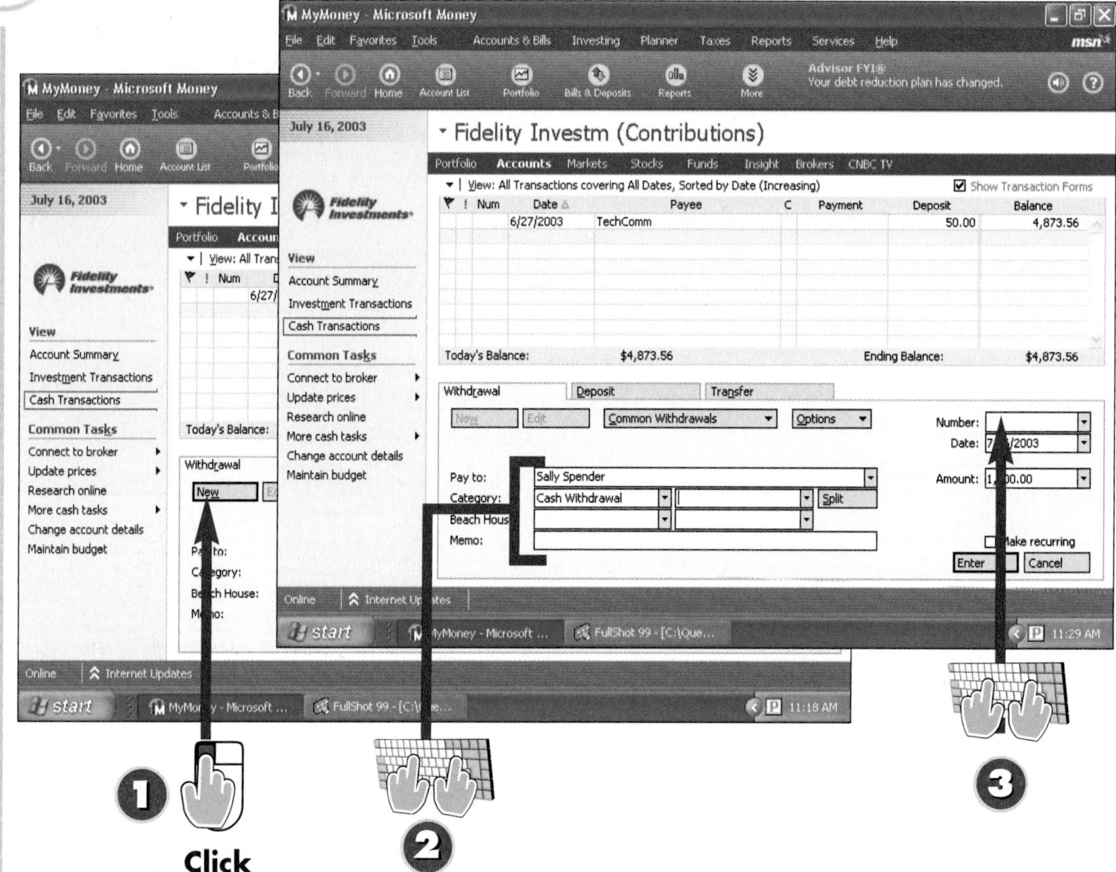

1. To record a cash withdrawal, be sure that the investment account you want to update is open and that the Withdrawal tab is visible. Then click **New**.
2. Enter the appropriate information in the **Pay to** and **Category** boxes. (Filling the **Memo** box is optional.)
3. If the withdrawal is to be made by check, type the check number in the **Number** box (this step is optional, but it's a good idea).

INTRODUCTION

When you get your investment statements in the mail, or as you make changes to your investment accounts, you can enter those activities in your Money investments roster. The process is just the same as entering transactions for your other accounts, as covered in Parts 4 and 5.

HINT

Downloading Statements Online
If you download your statements online into Money, you won't have to enter account activity by hand. Even so, it's good to know how to do it.

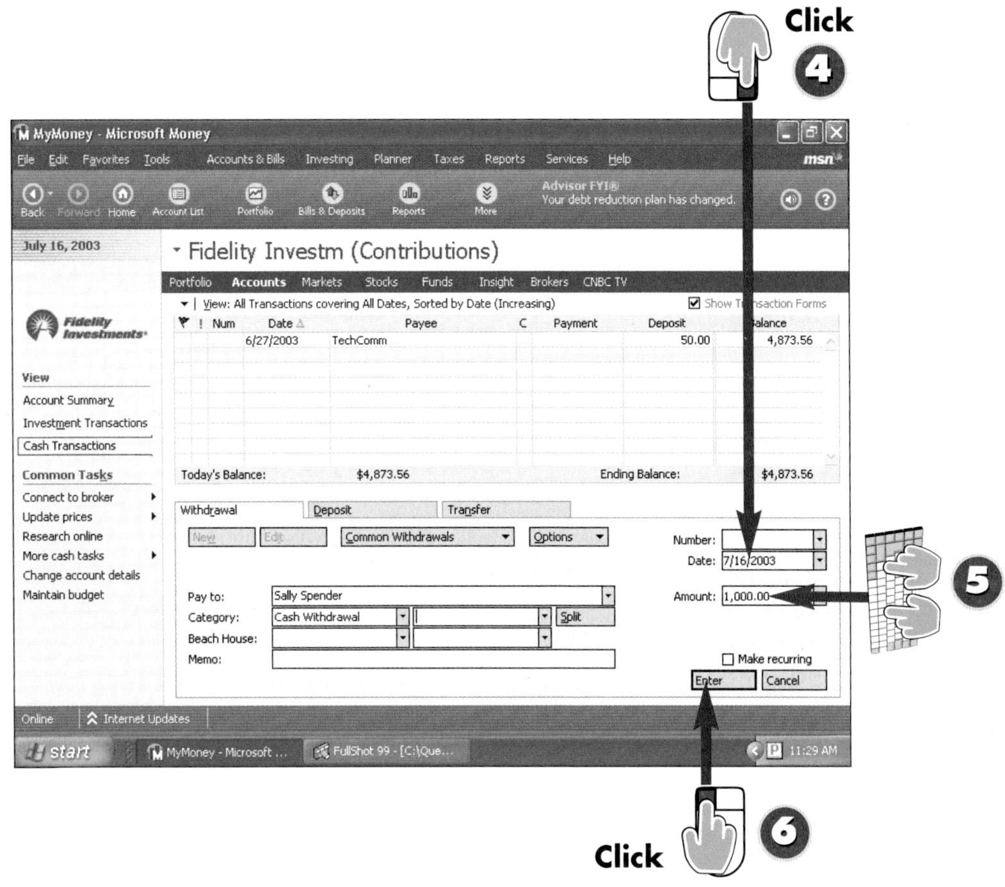

4. If the current date is not the date of the transaction, type the transaction date in the **Date** box.

5. In the **Amount** box, type the amount of the withdrawal.

6. Click **Enter**.

See next page

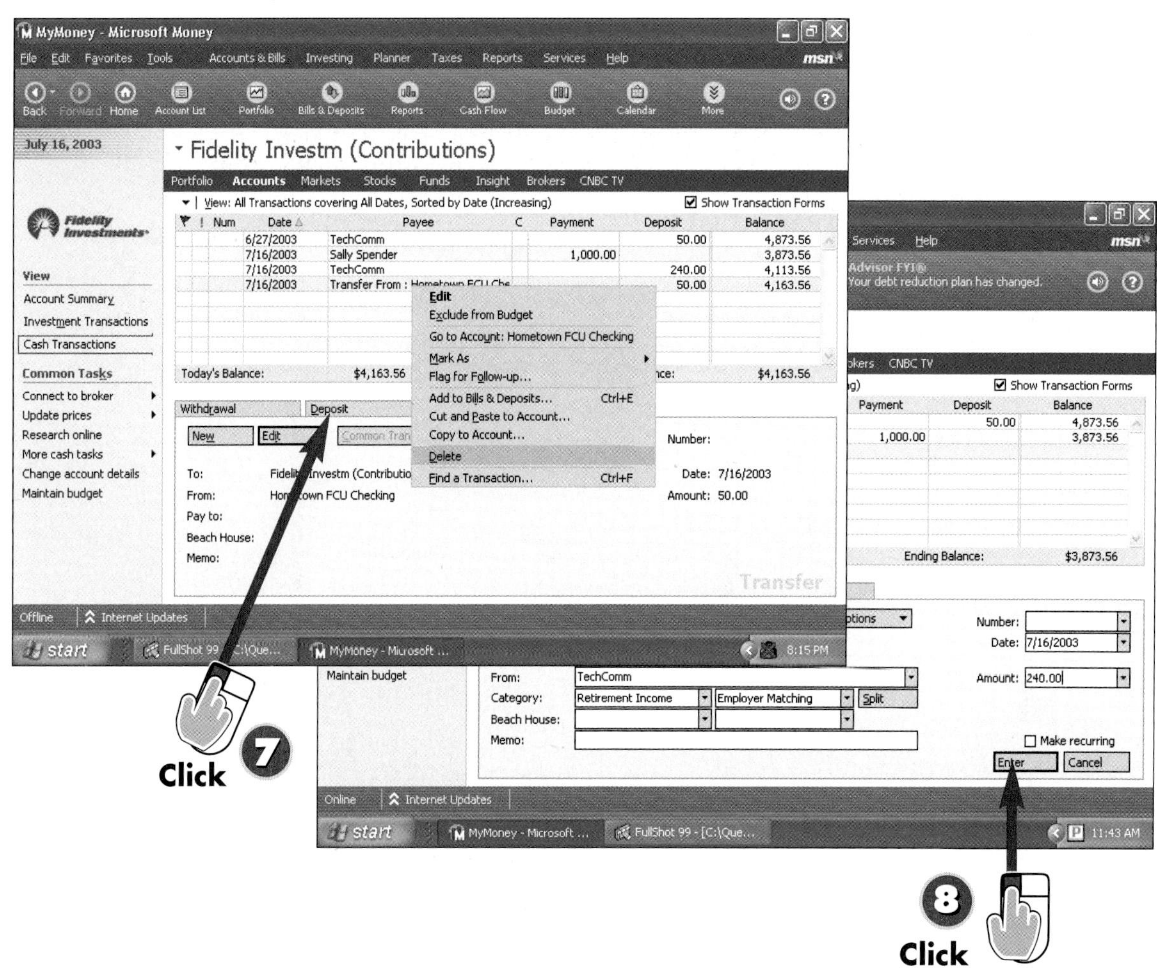

7 To record a deposit, click the **Deposit** tab and click **New**.

8 Enter the deposit information just as you did the withdrawal information. When you are finished, click **Enter**.

TIP

Adding Recurring Transactions

If a withdrawal, deposit, or transfer occurs on a regular basis, click the **Make recurring** check box to select it. Money adds the transaction to the Manage scheduled bills and deposits window and sets up a timely reminder under Bills & Deposits on the main Money home page.

TIP

Editing Transactions

To make changes to a withdrawal, deposit, or transfer after you click **Enter**, select the transaction and click the **Edit** button on the Withdrawal, Deposit, or Transfer tab. Then make your changes.

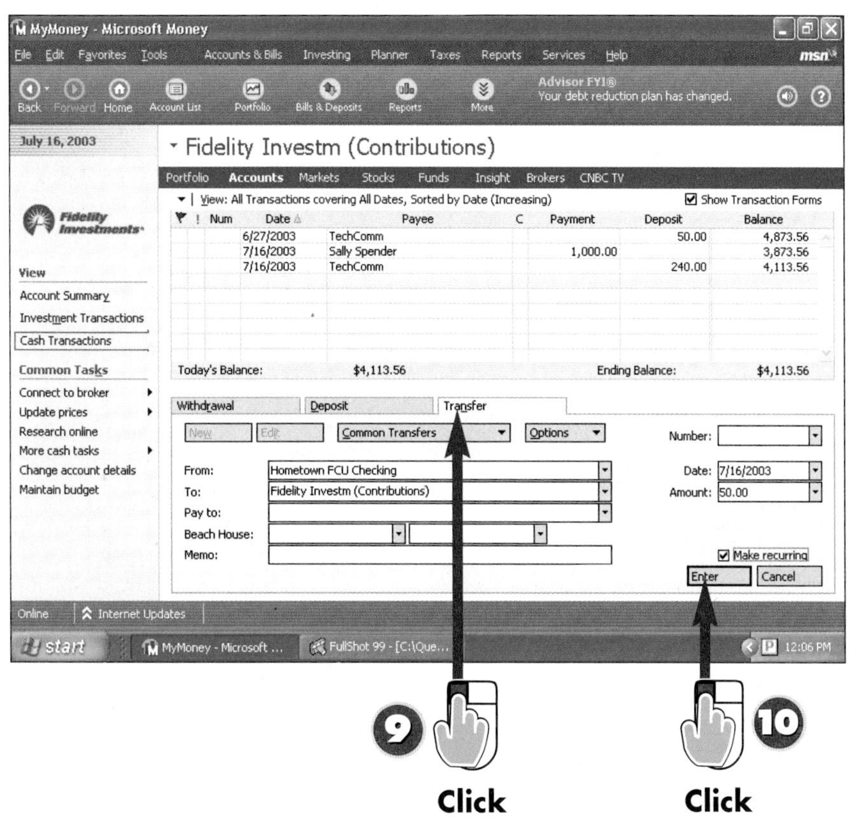

9 To record a transfer, click the **Transfer** tab and click **New**.

10 Enter the transfer information just as you did the withdrawal and deposit information. When you are finished, click **Enter**.

TIP

Deleting Transactions
To delete a transaction, right-click the transaction in the list and select **Delete**. A message appears asking if you want to delete the transaction. Click **Yes**.

Recording Investment Transactions

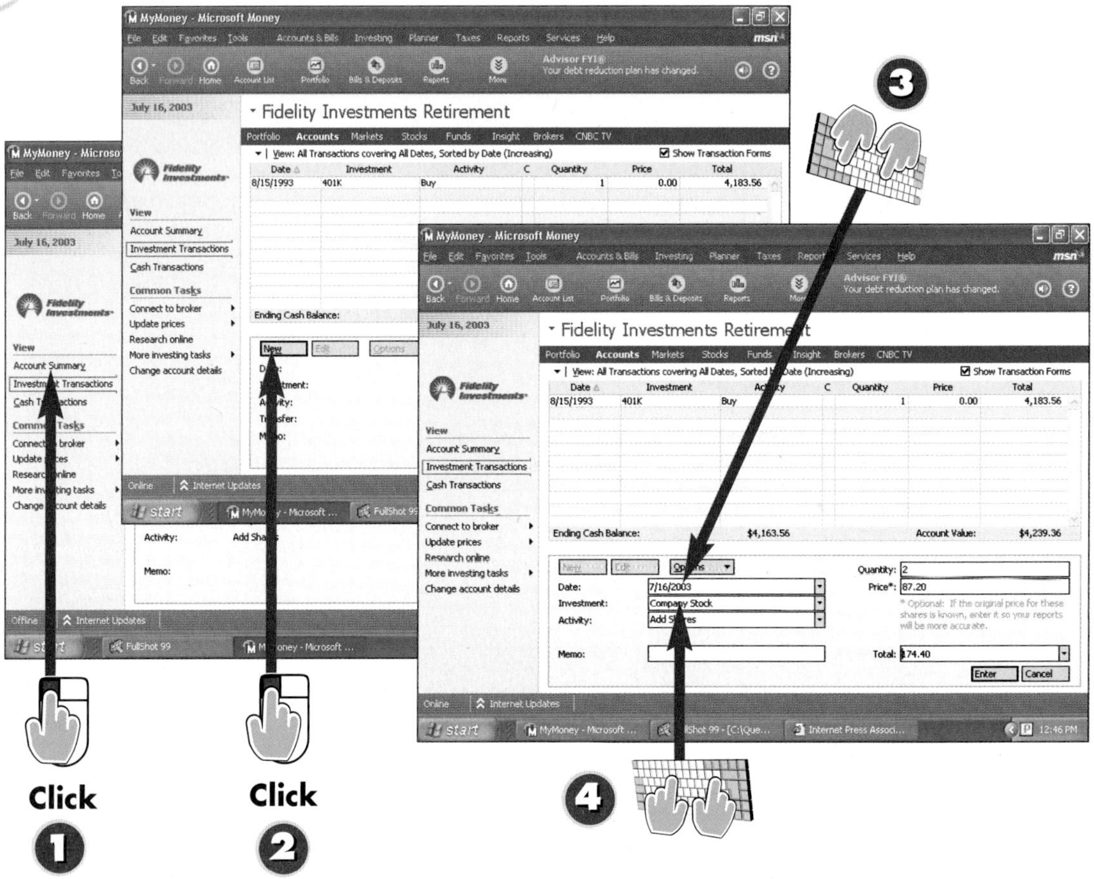

1. To record an investment transaction, be sure the investment account you want to update is open. Then, under **View**, click **Investment Transactions**.

2. Click **New**.

3. If the current date is not the date of the transaction, type the transaction date in the **Date** box.

4. Enter the investment type in the **Investment** box, or click the box's down arrow to select the investment type from the list.

INTRODUCTION

You record investment transactions the same way you recorded cash transactions in the previous task, but using the Investment Transactions view of the Portfolio page.

TIP

Entering Investment Transactions

The options you see when entering a new investment transaction differ depending on what type of investment you enter in the Investment box. As a result, the options you see may differ from what you see here.

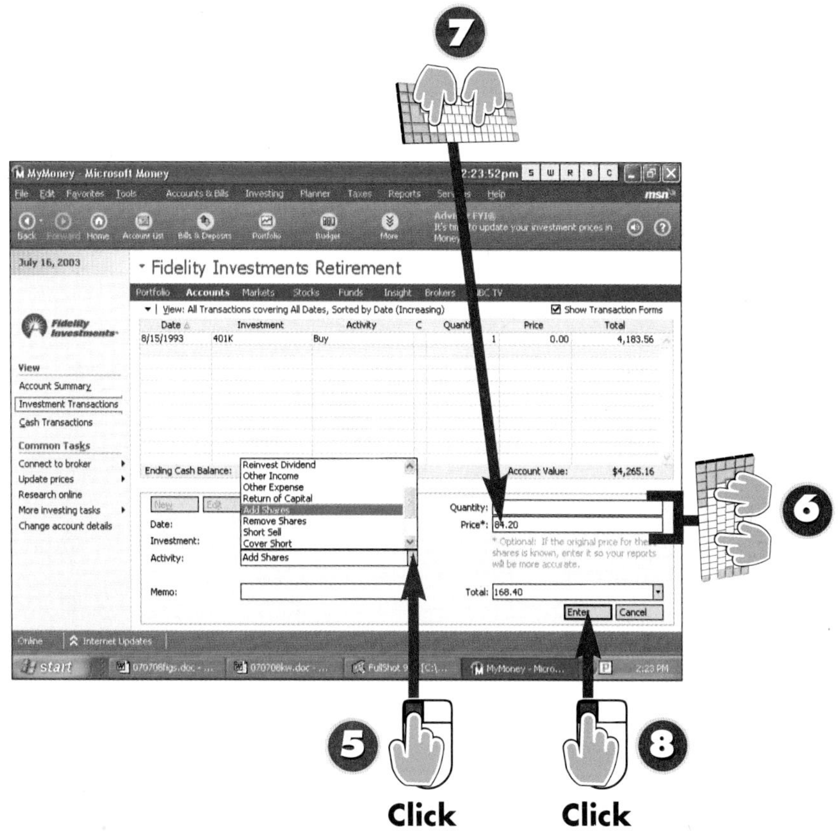

5 Click the **Activity** down arrow and select the activity you want to record (the example shown has **Add Shares selected**).

6 In the **Quantity** box, type the number of shares involved in the transaction. Then type the price of each share, if known, in the **Price** box.

7 Type the total amount of the transaction in the **Total** box.

8 Click **Enter**.

TIP

Editing Transactions
To make changes to a transaction after you click **Enter**, select the transaction in the list, and click the **Edit** button. Then make your changes.

HINT

Deleting Transactions
To delete a transaction, right-click the transaction in the list and select **Delete**. A message appears asking you if you want to delete the transaction; click **Yes**.

Adding New Investments

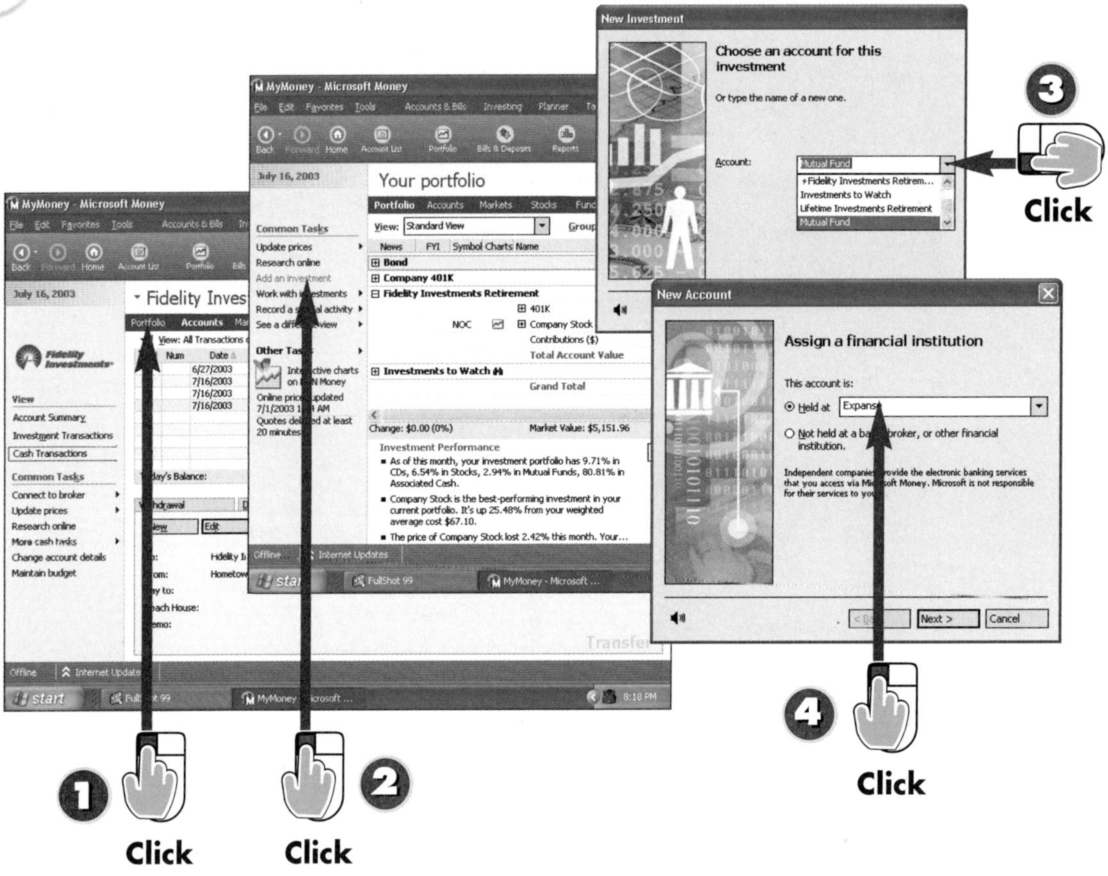

1. From the menu bar at the top of the Portfolio window, click **Portfolio**.

2. Under **Common Tasks**, click **Add an investment**.

3. Click the **Account** down arrow and choose the type of account you are adding (this example uses a mutual fund) or type the name of the new account. Then click **Next**.

4. Specify whether the account is held at a financial institution and, if so, type the name in the **Held at** box. Otherwise, click **Not held at**. Then click **Next**.

End

INTRODUCTION

If you have new investments to add, you can enter that information using your portfolio as well as through your account list. You already know how to enter a new account through your account list; now let's go through the process using your portfolio.

TIP

Your Options May Vary

The options you see when setting up a new investment differ depending on what type of investment you choose in step 3. As a result, what you see in this example may differ from what you see when you set up your own investment account.

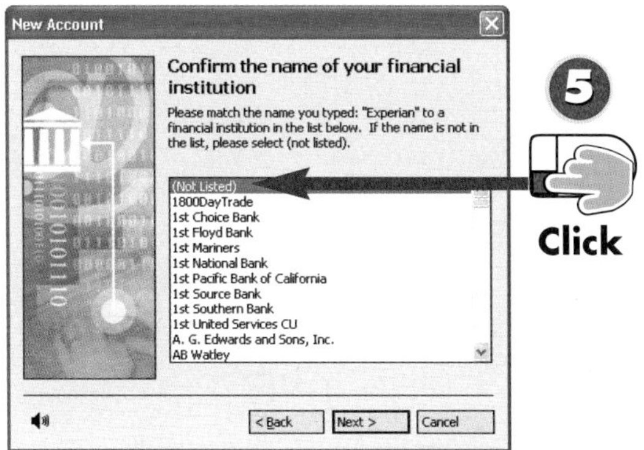

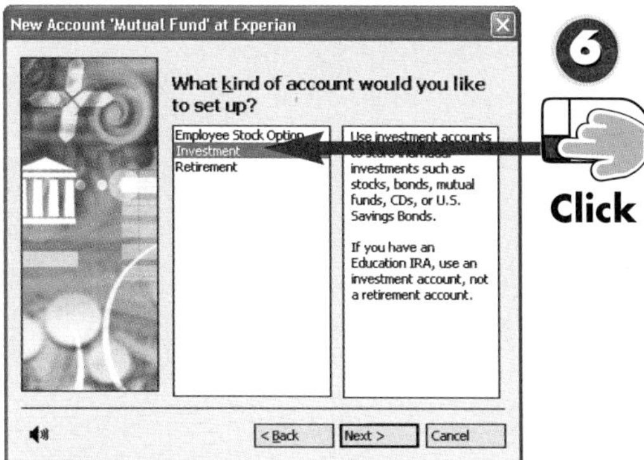

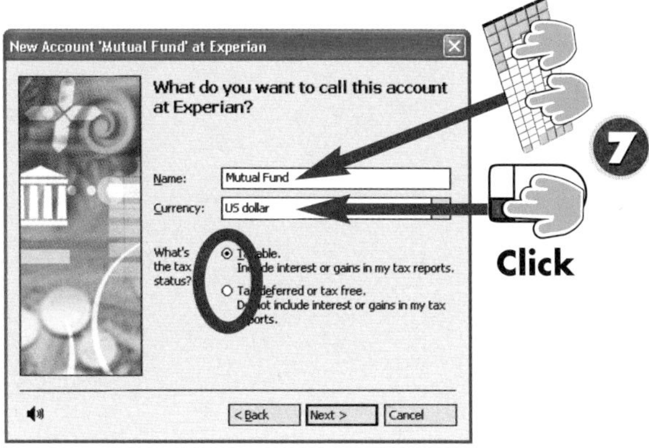

5 If you specified that the account is held at a financial institution, confirm the name of that financial institution by clicking it, and click **Next**.

6 In the left pane, click the type of investment account you are setting up (a brief explanation of the investment account appears in the right pane). Then click **Next**.

7 Type any name you want for the account in the **Name** box, click the **Currency** down arrow to select the currency type, and select the tax status. Then click **Next**.

See next page

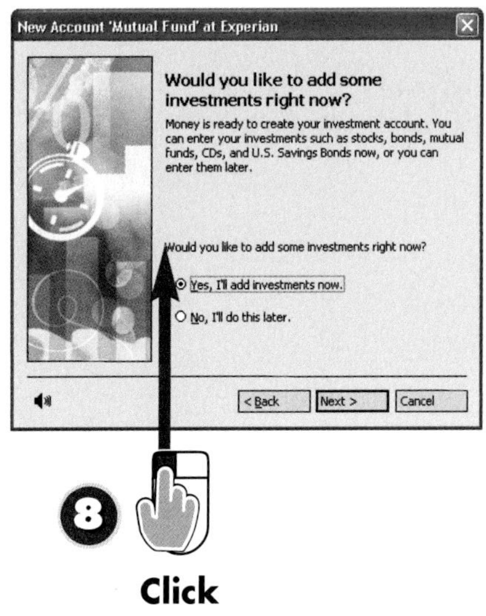

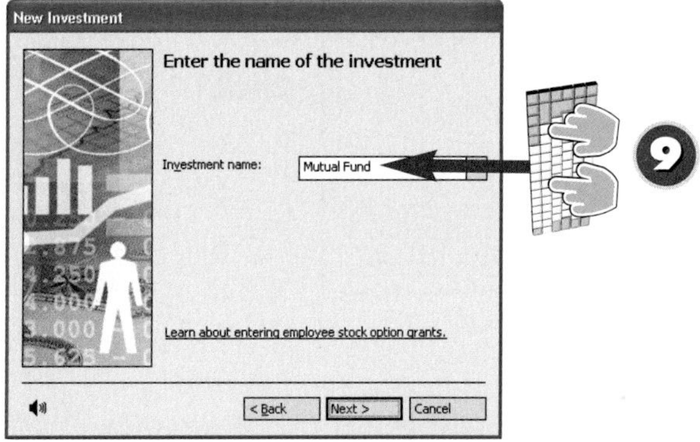

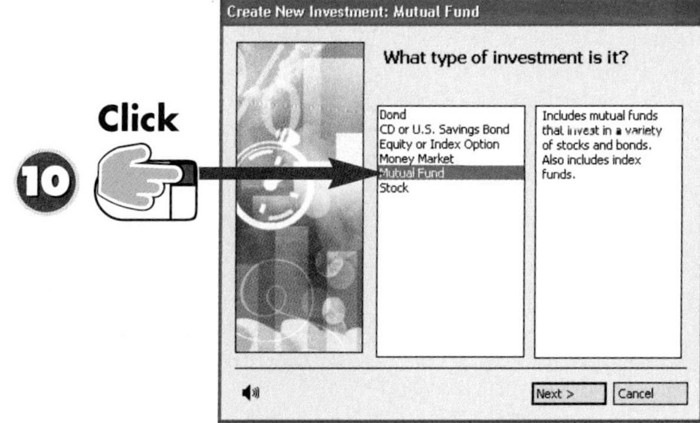

8 To add the investments for the new account now, click **Yes**, and then click **Next**. To enter the investments later, click **No** to finish the wizard.

9 If you selected **Yes** in step 8, type an identifiable name (here, **Mutual Fund**) for the investment in the **Investment name** box, and click **Next**.

10 In the left pane, select the type of investment you want to add (a brief explanation of the investment type appears in the right pane), and click **Next**.

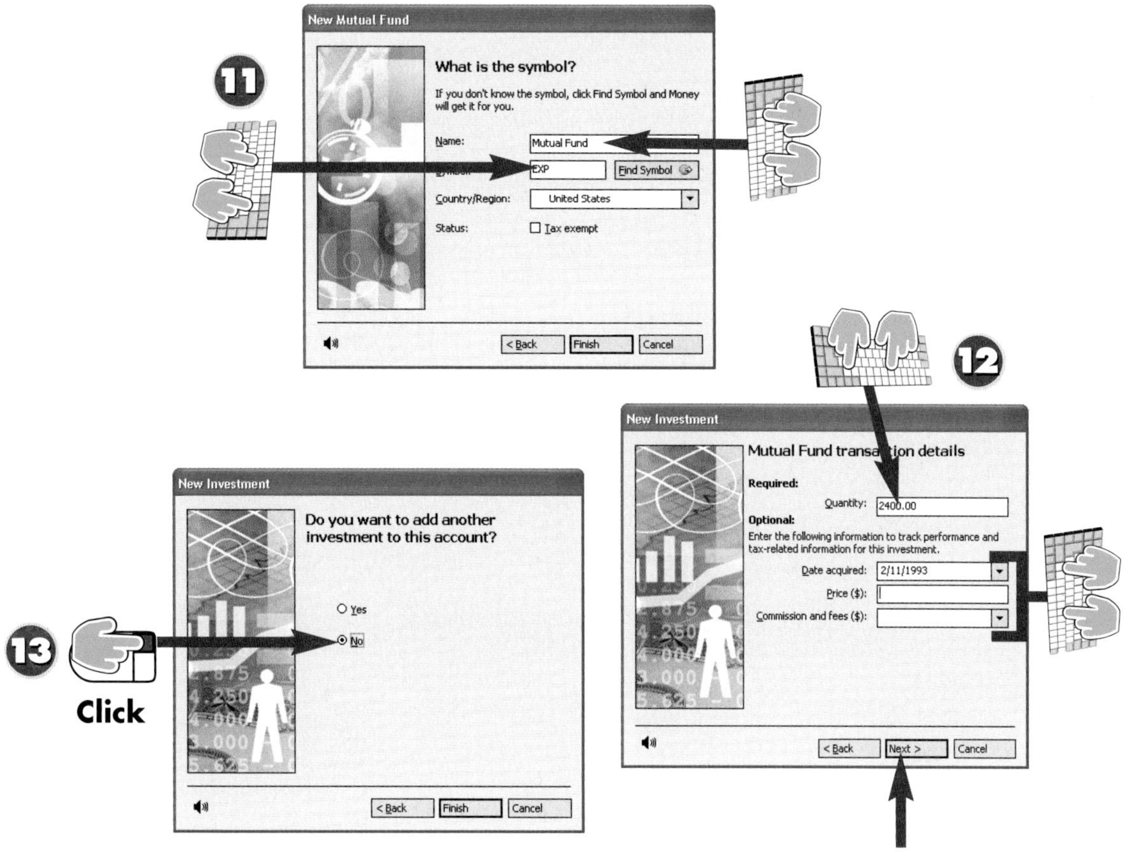

11 Specify a name for the new investment account, its stock symbol, and whether the investment is tax exempt by clicking the **Tax exempt** check box. Then click **Finish**.

12 Enter the quantity of shares or the investment's value (depending on the investment type), the date you acquired it, the price, and any fees paid. Then click **Next**.

13 To add another investment, click **Yes**, and repeat steps 2–11. If you are finished adding investments, click **No**, and then click **Finish**.

TIP

Finding the Symbol
If you don't know the stock symbol for the investment, click the **Find Symbol** button to search for it. You must be connected to the Internet to perform the search.

Updating Investment Prices

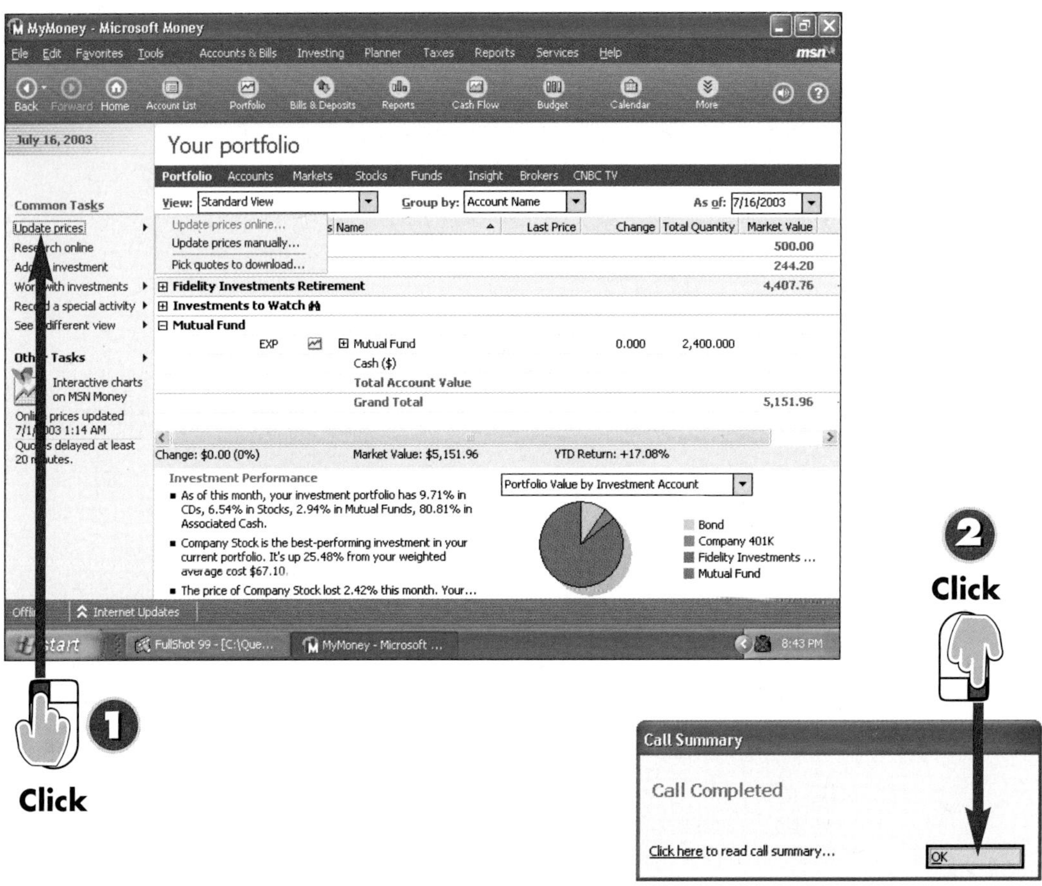

1. Click **Update prices** and select **Update prices online** to download and update all prices. (Money will display various messages to show the progress.)

2. When the download is complete, click **OK**.

End

INTRODUCTION

To make sure Money calculates the latest prices for your investments, you should update the quotes periodically. Note, however, that there is a 20-minute delay in the update process; that is, the quote you receive will be 20 minutes old. You must be connected to the Internet to perform this procedure.

HINT

Update Options
There are two other update options you can experiment with: **Update prices manually** downloads the prices and allows you to enter them yourself; **Pick quotes to download** lets you pick and choose quotes to download.

Finding Investment and Financial News

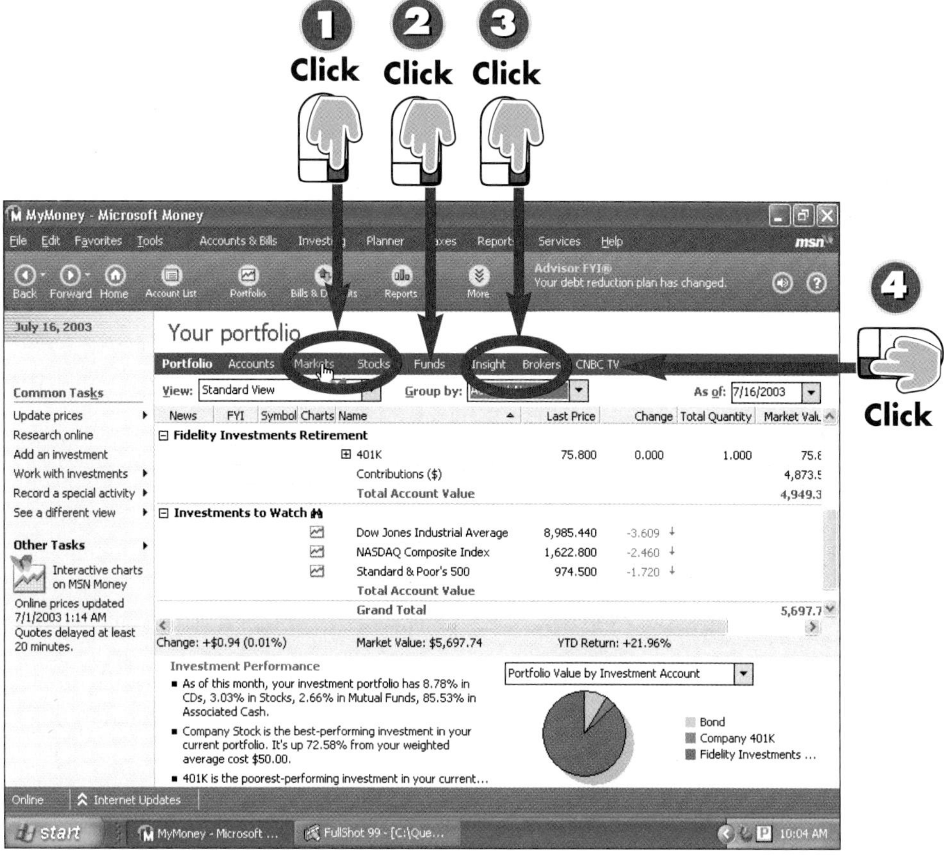

1. Click on the **Markets** or **Stocks** link to find information about general market conditions or individual stocks.

2. Click on the **Funds** link to gather information on mutual funds.

3. Click on the **Insight** link for investment strategies and information; click on the **Brokers** link to find someone to create a strategy for you.

4. Click on the **CNBC TV** link to get up-to-the-minute news on investments and stocks.

INTRODUCTION

In case you want to learn more about investing, explore strategies, check on stock or market trends, or find a broker to help you, you'll find links to all of this information and more in your portfolio. Be sure you are connected to the Internet before trying any of the links.

PART 9

Analyzing Your Finances

Money offers several ways to analyze every aspect of your finances in the past, the present, and the future by using reports. By now, you've entered almost all the financial information necessary to take advantage of the many reports available in the Reports Gallery. You can view reports, customize them, and even create a favorites list so that you can quickly access the reports you find most useful. You can also print reports to maintain for your own records. Using reports is yet another way to take hold of your spending habits, future goals, and a great deal more.

The Reports Gallery

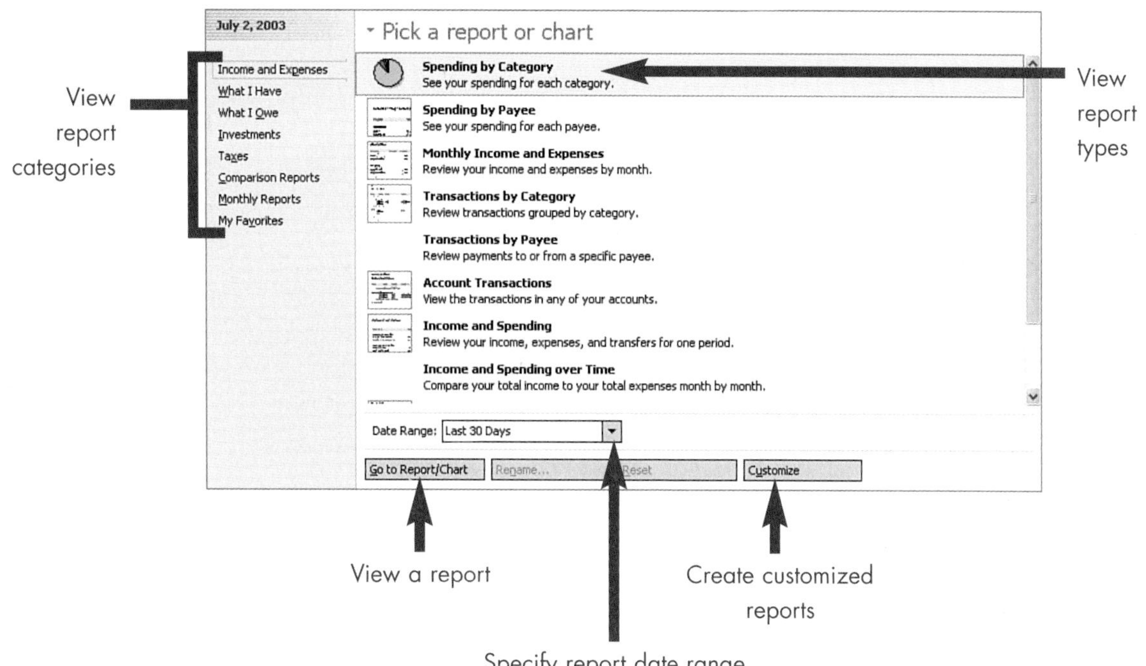

Viewing Reports

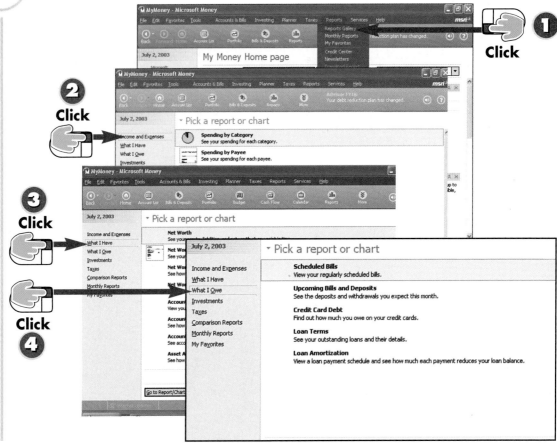

1. To access the Reports Gallery, open the **Reports** menu and choose **Reports Gallery**.
2. Click the **Income and Expenses** link to see what reports are available for analyzing how your income stacks up to your expenses.
3. Click the **What I Have** link to see a list of reports designed to help you determine what money you have, where it's located, where it has been, and where it's going.
4. Click the **What I Owe** link to see a list of reports designed to help you keep track of who you owe, how much you owe, and loan details.

INTRODUCTION

There are many different types of reports, and many ways you can use them. In this task, you'll learn the basics of using reports; then, you can spend as much time as you like looking through them on your own. Money's reports are categorized by subject, with each category offering several reports from which to choose.

5 Click

July 2, 2003

Income and Expenses
What I Have
What I Owe
Investments
Taxes
Comparison Reports
Monthly Reports
My Favorites

Pick a report or chart

Portfolio Value by Investment Account
See your current investment holdings and any unrealized capital gains and losses.

Portfolio Value by Investment Type
See how your investments are allocated between stocks, mutual funds, cash, and other investments.

Performance by Investment Account
See your investments by brokerage or other account and compare the annual rates of return.

Performance by Investment Type
See your investments by investment type, such as stocks or bonds, and compare the annual rates of return.

6 Click

July 2, 2003

Pick a report or chart

Tax-Related Transactions
View transactions that may affect your income taxes.

Capital Gains
See your capital gain or loss from investment sales in non-retirement accounts.

Loan Interest
See your total interest expense on a loan for each year.

Tax Software Report
See your tax-related information that you can export to a tax preparation program or print and enter by hand.

7 Click

July 2, 2003

Pick a report or chart

Spending by Category Comparison
Compare what you spend by category in two different time periods.

Spending by Payee Comparison
Compare what you spend by payee in two different time periods.

Income and Spending Comparison
Compare your overall financial situation during two different time periods.

Click 8

July 2, 2003

Pick a report or chart

Report for July, 2003 (in progress)
Report for June, 2003
Report for May, 2003
Report for April, 2003
Report for March, 2003
Report for February, 2003
Report for January, 2003
Report for December, 2002
Report for November, 2002
Report for October, 2002
Report for September, 2002
Report for August, 2002
Report for July, 2002
Report for June, 2002
Report for May, 2002
Report for April, 2002
Report for March, 2002
Report for February, 2002
Report for January, 2002
Report for December, 2001

Go to Report/Chart | Rename... | Reset | Customize

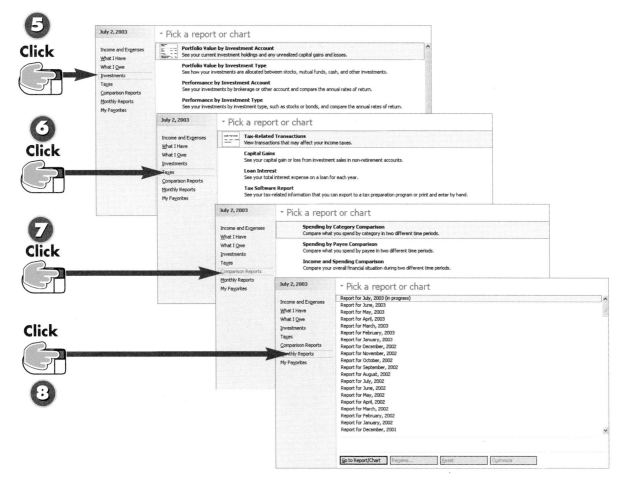

5 Click the **Investments** link to view a list of reports that let you analyze your investments' current status and their outlook for the future.

6 Click the **Taxes** link to see what types of reports are available for analyzing tax-related transactions and other information.

7 Click the **Comparison Reports** link to see a list of reports that let you view and compare your spending and income for specific time periods.

8 Click the **Monthly Reports** link to see reports for analyzing your overall financial situation.

9 Click the **My Favorites** link to see a list of your favorite and most-used reports. (If you have not yet set up any favorite reports, this screen will be blank.)

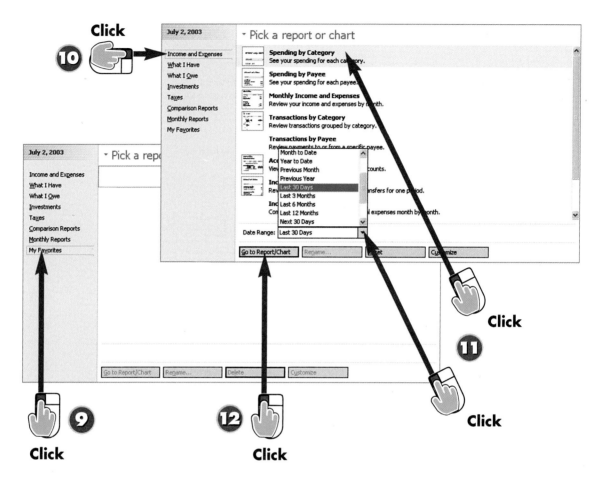

10 To view a report, click a report category that interests you (in this example, **Income and Expenses**).

11 Click the report that you would like to view (here, **Spending by Category**). If necessary, click the **Date Range** arrow and select the time the report should include.

12 Click **Go to Report/Chart**.

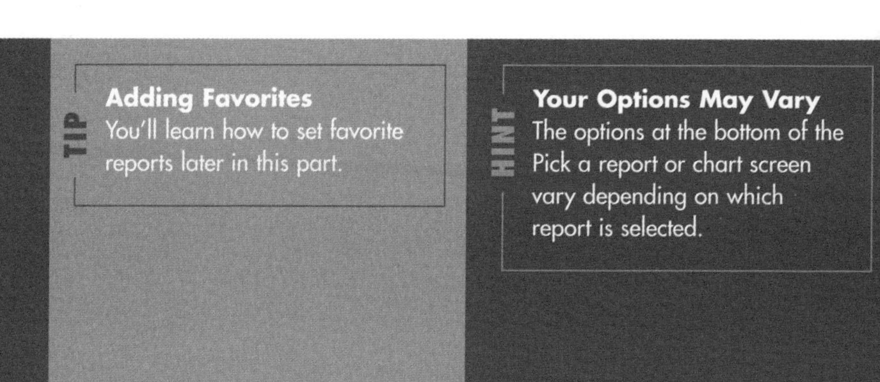

TIP

Adding Favorites

You'll learn how to set favorite reports later in this part.

HINT

Your Options May Vary

The options at the bottom of the Pick a report or chart screen vary depending on which report is selected.

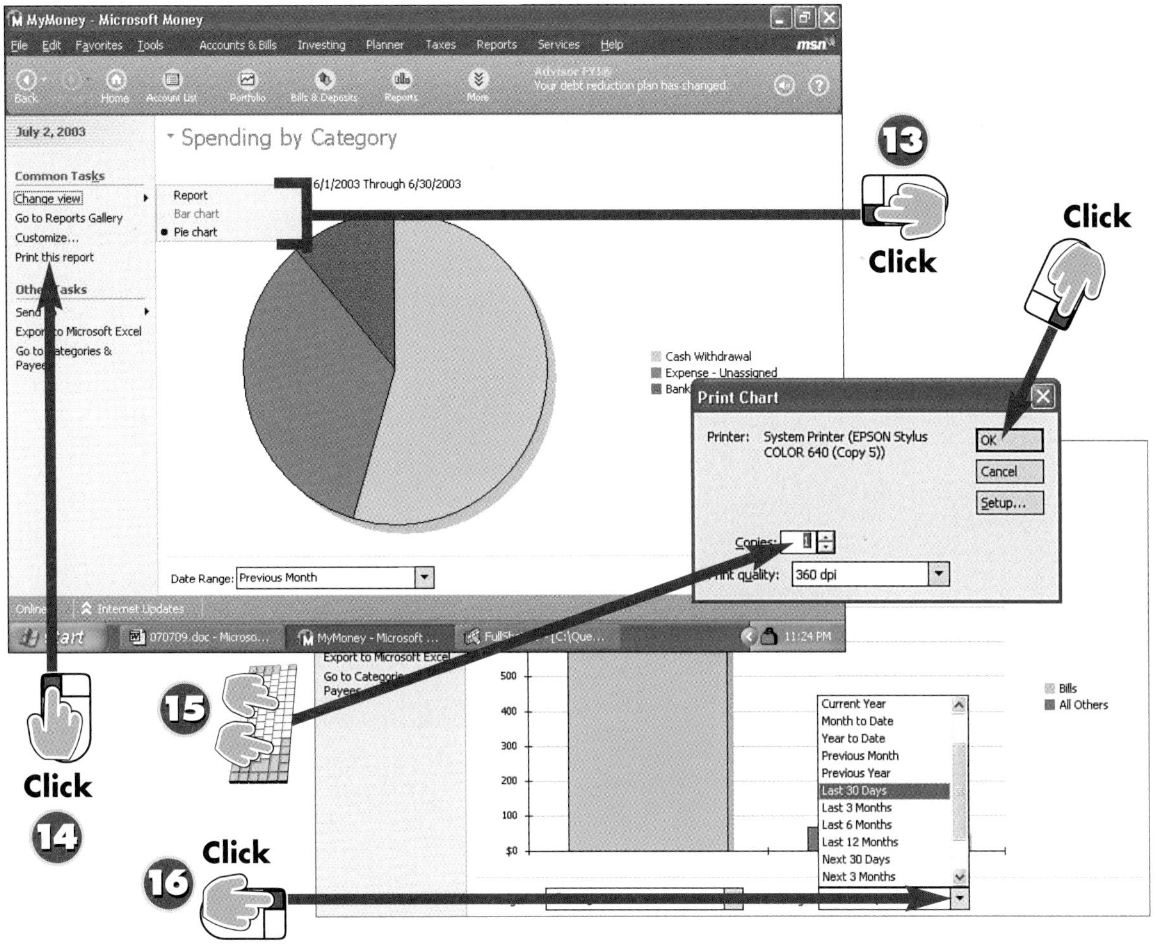

13 To change the layout of the report click the **Change view** link in the Common Tasks area and select **Report**, **Bar chart**, or **Pie chart**, depending on your needs.

14 To print the report, click the **Print this report** link.

15 A Print dialog box (here, Print Chart) opens. Specify how many copies of the report you want to print and click **OK**.

16 To change the range of dates featured in the open report, click the **Date Range** down arrow and choose a new range from the list that appears.

HINT

Export Options
Other options for reports include exporting them to an Excel file using the **Export to Microsoft Excel** option. You can also use the **Send to** options to send the report via email as a file attachment or to send the report to your desktop, enabling you to quickly access the report by double-clicking its desktop icon.

TIP

Returning to the Reports Gallery
Use the **Back** button or the **Reports** button on the Money toolbar to return to the Reports Gallery to view more reports.

Customizing Reports

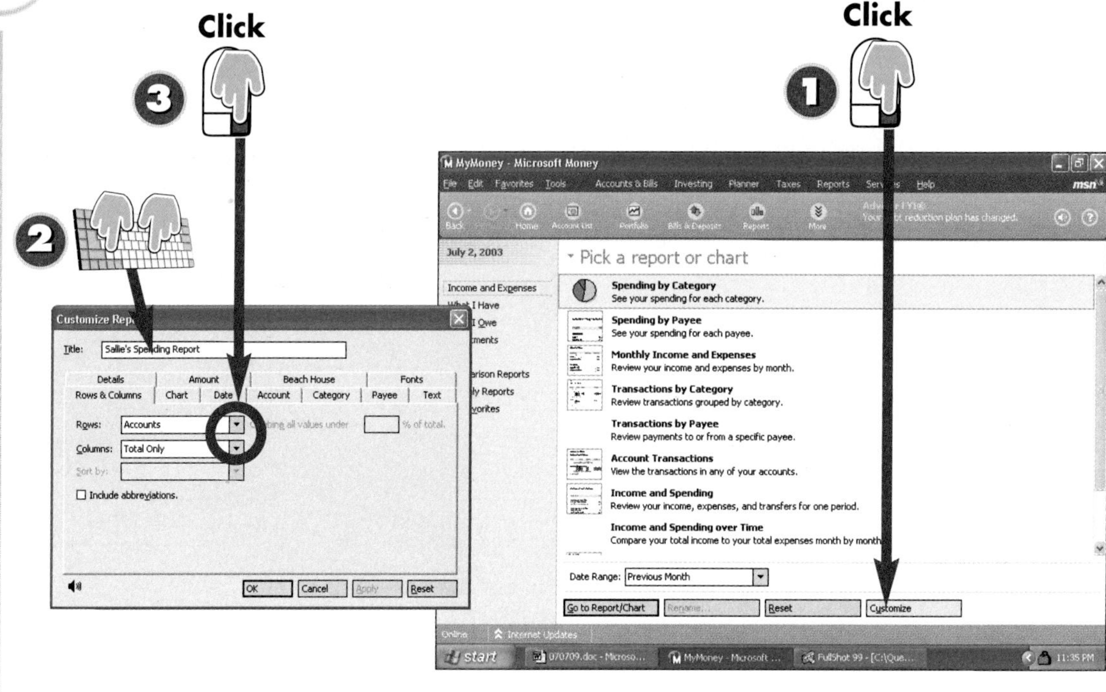

1. Click the appropriate report category (here, **Income and Expenses**) and the report you want to customize (here, **Spending by Category**). Click **Customize**.
2. In the Customize Report dialog box's **Title** field, type a name for your report.
3. Click the **Rows** and **Columns** down arrow and select what you want to appear in the report's rows and columns.

INTRODUCTION

You can customize reports to meet your unique financial reporting needs. For example, you can customize the Spending by Category report to analyze and, if necessary, change how much you spend for the categories you choose and for a given timeframe, as covered in this task. (Be aware that the options available vary depending on what type of report you are customizing.)

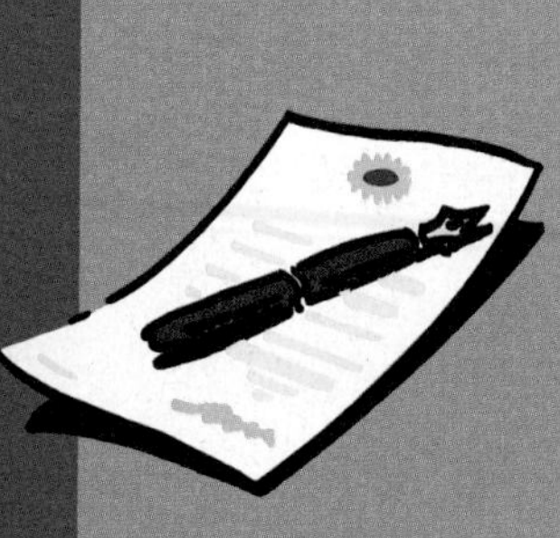

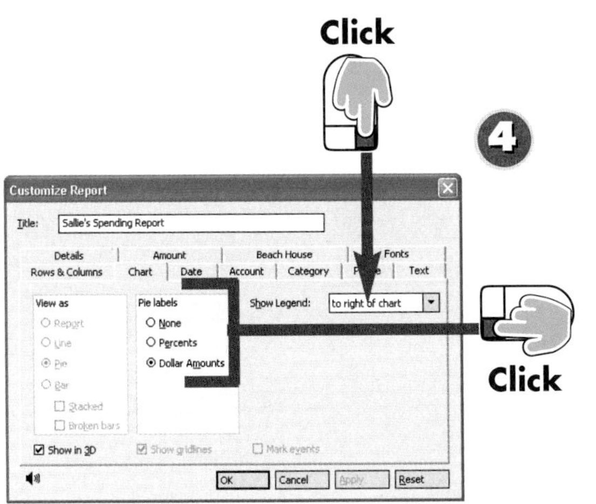

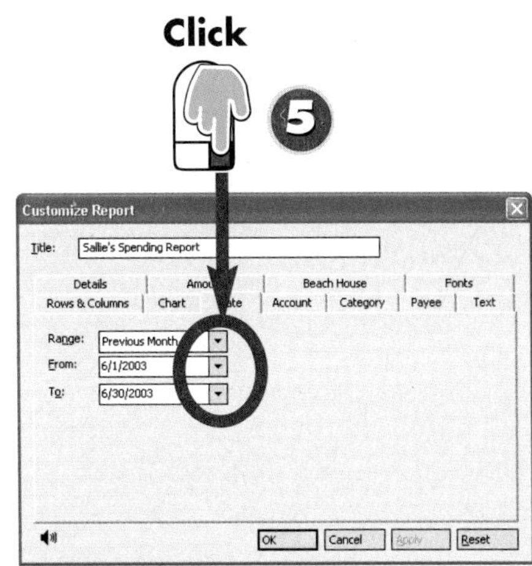

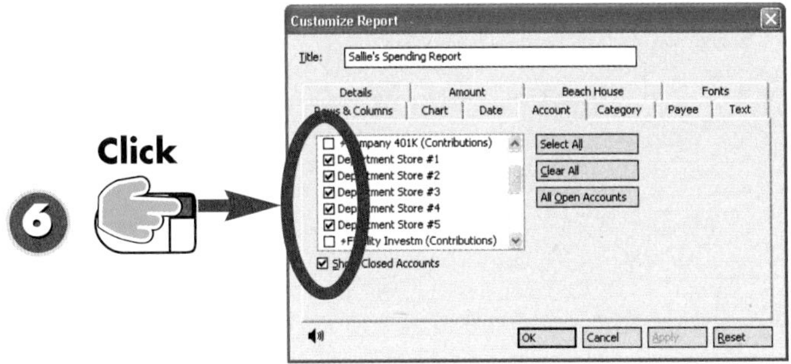

4. Click the **Chart** tab, and choose the desired option in the **Pie labels** area. Then, click **Show Legend** and choose where you want the legend to appear.
5. Click the **Date** tab, and then use the **Range**, **From**, and **To** drop-down lists to select the date range you want the report to include.
6. Click the **Account** tab and uncheck any accounts you do not want to include in your report.

See next page

TIP

Choosing Accounts
To include all available accounts in your report, click **Select All** in the Account tab (see step 6). To clear all the check boxes in the Account tab, click **Clear All**. If you want to see only open accounts, click **All Open Accounts**.

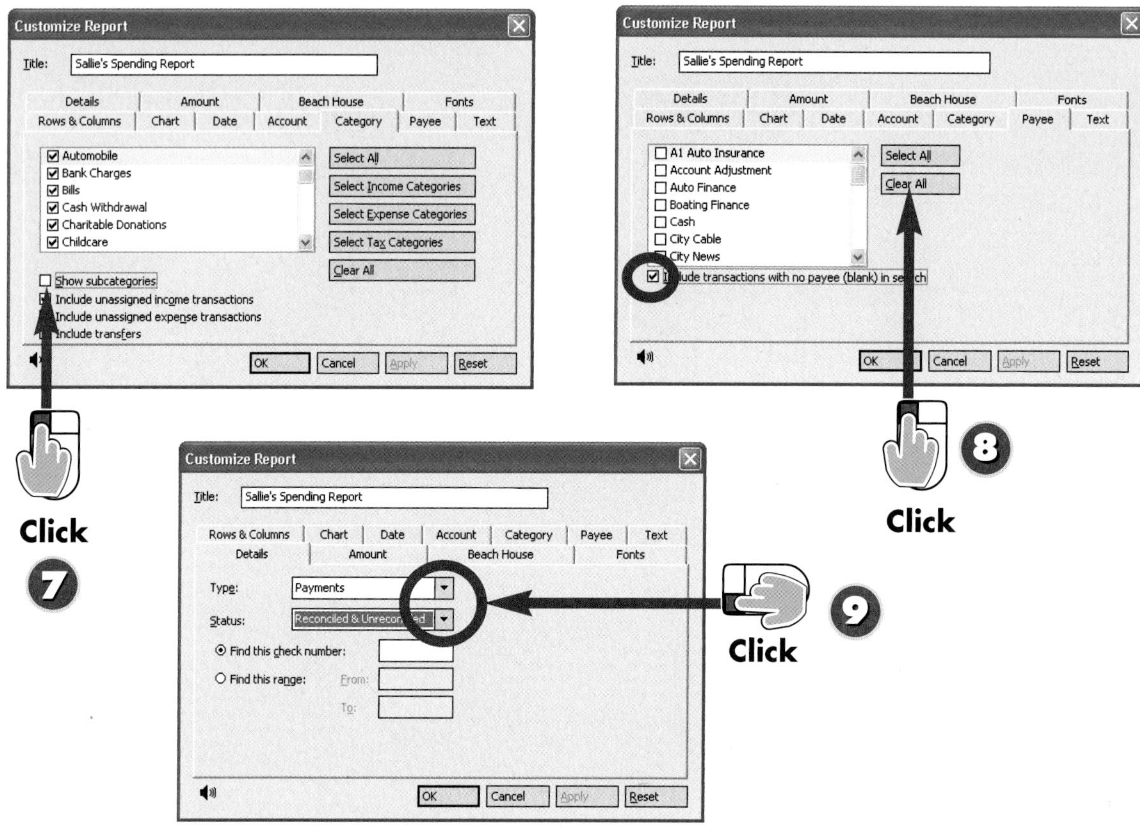

7. Click the **Category** tab. To customize your report to omit any subcategories, click the **Show subcategories** check box to uncheck it.

8. Click the **Payee** tab. Click **Clear All**, and mark the **Include transactions with no payee (blank) in search** check box.

9. Click the **Details** tab. Then, choose **Payments** from the **Type** drop-down list and **Reconciled & Unreconciled** from the **Status** drop-down list.

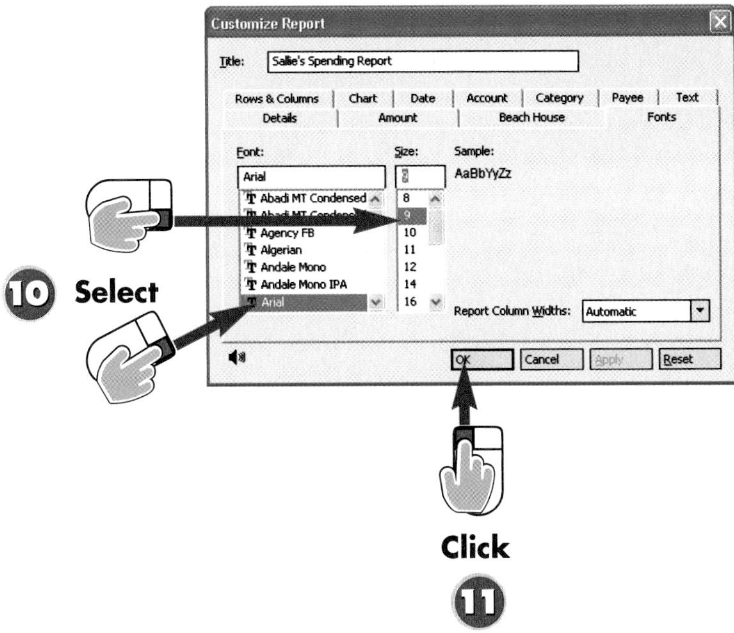

10 Click the **Fonts** tab, and use the **Font** and **Size** lists to select a font and font size.

11 Click **OK**.

12 To make additional changes to this report, repeat steps 1–11.

HINT

Using the Text and Amount Tabs

Use the Text tab in the Customize Report dialog box to include in your report only those transactions containing the text that you specify. For only a dollar amount or range, use the Amount tab.

TIP

Using the Text and Amount Tabs

Use the Text tab in the Customize Report dialog box to include in your report only those transactions containing the text that you specify. To create a report that includes only transactions of a specific dollar amount or range, use the Amount tab.

Creating a Favorite Reports List

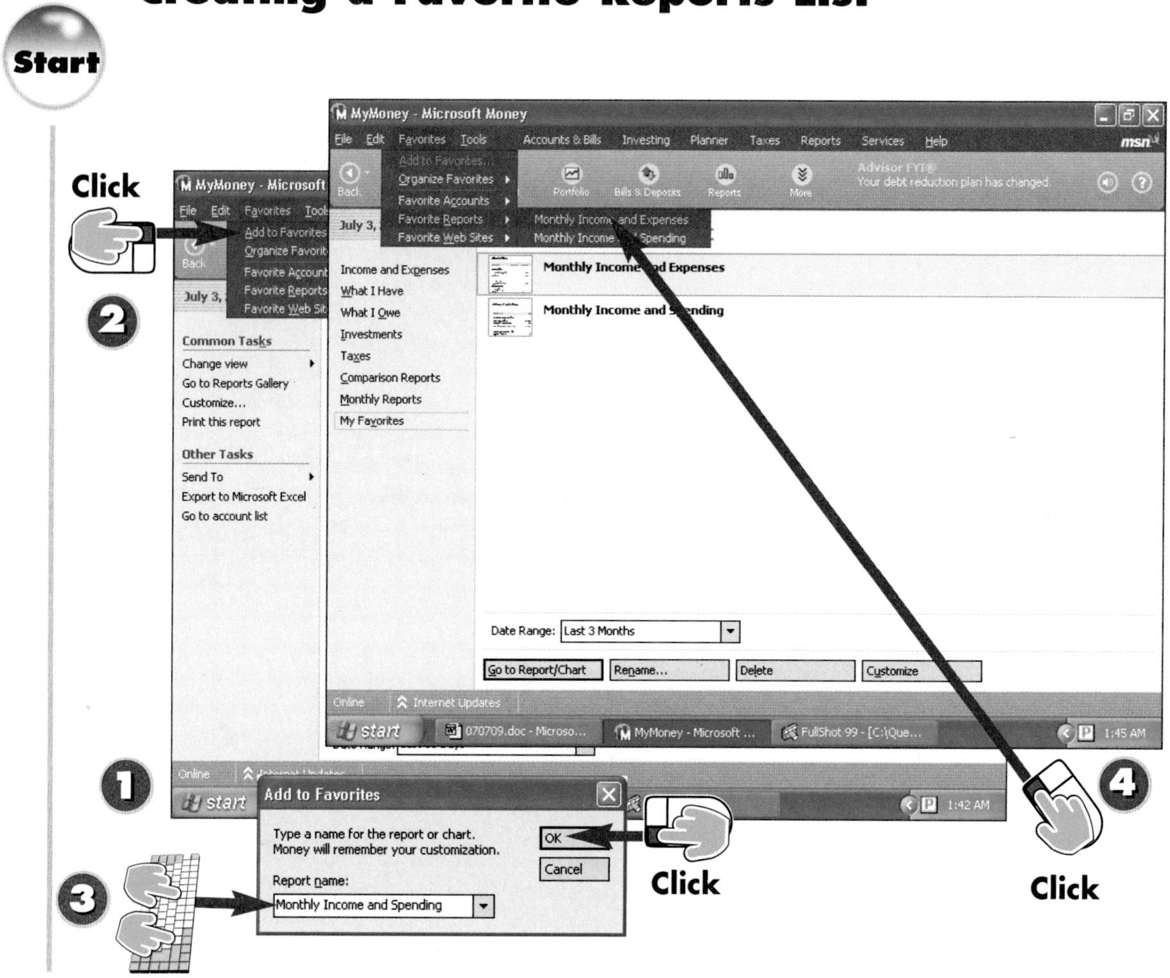

1. View or create the report you want to save as a favorite (see the preceding tasks in this part for details on how to view or create a report).
2. Open the **Favorites** menu and choose **Add to Favorites**.
3. Type a name for the report in the **Report name** box (or click the **Report name** down arrow and choose a name from the list), and then click **OK**.
4. To access the report, open the **Favorites** menu, choose **Favorite Reports**, and select the report's name from the submenu that appears.

INTRODUCTION

After you view a report or create a customized one, you can save it in your favorite reports list. It's a good idea to do so if you know that you will use the report again and as it is set up; that way, you won't have to search for it or create it all over again.

TIP

Accessing Your Favorites

Another way to access your favorite reports is by clicking the **My Favorites** link in the Report Gallery.

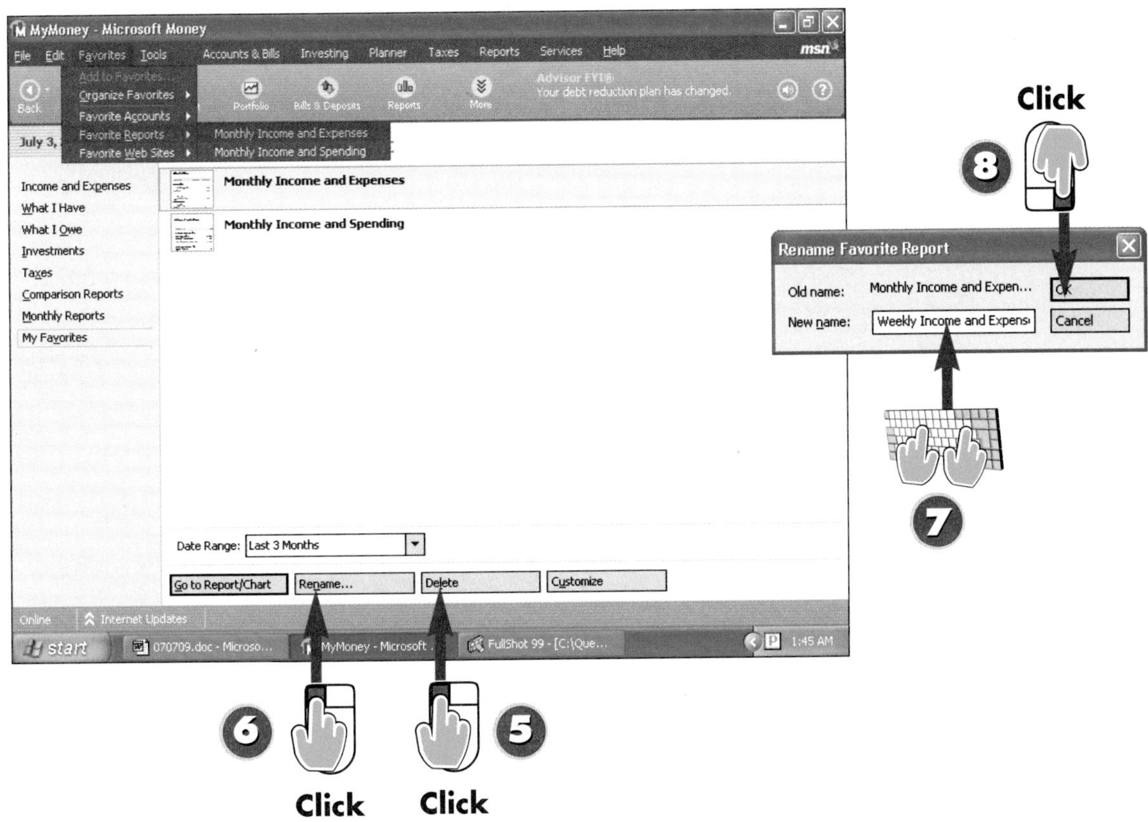

5. To remove a report from your favorites—and from Money—click the report in the favorites list, and click **Delete**.
6. To change the name of a report, click the report in the favorites list, and click **Rename**. The Rename Favorite Report dialog box opens.
7. Type a new name for the report in the **New name** box.
8. Click **OK**.

PART 10

Managing Your Taxes

While you are still thinking about investments and saving money, let's take a look at your taxes and where you can save some money with deductions. If you enter all your tax information into Money, it will help you find deductions you can take, estimate capital gains and/or potential losses, and show you what the most recent tax rates are. Money keeps track of the previous year's taxes as well as those for the current year, and can project what your potential refund or payment might be. This helps you plan your withholding and possibly avoid paying, or make plans for that nice refund. All the information you enter can be used later to export and file your taxes.

My Money and Taxes

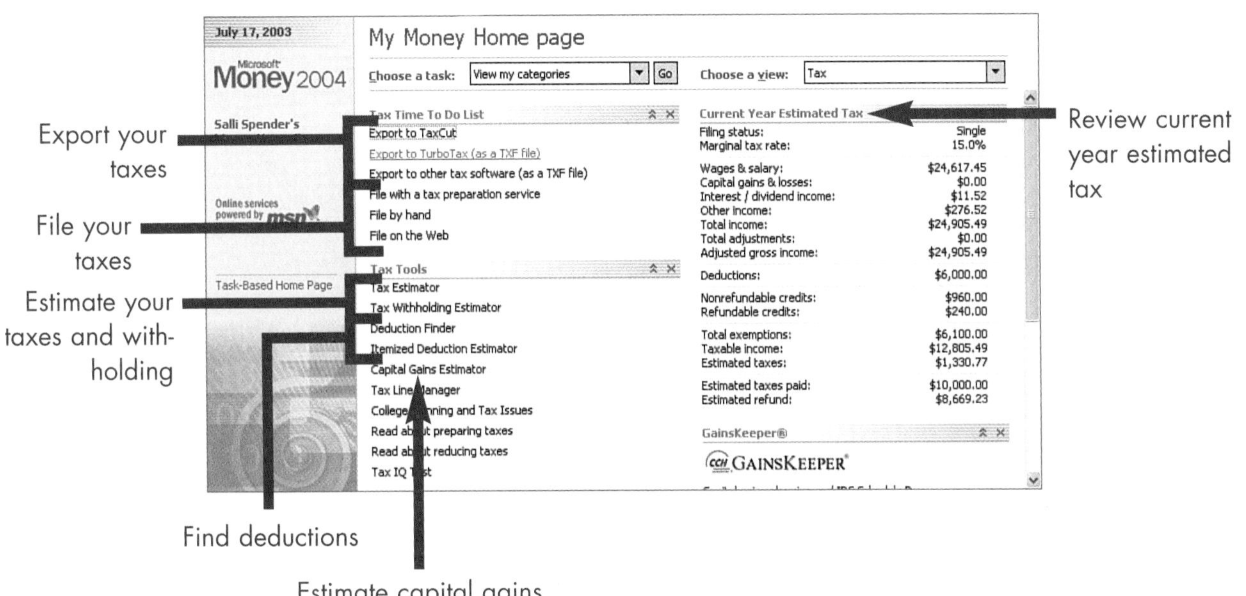

Entering Your Tax Information

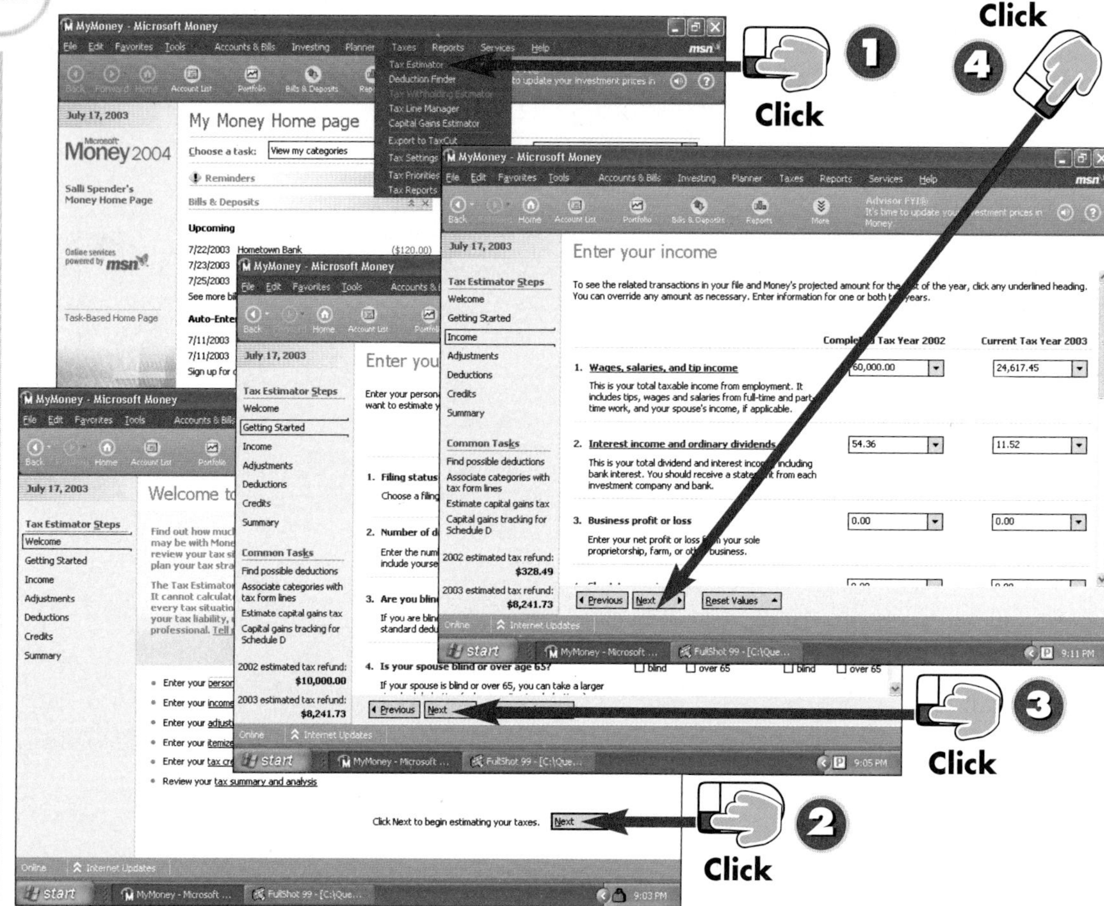

1. Open the **Taxes** menu and choose **Tax Estimator**.
2. Listen to or read the overview and click **Next**.
3. Read through all questions and enter the appropriate answers for both last year and this year, then click **Next**.
4. Enter your income information for last year and this year, then click **Next**.

INTRODUCTION

All the information you've entered thus far can be used for tax purposes (Money even allows you to flag any accounts that are factored into your taxes). There remains, however, some information you need to enter to make your tax information complete. To do so, you will need your previous year's tax information, and any tax information you have for the current year.

TIP

Estimating Income

If you are not certain about your income for this year, estimate as best you can. You can always come back later and change the figures.

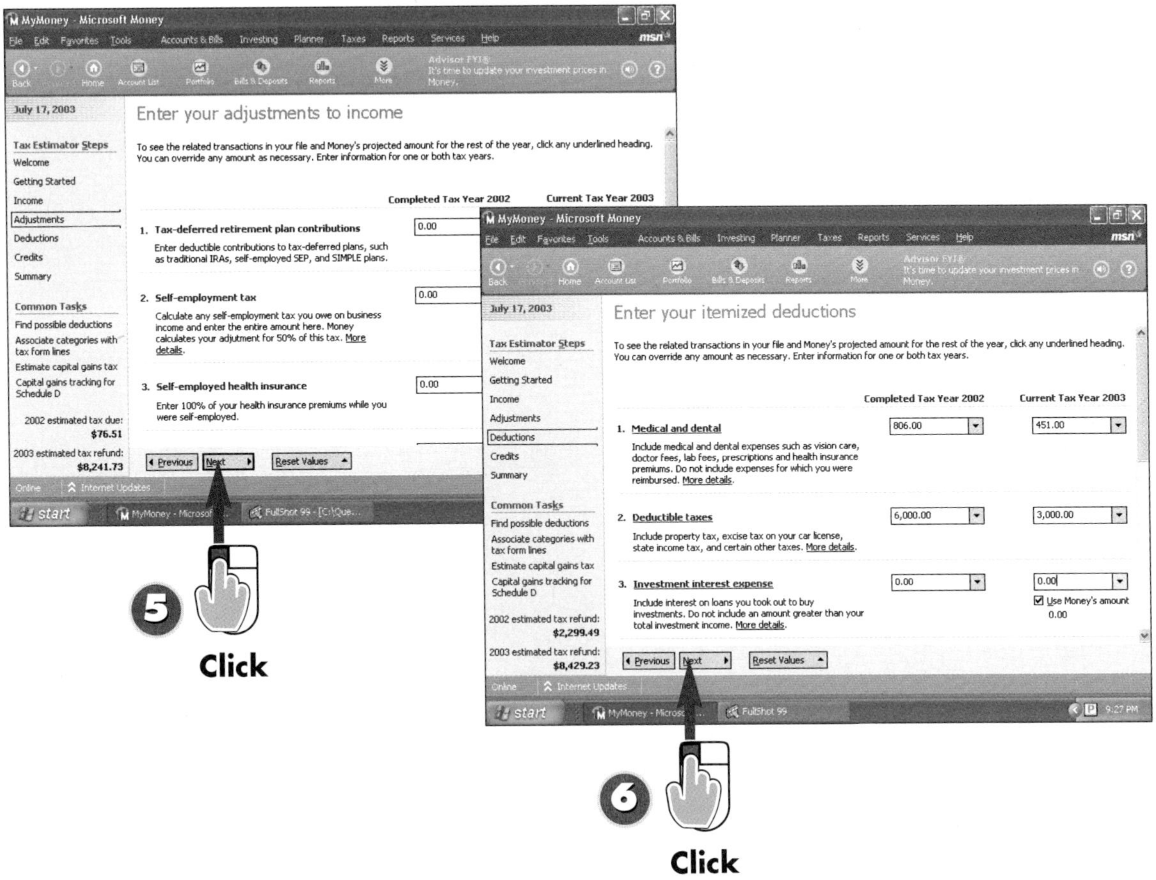

Click

Click

5 Enter any adjustments and click **Next**.

6 Enter your itemized deductions and click **Next**.

See next page

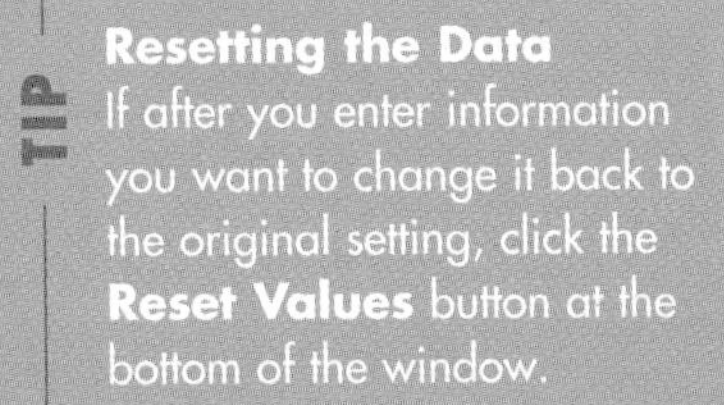

TIP

Resetting the Data
If after you enter information you want to change it back to the original setting, click the **Reset Values** button at the bottom of the window.

HINT

Changing Information
To go back and review or change information you already entered, click **Previous**, make your changes, and then click **Next** until you return to where you left off.

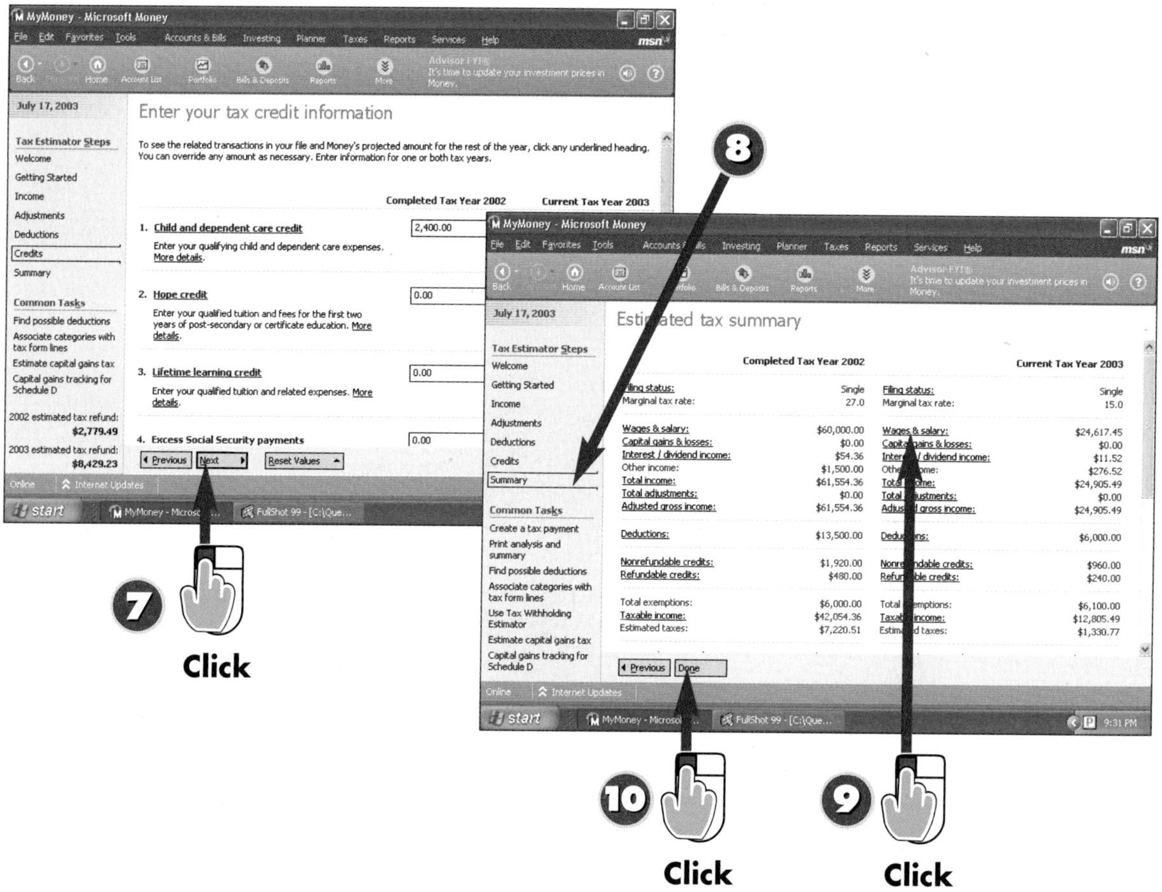

7. Enter your credits and click **Next**.
8. Review your tax summary. Scroll down if needed to see all information.
9. To revise specific tax information, click on a link and make your changes.
10. Click **Done** when you are finished.

Reviewing Possible Tax Deductions

Click 1

Click 2

Click 3

Click 4

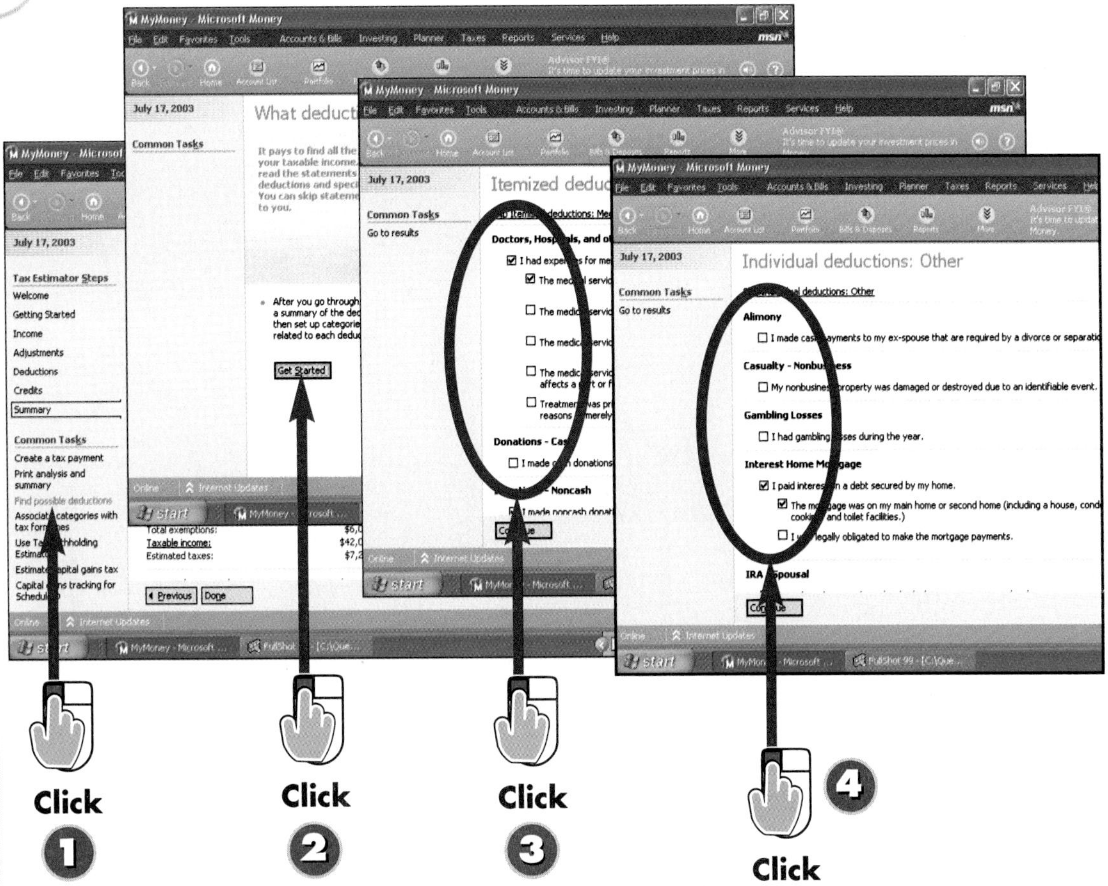

1. Click the **Find possible deductions** link on the left side of the screen.
2. Listen to or read the overview and click **Get Started**.
3. Select applicable itemized deductions by clicking each check box that applies. Then click **Continue**.
4. Select applicable individual deductions by clicking each check box that applies. Then click **Continue**.

See next page

INTRODUCTION

Money can help you find tax deductions based on the information you've entered thus far and the information you provide in this task.

HINT

Expanding Options

When you make selections, an option may expand into more options. Be sure to read them all and select only the ones that apply.

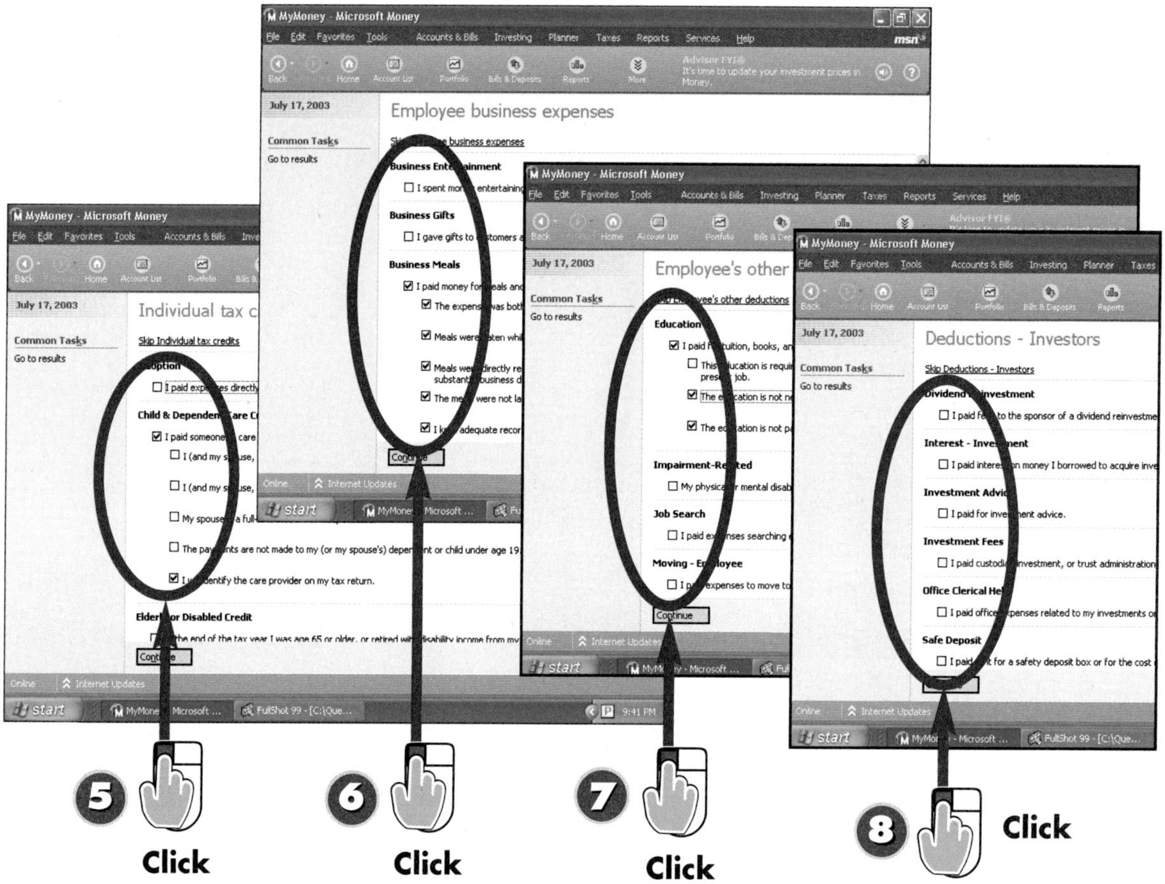

5 Click

6 Click

7 Click

8 Click

5 Select credits by clicking each check box that applies. Then click **Continue**.

6 Using the check boxes, select employee business expenses, if applicable, and click **Continue**.

7 Using the check boxes, select employee deductions, if applicable, and click **Continue**.

8 Using the check boxes, select any investor-related deductions and click **Continue**.

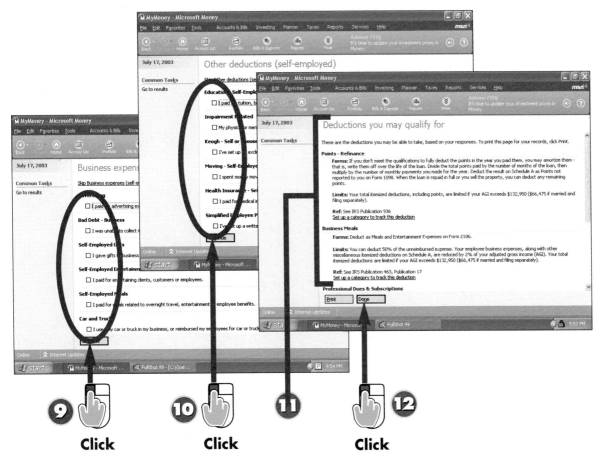

9. If you are self-employed, click the check boxes next to any self-employment deductions that apply and click **Continue**.

10. If you are self-employed, click the check boxes next to any other applicable deductions and click **Continue**.

11. Review the deductions you may qualify for, links to additional information, and advice at the bottom of the page. Scroll down if needed to see all the information.

12. Click **Done**.

End

TIP

Printing the Summary

To print the summary for your reference, click the **Print** button at the bottom of the page.

Reviewing or Estimating Capital Gains

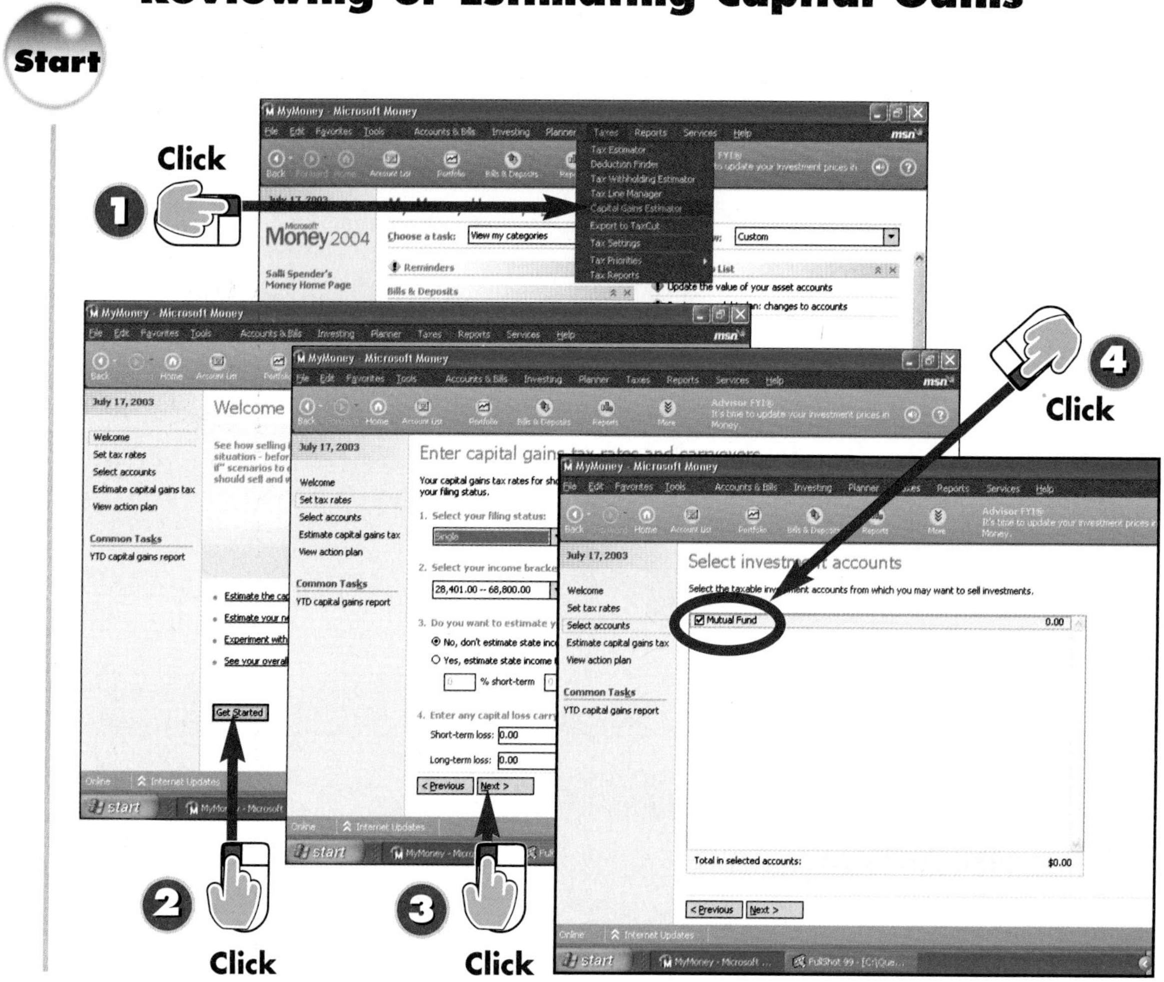

Click

Click

Click

Click

1. Open the **Taxes** menu and choose **Capital Gains Estimator**.
2. Listen to or read the overview and click **Get Started**.
3. Answer the questions about your filing status, tax filing, and enter any requested capital gain/loss information. Then click **Next**.
4. Click the check box next to the investment(s) you are considering selling and click **Next**.

INTRODUCTION

Another area that might help you with your taxes is capital gains or losses. By entering information on investments you are thinking of selling, Money can determine whether the sale would be advantageous and what tax liability you might have.

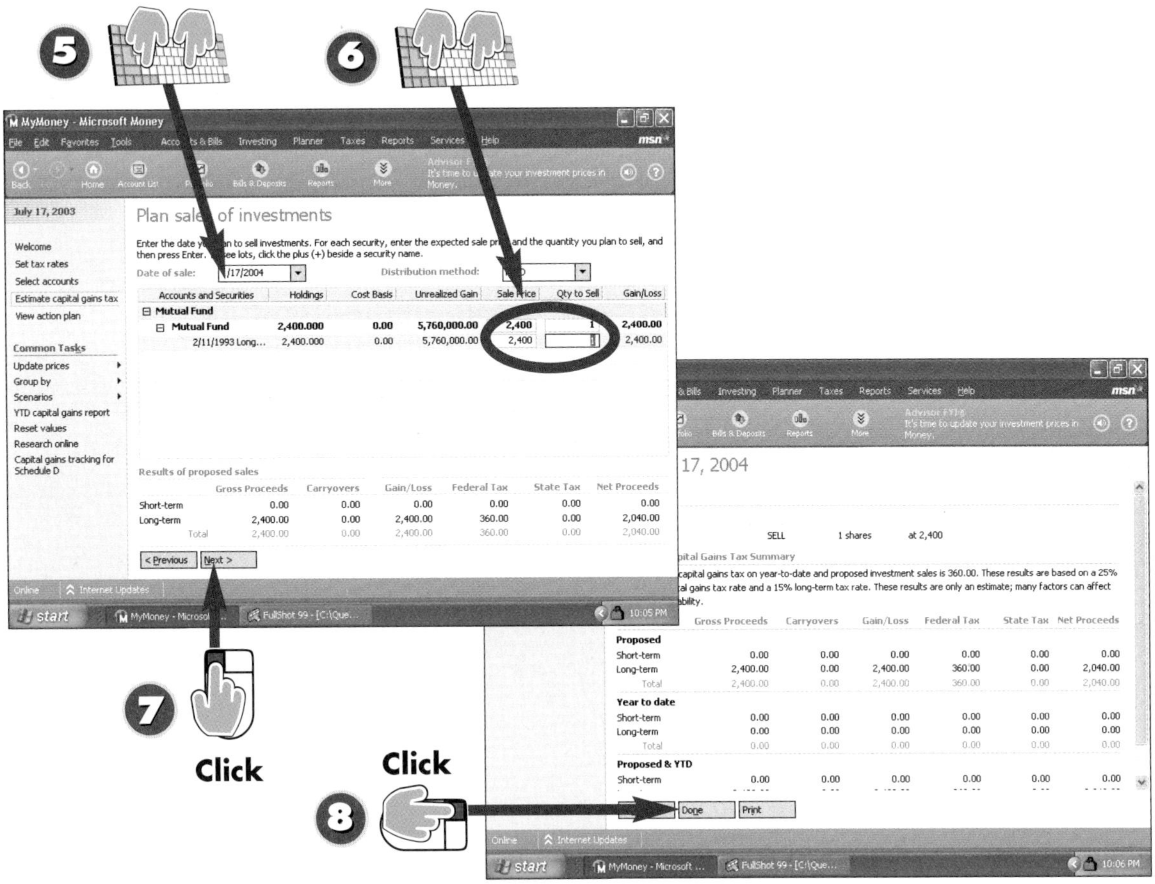

Click

Click

1. In the **Date of sale** field, type the date on which you are thinking of selling the investment(s).
2. Click the plus sign (**+**) to expand the investment information, and then type the sale price and quantity in the **Sale Price** and **Qty to Sell** boxes.
3. When you are satisfied with your selections, click **Next**.
4. Review your summary, click **Print** to print it for your reference, and click **Done** when you are finished.

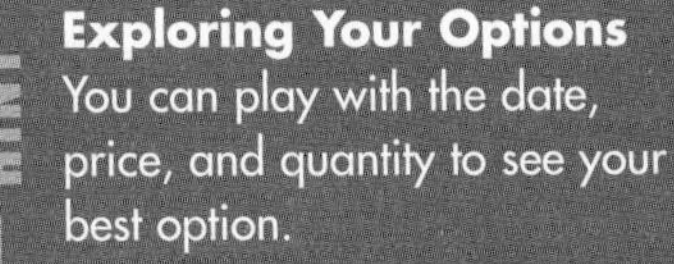

HINT

Exploring Your Options
You can play with the date, price, and quantity to see your best option.

TIP

Changing the Distribution Method
To change the distribution method, click the **Distribution method** down arrow in the window shown for steps 5–7 and make another selection.

HINT

Getting the Latest Prices
To get the latest prices, click the **Update prices** link in the Common Tasks area of the Plan sales investments window and select how you want to download them. Be sure you are connected to the Internet.

Start

Reviewing Your Filing Status and Tax Rates

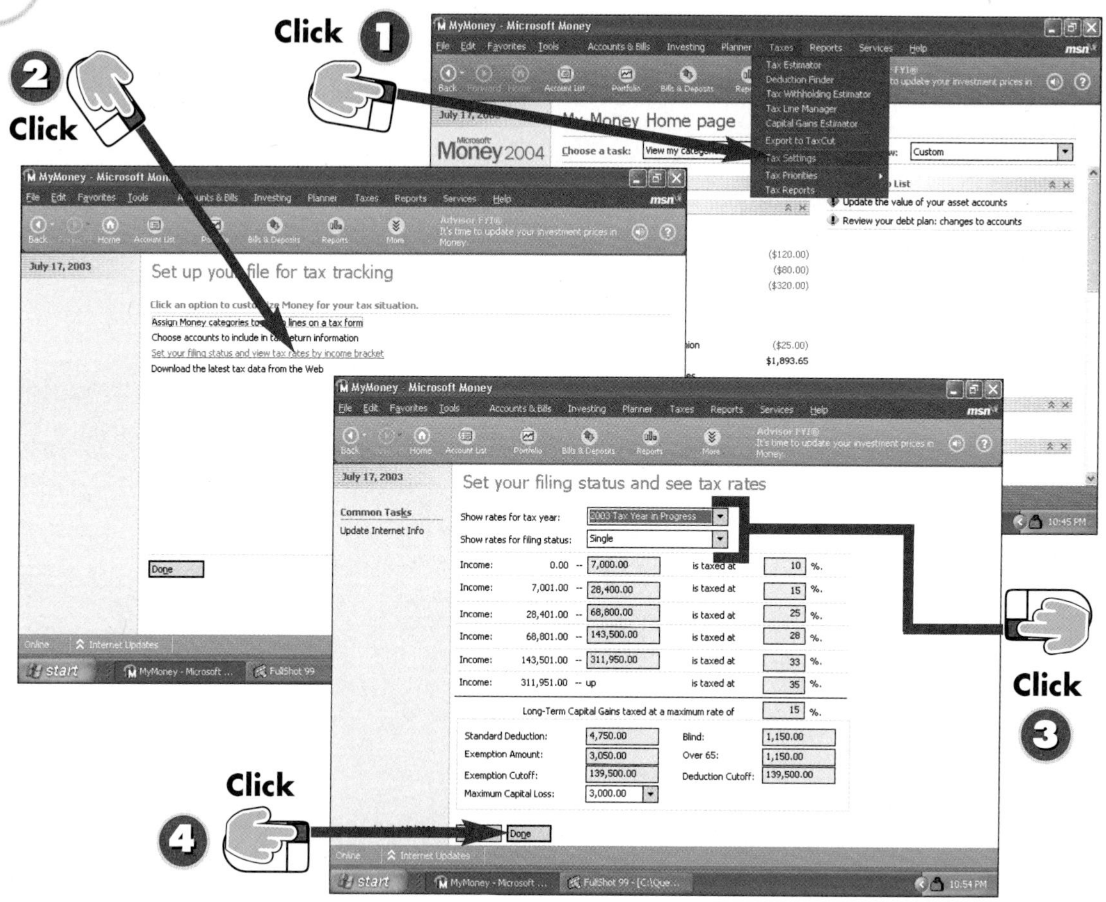

1. Open the **Taxes** menu and choose **Tax Settings**.
2. Click the **Set your filing status and view tax rates by income bracket** link.
3. To view rates for a different year, click **Show rates for tax year** and select a new year. For a different status, use the **Show rates for filing status** list.
4. Click **Done**.

INTRODUCTION

If you want to review your filing status or view the latest tax rates for each tax bracket, maximums for deductions and exemptions, and maximum capital gains rates, check out the tax settings. You can also review tax rates and information for other filing statuses.

TIP

Exploring Other Tax Features

To explore other tax features, click **Assign Money categories to match lines on a tax form** on the screen shown in step 2 to view the categories you set up and the ones you can use for your taxes. Click **Choose accounts to include in tax return information** to review and select the accounts you can use for your taxes. Click **Download the latest tax data from the Web** to get the latest tax rates.

Exporting Tax Information

Click

Click

Click

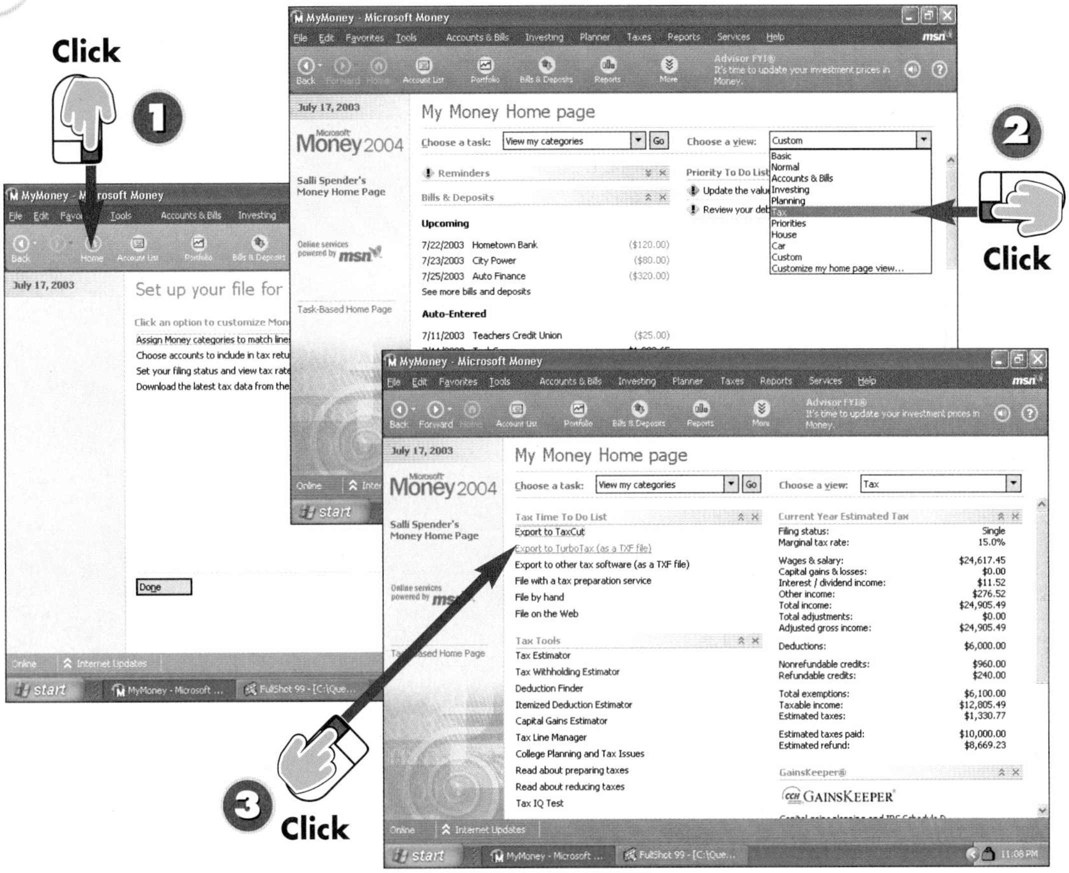

1. Click the **Home** button on the main Money toolbar.

2. Click the **Choose a view** down arrow and select **Tax**.

3. Under **Tax Time To Do List**, click the link that best describes how you want to export your tax information.

See next page

INTRODUCTION

Whether you have someone else do your taxes or you do them yourself by hand or using tax software, you can export all the tax information you've entered into Money to give you head start.

TIP

Obtaining the Latest Rates

To be sure you have the latest rates, connect to the Internet, open the **Tools** menu, click **Internet Updates**, and choose **Update Now**.

HINT

Saving Time

Exporting your tax information from Money saves you time and ensures accuracy because all the information is exported in a file you can use no matter how you file your taxes.

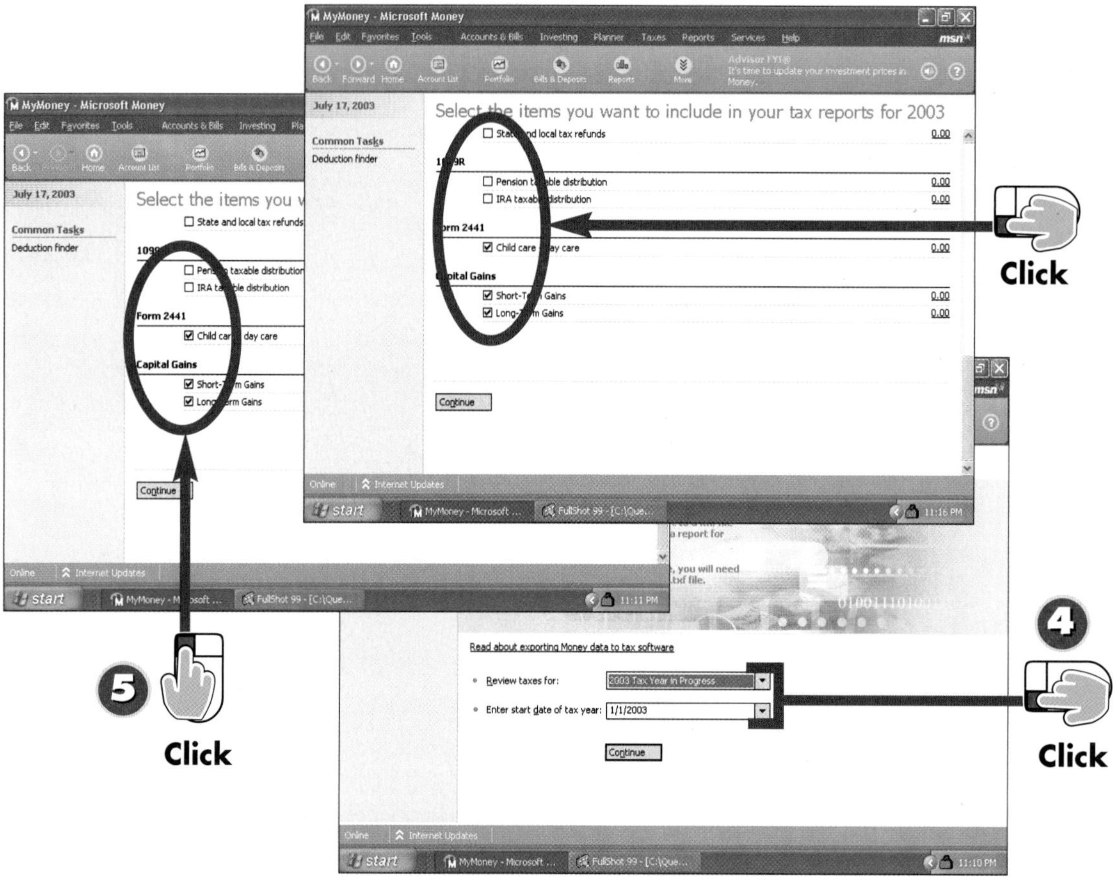

4. If necessary, change the tax year by clicking the **Review taxes for** down arrow and choosing the appropriate year, and click **Continue**.
5. Scroll through the list and click the check box next to each item you want to include for your taxes. Then click **Continue**.
6. Continue clicking the check boxes next to the items you want to include in your taxes, then click **Continue**.

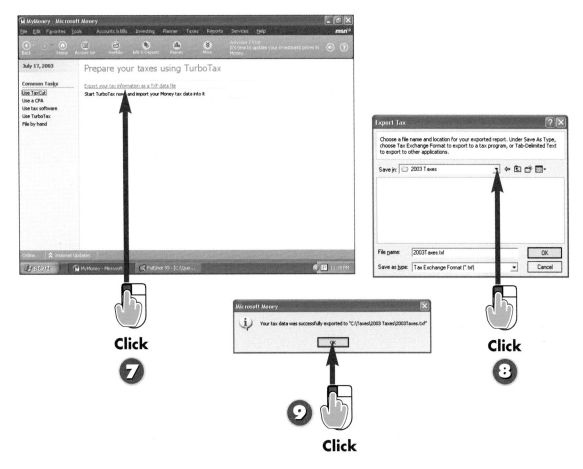

7 Click the **Export your tax information as a TXF data file** link to export your tax file.

8 Click the **Save in** down arrow, select a folder to save your tax file, and click **OK**. Money notifies you that the tax data was successfully exported.

9 Click **OK**.

TIP

Starting Your Tax Program

If you want to start the tax program (here, TurboTax) you use to automatically import your tax information, click **Start TurboTax now, and import your Money tax data into it**.

PART 11

Planning for the Future

All accounts are accounted for, a budget is in place, a debt-reduction plan is under way, and taxes are entered and ready to roll. In other words, your finances are under control. So, what's left? Let's gaze into the crystal ball and see what's in store for your financial future. You can plan for retirement, a child's education, that dream house, or whatever else may lie ahead.

The Lifetime Planner

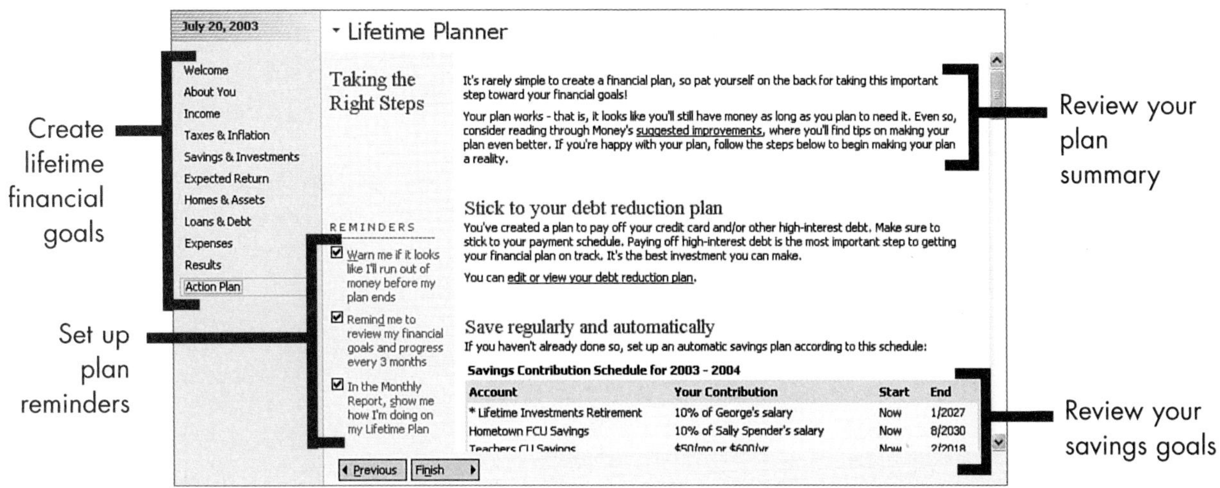

Entering Your Family Information

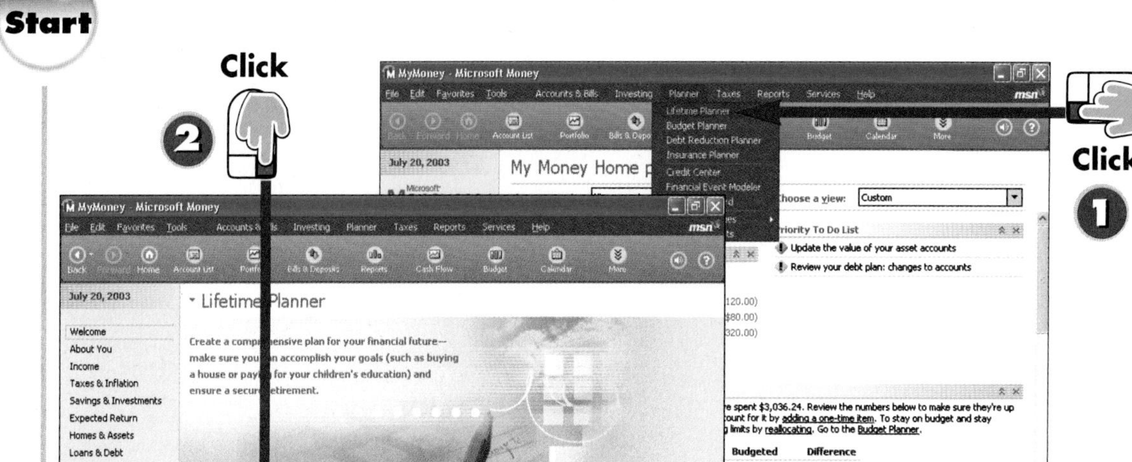

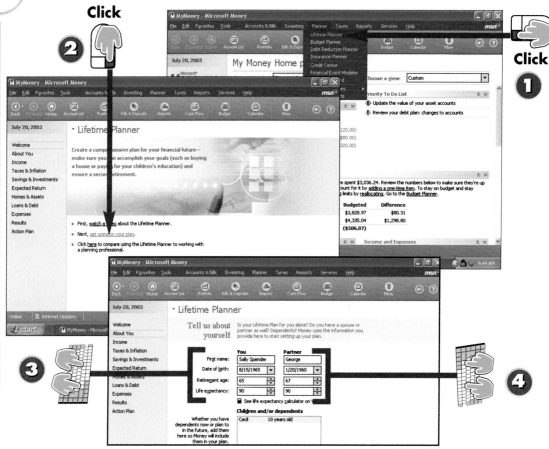

1. Open the **Planner** menu and choose **Lifetime Planner**.
2. Listen to or read the overview. When you're finished, click the **get going on your plan** link.
3. Review your personal information, making changes as needed.
4. If necessary, use the boxes in the **Partner** column to add information about a spouse or partner.

INTRODUCTION

The first step in creating a plan for your financial future is to tell Money who will be contributing to that future and any dependents for which you are responsible. You will also be asked to specify the age at which you plan to retire. Money uses this information to show you what your financial situation looks like from here on out.

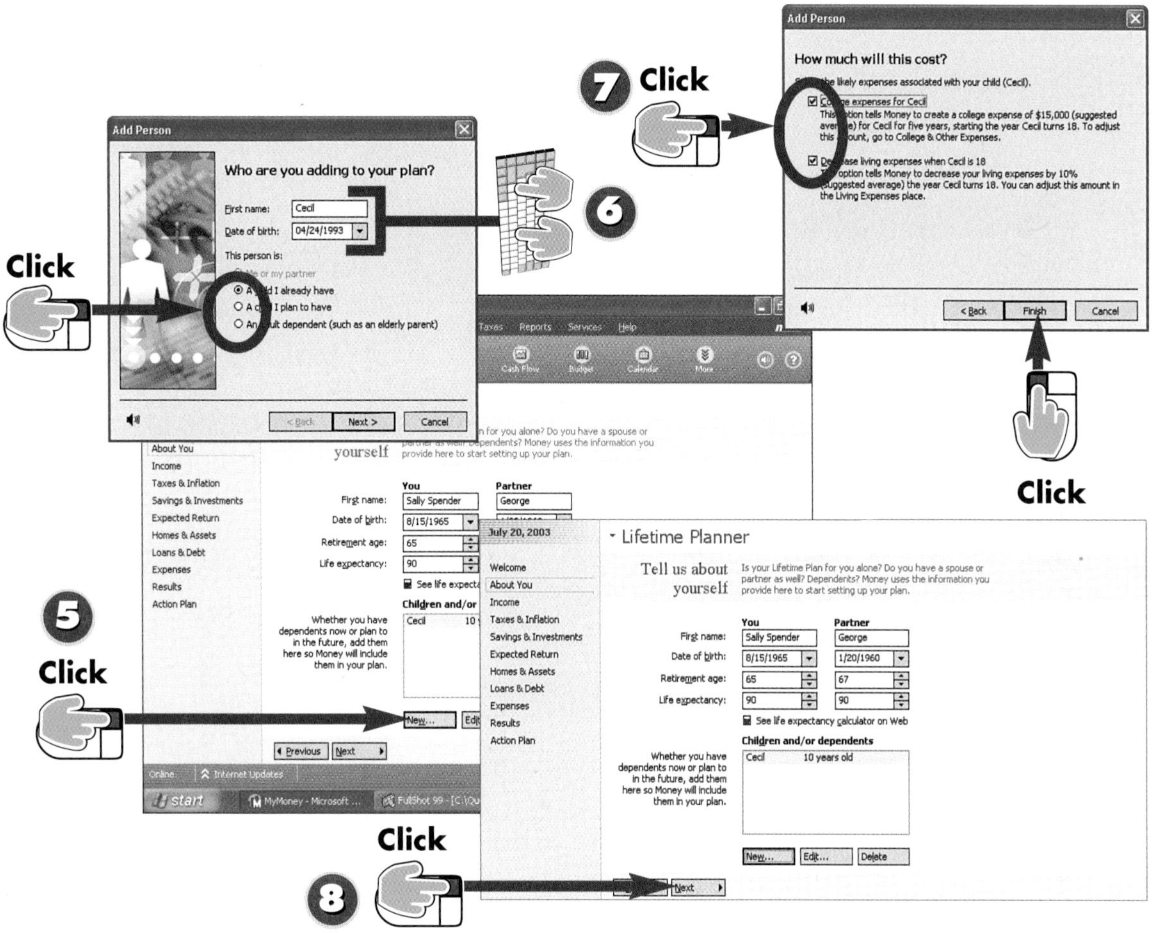

5 To add dependents, click the **New** button. The Add Person dialog box appears.

6 Enter the dependent's name and date of birth, and select one of the **This person is** options. Then click **Next**.

7 Click the check box next to each expense you want to plan for. Then click **Finish**.

8 To add additional dependents, repeat steps 5–7 for each dependent. When you are finished, click **Next**.

TIP

Determining Life Span
Money uses standard life-expectancy ages to determine approximately how long you and/or your partner will live. The retirement age and life-expectancy ages are used to determine social security and financial projections.

TIP

Changing Dependent Information
To change dependent information, select the dependent's name in the **Children and/or dependents** list and click **Edit**, or click **Delete** to remove the dependent.

Entering Income Information

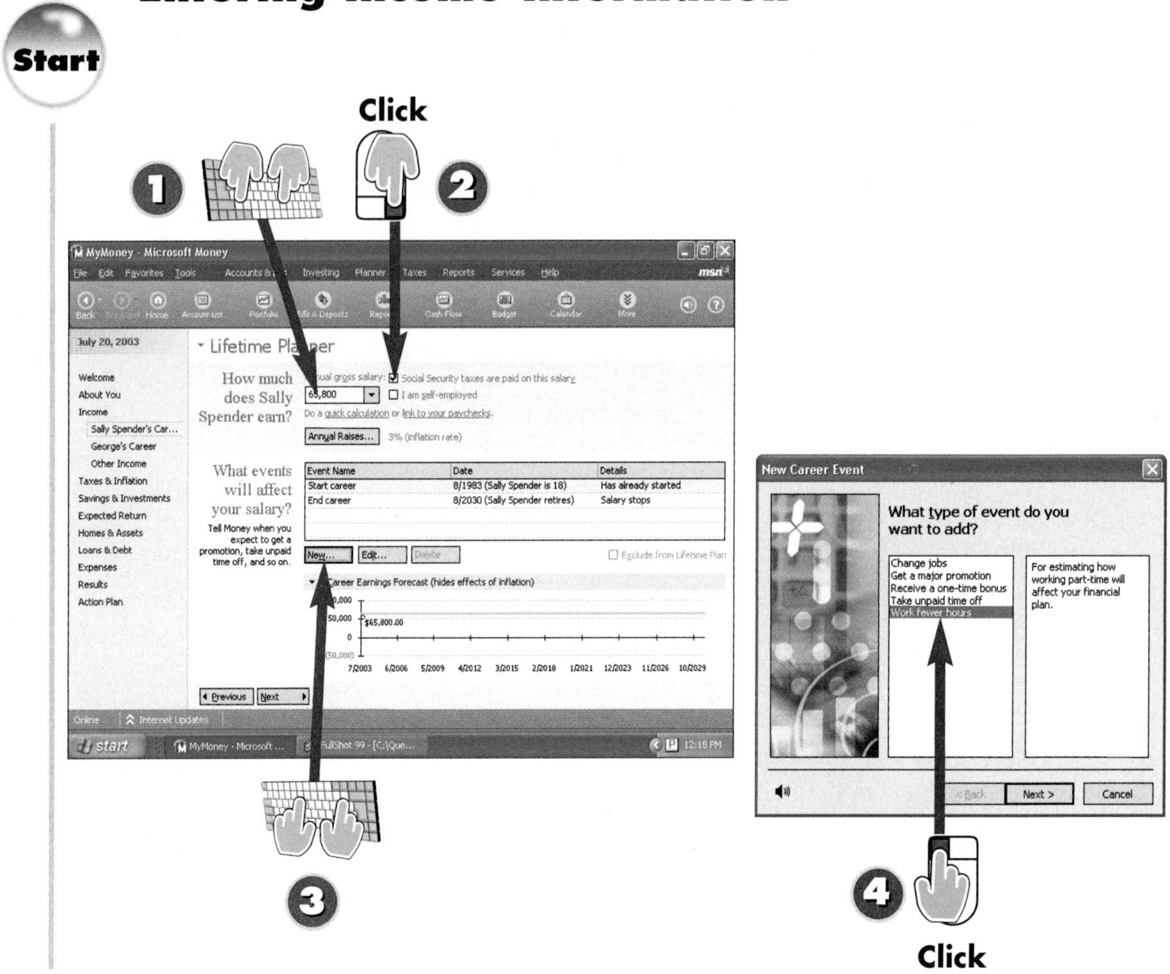

Click

Click

1. To change your salary, type the new figure under **Annual gross salary**.

2. If applicable, click the **Social Security taxes are paid on this salary** and **I am self-employed** check boxes.

3. To add a new event, such as a reduction in your work hours, click the **New** button. The New Career Event Wizard opens.

4. In the left pane, click the type of event that best describes the one you want to add (a brief description appears to the right), and then click **Next**.

INTRODUCTION

After you've entered your family information, you're ready to enter and/or update your income information along with that of your spouse's or partner's (if applicable). Money uses information you entered for your accounts to create a salary figure for you, which it uses to project future income for as long as you plan to work. You can play around with different scenarios—for example, cutting your work hours—to see how that would affect your financial future.

TIP

Determining Exact Salary
If the salary listed in the Annual gross salary box is incorrect, but you do not know your exact salary, click **quick calculation** or **link to your paychecks** to figure it out.

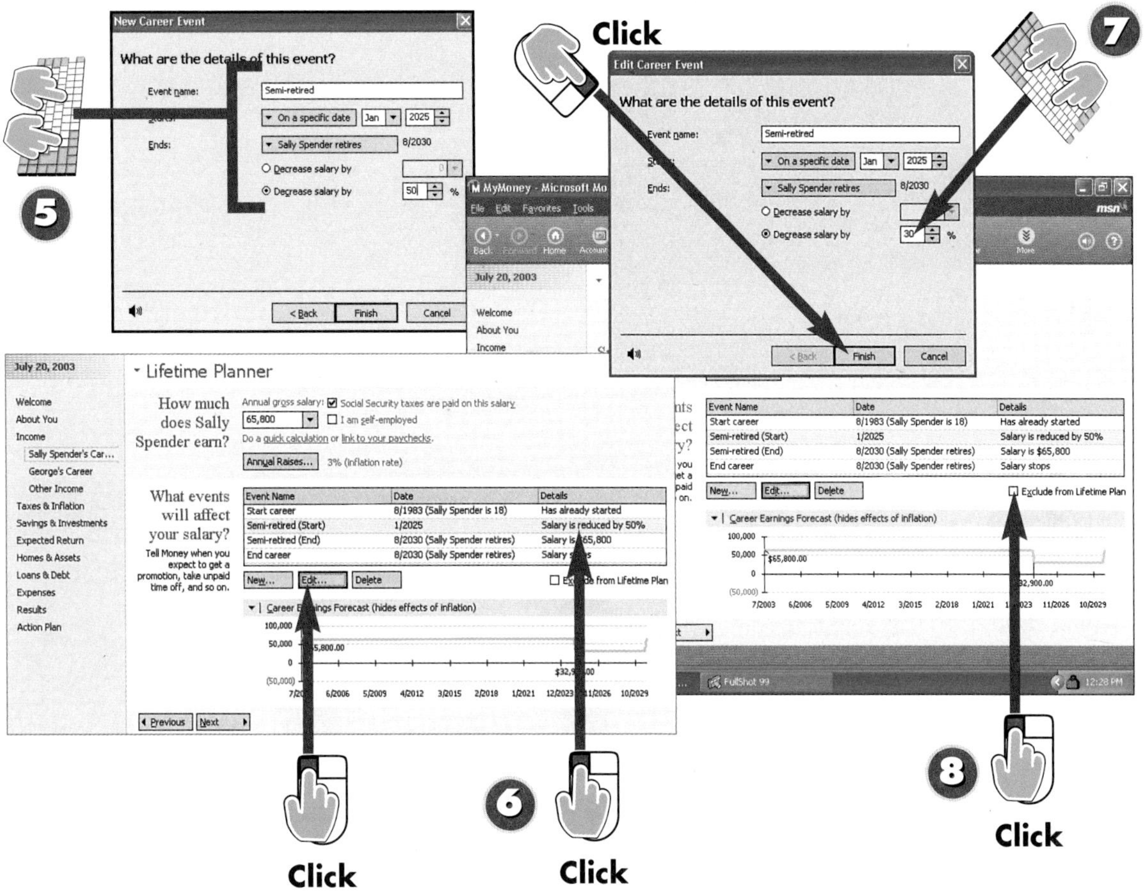

5. The wizard asks you questions related to the type of event you are adding. Select or type the answers to the questions, and click **Finish**.
6. To change event information, click the event in the list and click the **Edit** button. The Edit Career Event dialog box opens.
7. Make changes to any of the information—for example the **Decrease salary by** percentage—click **Finish**. Money updates your earnings forecast accordingly.
8. If you want Money to exclude an event from the results of your plan, select the event from the list and click the **Exclude from Lifetime Plan** check box.

See next page

HINT

Viewing Your Salary Forecast

Your salary forecast appears at the bottom of the Lifetime Planner screen. Click the **Career Earnings Forecast** down arrow to change the view.

TIP

Annual Inflation Percentage

To review or change the annual inflation percentage that determines your projected salary increases, click the **Annual Raises** button in the screen shown for steps 7–8.

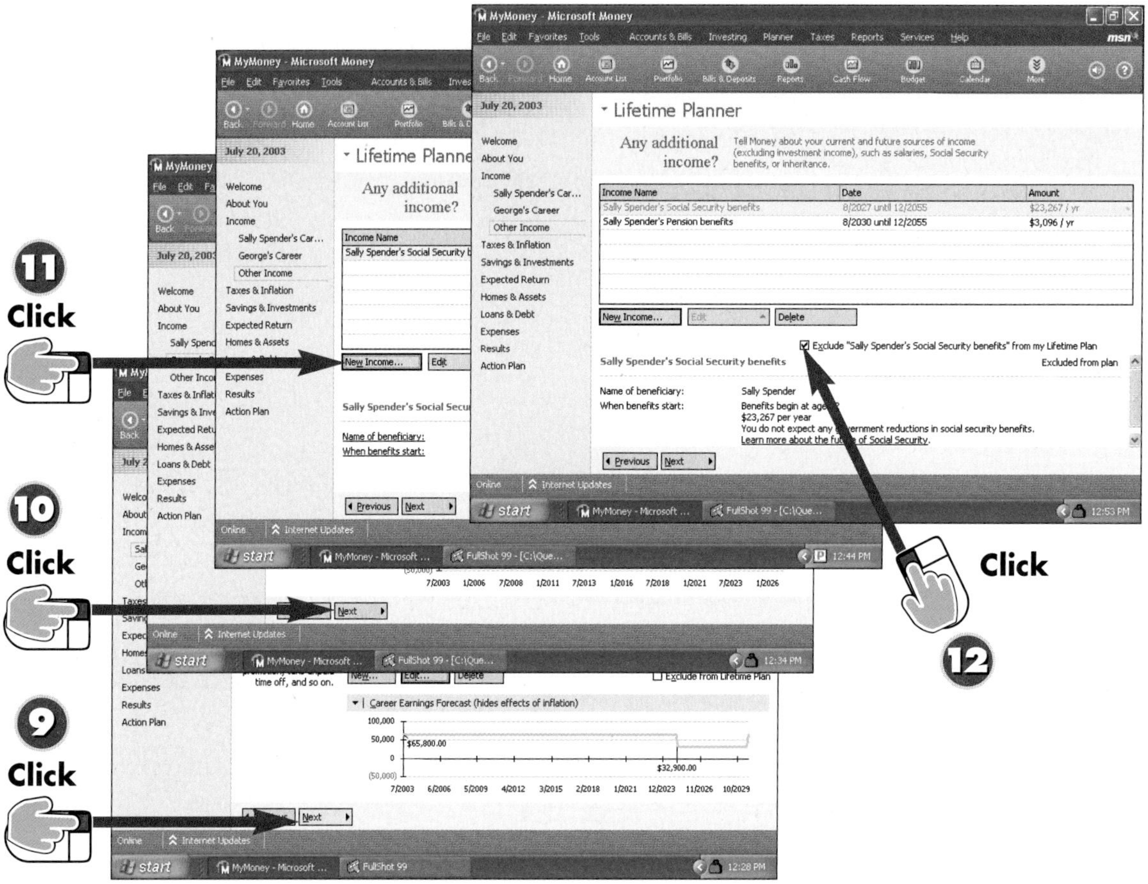

9 Click **Next**.

10 If applicable, enter your spouse or partner's information just as you did your own in steps 1–8. Then click **Next**.

11 To add future income, click the **New Income** button. The New Income Wizard opens; answer the questions and click **Finish** when you are done.

12 To exclude future income, such as social security, from your plan, select the income and click the **Exclude income name from my Lifetime Plan** check box. Then click **Next**.

Specifying Taxes and Inflation

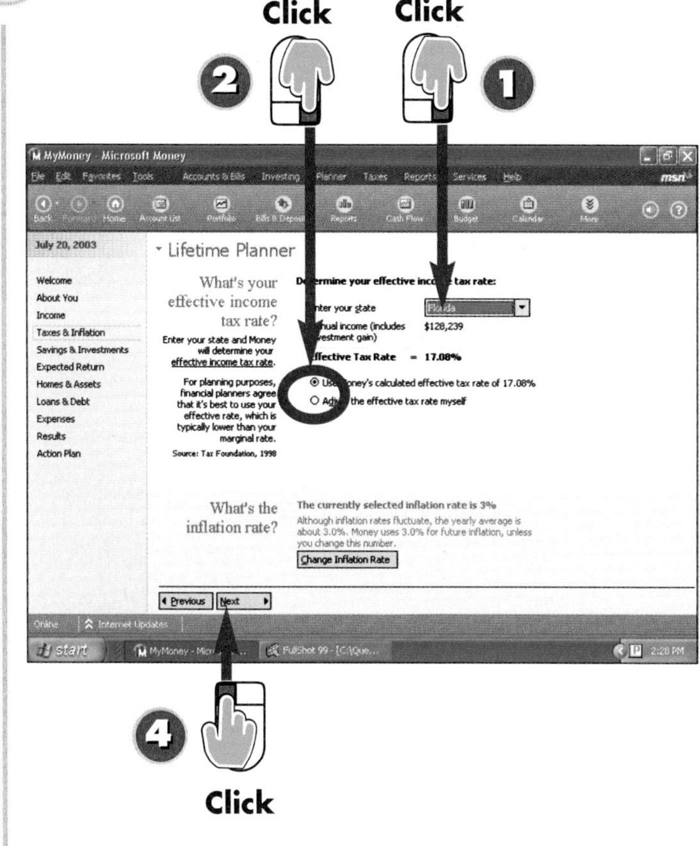

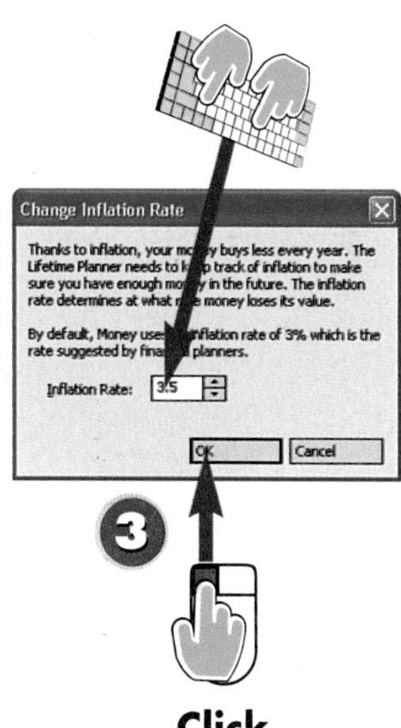

1. Click the **Enter your state** down arrow and select your state of residence from the list that appears.
2. To specify the tax rate for your state, click **Use Money's calculated effective tax rate of x%** (recommended) or **Adjust the effective tax rate myself**.
3. To change the inflation rate, click the **Change Inflation Rate** button and on the Change Inflation Rate dialog box, enter the rate you want to use, and click **OK**.
4. Click **Next**.

INTRODUCTION

After you've finished entering your family and income information, it's time to tell Money where you live—specifically, in what state. This enables Money to determine your state tax rate. You can also use this window to change the inflation rate that Money uses to calculate future earnings (the default rate is 3%).

TIP

Adjusting the Effective Tax Rate

If you choose the **Adjust the effective tax rate myself** option in step 2, a box with the current rate appears next to a slider bar. Click in the box and type a different rate if you want to change it.

Entering Savings and Investment Information

Start

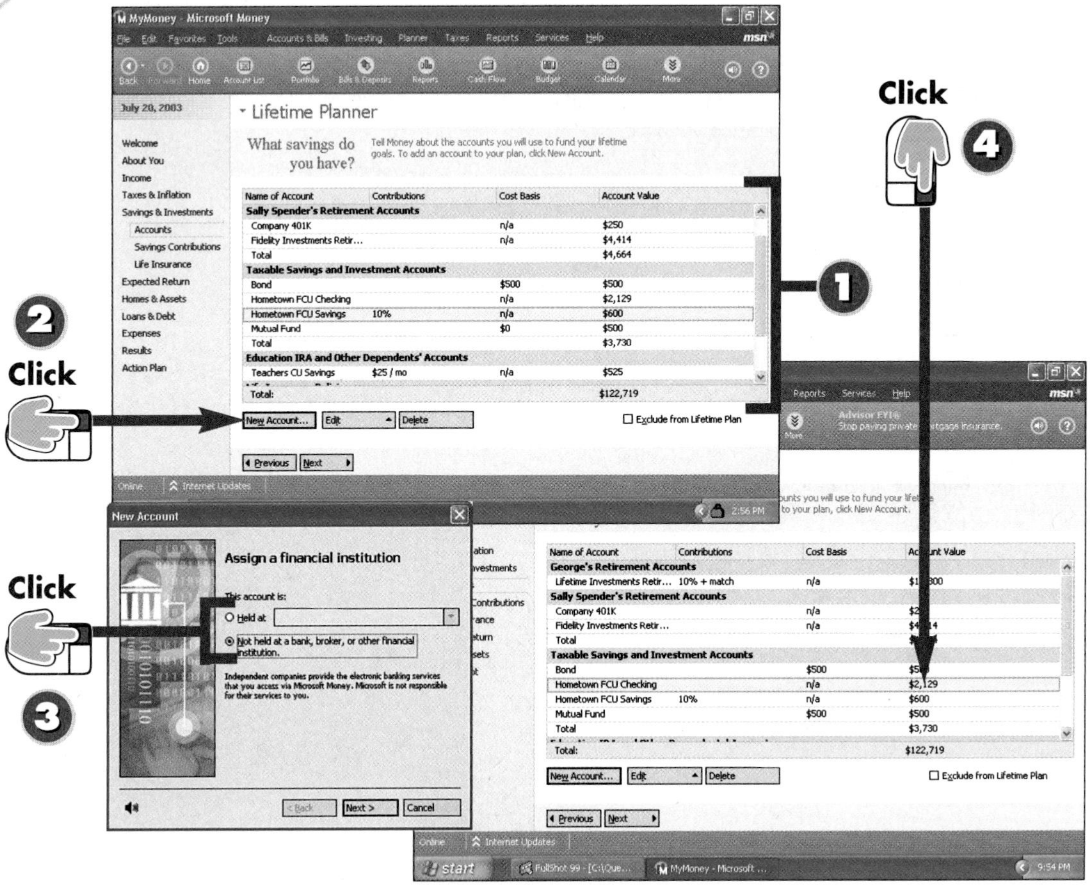

1. After reviewing all your accounts, decide which ones you need to update, add, remove, or exclude from your plan.
2. To add a new account, click the **New Account** button. The New Account Wizard opens.
3. The wizard asks you a series of questions. Answer them, clicking **Next** to proceed to the next question, and then click **Finish**.
4. To exclude an account from your plan (but not remove it from Money), select the account and click the **Exclude from Lifetime Plan** check box.

INTRODUCTION

The fourth step in creating your lifetime plan is to review and, if necessary, update your savings and investment information. Money makes it easy to do so by pulling together all your savings and investment accounts, contributions, and balances for you to review. You can also add new accounts.

HINT

Adding a New Account

The New Account Wizard in step 3 is the same wizard you used in Part 4. If you need help remembering how to add a new account, see "Adding a New Account" in Part 4.

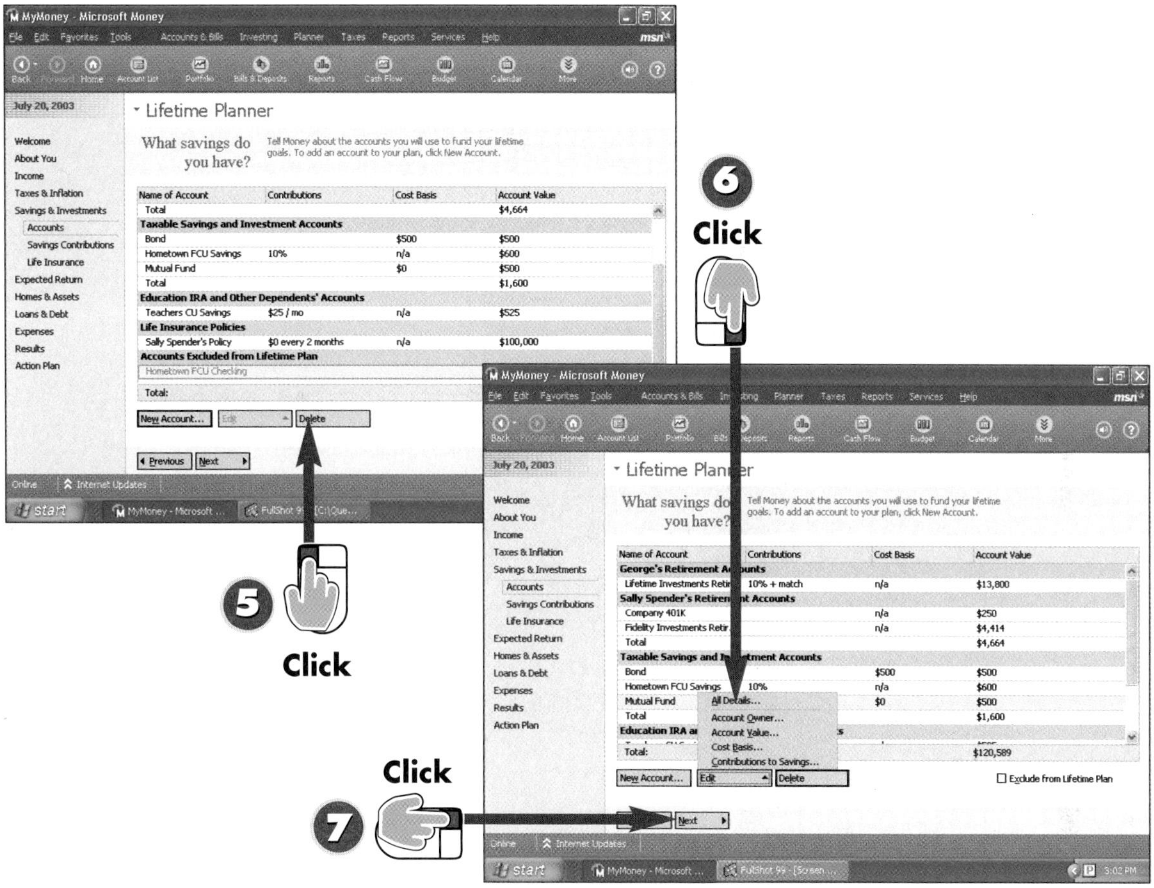

5 To delete an account from Money, select the account and click the **Delete** button.

6 To update information for an account, select it, click the **Edit** button, and make a selection from the menu that appears.

7 When you are finished reviewing and updating all your accounts, click **Next**.

Reviewing and Changing Savings Contributions

Click

Click

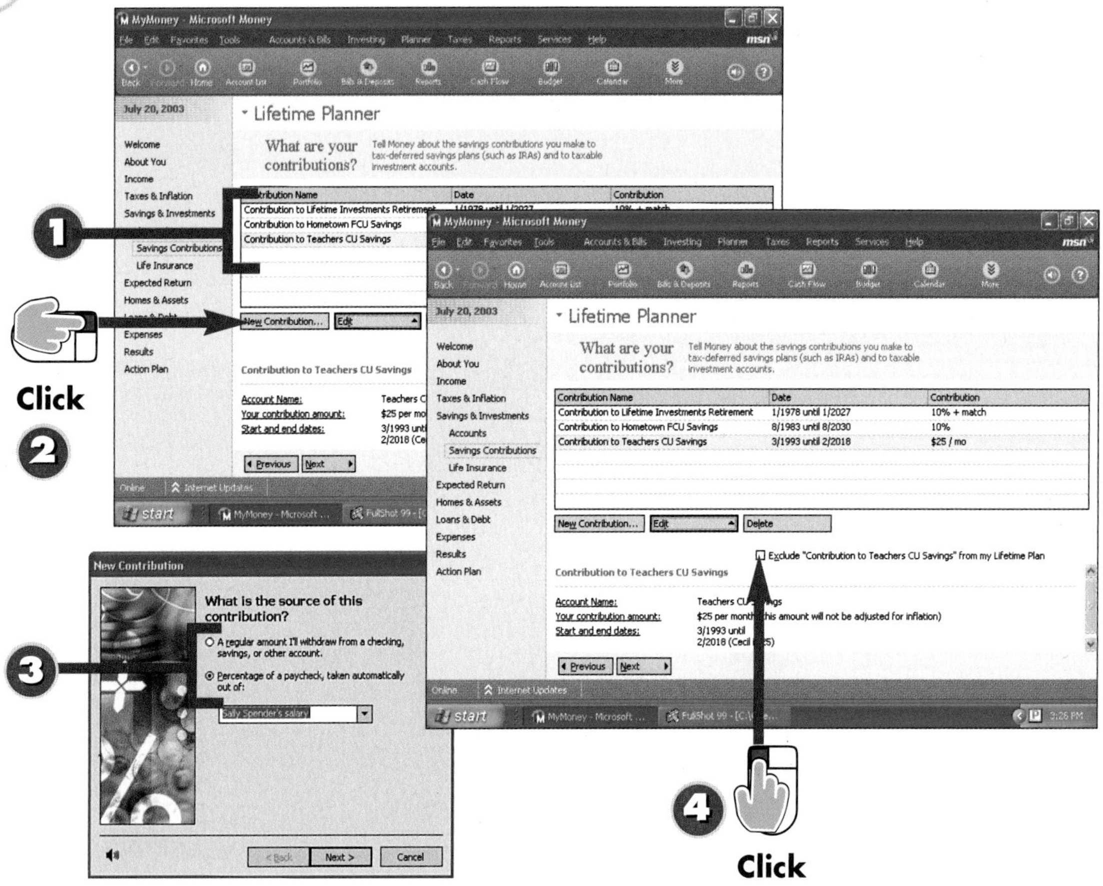

1 After reviewing all your contributions, decide which accounts you need to update, add, remove, or exclude from your plan.

2 To add a new contribution, click the **New Contribution** button. The New Contribution wizard opens.

3 The wizard asks you a series of questions. Answer them, clicking **Next** to proceed to the next question, and then click **Finish**.

4 To exclude an account to which you make contributions, select the account and click the **Exclude contribution name from my Lifetime Plan** check box.

INTRODUCTION

In the Savings Contributions portion of the Lifetime Planner, Money enables you to review your savings and investment contributions, and if necessary, to add, edit, exclude, or delete contributions.

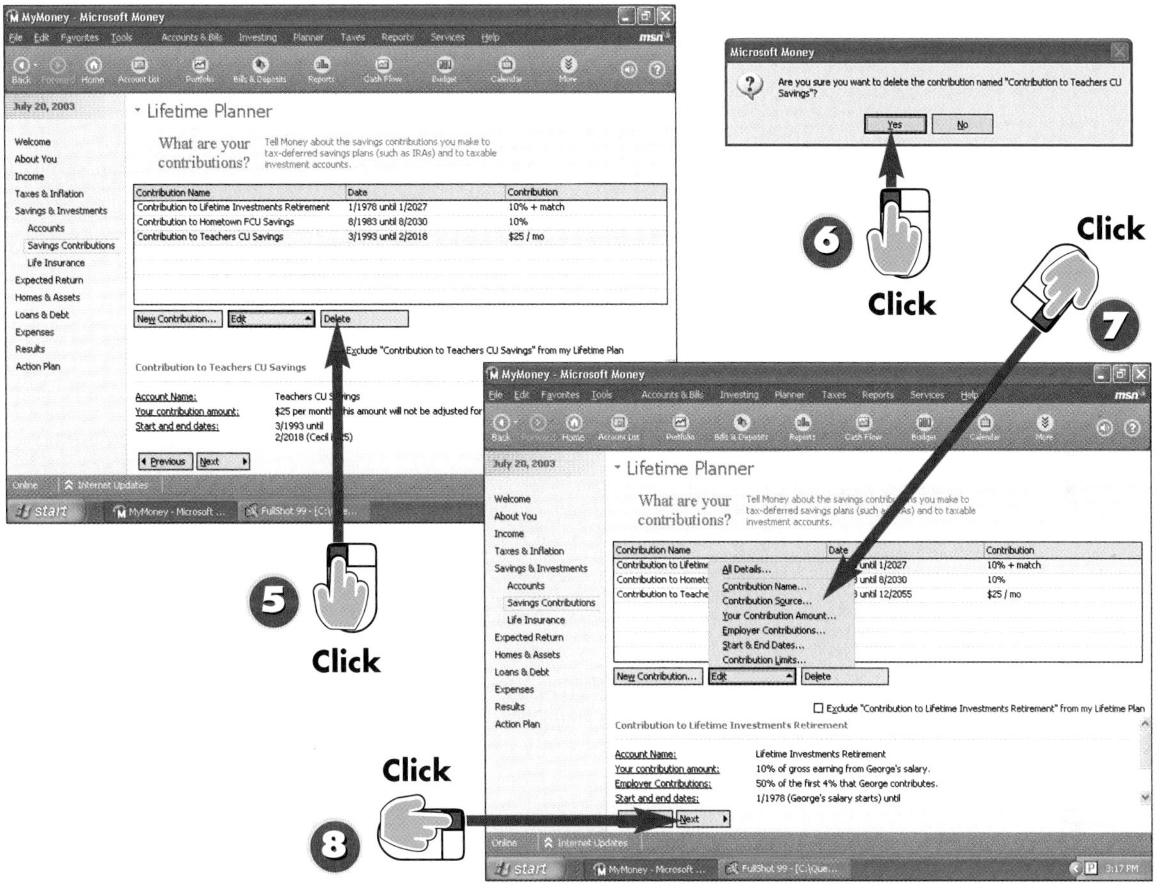

5 To delete a savings plan to which you make contributions from Money, select the savings plan and click the **Delete** button. A confirmation message appears.

6 Click **Yes** to delete the savings plan.

7 To update contribution information for a plan, select the plan, click the **Edit** button, and make a selection from the menu that appears.

8 When you are finished updating all your plans, click **Next**.

TIP

Reviewing the Summary

When you select a savings or investment account, a summary appears at the bottom of the page. You can click the links in the summary to review the information or make changes, if needed.

Reviewing and Changing Life Insurance Policies

Start

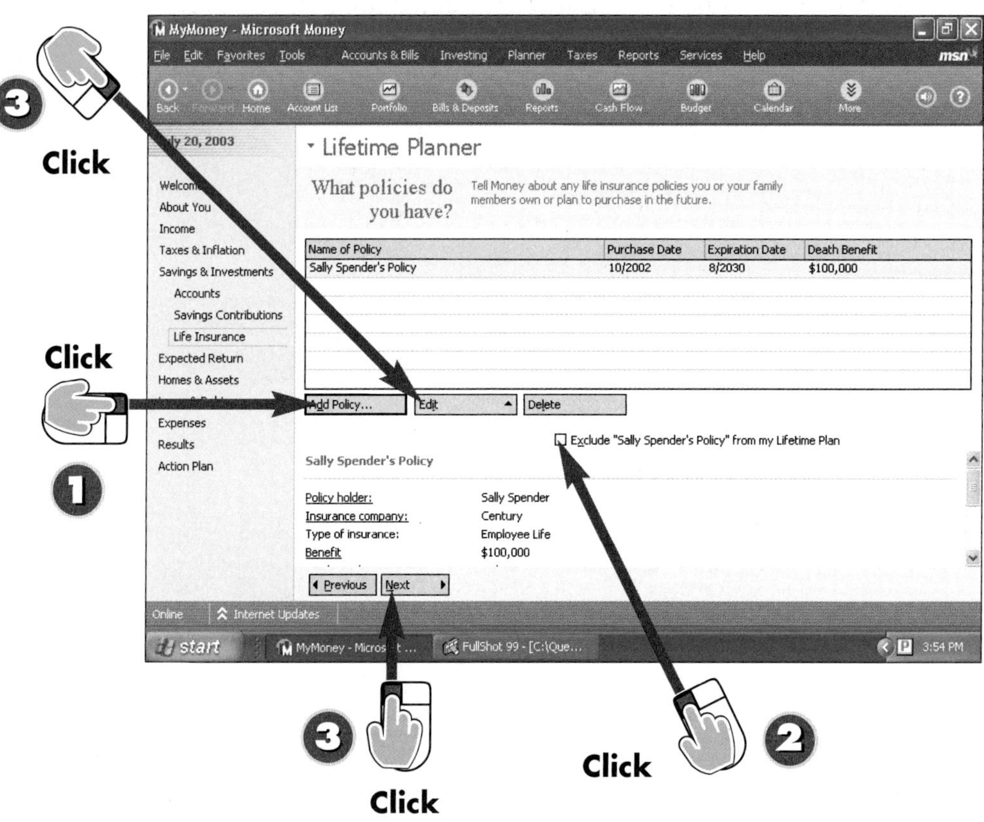

1. To add a new policy, click the **Add Policy** button. The New Policy wizard opens; answer all the wizard's questions, clicking **Next** to proceed, and then click **Finish**.
2. To exclude a policy from your plan, select the policy and click the **Exclude name of policy from my Lifetime Plan** check box.
3. To update a policy's information, select it, click the **Edit** button, and make a selection from the menu that appears.
4. Click **Next**.

End

INTRODUCTION

A critical aspect of creating a lifetime plan is assessing your life insurance policies. Money's Lifetime Planner enables you to review your existing insurance policies and to make changes as needed. You can also add new policies.

TIP

Viewing Detailed Information

Detailed information about the selected policy appears at the bottom of the page. Click a link to review the information or make changes, if needed.

HINT

Deleting Policies

To remove a life insurance policy from your plan, select the plan from the list and click the **Delete** button. A confirmation message appears. Click **Yes** to delete the plan.

Entering Expected Returns on Investments

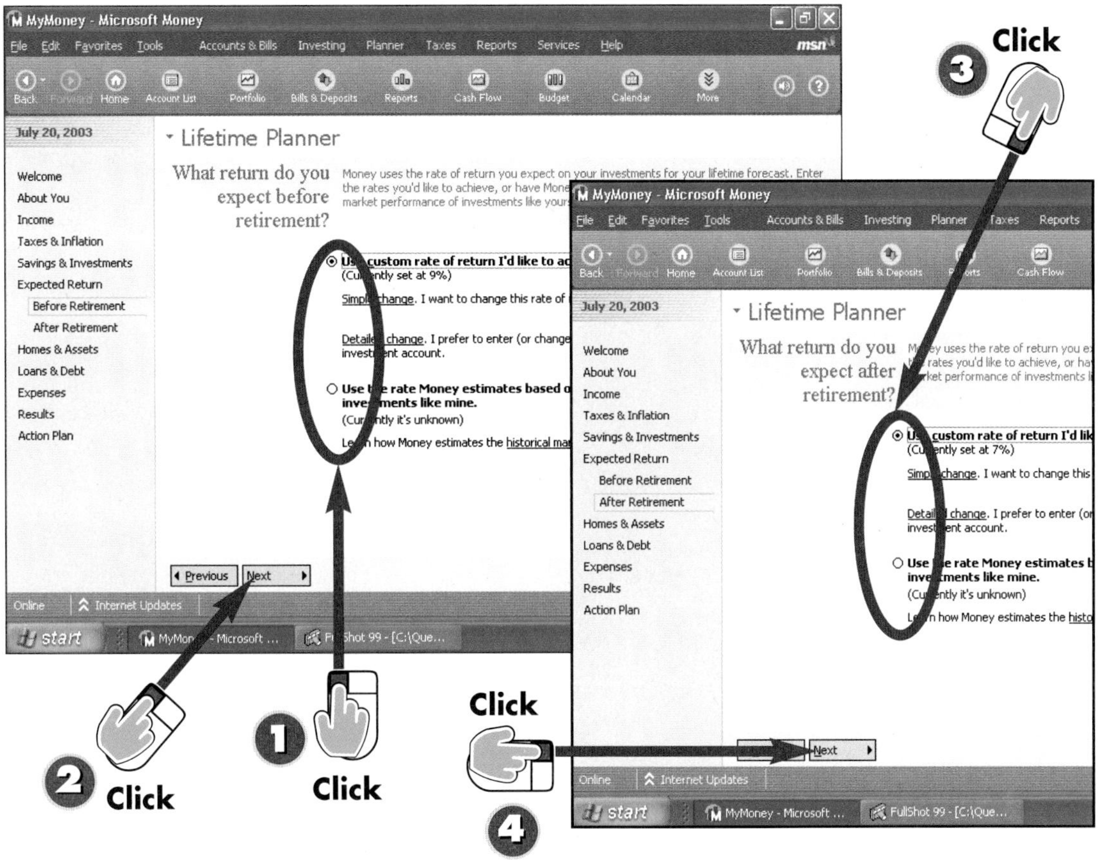

1. In the Before Retirement screen of your Lifetime Planner, click **Use custom rate of return...** or **Use the rate Money estimates...**.
2. Click **Next**.
3. On the After Retirement portion of your Lifetime Planner, click **Use custom rate of return...** or **Use the rate Money estimates...**.
4. Click **Next**.

INTRODUCTION

Money's Lifetime Planner next asks you to specify the rate you expect for the return on your investments. Money can determine the rate of return, or you can enter your own.

TIP

Changing Rates

If you selected the first rate of return option in steps 1 and 3, and want to change the rate for all accounts in your lifetime plan in one fell swoop, click the **Simple change** link and enter the new rate. To change the rates for specific accounts in your lifetime plan, click the **Detailed change** link and change the rates for the desired accounts.

Setting Up Homes and Assets

Start

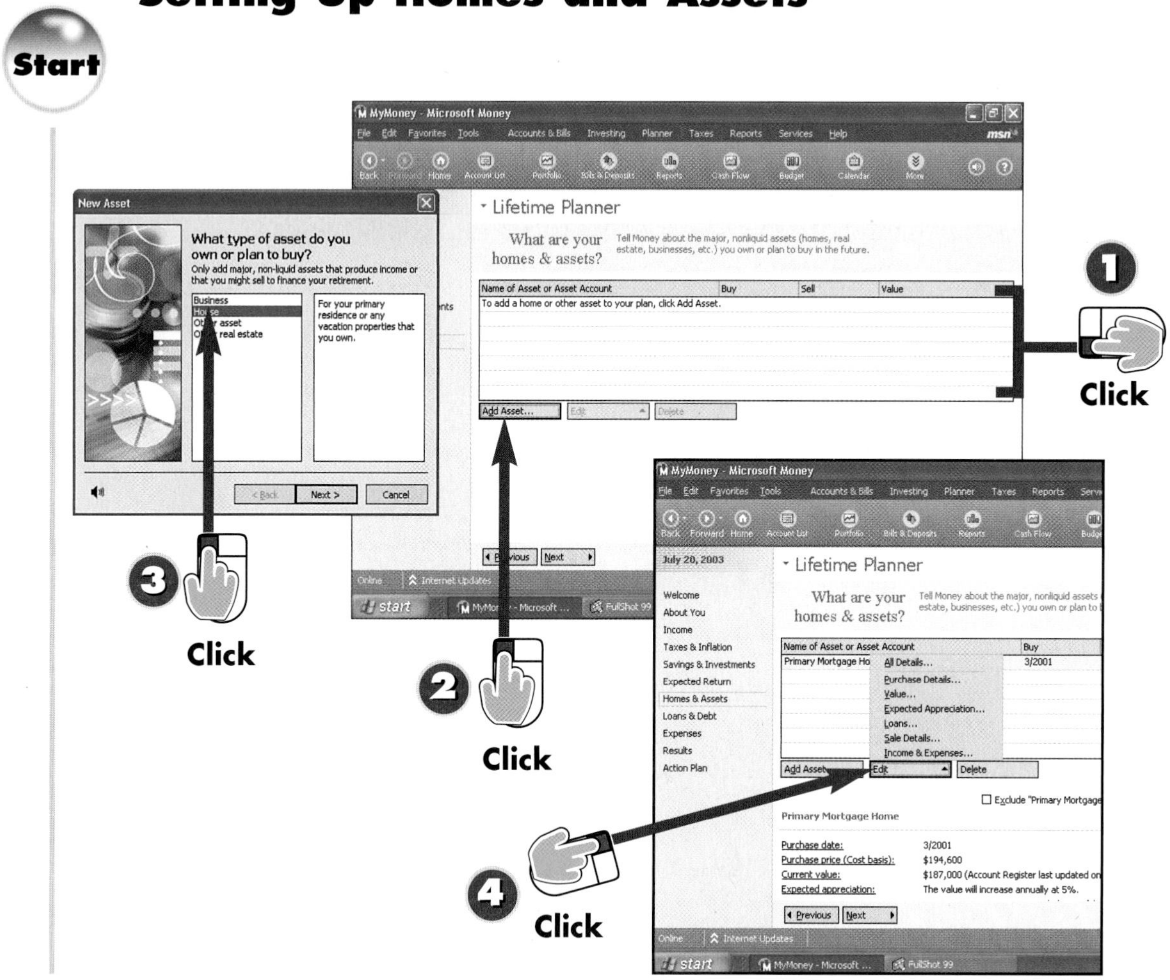

1. With your asset information in hand, decide which assets you want to add to the Lifetime Planner.

2. To enter a new asset, click the **Add Asset** button. The New Asset Wizard opens.

3. The wizard asks you a series of questions. Answer them, clicking **Next** to proceed to the next question, and then click **Finish**.

4. To update an asset's information, select it, click the **Edit** button, and make a selection from the menu that appears.

INTRODUCTION

The Homes and Assets portion of Money's Lifetime Planner asks you to provide information about any property you own, and about any other assets.

TIP

Viewing Detailed Information

Detailed information about the selected home or asset appears at the bottom of the page. Click a link to review the information or make changes, if needed.

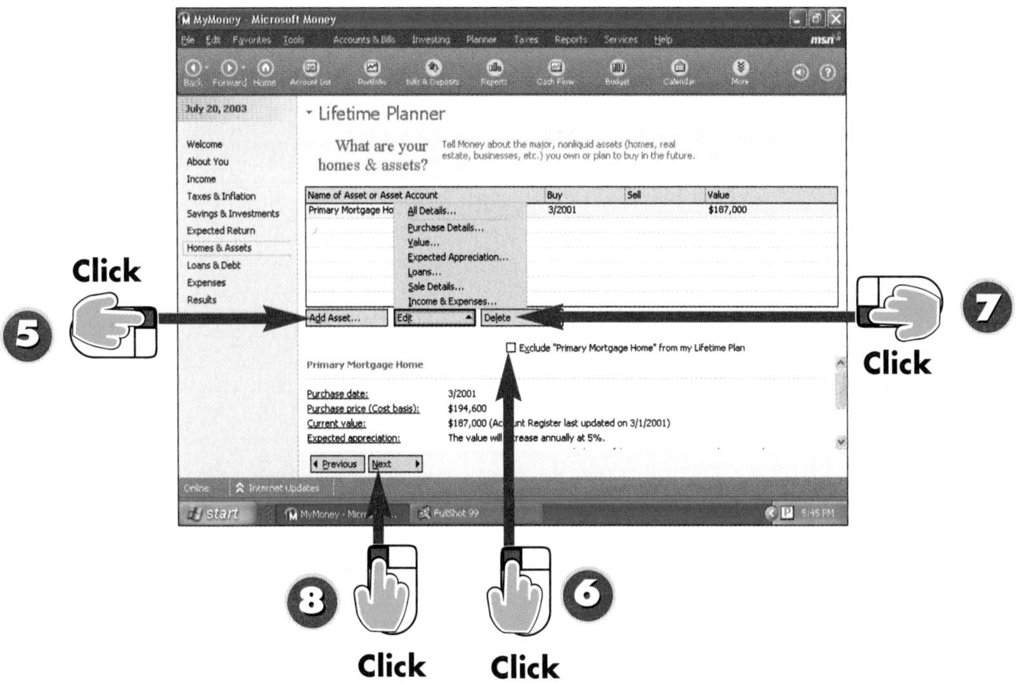

5 Repeat step 1 for each asset/property you own or are thinking about buying.

6 To exclude an asset from your plan, select the asset, and click the **Exclude name of asset from my Lifetime Plan** check box. Repeat as needed.

7 To delete an asset from Money, select the asset and click the **Delete** button. A confirmation message appears; click **Yes** to delete the asset.

8 When you are finished making your changes, click **Next**.

Reviewing and Changing Your Debt Information

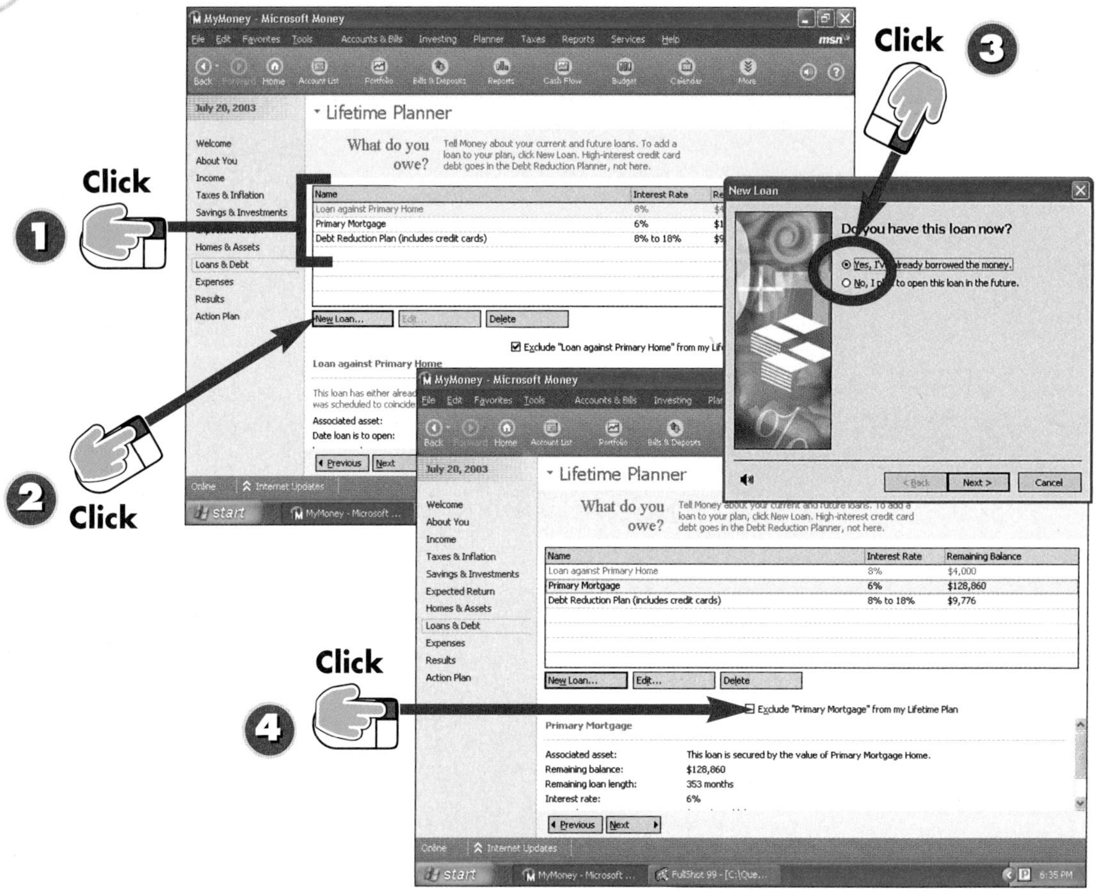

1. After reviewing all your loans, decide which loans you need to update, add, remove, or exclude from your plan.

2. To add a loan, click the **New Loan** button. The New Loan Wizard opens.

3. The wizard asks you a series of questions. Answer them, clicking **Next** to proceed to the next question, and then click **Finish**.

4. To exclude a loan from your plan, select the loan, and mark the **Exclude loan name from my Lifetime Plan** check box. Repeat as needed.

INTRODUCTION

The Loans and Debt portion of the Lifetime Planner involves reviewing your total debt, including any loans, and deciding where you need to make changes, if at all. As with all the other steps you've already completed in the Lifetime Planner, you can add new loan accounts and specify what, if any, debt you want to exclude from your plan.

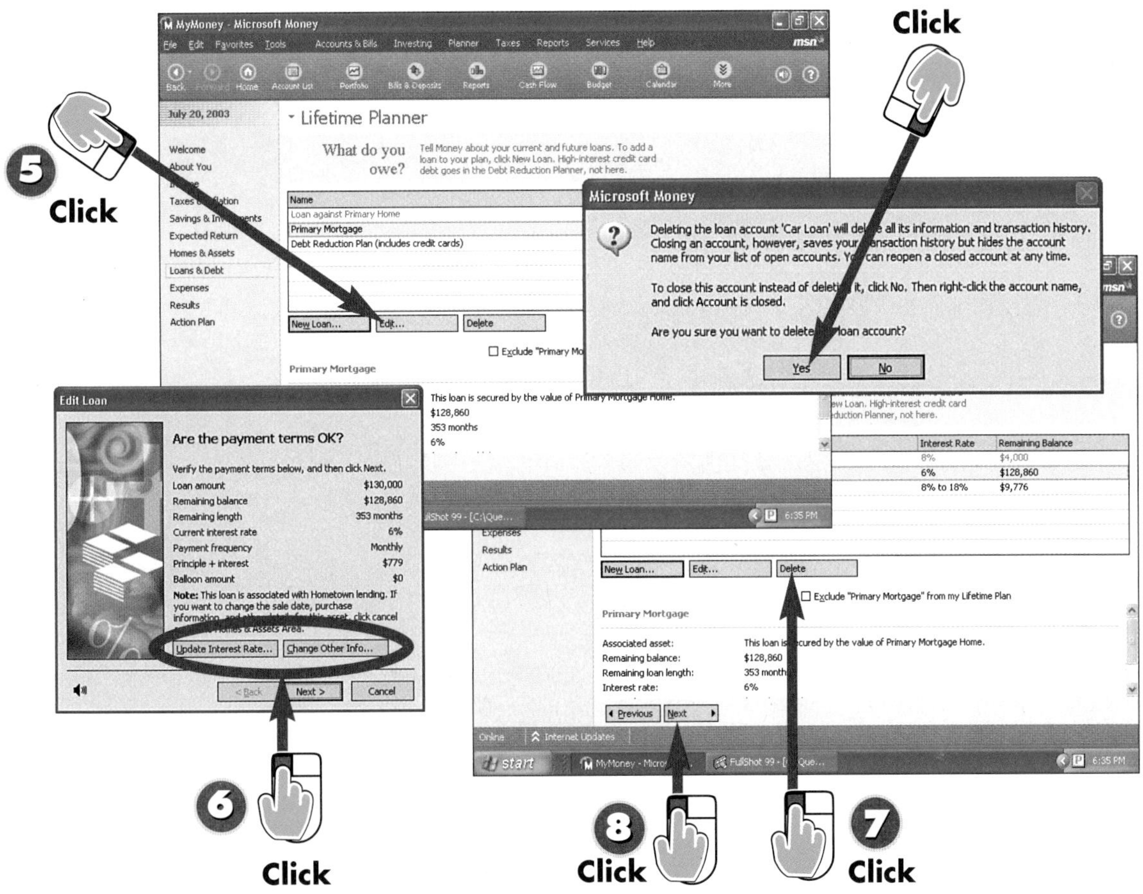

5 To update a loan's information, select it from the list and click the **Edit** button. The Edit Loan dialog box opens.

6 Make your changes, and click **Next** to make additional loan changes. Then click **Finish** when you are done.

7 To delete a loan from Money, select the loan and click the **Delete** button. A confirmation message appears; click **Yes** to delete the loan.

8 Click **Next**.

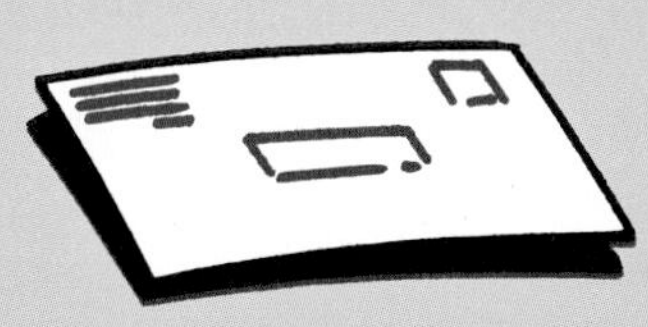

TIP

Viewing Detailed Information

Detailed information about a selected loan appears at the bottom of the page. Click a link to review the information or make changes, if needed.

Reviewing and Changing Expenses

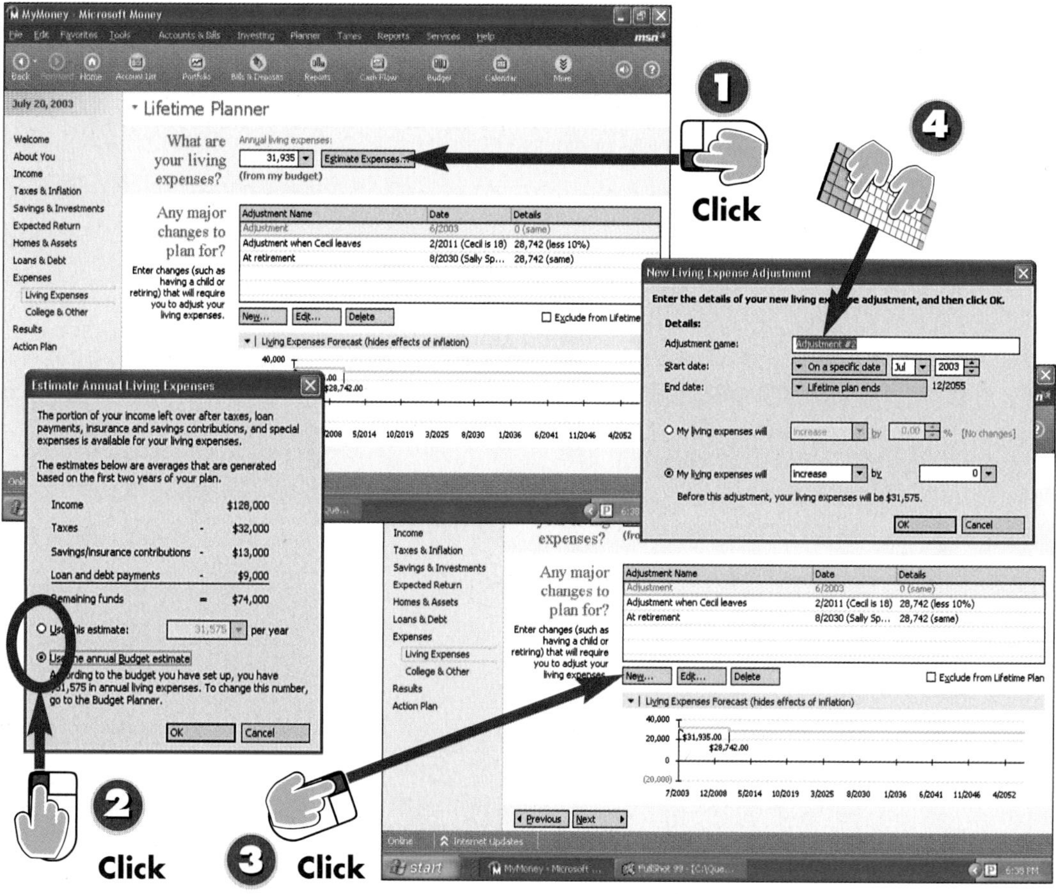

1. To change your living-expenses estimate, click the **Estimate Expenses** button. The Estimate Annual Living Expenses dialog box opens.
2. Click **Use this estimate** and enter a figure (or click **Use the annual Budget estimate** to use the figure Money created from your budget). Then click **OK**.
3. To add a new living-expense adjustment to your plan, click the **New** button. The New Living Expense Adjustment dialog box opens.
4. Enter a descriptive name for the adjustment in the **Adjustment Name** box.

INTRODUCTION

Before you review your entire lifetime plan, you must assess your current and future expenses. There are two parts to this process. The first is to review your expenses and make changes as needed. To help you, Money compiles the expense information from your budget and displays the sum total of the combined expenses. The second part of this process is to determine any other expenses, such as college funding, that may arise in the future.

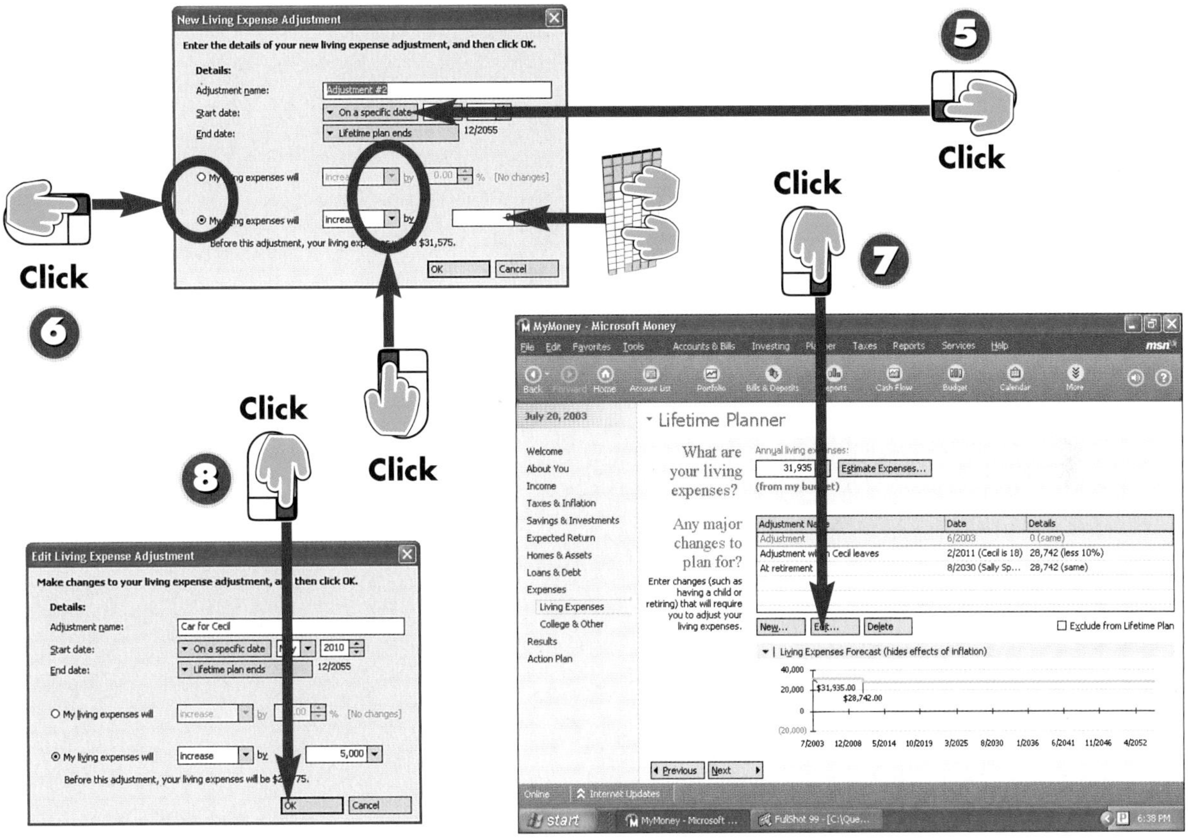

5 Click the **Start date** and select the date type. Then, click the month you want, and then enter the day and year the adjustment will take effect.

6 Select a living expense option (percentage or amount), select **decrease** or **increase**, and enter the percentage or amount in the next box. Then click **OK**.

7 To make changes to an adjustment, select it from the list, click the **Edit** button, and make a selection. The Edit Living Expense Adjustment dialog box opens.

8 Make your changes to the adjustment as you did in steps 4–6 to create an adjustment. Then click **OK**.

TIP

Viewing the Expense Forecast

Your expense forecast appears at the bottom of the page. Click the **Living Expenses Forecast** down arrow to change how it is displayed.

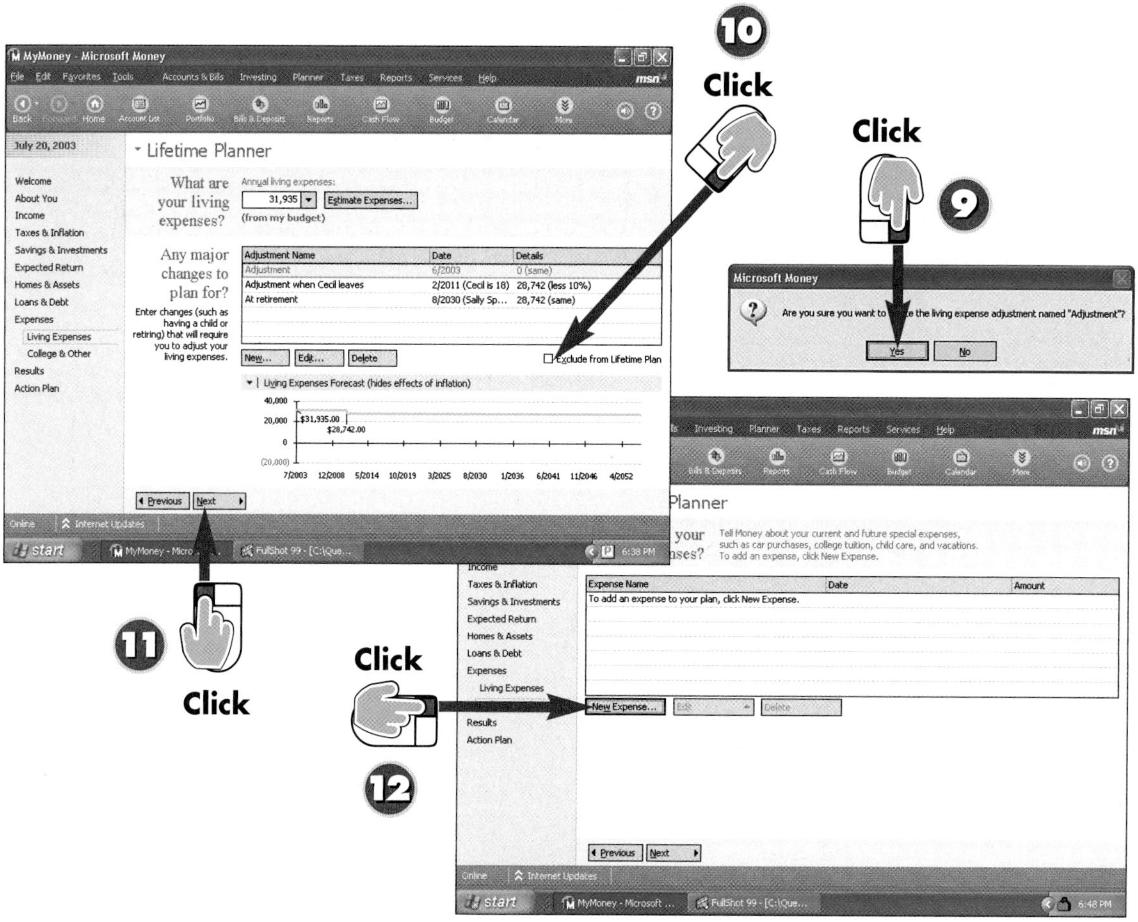

Click

10

Click

9

Click

11

Click

12

9 To permanently remove an adjustment from Money, select it and click the **Delete** button. A confirmation message appears; click **Yes** to delete the adjustment.

10 To exclude an adjustment from your plan, select the adjustment and click the **Exclude from Lifetime Plan** check box.

11 Click **Next**.

12 To add a new expense, such as college expenses, click the **New Expense** button. The New Expense Wizard opens.

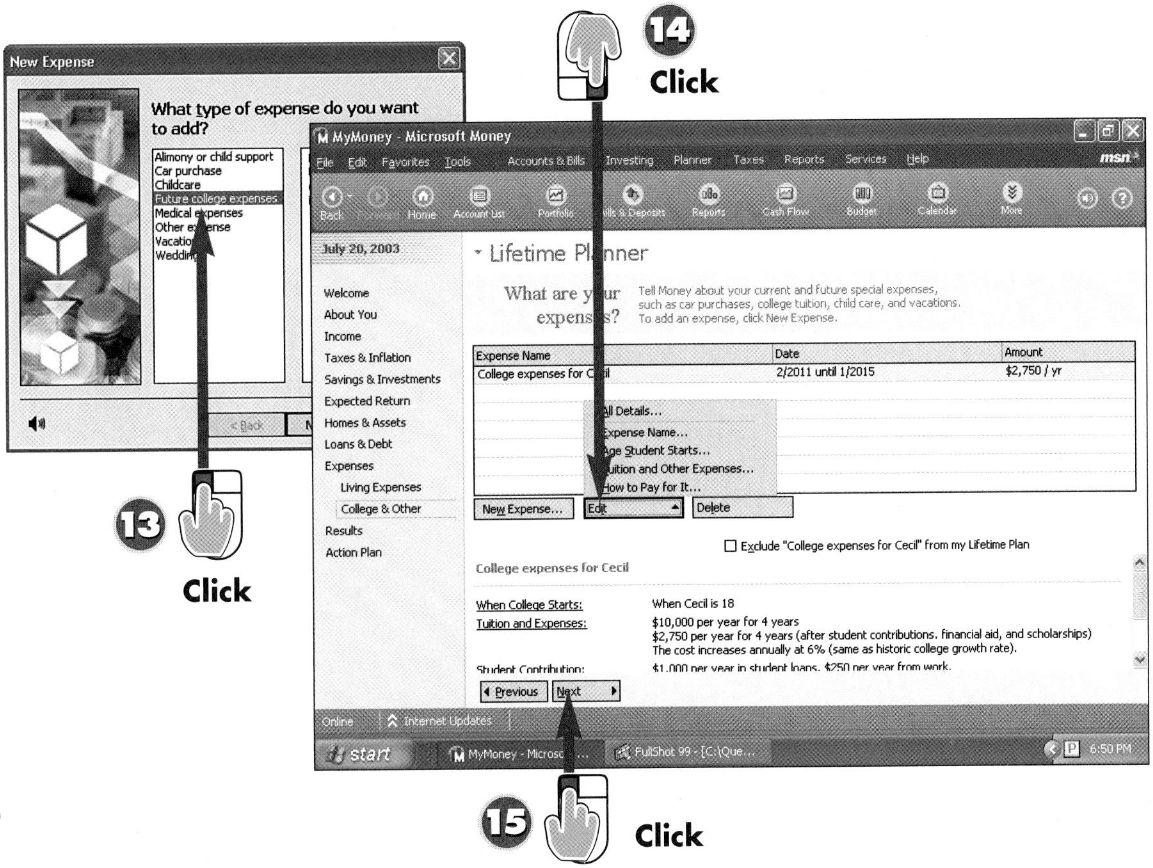

14 **Click**

13 **Click**

15 **Click**

13 The wizard asks you a series of questions. Answer them, clicking **Next** to proceed to the next question, and then click **Finish**.

14 To update an expense, select it, click the **Edit** button, and make a selection from the menu that appears.

15 When you are finished adding, changing, and updating expenses, click **Next**.

Reviewing and Changing Your Plan Results

Start

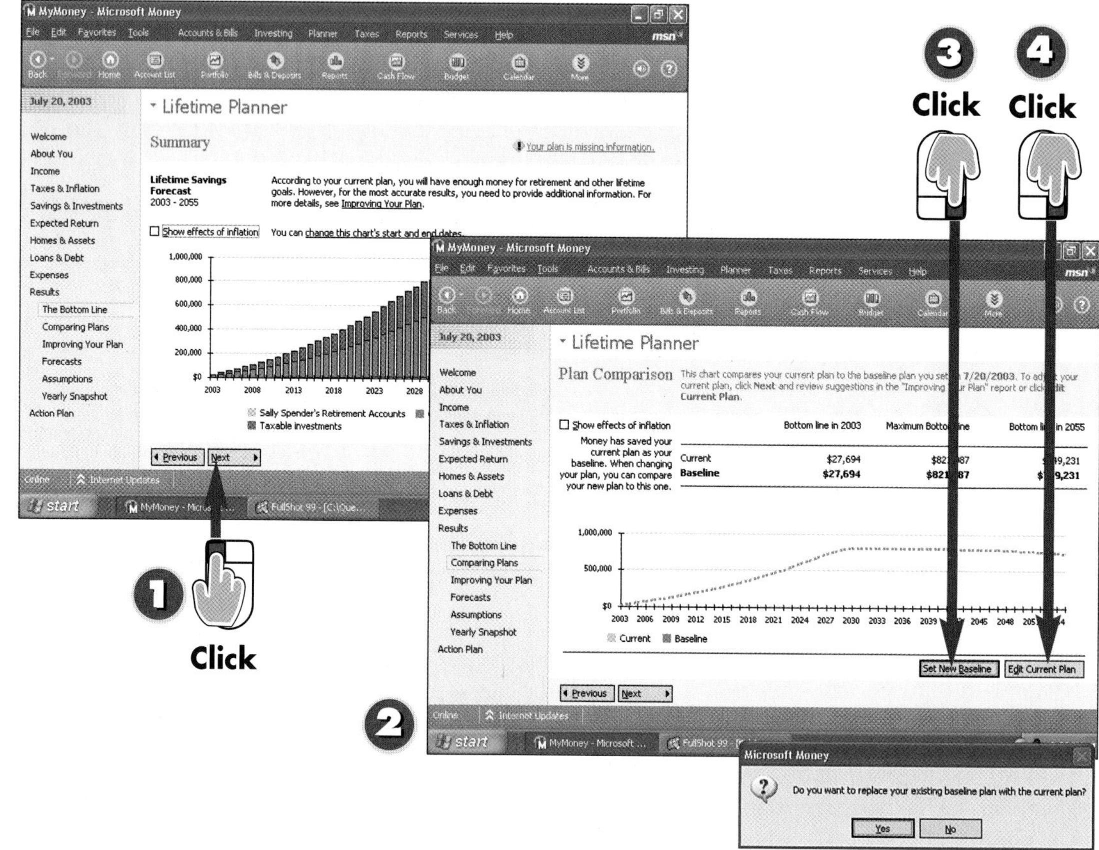

1. Review your plan summary (be sure to read the paragraph at the top that explains anything you need to know about it). Then, click **Next**.
2. If you previously created a lifetime plan, you can compare it (baseline) with the one you just created (current) to see which one you want to use.
3. To choose a plan, click the **Set New Baseline** button. A confirmation message appears; click **Yes** to use the current plan or **No** to use the baseline plan.
4. To make changes to your plan, click the **Edit Current Plan** button and make the changes. The What do you want to change in your Lifetime Plan? window opens.

INTRODUCTION

The moment has come for you to see the results of all your hard work. Money provides you with a summary of your retirement accounts, lets you know whether you need to go back and make changes, and whether you will be able to meet your financial goals based on the information you've provided thus far.

TIP

Baseline Versus Current
If you've already created a lifetime plan, Money calls it your *baseline plan*, and calls the plan you are creating now your *current plan*.

HINT

Tweaking Your Plan Results
If necessary, click **change this chart's start and end dates** in step 1. To see how inflation could affect your accounts, mark the **Show effects of inflation** check box.

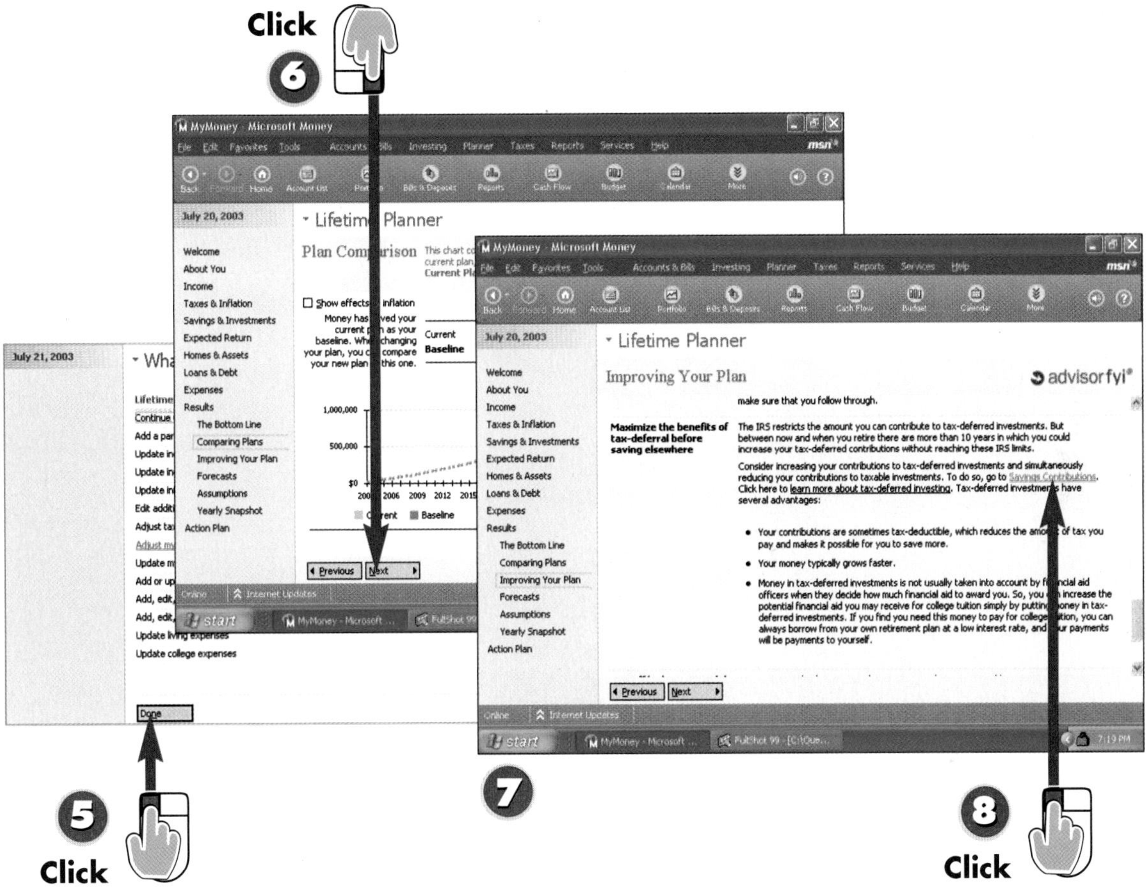

Click 6

Click 5

7

8 Click

5 Click a link, make your changes, and click **Done**. Repeat for any other changes you want to make, and then click **Done** on the Lifetime Plan change window.

6 Click **Next**.

7 Read the information that Money provides about how you can improve your plan. Scroll down to review all of it.

8 If necessary, click on one of the many links that Money provides to enable you to go back and make additional changes or review information.

See next page

TIP

Experimenting

Creating more than one lifetime plan, based on different scenarios, is a great way to see what you need to do in order to reach your lifetime financial goals. The line graphs shown in step 2 allow you to see at a glance how the plans compare over the course of your lifetime. If you want to create another plan, repeat the tasks in this part. Then, when you reach this task, you'll be able to compare the plans.

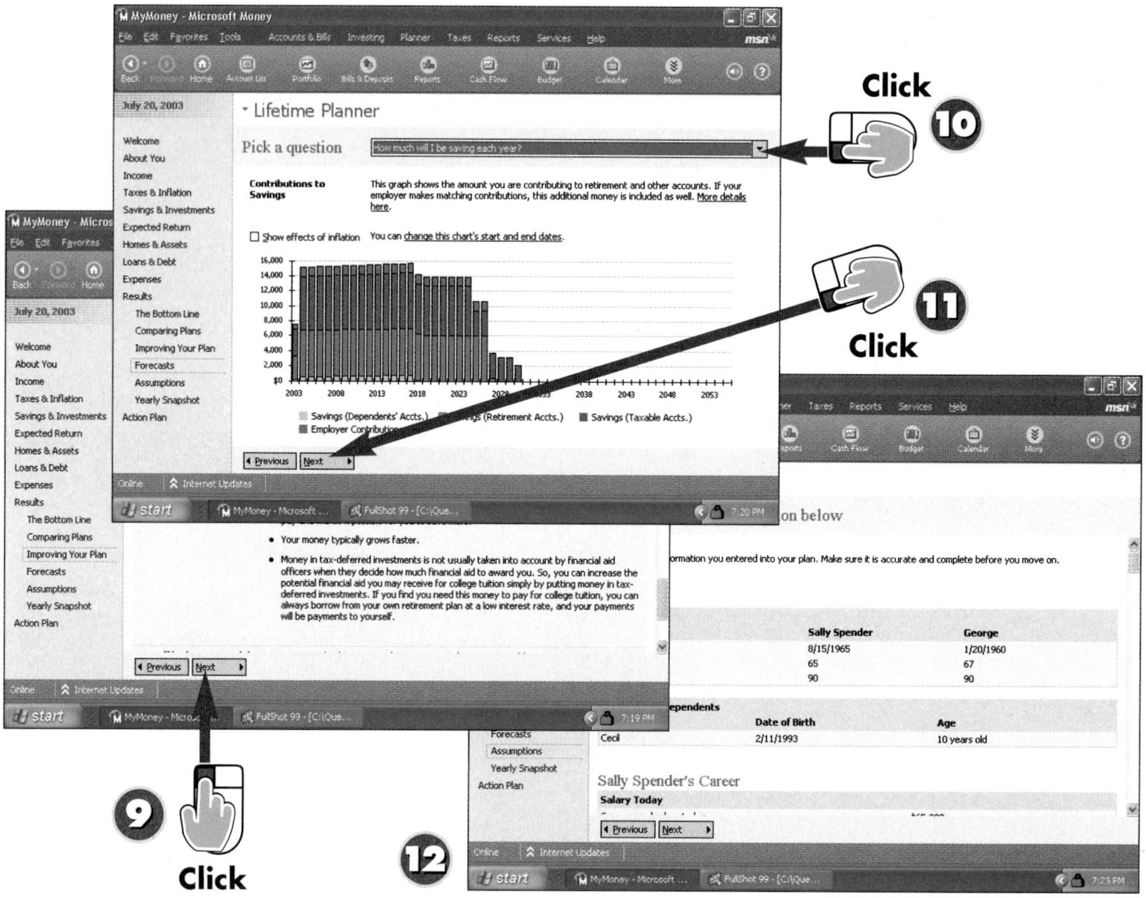

Click 10

Click 11

9 Click

12

9 Review or change any information and click **Results** to return to the planner. If the link you clicked in step 7 goes to the Internet, click the **Back** button, then click **Next**.

10 To get answers to questions you may have about your plan, click the **Pick a question** down arrow and choose a question from the list that appears.

11 Review your savings contribution summary. When you are finished, click **Next**.

12 Money displays all the personal information you entered while setting up your plan. Review the information to make sure it is complete and accurate.

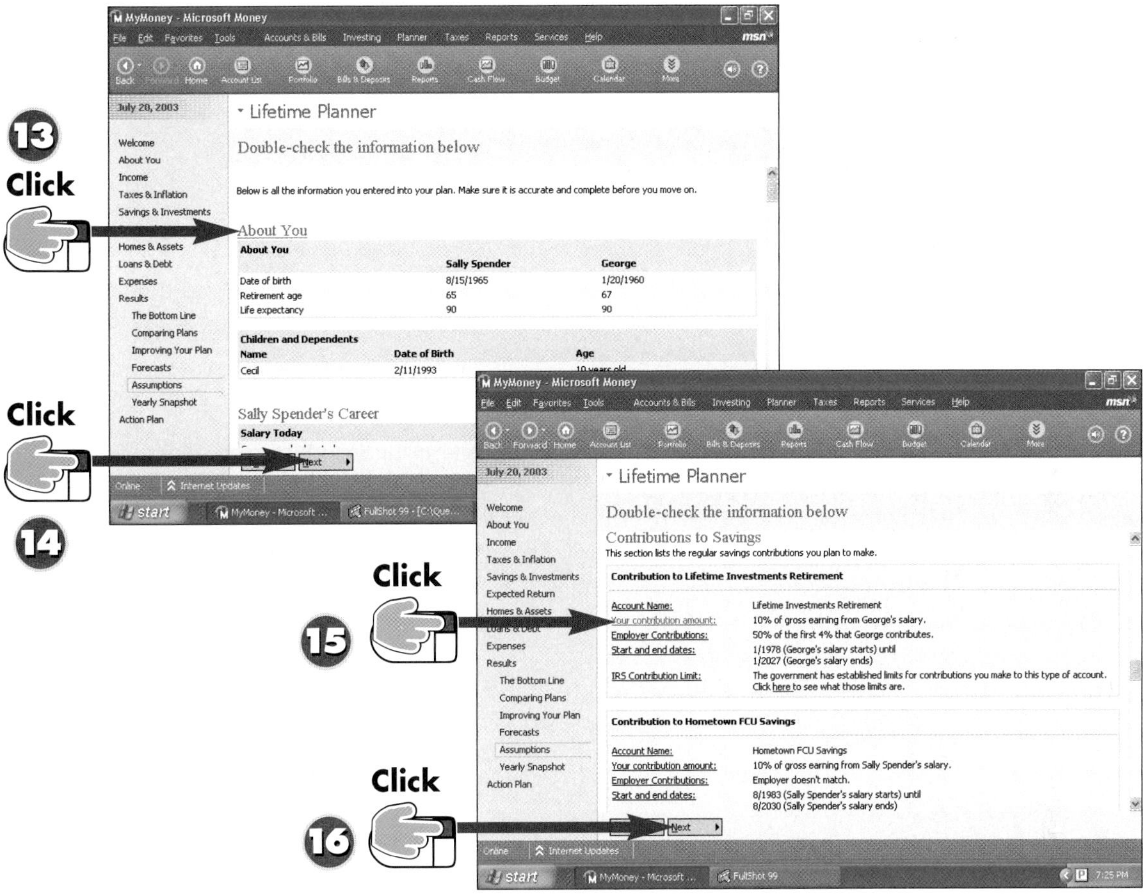

13 To make changes to any of the information, click the category heading, make your changes, and click **Results** on the left side of the window to return to the results.

14 Click **Next**.

15 Review your savings information. If you see something you want to change, click the link next to the contribution to go to that area, and make your changes.

16 Click **Next**.

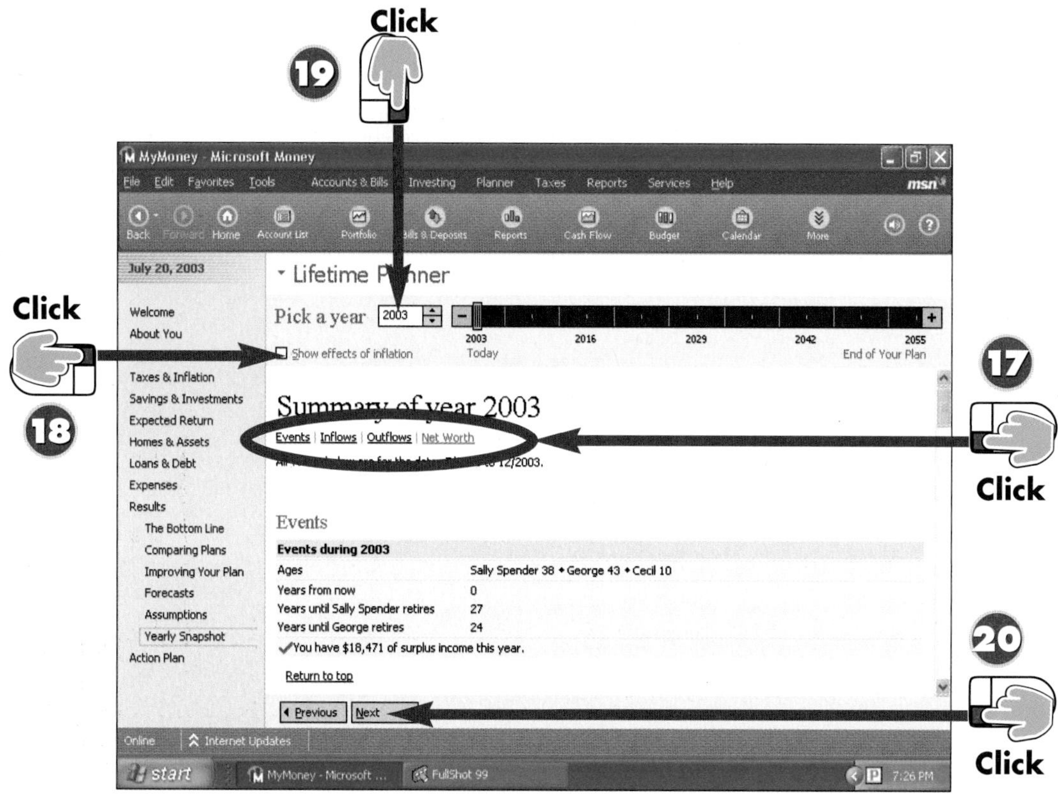

17 Review your yearly plan summary by either scrolling down or clicking the **Events**, **Inflows**, **Outflows**, or **Net Worth** short-cut links.

18 To see the effects of inflation on your financial outlook, click in the **Show effects of inflation** check box.

19 Type a year in the **Pick a year** spin box to see what your finances will look like during that year.

20 Click **Next**.

Putting Your Plan into Action

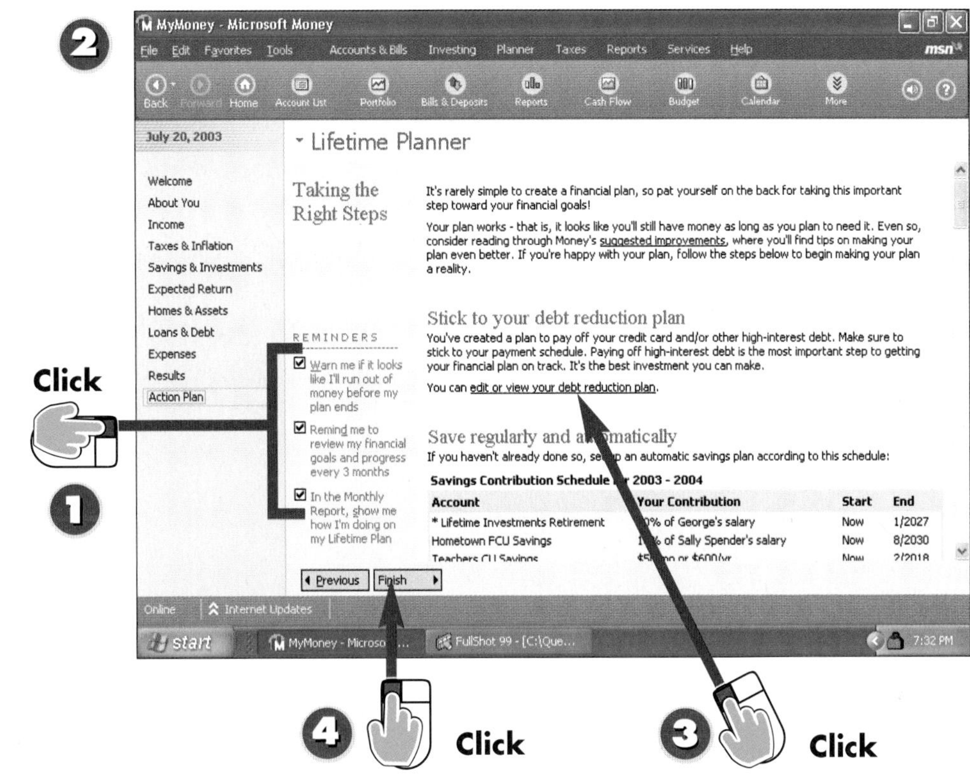

1. Click the check boxes under **Reminders** if you want Money to place reminders related to your lifetime plan on your home page to help you reach your goals.
2. Give your plan a final once-over by reading through the information in the main part of the screen.
3. Click any of the links that Money provides if you want to tweak your information or learn more about a particular topic.
4. When you are satisfied with your plan, click **Finish**.

INTRODUCTION

Now all that's left to do is put your plan into action. Don't worry, you can always make changes later; you should review and re-evaluate your plan from time to time anyway. Return to this part and repeat the appropriate tasks when it's time to update your plan.

TIP

Tweaking the Plan
To change the start and end dates for your accounts, click **change this chart's start and end dates**. To see how inflation could impact your accounts, select the box next to **Show effects of inflation**.

PART 12

Planning for and Managing Major Purchases

If you are in the market to buy a house—or are considering obtaining a loan for other purchases—and aren't sure how much you can afford, you can use Money's House and Loan area to get the answers you need. You can also use this area to keep track of your household items, a feature that can come in really handy for insurance purposes. Another nice feature is the loan comparison. By comparing loans, you can see ahead of time how much you will end up paying back, determine what the best terms are for you, and enable yourself to plan ahead.

The House and Loan Tasks

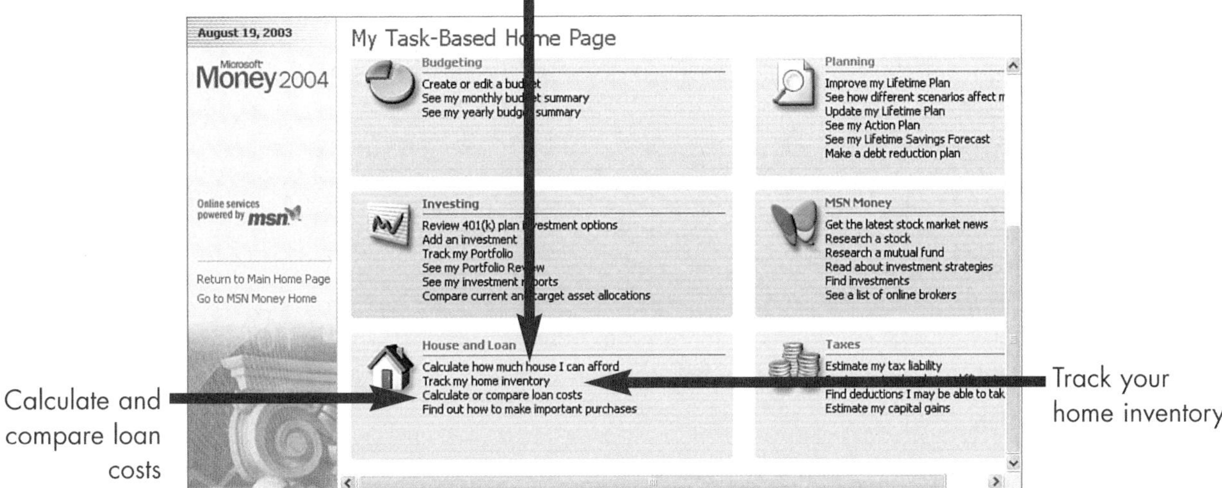

Determining How Much House You Can Afford

Start

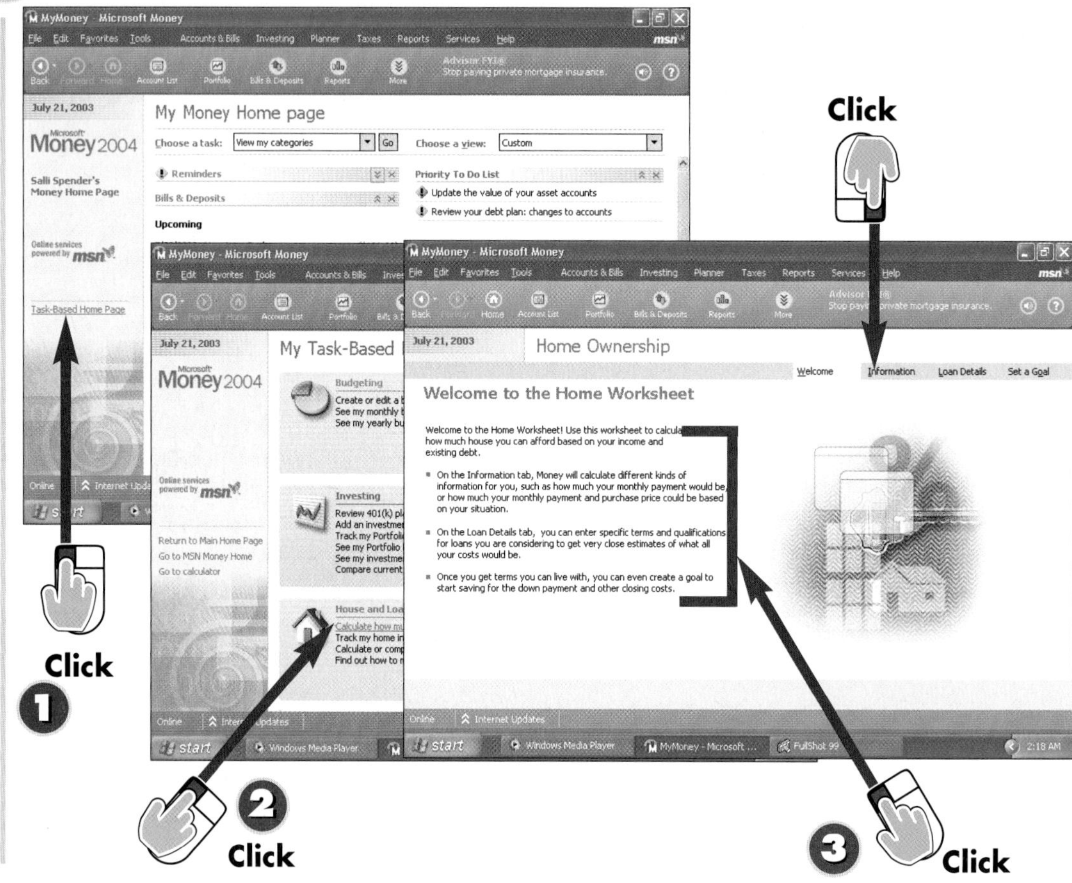

1. In the My Money home page, click the **Task-based Home Page** link on the left side of the window.
2. In the **House and Loan** area of the task-based home page, click the **Calculate how much house I can afford** link. Money opens the Home Worksheet.
3. Listen to or read the home worksheet information on the left side of the window. Then click the **Information** link.
4. Click the **Calculate** down arrow and select how you want Money to calculate the house costs.

INTRODUCTION

You can use Money's Home Worksheet to quickly and easily determine just how much house you can afford. This feature is really nice because it doesn't require much work on your part. All the information you've already entered in Money is recycled and used here.

TIP

Editing the Home Worksheet

Money automatically fills in most of the information in the Home Worksheet based on all the financial information you have already entered into Money. If you want to change it, click in the box you want to change and type the new information.

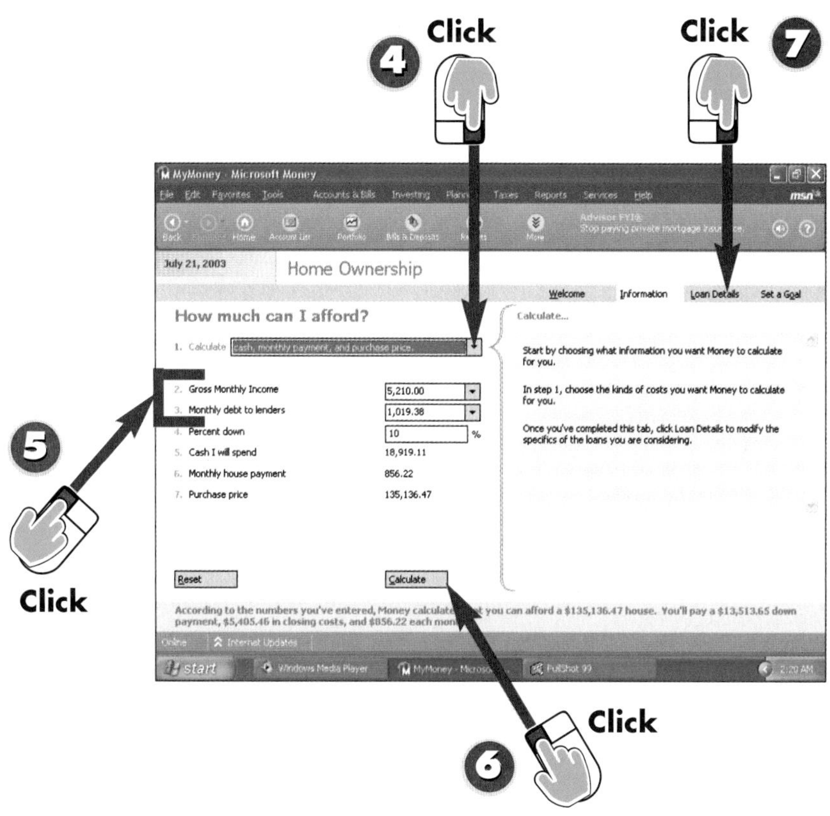

5 Change the figures, if needed, in the **Gross Monthly Income**, **Monthly debt to lenders**, and **Percent down** boxes.

6 Click the **Calculate** button to see how much cash you would need to put down, the monthly house payment, and purchase price.

7 Repeat steps 5–6 to adjust the figures. To change the loan details, click the **Loan Details** link.

8 Confirm or change the details of the loan, such as the length of the loan, the interest rate, and so on.

See next page

TIP

Getting Explanations
Click in one of the boxes under **Confirm the details of the loan** to see an explanation for that box. In step 8, the explanation is shown for the **Property taxes** box.

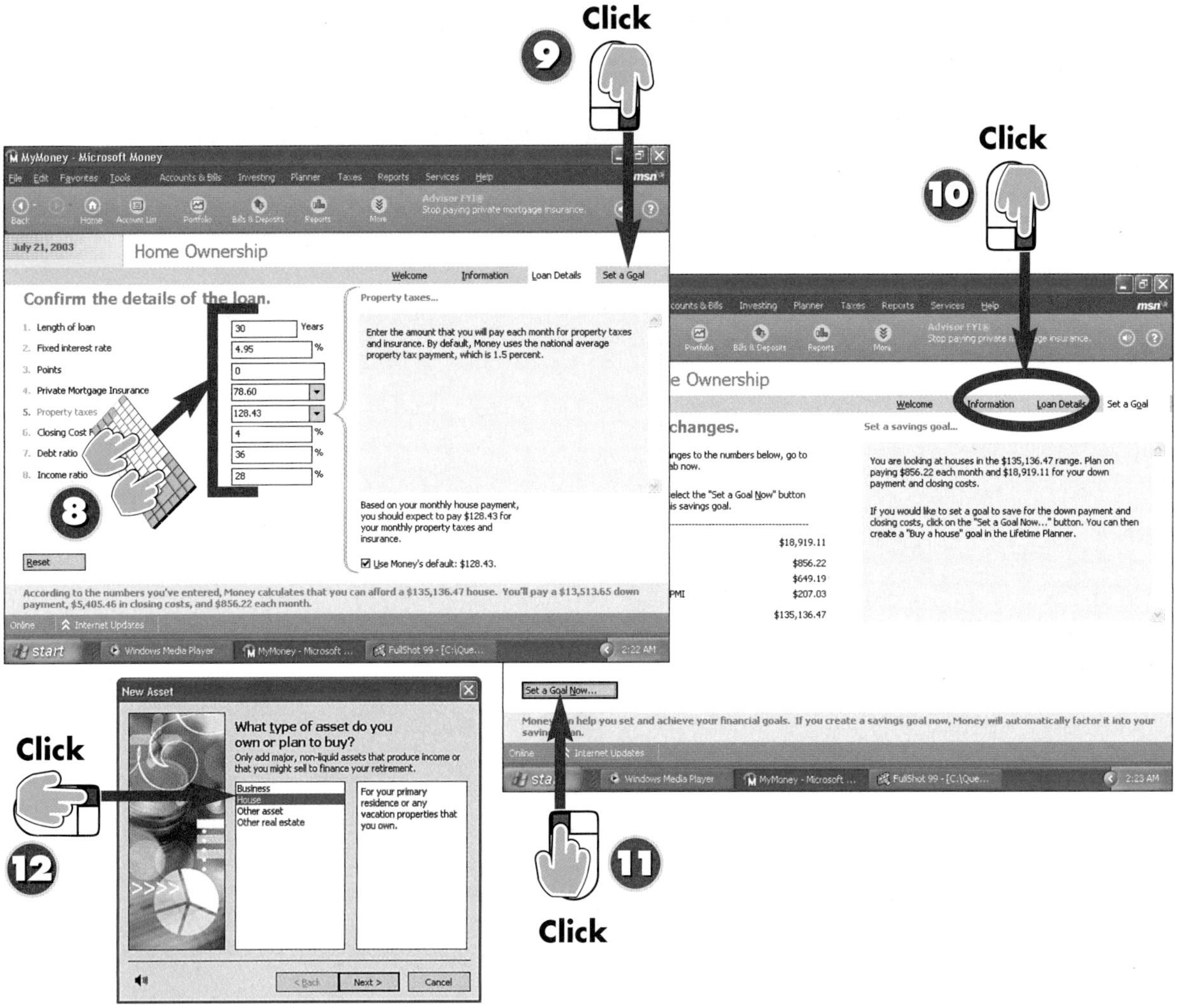

9 Money displays the loan totals at the bottom of the page; read them over. To plan for the loan, click the **Set a Goal** link.

10 To go back and adjust any of the loan costs, click either the **Information** or **Loan Details** link to make your changes.

11 When you are finished making changes, click the **Set a Goal Now** button to add the goal to your lifetime plan. Money opens your plan and the New Asset wizard.

12 The wizard asks you a series of questions. Answer the questions, clicking **Next** to go to the next question. Click **Finish** when you are done.

TIP

Clearing the Loan Details
Click the **Reset** button on the window shown in steps 8 and 9 to clear the current loan details and enter new ones.

Taking Inventory

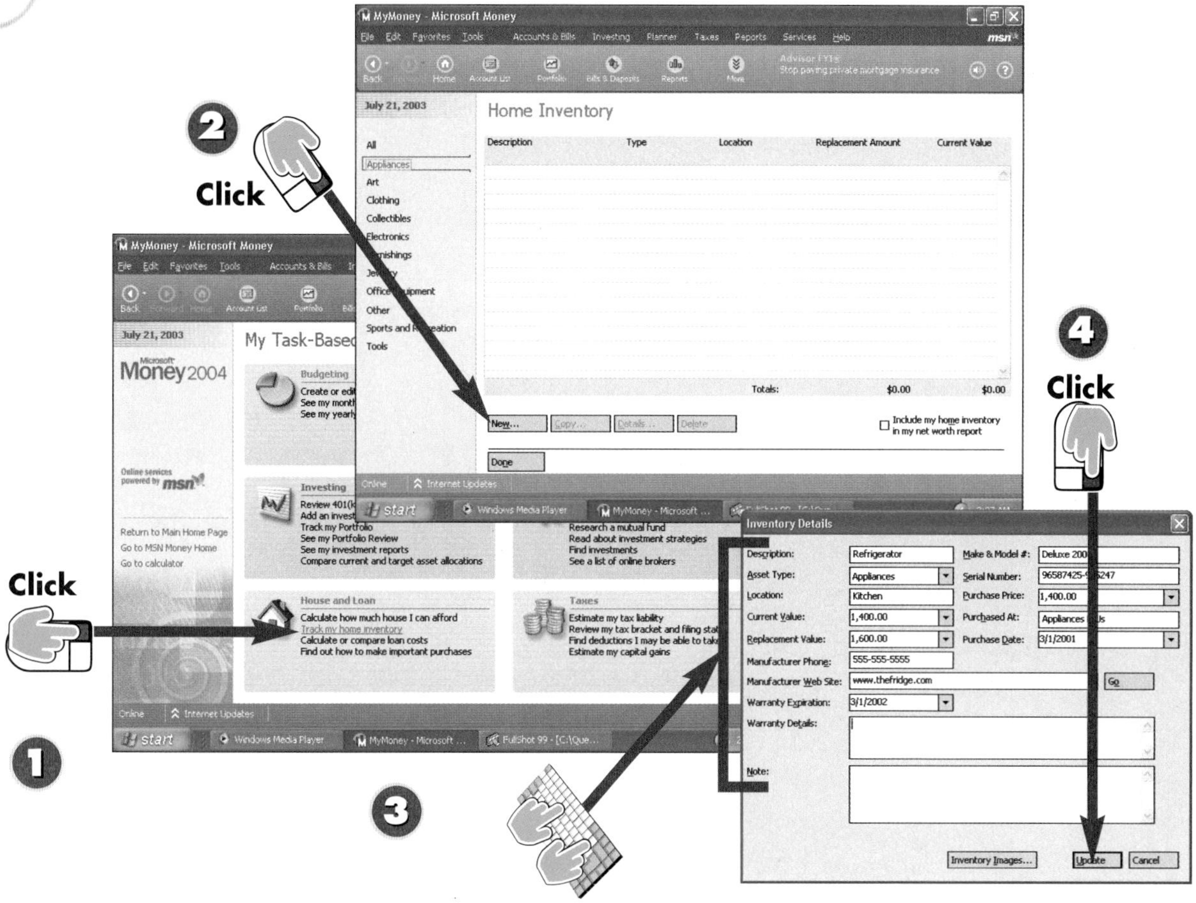

1. On the My Money home page, click the **Task-based Home Page** link. Then click the **Track my home inventory** link in the **House and Loan** area.
2. On the left side of the window, click the category for which you want to add a new item (here, **Appliances** is shown) and click the **New** button.
3. Type everything you know about the item you want to inventory. (If you're missing some information, don't worry; you can come back and enter it later.)
4. Click the **Update** button.

See next page

INTRODUCTION

Whether you own a house or not, you most likely have plenty of items you should keep track of for insurance purposes. Before you start taking inventory, be sure you have receipts and the make and model (if applicable) of the items you are entering.

Start

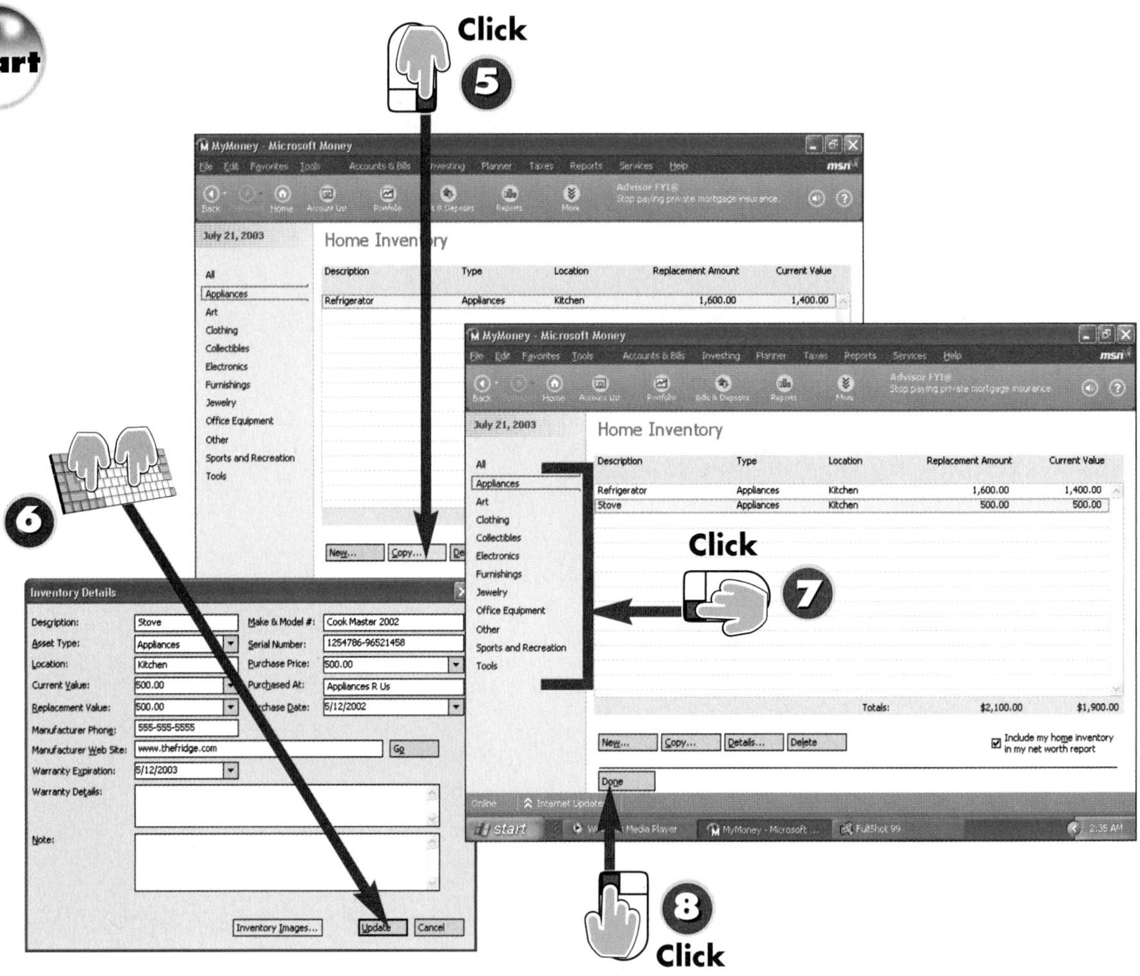

Click 5

Click 7

6

Click 8

5 To copy an item you've already entered to use as a template for a new item, select the item you want to copy from the list and click the **Copy** button.

6 Type over the copied information to enter the details of the new item, and click the **Update** button.

7 Continue adding all the items you want to inventory for each category listed on the left side of the window.

8 When you are finished entering all of your items, click **Done**.

TIP

Including Assets
If you want an item to be included as part of your overall net worth, select it and then click the **Include my home inventory in my net worth report** check box.

TIP

Removing an Item
To remove an item from the inventory, select it and click the **Delete** button. A confirmation message appears; click **Yes** to delete the item.

TIP

Updating Item Details
To review and/or change information for an item, select it and click the **Details** button. Make your changes in the Inventory Details dialog box and click **Update** when you're finished.

Comparing Loans

Click 2

Click 3

Click 1

4

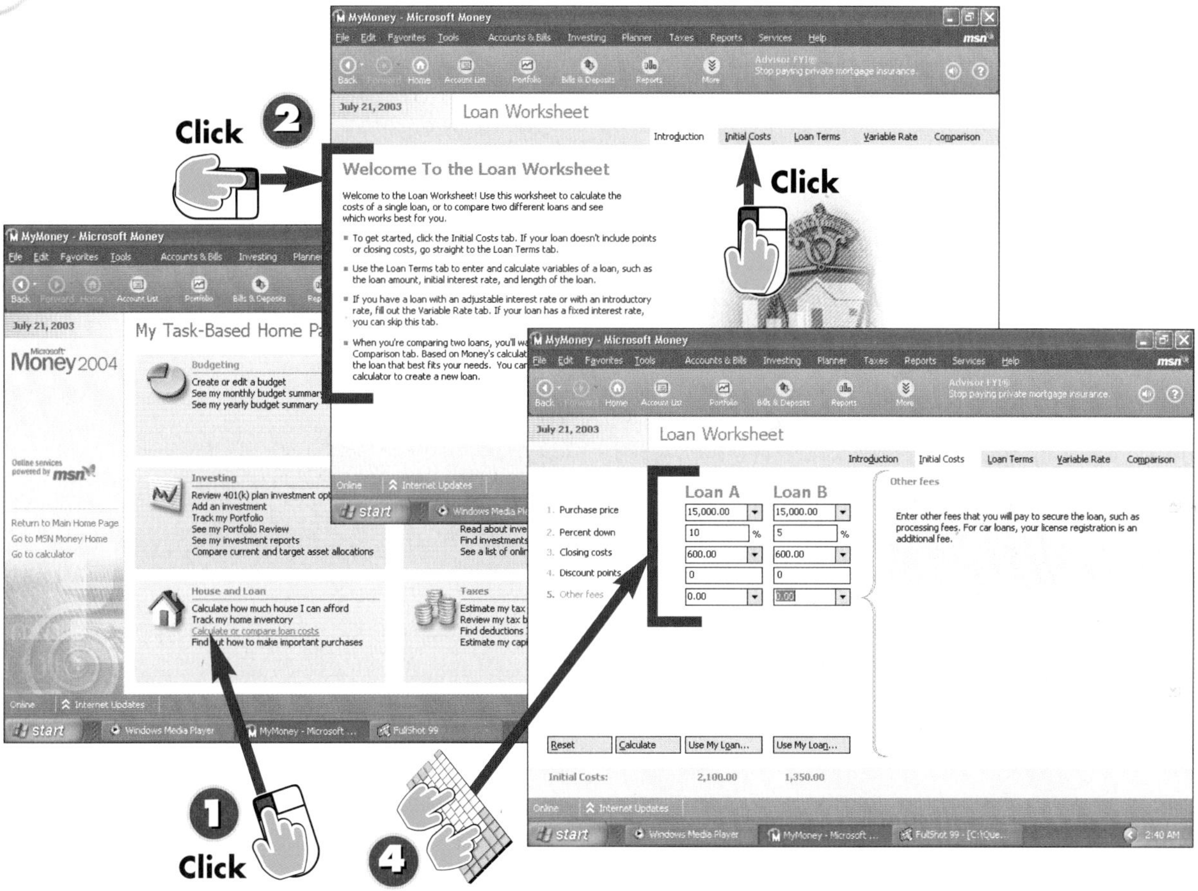

1. On the My Money home page, click the **Task-based Home Page** link, and click the **Calculate or compare loan costs** link in the **House and Loan** area.
2. Money opens the Loan Worksheet. Listen to or read the information on the left side of the window.
3. Click the **Initial Costs** link.
4. Enter the initial loan costs for both loans.

See next page

INTRODUCTION

If you are considering buying a house, getting a loan to remodel your house, or some other expensive item, Money's Loan Comparison feature is a great way to see what type of loan will work best for you.

TIP

Viewing Explanations
Click in one of the boxes under Loan A or Loan B to see an explanation for that box. In step 3, the explanation is shown for the Other fees box.

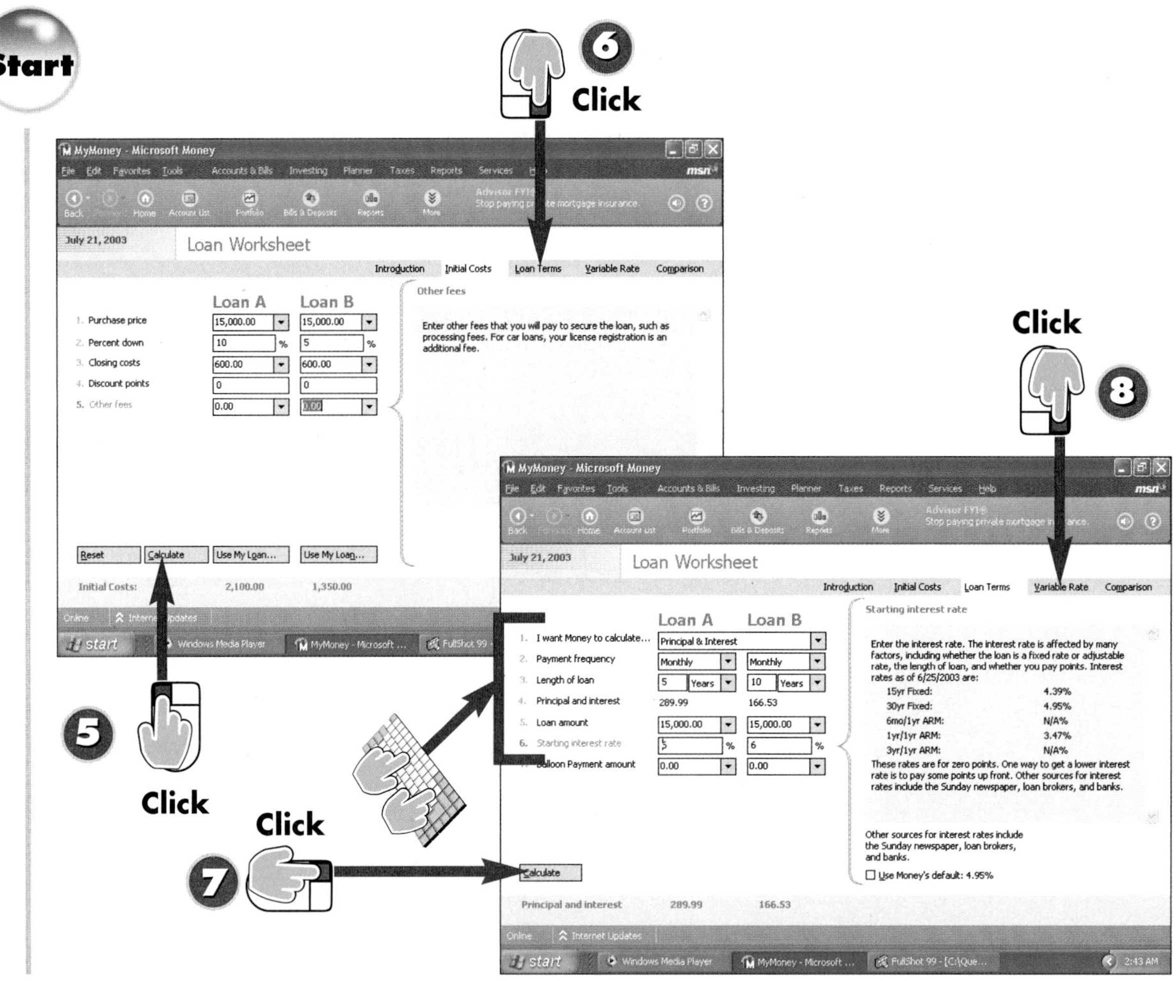

5 Click the **Calculate** button to see the results of both loans at the bottom of the window next to **Initial Costs**.

6 Click the **Loan Terms** link.

7 Enter the loan terms and click the **Calculate** button. Experiment by entering different terms.

8 To experiment with a variable rate, click the **Variable Rate** link. If you are not interested in a variable-rate loan, skip to step 11.

TIP

Comparing Loans
On the screen shown in steps 4–6, click the **Use my loan** button under the details for either loan A or loan B (or both) to compare existing loan accounts.

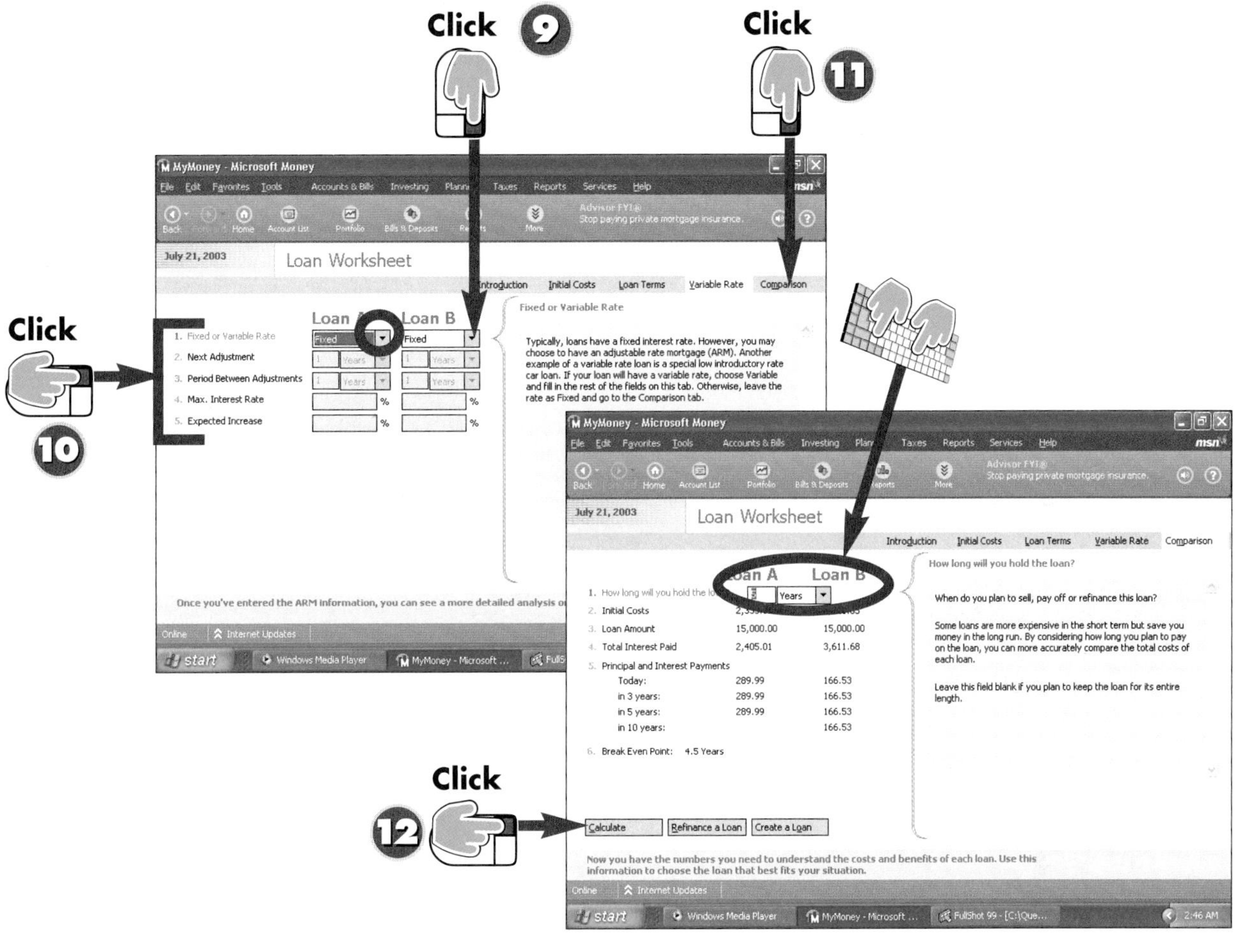

Click 9

Click 11

Click 10

Click 12

9 Click the **Fixed or Variable Rate** down arrow for both loan A and loan B and select **Variable**.

10 Enter the variable-rate information for both loan A and B.

11 Click **Comparison**.

12 Enter how long you expect to keep the loan, and click **Calculate**. The results of the loan comparison are displayed in lines 2–6.

TIP

Getting Refinance Information

If you want to see the results of refinancing a loan, click the **Refinance a Loan** button on the window shown in step 12. To create a new loan account, click the **Create a Loan** button.

Money Extras

With Money, you can research all kinds of financial information, go shopping, get hooked up with online banking, or just read up on the latest financial news. You can also get your credit report, monitor your credit for a year for free, and get some good advice on how to better your credit and protect yourself. In this part, you'll explore some of Money's extra features.

Another area you'll learn about in this part is the Purchase wizard. You can use the Purchase wizard to see what it would take to buy an expensive item, remodel your house, take that vacation you've been dreaming of, or just loan a friend some money. You can also get advice on taking out loans, as well as get buying tips. Planning your purchases or loans is a great way to know where your money is going so you can make some well-thought-out financial decisions.

Financial Services

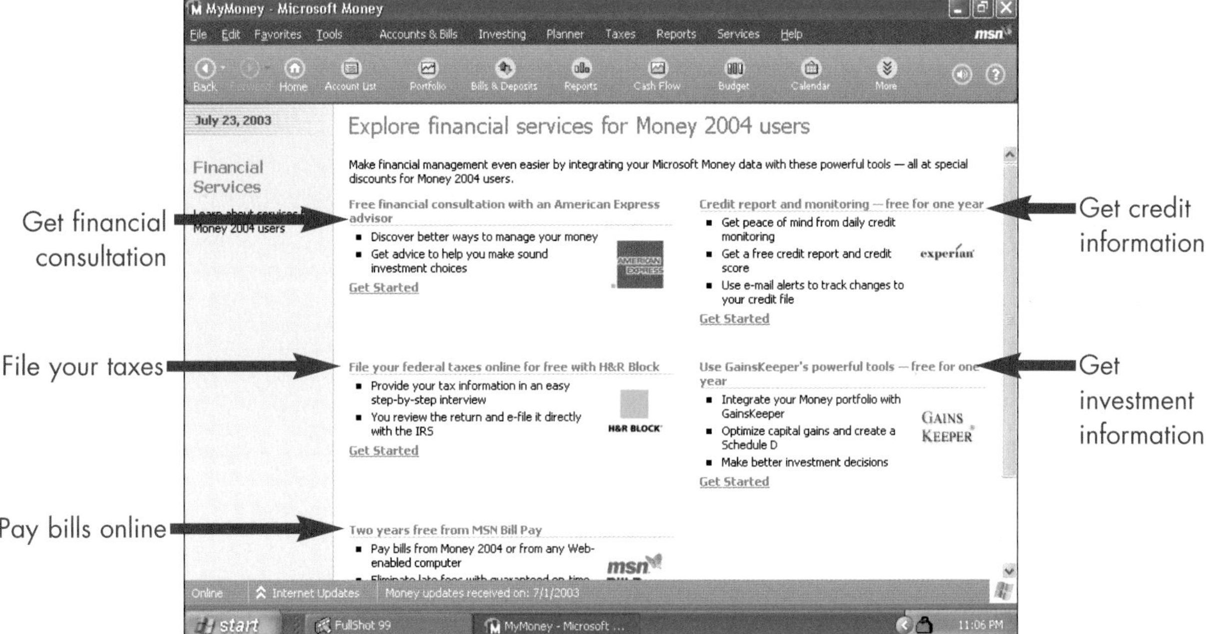

Exploring Money Services

Start

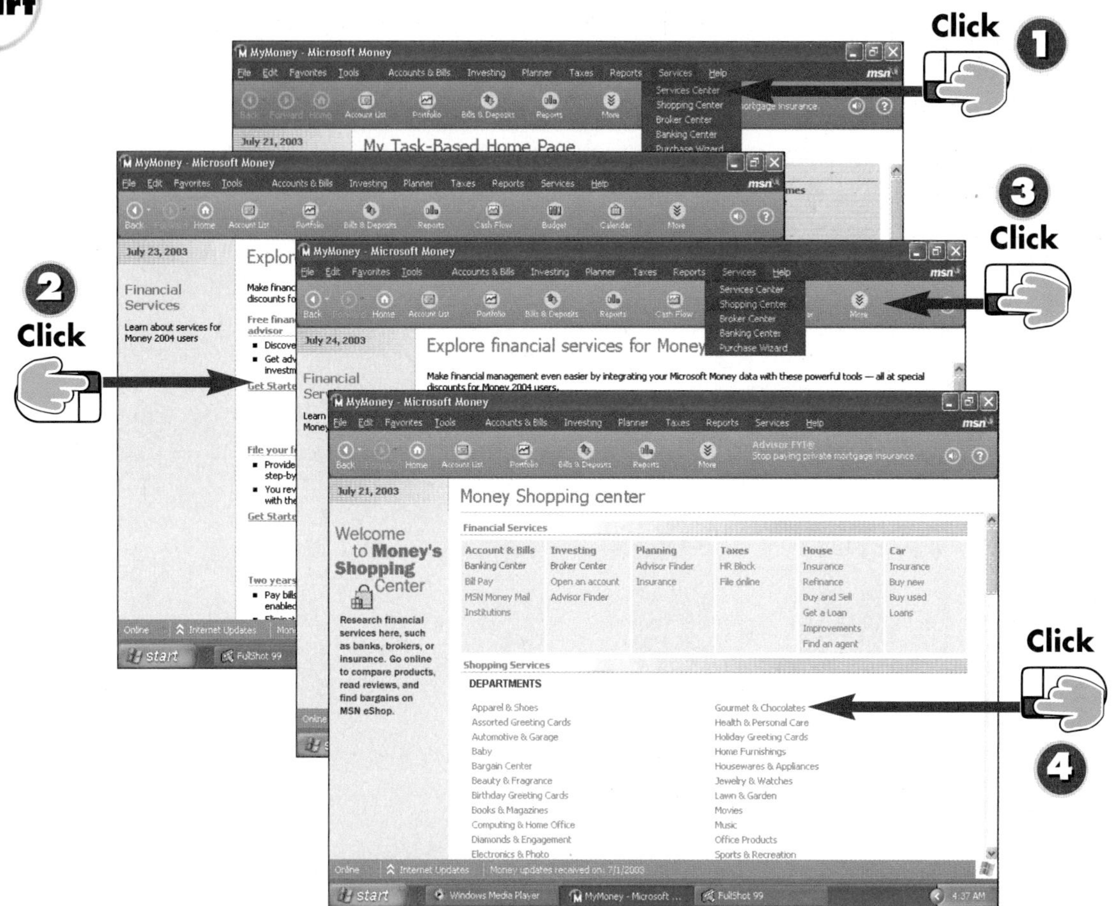

1. Open the **Services** menu and choose **Services Center**.

2. Read through all the services Money provides. To get information about a service, click the **Get Started** link under the service category you want to see.

3. Open the **Services** menu and choose **Shopping Center**.

4. Review the shopping categories. If you want to shop for products in a certain category, such as Gourmet & Chocolates, click the category link.

INTRODUCTION

Money Services provides you with links to all kinds of information related to your finances. Most options listed under the Services menu are accessible through the Internet. So, get connected before you try the links.

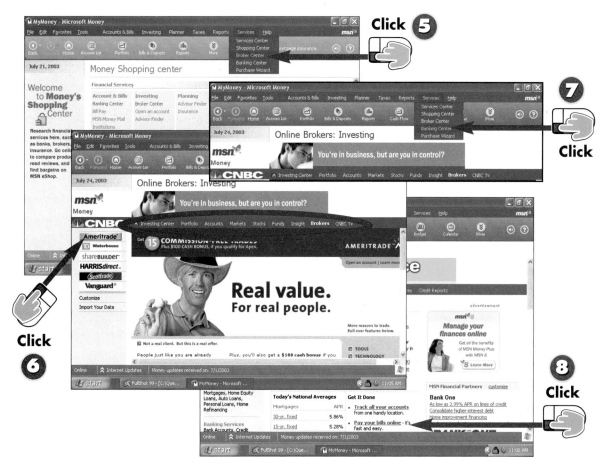

5. Open the **Services** menu and choose **Broker Center**.

6. Click links on the Online Brokers: Investing page to find information about broker services, investments, and the like.

7. Open the **Services** menu and choose **Banking Center**.

8. Click links on the Banking & Bills Home page to read about banking services, interest rates, loans, and more.

See next page

TIP

Accessing the Portfolio

From the menu bar encircled on the image shown in step 6, you can access some of your portfolio and account information. For example, clicking the Portfolio link opens your portfolio window in Money.

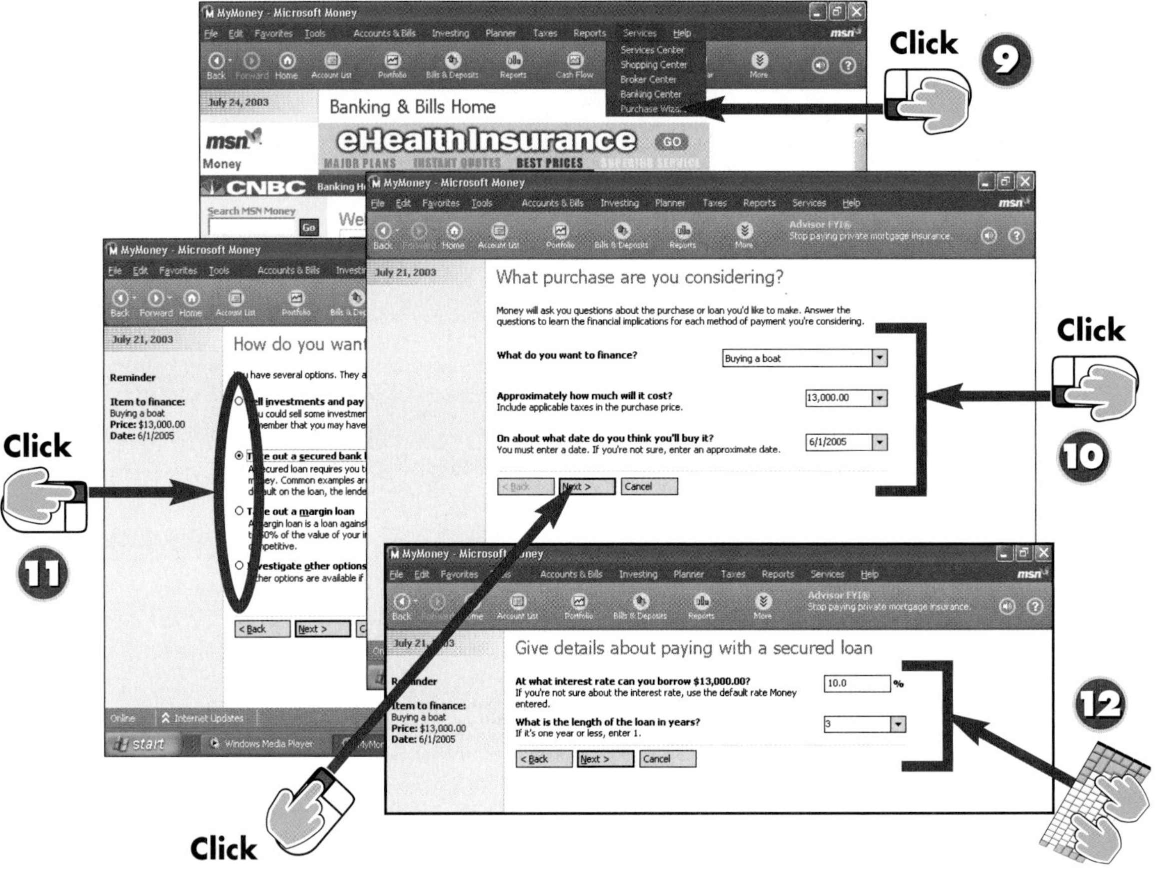

9 To experiment with financing a purchase, open the **Services** menu and choose **Purchase Wizard**.

10 Using the drop-down lists, select the item you want to finance, the amount, and the date. Then click **Next**.

11 Select how you want to pay for the purchase, and click **Next**.

12 Enter the interest rate and loan length, and then click **Next**.

TIP

Clicking the Headings

Click the headings (for example, **My Accounts**) on the left side of the Banking Center page shown in step 9 to access some of your accounts, use online services, and view financial information.

TIP

Trying Different Figures

If after reviewing the results you want to try different figures, click **Try Another**. Click **Print** to print the results.

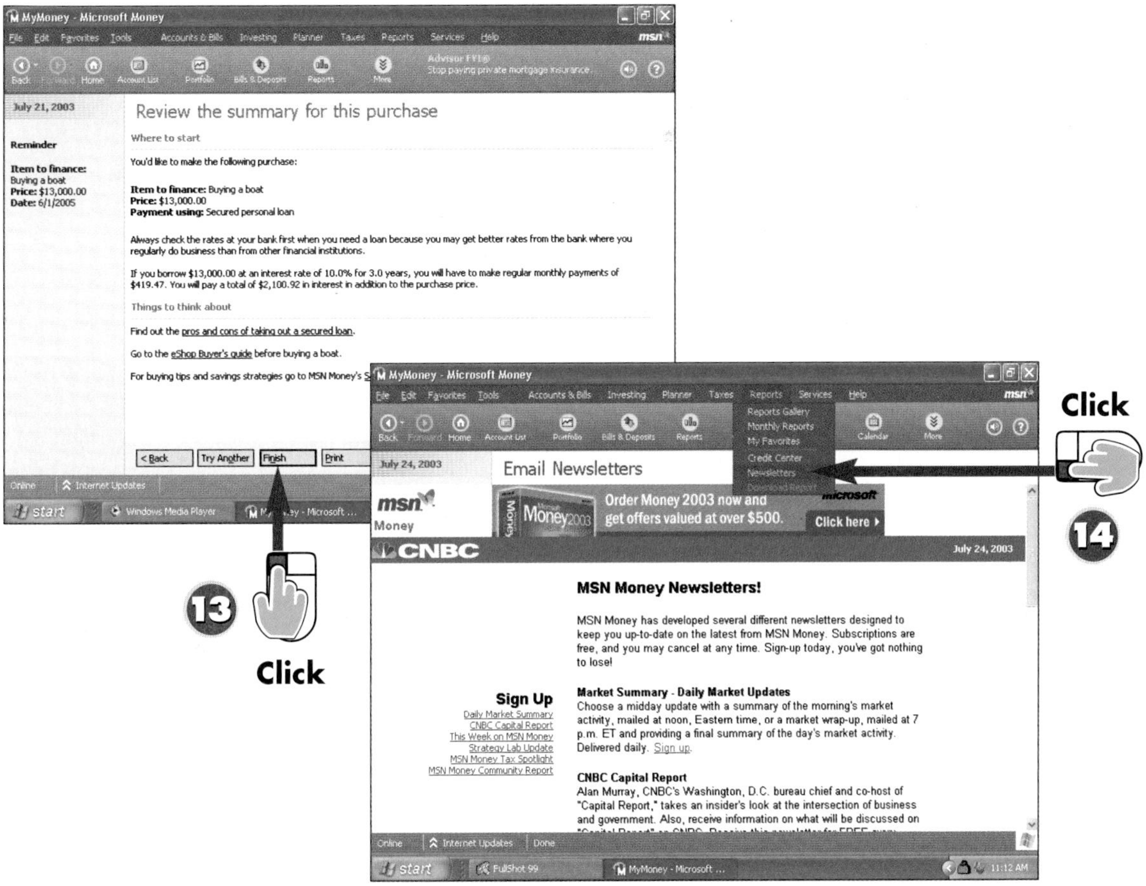

13 Money outlines your payment information. After you've read it, click **Finish**.

14 To read up on everything financial, check out Money Newsletters by opening the **Reports** menu and choosing **Newsletters**.

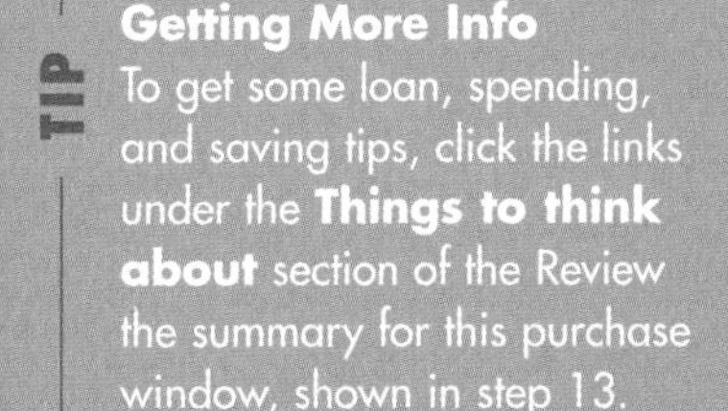

TIP

Getting More Info

To get some loan, spending, and saving tips, click the links under the **Things to think about** section of the Review the summary for this purchase window, shown in step 13.

TIP

Reading Reports

Notice on the left side of the Money newsletter page in step 14 that there are more links you should check out for other financial-related reports and news items. Click a link to find out more.

Checking Your Credit

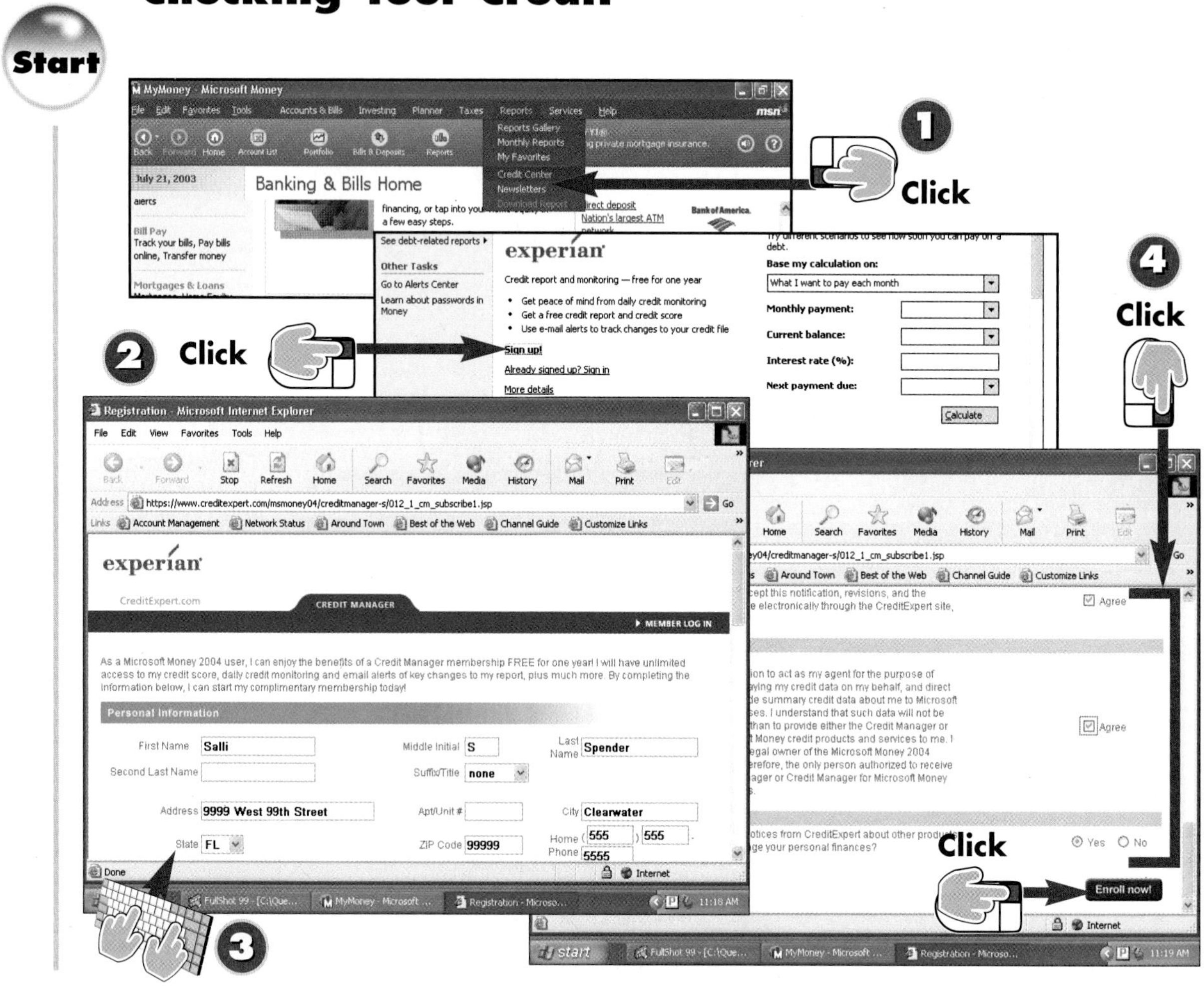

Start

1 Open the **Reports** menu and choose **Credit Center**.

2 To check your credit and sign up for credit monitoring, click the **Sign up** link. Your browser opens the Experian Web site.

3 Enter your personal information in the spaces provided, then scroll down.

4 Read the questions carefully and click the option buttons and check boxes on the right to answer them. When you're finished, click the **Enroll now** button.

INTRODUCTION

Keep your finger on the pulse of your credit activity by checking your credit, getting credit advice, and signing up for services that allow you to monitor your credit using Money's Credit Center. You get the first year of credit monitoring for free.

TIP

Getting More Information
For more information about Experian's credit monitoring, click the **More details** link beneath the **Sign up** link shown in step 2.

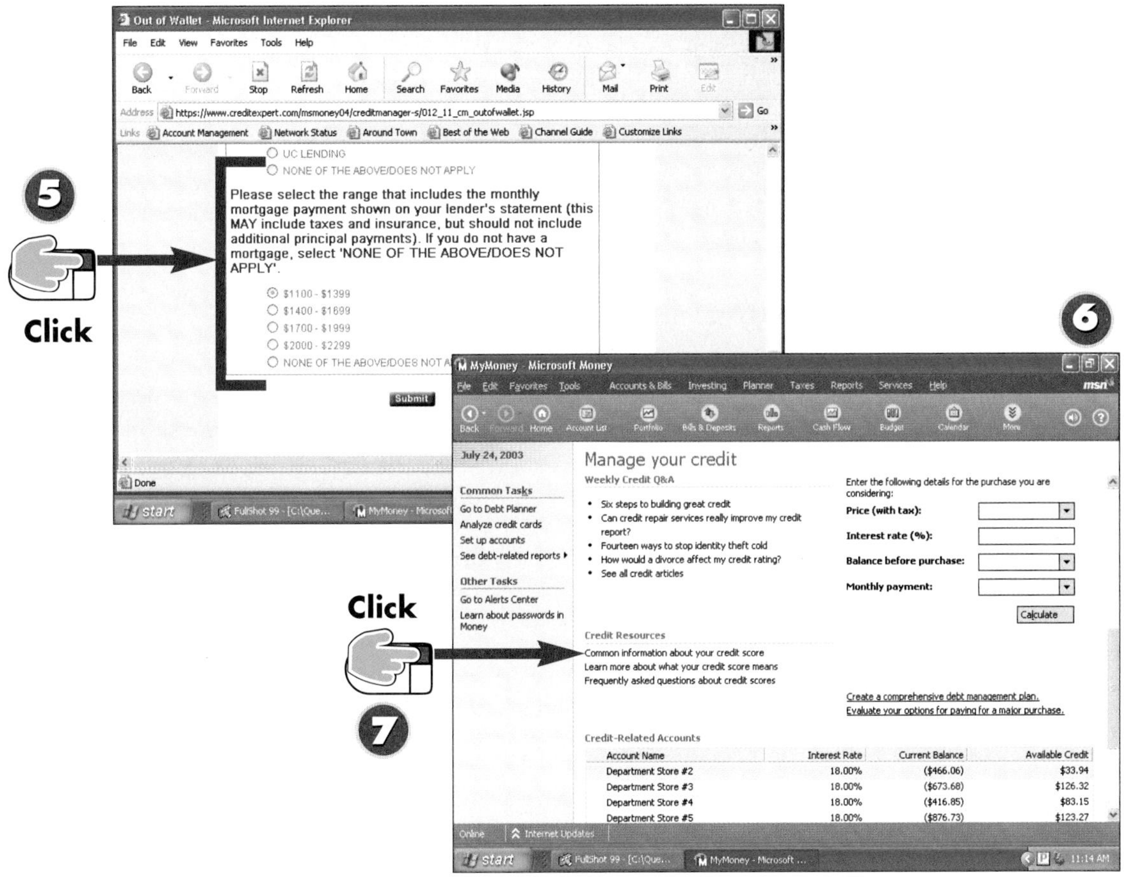

5 Click

6

Click 7

5. On the Congratulations page, scroll down and answer yet more questions by clicking the appropriate options. Then click the **Submit** button.

6. When you are finished checking your credit, close your browser. Money should still be open to the Manage your credit window.

7. Click the links on the page to read credit-management advice and information, or even review your credit accounts.

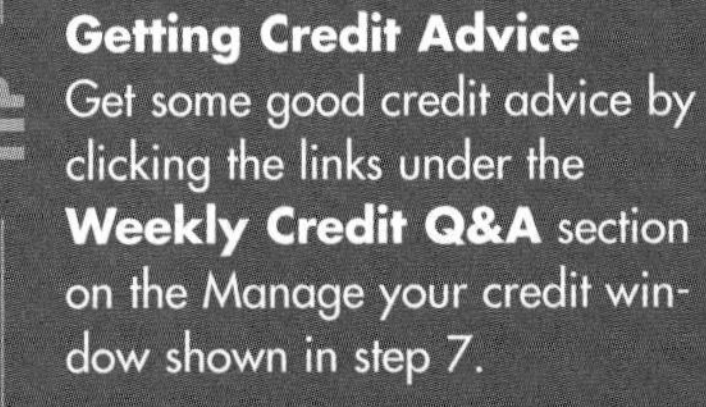

TIP

Getting Credit Advice

Get some good credit advice by clicking the links under the **Weekly Credit Q&A** section on the Manage your credit window shown in step 7.

Glossary

Numbers and Symbols

401K A savings plan offered by a corporation to its employees, which allows employees to save tax-deferred income for retirement purposes. Some employers will contribute to the employee's 401K by matching the employee's contribution.

A–B

Advisor A feature in Money that alerts you to important information or actions you should take—for example, financial advice, reminders to update quotes or your accounts, and so on. The Advisor displays messages on the Money toolbar and on your home page.

backing up To copy a file to an alternate location, such as a *floppy disk*, to save in case the file cannot be retrieved from its primary location.

bond A debt instrument issued for a specific amount and period of time—usually more than one year—that the government uses to raise capital. You can buy bonds from the federal government, states, cities, corporations, and many other types of institutions. A bond gains interest over the period of time you have it; after it reaches maturity, you get your money back and any interest that accrued during the time you had it.

broker A licensed individual or firm that acts as an intermediary between a buyer and seller of investments or financial services, and usually works on commission.

browse To explore the *World Wide Web* on the Internet, viewing Web pages through a *browser*. This is also known as "surfing" or "cruising the Net."

browser A program such as Internet Explorer or Netscape Navigator that enables you to view Web pages.

budget An itemized spending and savings plan you can set up in Money using the Budget Planner to streamline your spending habits in order to reduce your debt and save money.

Budget Planner A tool you use in Money to create and plan a budget for your finances. Money then tracks all your spending and savings and reminds you when you are not sticking to your budget.

C

capital gains The amount of an asset's or investment's selling price that exceeds the purchase price, producing a profit if sold.

Cash-flow forecast A feature in Money that shows you how much money you have for each of your accounts for a specific time period, ranging from the current date to the immediate future. The cash-flow forecast is based on all the accounts, bills, and income information you've entered in Money.

CD Certificate of Deposit, which is a short-term, interest-bearing, and insured type of savings. It offers higher rates of return, but ties up funds for an agreed-upon time frame (anywhere from three months to six years).

check box A small, square box used to select objects in a software program or on a Web page. Clicking an empty check box inserts a check mark there, indicating that the object or option next to the check box is selected. Clicking a check box that already has a check mark in it removes the check mark, indicating that option is not selected.

classification A term used in Money to describe a way to organize your finances. For example, you can create up two classifications for specific expenses, such as a rental property.

cut To remove text or an object from a document or file. When cut, the text or object can be *pasted* elsewhere, such as in another file.

D

Debt Reduction Planner A tool you use in Money to create a plan to reduce or completely eliminate debt. Money incorporates the plan into your budget (assuming you set one up), tracks all your spending and savings, and reminds you when you are not sticking to your plan.

debt-to-income ratio The percentage of your debt compared to your income. Standard, acceptable debt is 36 to 42 percent. Anything beyond that is headed for trouble. You can figure your monthly debt-to-income by multiplying your monthly income by .38 (standard percentage of debt).

deduction An expense approved by the IRS (Internal Revenue Service) that can be subtracted from your gross income, for example for charitable gifts.

Deduction Finder A tool you use in Money to find deductions you can take on your taxes. After you answer a series of questions, Money uses the information you enter to determine the deductions for which you most likely qualify.

desktop The area on your computer that is visible when no applications are open. Your desktop contains icons that link to files or applications.

dialog box A box that pops up in Windows programs to provide the options necessary for completing a particular task. Different tasks display different dialog boxes.

dial-up service Internet service that is accessed usually through a modem, which dials a specific number to connect to the Internet provider's server, allowing users to cruise the Internet, access email, and so on.

diskette *See **floppy disk**.*

Dow Jones Industrial Average An indicator of the overall condition of the stock market. The Dow average is determined by *Wall Street Journal* editors who add up all the prices of all the stocks and divide them by the number of stocks in the index.

download To copy information, such as a file, from a server computer to your computer. *See also* ***upload***.

E

email address The Internet address an email program uses to send email messages to a specific Internet user.

exemption A reduction of your taxable income approved by the IRS that you can take on your taxes.

export To copy a file or other information from the current location to another location—for example, from your computer to a Web site or from Money to Excel.

F

Favorites list A list of your most-used files or other information, such as reports. Browsers such as Internet Explorer allow you to create a Favorites list for all the Web sites you frequent most.

fixed-rate loan A loan whose interest rate stays the same for the entire term of the loan.

floppy disk A square diskette inserted in your computer's A: drive, used to store files and information. It can be inserted and removed so that you can take the disk with you or keep backups of your files for safekeeping.

G–H

gross pay The total amount of income before taxes, benefit costs, and other expenses are taken from it.

home page Refers to the starting point for all your accounts and financial information in Money. Web sites also have home pages. In this book, however, home page refers to your Money home page.

hyperlink *See* ***link***.

I

icons (desktop) Small pictures or symbols that represent software applications, such as Money, that are placed on your desktop or on your taskbar when a software system is installed on your computer. Clicking an icon opens the software system.

import To copy a file or other information from another location to a current location, for example, from a Web site to your computer, or from Quicken to Money.

Internet A large network of computers connecting universities, research institutions, governments, businesses, and private individuals in order to exchange messages, share information, engage in commerce, and more.

investment An item purchased for income or capital appreciation.

J–L

Lifetime Planner A tool you use in Money to create a plan to attain lifetime goals, such as for retirement. Money incorporates the plan into your budget (assuming you set one up), tracks your spending and savings, and reminds you when you are not sticking to your plan.

link Short for hyperlink, an object or text (typically underlined) on a Web page or document that, once clicked, enables the user to view another location on the page or document, view a different document or page, download a file, or trigger some other action.

M

menu A list of choices on a computer screen. A user selects one choice to perform an action within a software application.

mutual fund An account you can purchase that is serviced by an investment company to raise money from stocks, bonds, and so on. You can sell mutual funds at any time, but the price of a share in a mutual fund changes daily, depending upon the performance of the securities held by the fund. There are many types of mutual funds, each providing different risks and benefits.

N

NASDAQ A computerized exchange system created to facilitate the buying and selling (also known as *trading*) of securities and commodities by providing stock brokers and dealers with current quotes. Trading on the NASDAQ exchange is done over a network of computers and telephones.

.NET Passport A login identification and password that allows you to access all .NET Passport–participating sites and services, such as Money's online banking features and a host of information. In addition, having a .NET Passport password provides some conveniences, such as keeping track of your password if you forget it.

net pay The total amount of income after taxes, benefit costs, and other expenses are taken from it.

O–P

online services Refers to those functions in Money that are accessed through the Internet.

payee The person or business to which a payment is made.

pie chart A chart that is circular and color-coded or divided in slices (like a pie), each slice representing different information, such as how your investments are spread out.

pop-up menu A software application menu that arises when clicked on.

portfolio A collection of investments owned by an individual that can include stocks, bonds, mutual funds, and so on.

Q

Quicken A software application similar to Money that you can use to manage your finances. Quicken files can be imported and used in Money, which means that if you are converting from Quicken to Money, you won't have to enter all your financial information again.

quote Refers to the percentage rates and stock prices that Money downloads from the Internet to ensure it has all the latest updates for your accounts. Money uses the quotes to update your accounts and predict your cash-flow forecast, among other things.

R

reminder A feature you use in Money to bring to your attention important information regarding your finances and to ensure that your finances are running smoothly. Reminders appear on your home page to warn you if you are going over budget, are running out of money, or need to pay a bill, among other things.

Reports Gallery An area of Money where you can view, print, save, or send various reports. The reports are all based on the accounts and financial information you've entered in Money.

S

scroll The process of moving through (up/down or left/right) a document or Web page by clicking the down or up arrows that appear on a scrollbar.

select Clicking on text, in a check box, or other option in order to indicate that you want to create, change, or manipulate information in some way. For example, you click in a check box to include its information for your accounts.

Setup Assistant A tool you use to set up a new Money file.

share A certificate that represents part ownership in a corporation or mutual fund.

split A term used in Money to refer to the process of dividing income or expense into two or more accounts or categories. For example, if you receive a direct deposit into your checking account and you have a portion of the deposit go to your savings account, you can tell Money to split the deposit and specify how much is to go in to each account.

stock An investment instrument that you can purchase from a corporation that offers it. The stock signifies an ownership or shareholder in a corporation, entitling the shareholder to make money from the corporation's assets and profits. The extent of ownership in the corporation is determined by the number of shares a person owns divided by the total number of shares.

symbol Refers to a company symbol used when checking quotes on the stock market.

T

Tax Estimator A tool you use in Money to estimate the taxes you'll pay for the current year. You enter your tax information for the previous year, which Money uses in combination with the other asset and account information you've entered to estimate how much your taxes will be.

toolbar A row of icons or buttons, usually near the top of the application's window. You click the buttons or icons to access information or perform tasks.

transaction Refers to a term Money uses to describe account activity that you enter in Money—for example deposits, bills you pay, and so on.

U

upgrade The updating of files and information to a newer format.

upload The act of copying information to a server computer from your computer. *See also* ***download***.

V

variable-rate loan A loan whose interest rate changes during the term of the loan.

view A term used in Money to refer to the information you see on a specific window. For example, in the Pick an account to use window, you can choose to see your accounts listed by name, type, favorites name, and so on, by changing the view.

W-Z

Web *See* ***World Wide Web***.

Web site A group of individual Web pages linked together to form a single, self-sufficient, multi-page location used to share information.

wizard An automated system, used to easily step you through a process, such as setting up account information in Money. There are many wizards you can use for setting up or changing much of the information you enter in Money—for example, accounts, loans, assets, investments, planning for large purchases, and so on.

World Wide Web (WWW or Web) A set of Internet computers and services that provide an easy-to-use system for finding information and moving among resources. The Web uses hyperlinks to allow you to move from site to site through the Internet. The nickname *Web* is befitting, considering that it links you to and from a menagerie of sites all over the world.

Index

A

Abbreviation box, 47

accessing

- accounts, 27
- bill information, 27
- favorite reports, 158
- files, 30
- help, 28
- investment information, 27
- Money, 4-5
- Money services information, 28
- planners, 27
- reports, 28
- Reports Gallery, 150
- tax-related information, 28
- Web help, 34

account balances

- discrepancies, handling, 92-93
- viewing, 46

account categories. *See also* categories

- adding, 60
- organizing, 58-59
- viewing, 58-59

account classifications, creating, 62

account lists, 45

- closing accounts from within, 54
- sorting, 91

Account List button, 46

account balances, entering, 12

account names, changing, 46

account numbers, changing, 72

Account tracking area, 47

account transactions, searching for, 87-89

account types, changing, 46

accounts. *See also* investment accounts

- accessing, 27
- adding notes about, 47
- adding spouse/partner accounts, 57
- adding spouse/partner information, 56
- adding to Favorites list, 47
- adding toolbar buttons for, 25
- balancing, 91-95
- bank accounts, 12
- bills, adding, 72-73
- closing from within account list, 54
- closing/reopening, 54
- credit card accounts, 13
- credit card accounts, closing, 54
- debt-reduction plan accounts, 124-127
- deleting, 55
- electronic pay accounts, 81
- entering information into, 12-14
- frequent-flyer accounts, 50-51
- information, reviewing, 46-48
- information, updating, 46-48
- investment purchase accounts, adding, 77
- new, adding, 52-53
- online accounts, setting up, 66
- opening, 26
- organizing, 26
- paying off, 122
- recording transactions, 70-71
- retirement accounts, 14
- sorting, 49
- specifying, 10-11
- updating, 35, 70
- viewing, 26

Accounts & Bills menu, 27

actions, reversing, 26

adding
- accounts (new), 52-53
- assets to financial plans, 188-189
- bills, 72-73
- to cash flow, 98
- categories, 41, 60
- deposits, 74-75
- frequent-flyer miles, 51
- goals, 108
- income (sporadic), 106
- investment accounts, 142-145
- investment purchase accounts, 77
- money transfers, 76
- paychecks, 74-75
- payees, 64
- recurring transactions in investment accounts, 138
- sub-categories, 60, 104
- tasks to task list, 39
- toolbar buttons, 25

Adjust Loan Payment Amount dialog, 79

adjusting
- budget information, 114-116
- printer settings, 32

Advanced Search tool, 87

advise, getting, 97

annual inflation percentage, determining, 179

arranging toolbar buttons, 24

assessing expenses, 192-195

audio help, turning off, 8

authorizing debt-reduction plans, 130-131

B

backing up files, 31

Balance dialog, 95

balances
- entering, 12
- viewing, 46
- viewing for downloaded statements, 67

balancing accounts, 91-95

bank accounts, 12

bank-account information, entering, 12

bank cards, 13

Banking Center, 215

baseline plans (lifetime plans), 196

bill details
- accessing, 27
- entering, 19-20
- modifying, 21

bill series, editing, 78

bills
- account information, editing, 86
- adding, 72-73
- deleting from list, 80
- entering details, 19-20
- paid bills, reviewing, 86
- paying online, 82
- recurring bills, updating, 78-79
- reminders, setting up, 90
- selecting, 73
- setting up payments, 18

bills and deposits list, deleting bills/deposits, 80

Broker Center, 215

brokers, connecting to, 135
Brokers link, 147
budget periods, viewing, 117
budget planners, 103
budget reports
customizing, 110
viewing, 110
budget summaries, reviewing, 109
budgeting expenses, 192-195
budgets
budget information, updating, 114-116
creating, 104-109, 116
deposits, adding, 111
editing, 114-116
funds, reallocating, 112-113
planning, 103
reminders, setting up, 118
viewing, 117
withdrawals, adding, 111
business days, 90
buttons (toolbar), adding, 25

Calculate how much house I can afford link, 204
calculating
debt, 122
mortgage payments, 204-206
calendar, hiding, 70
calendar months, viewing, 70
capital gains
estimating, 168-169
reviewing, 168-169
cash flow, adding to, 98
cash flow projections, 96-97
customizing, 100
editing, 99
reviewing, 96-97
revisiting, 119
Cash Flow Scenarios, 100-101
cash withdrawals, recording in investment accounts, 136
categories. *See also* account categories
adding, 60
adding previously removed categories, 42
deleting, 42, 61, 104
details of, viewing, 59
expanding/collapsing, 42
moving, 59
opening, 42
organizing, 58-59
rearranging, 41
renaming, 61
sub-categories, adding, 104
sub-categories, selecting, 105
updating, 41
updating information in, 42
viewing, 58-59
categorizing transactions, 71
changing
account names, 46
account types, 46
distribution methods, 169
home page view, 43
passwords, 33
check numbers, tracking, 71
checking credit activity, 218-219

checks
- ordering, 83
- print options, modifying, 85
- printing, 83-85
- set-up options, modifying, 85
- test prints, 84
- writing, 83-85

choosing currencies, 125

classifications, 62

closing accounts, 54

CNBC TV link, 147

collapsing categories, 42

Common Tasks, 135

comparing loans, 209-211

Comparison Reports link, 151

connecting to brokers, 135

Contact bank or broker links, 86

converting files from previous versions, 5

creating
- account classifications, 62
- budgets, 104-109
- debt-reduction plan accounts, 124-127
- debt-reduction plans, 122
- favorite reports list, 158-159
- financial plans, 176-181

credit advice, 219

credit card accounts, 13
- closing, 54
- updating information, 47

Credit Center, 218-219

credit monitoring, 218-219
- Experian, 218

currencies
- choosing, 125
- tracking, 9

Customize Cash Flow link, 100

customizing
- budget reports, 110
- cash flow projections, 100
- home page task list, 39-40
- reports, 154-157
- toolbar, 24-25

D

data, resetting original data, 163

debt. *See also* budgets; debt-reduction plans
- calculating, 122
- paying off, 128
- reducing, 120
- summarizing, 128

debt information, editing, 123

Debt Reduction Planner, 121
- audio help, turning on/off, 122
- Results area, 129

debt-reduction plans, 120
- account information, editing, 123
- accounts, adding, 122
- accounts, creating, 124-127
- accounts, deleting, 124-127
- accounts, removing, 122
- authorizing, 130-131
- creating, 122
- implementing, 130-131
- results, viewing, 129

deductions
- finding, 160, 165-167
- reviewing, 165-167
- tracking, 74

default home page, viewing, 43

deleting
- accounts, 55
- categories, 42, 61, 104
- debt-reduction plan accounts, 124-127
- payees, 65
- toolbar buttons, 25
- transactions, 93

dependent information, editing, 177

deposit series, editing, 78

deposits
- adding, 74-75
- adding to budget, 111
- deleting from list, 80
- recording in investment accounts, 138
- recurring deposits, updating, 78-79

determining
- annual inflation percentage, 179
- life-expectancy age, 177
- living expenses, 193
- mortgage payments, 204-206
- rates of return, 187
- retirement age, 177

distribution methods, changing, 169

downloaded statements, viewing, 67

downloading
- online statements, 67
- statements, 92
- stock quotes, 135

E

earnings forecasts, updating, 179

Edit account number link, 72

Edit address link, 72

Edit Career Event dialog, 179

Edit Expense Adjustment dialog, 193

Edit Loan dialog, 191

Edit menu, 26

Edit payee information link, 76

editing
- bill series, 78
- budgets, 114-116
- cash flow projections, 99
- debt information, 123
- debt-reduction plan account information, 123
- dependent information, 177
- deposit series, 78
- expenses, 115
- financial plans, 196
- Home Worksheet, 204
- income, 114

electronic bill payment status, 86

electronic payments, setting up, 81

electronic transfers, 82

End User Agreement (EULA), 4

End User Agreement dialog, 4

entering
- account balances, 12
- bank account information, 12
- bill details, 19-20
- income information, 16-17, 178-180
- information into accounts, 12-14
- investment information, 182-183
- money transfer classifications, 76

payee information, 82
savings information, 182-183
service charges, 92
tax information, 162-164
transfers, 76

estimating
capital gains, 168-169
expenses, 123
taxes, 162

EULA (End User Agreement), 4

executing financial plans, 201

expanding categories, 42

expense forecasts, 193

expenses
assessing, 192-195
editing, 115
estimating, 123
setting up, 19-20

Experian, 218

Experian's credit monitoring, 218

exploring Money Services, 214-217

exporting
reports, 153
tax information, 171-173

favorite reports list, creating, 158-159

Favorites list, 47

Favorites menu, 26

File menu, 26

files
accessing, 30
backing up, 31
converting from previous versions, 5
creating, 5, 29
opening, 4-5, 26, 30
printing, 32
Quicken, importing, 6
saving, 5
updating, 35

filing status, reviewing, 170

finance reports, viewing, 151

finances
tracking, 9
what-if situations, 100-101

financial information, updating, 35

financial institutions, researching, 86

financial news
finding, 147
Money newsletters, 217

financial planning
assets, adding, 188-189
assets, updating, 188
baseline plans, 196
contributions, adding, 184
contributions, deleting, 185
contributions, excluding, 184
contributions, updating, 185
current plans, 196
debt, reviewing, 190-191
dependent information, editing, 177
entering family information, 176
entering income information, 178
expenses, adding, 192
expenses, assessing, 192-195
expenses, editing, 193
inflation rate, modifying, 181
investment information, entering, 182-183
life insurance policies, 186
life-expectancy age, 177

loans, adding, 190
loans, deleting, 191
loans, editing, 191
loans, excluding, 190
plans, creating, 176-181
plans, editing, 196
plans, executing, 201
rates of returns, entering, 187
retirement age, 177
reviewing plans, 196-200
savings information, entering, 182-183
state tax rates, determining, 181
tax rates, adjusting, 181
yearly plan summaries, 200

financial plans, creating, 176-181

financial priorities, 10-11

financial reports
customizing, 154-157
viewing, 150, 153

financial tracking, 9

financial-tracking information, setting up, 9

Find a transaction link, 87

Find and Replace wizard, 87-89

Find Symbol button, 145

finding
credit advise, 219
deductions, 160, 165-167
financial news, 147
stock symbols, 145
transactions, 87

Forecast your cash flow window, 98

forecasting. *See also* planning
cash flow, 96-97
expenses, 193
what-if situations, 100-101

forecasts (cash-flow), revisiting, 119

frequent-flyer accounts
modifying, 51
setting up, 50-51

frequent-flyer miles (points)
adding, 51
tracking, 50

funds
excess funds, saving, 108
reallocating, 112-113
transferring, 82

Future Loan Payment dialog, 79

future planning. *See also* financial planning
entering information for, 176-177

G-H

getting advice, 97

getting help, 34

Go to calendar, 70

goals
adding, 108
setting up, 108

grouping investment accounts, 134

gross pay, tracking, 16

handling account balance discrepancies, 92

help
accessing, 28, 34
audio help, turning off, 8
electronic transfer help, 82

Help menu, 28

Help on the Web, 34

help videos, viewing, 34
hiding calendar, 70
home inventory
removing items from, 208
tracking, 207-208
home page, 36
categories, adding/removing, 41
categories, rearranging, 38
changing, 43
default, viewing, 43
task list, customizing, 39-40
home page views, 38
Home Worksheet, 204-206
House and Loan feature, 202
House and Loan Tasks, 203

implementing debt-reduction plans, 130-131
importing Quicken files, 6
income
adding, 106
editing, 114
tracking, 16
viewing, 107
Income and Expenses link, 150
income information, entering, 16-17, 178-180
inflation, effects of, viewing, 200
Insight link, 147
installing Money, 3
insurance policies, home inventory, tracking, 207-208
interest rates, 126
Investing menu, 27
investment accounts
adding, 142-145
cash transactions, deleting, 139
cash transactions, editing, 138
cash transactions, recording, 136-138
grouping, 134
recurring transactions, adding, 138
summaries, 135
transactions, editing, 141
transfers, recording, 139
investment contributions, 184-185
investment news, finding, 147
investment prices, updating, 146
investment transactions, recording using Transactions view, 140-141
investments
managing, 132
performing common tasks, 135
reviewing, 134-135
Investments link, 151

keyboard shortcuts, 26, 32

life insurance policies, 186
life time planning. *See* financial planning
life-expectancy age, determining, 177
Lifetime Planner, 174-175. *See also* financial planning
Home and Assets portion, 188-189
Loans and Debt portion, 190-191
plan summaries, reviewing, 196-200
Savings Contributions, modifying, 184-185

lifetime plans, 197. *See also* financial planning

links

Brokers link, 147
Calculate how much house I can afford, 204
CNBC TV link, 147
Comparison Reports link, 151
Contact bank or broker, 86
Customize Cash Flow link, 100
Edit account number link, 72
Edit address link, 72
Edit payee information link, 76
Find a transaction link, 87
Go to calendar link, 70
Income and Expenses link, 150
Insight link, 147
Investment link, 151
Markets link, 147
Monthly Reports link, 151
My Favorites link, 152
Pay Record Bills and Deposits, 70
Print this report link, 153
See payee details link, 86
Stocks link, 147
Task-based Home Page link, 204
Taxes link, 151
What I Have link, 150
What I Owe link, 150

lists

account list, 45
Favorites list, 47

living expenses, determining, 193

loan comparison feature, 202, 209-211

Loan Worksheet, 209

loans

comparing, 209-211
Loan Comparison feature, 209-211
refinance loans, 211
reviewing, 190-191

Manage scheduled bills and deposits window, 72

managing

budgets, 104-109, 118
investments, 132
payments (adjustable), 72
taxes, 160

Markets link, 147

menu bar, 23

menus, 26

Microsoft Money Help, 23, 34, 82

Microsoft Money Home Page, 23, 36

Microsoft Money, installing 3

Microsoft Money Web site, 83

miles. *See* frequent-flyer miles (points)

modifying

account numbers, 72
bill details, 21
bill reminders, 90
bills (recurring), 78-79
budget information, 114-116
check printing options, 85
check set-up options, 85

deposits (recurring), 78-79
frequent-flyer accounts, 51
passwords, 33
report layout, 153

money, transferring, 76

Money Help, 23, 34, 82

Money Home Page, 23, 36

Money, installing 3

Money Services, exploring, 214-217

money transfers
classifications, entering, 76
entering, 76
setting up, 82

Money User's Guide, 34

Money's Credit Center, 218-219

monitoring credit, 218-219

Monthly Reports link, 151

mortgage payments, calculating, 204-206

moving
categories, 59
forward/backward one page, 24
toolbar buttons, 24

My Favorites link, 152

N-O

.NET Passport, 8

.NET Passport passwords, 33

.NET passwords, 7

net pay, tracking, 16

New Account wizard, 124

New Asset Wizard, 188

New Living Expense Adjustment dialog, 192

New Loan Wizard, 190

New Policy Wizard, 186

news alerts, setting up, 10

online accounts, setting up, 15, 66

online bill payments, 81-82

online research, 135

online services
bill payment, 82
fund transfers, 82
setting up, 15, 66

Online Services Manager window, 81

online statements, downloading, 67

online User's Guide, 34

opening
accounts, 26
categories, 42
files, 4-5, 26, 30
Money, 4-5
portfolio window, 215

ordering checks, 83

organizing
accounts, 26
categories, 58-59
toolbar buttons, 24

P

Password Manager, 33

passwords
changing, 33
.NET passwords, 7

online bill payments, 81
setting up, 7-8, 33
standard passwords, 7

pay (net/gross), tracking, 16

Pay Record Bills and Deposits link, 70

paychecks, adding, 74-75

payee information
entering, 82
updating, 63

payees
adding, 64
deleting, 65
renaming, 63

paying off
accounts, 122
debt, 128

payments
electronic, setting up, 81
entering details of, 19-20
managing, 72-73
managing adjustable payments, 72

Pick an account to use window, 83

Planner menu, 27, 104

planners
accessing, 27
budget planners, 103
Debt Reduction Planner, 121
Lifetime Planner, 175

planning
budgets, 103
purchases, 212

plans
debt-reduction plan accounts, creating, 127
debt-reduction plan accounts, deleting, 127
debt-reduction plans, 120
debt-reduction plans, authorizing, 130-131
debt-reduction plans, creating, 122
debt-reduction plans, views, 129
lifetime plans, 196

Play what-if with cash flow window, 100

points. *See* frequent-flyer miles (points)

Portfolio link, portfolio window, opening, 215

Portfolio page, 133
adding accounts using, 142-145
Transactions view, recording transactions, 140-141

Print this report link, 153

printer settings, adjusting, 32

printing, 32
check, 83-85
shortcuts, 32

projections
cash flow, 96-97
cash flow, editing, 99

Purchase Wizard, 212
financing purchases, 216-217

purchases, planning, 212

Q-R

Quicken files, importing, 6

quotes. *See* stock quotes

reallocating funds, 112-113

rearranging
categories on home page, 38
tasks in the task list, 39

recording
cash transactions in investment accounts, 136-138
investment transactions using Transactions view, 140-141
transactions, 70-71

reducing debt, 120

refinancing loans, 211

reminders
bill reminders, setting up, 90
budget reminders, setting up, 118

removing
categories, 41-42, 104
tasks from task list, 39
toolbar buttons, 25
transactions, 93

renaming
categories, 61
payees, 63

reopening accounts, 54

reports
accessing, 28
budget reports, customizing, 110
budget reports, viewing, 110
Comparison Reports link, 151
customizing, 154-157
exporting, 153
favorite reports list, 158-159
favorite reports, accessing, 158
Income and Expenses link, 150
Investment link, 151
layout of, modifying, 153
Monthly Reports link, 151
My Favorites link, 152
Print this report link, 153
printing, 32
Taxes link, 151
viewing, 150-153
What I Have link, 150
What I Owe link, 150

Reports Gallery, 149
accessing, 150

Reports menu, 28

researching financial institutions, 86

resetting original data, 163

Results area (Debt Reduction Planner), 129

retirement. *See also* financial planning
retirement accounts, 14
retirement age, determining, 177
retirement planning, 176-177

reversing actions, 26

reviewing
account information, 46-48
bills (paid), 86
budget summaries, 109
capital gains, 168-169
cash flow projections, 96-97
debt information, 190-191
deductions, 165-167
filing status, 170
financial plan summaries, 196-200
investments, 134-135

salary. *See* income

salary forecasts, viewing, 179

saving
excess funds toward goals, 108
files, 5

searching for transactions, 87-89

selecting
- bills, 73
- sub-categories, 105
- transaction types, 93

service charges, entering, 92

Services Center
- Banking Center, 215
- Broker Center, 215
- information about services, 214
- Money's services, 214
- Shopping Center, 214

Services menu, 28

setting up
- account information, 12-14
- accounts (new), 52
- bill payments, 18
- bill reminders, 90
- budget reminders, 118
- electronic payments, 81
- expenses, 19-20
- financial-tracking information, 9
- frequent-flyer accounts, 50-51
- goals, 108
- Money, 3
- .NET Passport passwords, 33
- money transfers, 82
- news alerts, 10
- online accounts, 15, 66
- passwords, 7-8, 33
- payees, 64
- spouse/partner accounts, 57

settings (printer), adjusting, 32

Setup Assistant, 3
- audio help, turning off, 8
- skipping, 8, 29
- starting, 7

shopping, 214

Shopping Center, 214

shortcuts, 26, 32

sign-in, skipping, 8

sorting
- account list, 91
- accounts, 49

sound, turning off, 8

spending
- estimating, 123
- viewing, 107

spouse/partner accounts, setting up, 57

starting
- Money, 4-5
- Setup Assistant, 7

statements
- downloaded statements, viewing, 67
- downloading, 92

stock quotes
- update options, 146
- updating prices, 135

stock symbols, finding, 145

Stocks link, 147

sub-categories, 60. *See also* categories

sum of splits, 79

summaries, investment accounts, 135

summarizing, debt, 128

T

task list
- customizing, 39-40
- tasks, adding/removing, 39
- tasks, rearranging, 39

task-based home page, 38

Task-based Home Page link, 204

tasks, adding/removing to task list, 39

tax features, 170

tax information
- entering, 162-164
- exporting, 171-173

tax rates, obtaining, 171

taxes
- capital gains, estimating, 168-169
- deductions, finding, 165-166
- estimating, 162
- filing status, reviewing, 170
- managing, 160
- tax feature, 170
- tracking, 160
- TurboTax, starting, 173

Taxes link, 151

Taxes menu, 28

thermometers, 118

toolbar, 23
- customizing, 24-25

toolbar buttons
- adding, 25
- descriptions, viewing, 24
- moving, 24
- removing, 25

Tools menu, 27

total transactions, 79

tracking
- check numbers, 71
- currency, 9
- deductions, 74
- finances, 9
- finances (spouse/partner), 56
- frequent-flyer miles, 50
- frequent-flyer points, 50
- home inventory, 207-208
- net pay, 16
- taxes, 160

transaction types, selecting, 93

transactions
- categorizing, 71
- deleting, 93
- disabling tracking, 90
- information, replacing, 89
- recording, 70-71
- reports, viewing, 88
- searching for, 87-89
- viewing, 63

transferring
- funds, 82
- money, 76

transfers, entering, 76

troubleshooting, 34

TurboTax, starting, 173

turning on/off
- audio help, 8
- Debt Reduction Planner Audio Help, 122
- voice commands, 8

TXF files, 173

undoing actions, 26

updating. *See also* editing

account information, 46-48
accounts, 35, 70
bills (recurring), 78-79
budget information, 114-116
categories, 41
deposits (recurring), 78-79
earnings forecasts, 179
files, 35
financial information, 35
investment information, 182-183
investment prices, 146
payee information, 63
savings information, 182-183

utilities, accessing via Tools menu, 27

viewing

account balance discrepancies, 93
accounts, 26
balances, 46
budget periods, 117
budget reports, 110
budgets, 117
calendar months, 70
categories, 58-59
category details, 59
debt-reduction plan results, 129
default home page, 43
downloaded statements, 67
help videos, 34
income, 107
reports, 150-153
salary forecasts, 179
spending, 107
transaction reports, 88
transactions, 63

views

home page, 38
task-based home page, 38

voice commands, turning off, 8

Web help, accessing, 34

What I Have link, 150

What I Owe link, 150

what-if situations, 100-101

Which account do you want to balance? window, 91

windows

Forecast your cash flow window, 98
Manage scheduled bills and deposits, 72
Online Services Manager, 81
Pick an account to use window, 83
Play what-if with cash flow window, 100
Which account do you want to balance?, 91

withdrawals, adding to budget, 111

wizards

account balancing wizard, 91
Find and Replace wizard, 87-89
New Account wizard, 124
New Asset Wizard, 188
New Loan Wizard, 190
New Policy Wizard, 186
Purchase Wizard, 212

writing checks, 83-85